MORTAL IMITATIONS OF DIVINE LIFE

SERIES EDITOR

John Russon

REREADING ANCIENT PHILOSOPHY

MORTAL IMITATIONS OF DIVINE LIFE

The Nature of the Soul in Aristotle's *De Anima*

ELI DIAMOND

NORTHWESTERN UNIVERSITY PRESS • EVANSTON, ILLINOIS

Northwestern University Press
www.nupress.northwestern.edu

Printed in the United States of America

10 9 8 7 6 5 4 3 2 1

Library of Congress Cataloging-in-Publication Data

Diamond, Eli, 1976–
Mortal imitations of divine life : the nature of the soul in Aristotle's De anima / Eli Diamond.
pages cm. — (Rereading ancient philosophy)
Includes bibliographical references and index.
ISBN 978-0-8101-3069-2 (cloth : alk. paper) —
ISBN 978-0-8101-3070-8 (ebook)
1. Aristotle. De anima. 2. Soul. 3. Movement (Philosophy) I. Title. II. Series: Rereading ancient philosophy.
B415.D53 2015
128—dc23

2014044415

♾ The paper used in this publication meets the minimum requirements of the American National Standard for Information Sciences—Permanence of Paper for Printed Library Materials, ANSI Z39.48–1992.

CONTENTS

ACKNOWLEDGMENTS

This book would never have been written without the Dalhousie University Classics Department, where I first encountered ancient philosophy as an undergraduate and a Master's student and where I now have the honor to teach. My understanding of Aristotle has been formed by the encounter with ancient, late-ancient, and medieval texts I received from wonderful teachers like Colin Starnes, Robert Crouse, Wayne Hankey, and Dennis House. These brilliant readers of ancient philosophy, along with their colleague James Doull, whom I only met once but whose short writings on Aristotle have been indispensable to me, have formed the way I approach the reading of any philosophical texts, and especially those of Plato and Aristotle.

When I returned after many years to teach in the Dalhousie Classics Department, I was delighted to discover that passion for the rigorous study of these philosophical texts was as strong as ever. This book was seriously improved through lively discussion with students in my graduate seminar on Aristotle's *De Anima* in 2008–09, and I am grateful to Luke Togni, Alex Plumb, Nicholas Hatt, Benjamin Lee, and Christopher McKelvie for their participation. Two undergraduate students who took that seminar, Benjamin Max Manson and Evan King, made particularly valuable corrections to my interpretation at important points, and I am grateful for their independent-minded and justified stubbornness that my reading was not adequate. In general, the philosophical passion of the wonderful undergraduate and graduate students in Dalhousie Classics has been a sustaining inspiration throughout the final stages of writing this book.

Many teachers, friends, and colleagues have helped me in all kinds of ways during the writing of this book: Michael Fournier, Jack Mitchell, Stephen Blackwood, Chike Jeffers, David Butorac, Matthew Robinson, Jim Gilbert-Walsh, David Peddle, Ian Stewart, Angus Johnston, Neil Robertson, Kyle Fraser, Francisco Gonzalez, Patricia Fagan, Eric Sanday, Eve Rabinoff—these scholars and philosophers have helped me in indispensable ways. Nathan Andersen and Greg Recco offered thoughtful responses and proposed revisions to the book which palpably improved the final product. I thank the editors at Northwestern University Press, Henry Carrigan, Peter Raccuglia, Nathan MacBrien, and Gianna Mosser, for their patient help. My deepest gratitude goes out to the editor of this series, John

Russon, for his tireless enthusiasm for the project and wise practical advice throughout.

I gratefully acknowledge the financial support of Canada's Social Sciences and Humanities Research Council, which was essential for carrying out this project. Some of the material in chapter 4 on theoretical mind has appeared in a slightly different and expanded form in my article "Aristotle's Appropriation of Plato's Sun Analogy in *De Anima*," in *Apeiron*, vol. 47, no. 3 (2014).

No living scholar of Aristotle has had a deeper impact on my understanding of Aristotle than Aryeh Kosman, and discovering his writings on Aristotle has been one of the joys of carrying out this project. I have deeply appreciated his subsequent encouragement and willingness to comment on parts of this book. One of my longest-standing and dearest philosophical friends, David Bronstein, has read certain parts of this book, and his meticulous suggestions have saved me from many serious mistakes. Nicholas Thorne read through the entire manuscript with great care and helped me make countless improvements with a generosity far beyond what I deserved. Michelle Wilband graciously proofread and edited an earlier version of the book and her improvements were indispensable. I am thankful to my student assistants, Bryan Heystee, Aaron Higgins-Brake, and Jacob Glover, who read through the penultimate version of the book with an eagle eye and found all kinds of small and large problems. Lois Bearden, Jack Bearden, and Jacquie de Mestral mercifully opened their Harbourville homes to me when I needed a quiet place to work.

I thank Tad Brennan and Souleymane Bachir Diagne for their helpful comments and encouragement as members of my doctoral supervisory committee. Tad Brennan taught a superb graduate seminar on Aristotle's *De Anima* at Northwestern University which was invaluable to me as a doctoral student, and Bachir Diagne's insistence that I take into account animal locomotion and the movement of the stars in my argument forced me to rethink the work as a whole in a completely new light. I am especially thankful to Richard Kraut, my Ph.D. thesis supervisor, who demonstrated to me exactly how to supervise and mentor a graduate student. His kind and conscientious help and the freedom he allowed me to pursue an intuition about Aristotle's psychology that must have initially appeared very strange provided the perfect conditions for writing the reading of *De Anima* that eventually turned into this book.

Finally, I would certainly never be a philosopher today if not for the loving education and encouragement of my parents, Joseph and Bonnie Diamond. My wife Kieva, through her unflagging love and patience, has helped me develop the Aristotelian sensitivity to the presence of the divine in everyday life. It is to her and our three boys Harlow, Abraham, and Simcha, that I dedicate this book.

PREFACE

> And further, life belongs to God. For the activity of mind is life, and God is activity. And the essential activity of God is life, the best life and an eternal life. We say then that God is a living being, eternal and best, so a life that is always continuous and eternal belongs to God. For this is God.
>
> καὶ ζωὴ δέ γε ὑπάρχει: ἡ γὰρ νοῦ ἐνέργεια ζωή, ἐκεῖνος δὲ ἡ ἐνέργεια: ἐνέργεια δὲ ἡ καθ' αὑτὴν ἐκείνου ζωὴ ἀρίστη καὶ ἀΐδιος. φαμὲν δὴ τὸν θεὸν εἶναι ζῷον ἀΐδιον ἄριστον, ὥστε ζωὴ καὶ αἰὼν συνεχὴς καὶ ἀΐδιος ὑπάρχειτῷ θεῷ: τοῦτο γὰρ ὁ θεός.

Hans-Georg Gadamer notes that Aristotle's thinking and conceptualization of the world is thoroughly determined by "the insight into the nature of what lives."[1] In Aristotle's analysis of the world, substances (οὐσίαι) are the most fundamental beings, and among substances, natural living beings, that is, plants and animals, exhibit this fundamental mode of substance-being most fully.[2] Being alive, we learn from the passage in *Metaphysics* XII cited above, belongs not only to natural living beings, but even to the divine first principle of all nature; in fact, this God, which is the very activity of mind, is not only the best life, but in some sense, life (ζωή) itself. Whether studying the natural world in minute empirical detail, the ethical-political dimension of human life, or the existence of divine separate substances, Aristotle remains, at heart, a philosophical biologist. For this reason, there is no better way into Aristotelian thought than through his treatise on the soul, the goal of which is to understand the nature of the cause of living beings.

What is it about living beings that Aristotle finds so astonishing and wondrous? His analysis of each living activity helps recall just how marvelous the organic realm is. In nutrition, a living being achieves its stability and independence not in isolation from but through its dependence on and exchange with its surrounding environment, with sunlight, air, water, nourishment. With the emergence of animal sensation, the world is taken into the organism without destroying it, leaving it as it is without even requiring direct contact with the objects of sense. Along with sensation comes self-movement, since the world is not simply assimilated neutrally or disinterestedly by the organism, but it exerts a push or pull on the animal, as an object of its desire or dread which moves it through the world. Finally, with the emergence of thinking we arrive at an activity whereby we can engage with the full range of objects in our world through a wholly inner act, no longer dependent on the constant presence of that world, on account of having internalized it.

My argument in this book is that Aristotle's analysis of these types of soul and their characteristic living activities is quietly theological throughout. That is, rather than simply being a series of unconnected activities or distinct kinds of soul, the ascending scale of kinds of soul actually constitute degrees of realization of what it means to be alive, and so each is only properly understood when seen in the light of the most completely realized living activity. This complete life is the Aristotelian God.

Lower levels of organic life on this analysis are traces, vestiges, reflections of higher activities, and ultimately of the highest, divine activity. At these lower levels, Aristotle identifies distinctions and structures which will emerge with greater clarity in the development through the higher living activities. While each kind of soul and activity is analyzed in itself, these discrete, focused analyses of each stage must be complemented by thinking through the commonalities and divergences between the levels. In doing so, a clear tendency in the development of organic life emerges, a movement towards increasing self-sufficiency and self-relatedness, towards a deepened ability to take in the world without losing either itself or the nature of its objects, towards being able to initiate its activities from within, without simply reacting to external stimuli—in a word, towards the *freedom* of a wholly self-sufficient, absolutely self-determined divine principle.[3]

In the simplest activities of life, even in the ingestion, digestion, and excretion of food, even in the rotation of an animal's knee joints while it moves through its environment,[4] Aristotle detects traces of the highest living principle. As with Heraclitus receiving his guests while warming himself at his kitchen hearth, Aristotle wants us to see that the highest divinity is present, however unclearly, in the most mundane, seemingly profane, activities.[5] As strange as this way of thinking may initially seem to us, Aristotle discovers, at the level of an organism's metabolic self-maintenance, an unchanging activity which prefigures the even more astonishing dynamic self-sufficiency exhibited in sensation, self-movement, and thinking. His analysis of these living activities concludes with the discovery of a divine principle as the fullest realization of that dynamically self-related mode of being he calls ἐνέργεια (*energeia*). In this divine, living principle, the aspiration inherent in these other organic activities is completely satisfied.

In thinking about the analysis undertaken in *De Anima* as quietly but constantly theological, it is important to note at the outset what this does *not* mean. First, it is very significant that Aristotle does not actually allow comparisons with the divine activity or even with higher natural activities to intrude on his analysis of each kind of soul. God is never imported into the argument as a criterion to measure the deficiency of a lower level of soul. Divine life is not the presupposition of his investigation, but rather the result which only emerges once he has identified the best and highest natural living activity. In fact, his analysis of each particular type of soul does not paint the picture of a series of deficient versions of something superior, but rather wonderfully successful realizations of precisely what that type of soul is. Biology must, at least initially, operate apart from any theological interest. Second, the sense in which the analysis of organic life is theological is very distant from any notion of "intelligent design." The theological point is decidedly not that the highest living being has designed other living beings. *De Anima* rather shows each stage of soul to *be* the very activity which is God, though with starkly varying degrees of success. The relation between theology and natural science one finds here is subtle and complex.

It is a common approach in the study of older thinkers to look for the contemporary relevance in the ways in which the older thought anticipates either some accepted scientific truth or some influential contemporary position. One starts with a contemporary standpoint and looks back to some important thinker to see if this view is present or at least anticipated there. Thus, if Aristotle can be seen either to anticipate some presently held philosophical position, or to offer good reasons why we might oppose it, then his views will have been shown to be of enduring philosophical interest. In this book I have attempted to proceed in the opposite way, approaching this central Aristotelian text with no expectation that Aristotle will have something to say about this or that contemporary debate. I have tried to allow the work itself to shape my sense of its mode of argumentation, its underlying structure, and its fundamental philosophical aim. The consequent effect of my reading of *De Anima* is thus to reassert its strangeness, its distance from the methods and sensibilities of contemporary philosophy. In other words, by making Aristotle's thinking about soul and mind strange and alien to prevailing tendencies in contemporary thinking, this interpretation of *De Anima* runs the risk of turning Aristotle's treatise into a curious artifact in the museum of antiquated thinking. This is especially true, since my explanation of Aristotle's arguments will occasionally show that these arguments as they stand could no longer simply be adopted by a contemporary standpoint. To cite just one example, I show how Aristotle's analysis of the soul's causal role in the movement of animals through space can only be fully understood in relation to the circular motion of those supra-lunary bodies which exhibit the kind of perfect, self-related, self-sufficient motion that animal and human locomotion (and ultimately, all changes in nature) implicitly strive to exhibit without ever fully succeeding.

This is a risk I am willing to assume, insofar as my guiding principle is ultimate fidelity to Aristotle's text, together with a refusal to read the parts in isolation from the whole. What follows is for the most part a careful reading of the *De Anima* which attempts to articulate the overall aim and structure of the work, though arriving at this more fundamental point demands many detailed interpretations of many particular passages. This interpretative work is obligatory, not only because Aristotle's style is dense and difficult. In any treatise, he is remarkably quiet and subtle about what he is most fundamentally doing, a feature of his writing which often is not fully appreciated. The answer to the question of *why* he is treating each topic where he treats it is more often than not left unstated. His careful attention to the particular phenomenon in question at any point in the argument often means he does not spell out for the reader the connection of that analysis to the unfolding argument as a whole. It is left to the attentive reader to make the connections explicit.

Reasserting the strangeness and distance of Aristotle's psychology from the methods and sensibilities of contemporary philosophy raises the question: what interest does this view of the soul that I here present as Aristotle's hold for the contemporary philosopher? In fact, I would argue it is precisely *through* these differences between contemporary and Aristotelian approaches to understanding life and soul that we may be genuinely instructed by the *De Anima*. Perhaps the chief reason for the strangeness of the *De Anima* lies in the fact that, like it or not, Aristotle is engaged in what we would now call the "philosophy of nature," and this philosophical genre is decidedly no longer in fashion. Of course, Aristotle would find the contrast between natural science and philosophy of nature strange, since it is only in a later period that a wholly empirical natural science contrasts itself with philosophy as non-empirical that the need for a philosophy of nature emerges. There is no doubt that if a philosophy of nature of the kind we find in Aristotle's *De Anima* is to be a legitimate enterprise, it must be endlessly open to what the careful empirical observation of nature teaches us. But this can surely be accomplished without excluding the desire that defines all speculative philosophy, the desire to grasp the whole or totality, according to ideas or structures that are not themselves simply empirically available, but which emerge through a global reflection upon the results of such careful empirical observation.

In his classic work *The Phenomenon of Life*, Hans Jonas calls for just this kind of philosophical reflection upon the totality of organic life, a movement "towards a philosophical biology." Aristotle is essential to this enterprise, since "his *De anima* is the first example of philosophical biology."[6] Of course, a *new* philosophical biology would necessarily look very different from Aristotle's. This is not only because the cosmology central to his thinking has been so radically overturned, but also because of the undeniable fact of the historical evolution of species. The taxonomy of natural kinds studied by Aristotle and taken by him to be eternal has been shown to have a historical genesis. Jonas writes:

> The terms on which his august example may be resumed in our time will be different from his, but the idea of stratification, of the progressive superposition of levels, with the dependence of each higher on the lower, the retention of all the lower in the higher, will still be found indispensable. One way of interpreting the scale is in terms of scope and distinctness of experience, of rising degrees of world perception which move toward the widest and freest objectification of the sum of being in individual percipients. Another way, concurrent with the grades of perception, is in terms of progressive freedom of action. The correlation and interpenetration of these two aspects—of perceiving and of acting, of the variety and adequacy of the one, the range and power of the other—is a constant theme for the empathic study of the many forms of life.[7]

If there is a philosophical biology to come, its task will be "to follow the unfolding of this germinal freedom in the ascending levels of organic evolution."[8] It may just be that Aristotle's *De Anima* lies simultaneously behind us *and* ahead of us, and that a deeper appreciation of the overall aim and structure of its argument, of its strangest and boldest claims, is well worth our philosophical time and effort.

MORTAL IMITATIONS OF DIVINE LIFE

Introduction

Aristotle opens his work on the soul with the following remark:

> Taking knowledge [εἴδησιν] to be among the beautiful and noble things, some more than others either because of its accuracy [ἀκρίβειαν] or because it relates to better and more wondrous objects, on account of both these factors the study of the soul would be rightly placed among the first things. (*De Anima* I.1.402a1–4)[1]

These opening lines of the work, as is usually the case in an Aristotelian treatise, are particularly charged with meaning. Aristotle is of course referring to the subject of the investigation, inquiry into the soul, and its importance for knowledge in general. But we should not forget that in investigating the soul, one of its primary activities is cognitive awareness—εἰδέναι. This knowledge verb, εἰδέναι, which also opens Aristotle's *Metaphysics* as the object of our universal natural desire, is a broad and inclusive one. With its etymological connection to the sense of vision it encompasses both intellectual and sensible modes of knowing, as well as theoretical and practical modes of knowing. Cognitive awareness of objects might be seen to constitute only one side of the fundamental division within the soul as cause of awareness and motion. As we will see in what follows, however, Aristotle shows how desire, which is responsible for moving the body through space, is itself simply a practical mode of cognition of an object as an end or goal for oneself. So another reason why the study of soul is of the highest importance is that it is the soul that is responsible for all awareness (εἴδησις), and *De Anima* will study precisely how this activity operates relative to the objects of its awareness. Thus the opening of *De Anima* does not merely offer a reflection upon the dignity of the study of soul in comparison with other objects of study, but already implicitly introduces one of the primary objects of concern for anyone studying soul: the different modes of our awareness of the world.

From the above passage we should also notice that while all knowledge is beautiful and honorable, Aristotle already suggests that there is a hierarchy of value between various kinds of knowledge. One kind of knowledge is more beautiful and honorable based on two criteria that Aristotle mentions here:

the accuracy or precision of this knowledge, and the goodness and wonder of its object. In other words, there are subjective conditions, the precision of that mode of knowing, and corresponding objective conditions, the goodness of the object known by that kind of knowledge, which will determine where a particular kind of awareness lies on this hierarchy of value.

In this book, I offer an interpretation of the *De Anima* which explains how and why Aristotle places ensouled beings and their various living activities on this hierarchy of value. Aristotle's central intention in *De Anima* is to discover the nature and essence of the soul—the principle of living beings. He says that "life" is spoken of in many ways, meaning that there are various activities which belong to and characterize living things, and when we ascribe one of these activities to a being, we are saying that it is alive in some way. The various kinds of soul and living activities do not constitute an unconnected variety, nor is there some activity which is simply identical in all the different kinds of living things. Soul as the principle of living being is ultimately understood only once it is grasped in its one activity which lies beyond its relation to body—active thinking—at which point we see what each lower level of soul is striving for with varying degrees of success, the end towards which all living activity naturally tends. Life is then clearly grasped as ἐνέργεια (*energeia*) or ἐντελέχεια (*entelecheia*)—an activity which is a self-relation, where the origin and end of its activity coincide, and where the being in question is completely preserved in the course of its activity. This is most clearly seen in the divine life, whose very essence is *energeia*, but is present in more and more explicit ways in ensouled beings as one moves through the hierarchy of living activities.

While it is not often recognized, Aristotle's *De Anima* is clearly divided into two conceptual halves, a division which Aristotle adopts from his philosophical predecessors, who recognized that the soul is above all defined by two activities: awareness and motion.[2] Living, ensouled beings can be marked off from unensouled beings by the fact that they are cognitively aware of their world, and that they move themselves through space. Thus soul is above all else the cause of the living being's cognition and self-movement. The significance of this distinction for Aristotle's conception of the soul and the structure of the *De Anima* has never been sufficiently appreciated. This division in the soul between awareness and self-motion, which lies at the root of the distinction in the *Nicomachean Ethics* between the theoretical and practical life, is prior to the division between the particular kinds of soul: nutritive, sensitive, and intellective. In fact, these kinds of soul or particular powers of soul, which usually get more attention in interpretations of *De Anima*, are contained within the more primary division between awareness and movement. The nutritive activity of soul which defines plants, although unconscious and stationary, manifests the structure of both consciousness and self-movement—primitively, but very precisely. With animals, the sensitive awareness which defines them takes on two forms: sensation of objects as they exist in themselves, that is, theoretical sensation; and "desiring" or practical sensations, which perceive objects as goals to be attained, as pleasant or good for the organism and hence as desirable. It is this sensible appetite or ἐπιθυμία, itself a certain mode of awareness, which is responsible for moving the non-rational animal body through space. Finally, in the intellectual soul of human beings, rational powers of cognition and motion emerge as distinct from these sensible powers. On the one hand there is the mind's theoretical thinking of the intelligible forms of objects, and on the other hand, the practical mind's rational desires for what is good for human beings in general. For both theoretical and practical soul, the higher powers presuppose the lower powers and depend on them: there is neither sensation of sensible forms without nutrition, nor any thinking of intelligible forms without learning through sensation, just as there are no sensible appetites without nutrition, and no rational desires without sensible desires. But despite this nesting of higher powers in lower powers in mortal beings, in the analysis of the summit of both these cognitive and locomotive hierarchies, Aristotle concludes with a reflection on the nature of *divine* living activity. I argue that the theoretical (or cognitive) and practical (or locomotive) powers correspond to the two sides of divine activity—God's self-thinking activity, and the perfectly circular motion of the outermost sphere of the fixed stars. The most fundamental aim of the *De Anima* is thus to show how every activity of the soul, whether nutritive, cognitive, or locomotive, obeys a common structure, while each level of the soul's activity approximates these two sides of God's activity with varying degrees of success.

Life and soul constitute an example of what Aristotle calls a πρὸς ἓν λεγόμενα (*pros hen legomena*) structure (often rendered in English as "core-dependent homonymy"), a structure in which various things are said to be living in relation to one thing which is the most complete and explicit meaning of life.[3] In the case of *De Anima*, this means that the various kinds of soul and the living activities they exhibit are all to be understood in reference to the most complete and explicit sense of living, the activity of thinking. This focal or core meaning of life is not the most common and primitive biological conception of life, the self-nourishment and self-maintenance characteristic of plants, but rather the highest and most complete sense of soul, its intellectual activity, which emerges in the human, but belongs most properly to the eternal self-contemplation of God.[4] The core meaning of life is divine contemplation, while the non-core instances (the hierarchy of different souls and living activities) are derivative of this focal meaning. Therefore the essence and nature of life lies in thinking, most perfectly exemplified for Aristotle in God's eternal thinking.

Another way of stating this thesis is that, for Aristotle, God's thinking and self-motion constitute the perfect paradigm of all living things, and each living being and its characteristic living activities approximate this paradigmatic or ideal kind of life to greater or lesser degrees. These various degrees constitute a hierarchy of living activities which are ordered in a series. Every kind of living being is striving to exhibit certain features of the summit of the series, the life of thinking, to the extent that it is able as determined by its own particular nature. For thinking exhibits certain characteristics: it remains the same throughout its activity; preserves the integrity of its object; initiates its activity from itself rather than being determined from outside; admits the greatest variety of different kinds of objects and the widest spectrum of contrariety; is itself most identical with its objects; remains continuously active; and is wholly incorporeal. I seek to show how at the lowest level of living activity, the nutritive soul characteristic of plants exhibits genuine vestiges of all these characteristics, but very obscurely and imperfectly. Through an analysis of the various activities and kinds of soul treated by Aristotle in his hierarchy of living activities, I show how these characteristics of the divine activity become progressively clearer and more explicit as one moves from nutrition, through the lower, more material senses of touch and taste to the higher, more cognitive senses of hearing and vision, and finally to theoretical and practical thought. According to my interpretation, the whole argument of the *De Anima* is thus an account of the unfolding of soul from its most primitive appearance in nutrition to its complete development in thinking, a development whose stages can also be observed in individuals through the development of the human embryo to mature adulthood.

On my reading of the *De Anima*, one of the most important tasks for the interpreter is identifying the parallels between the various levels of ensouled beings, in order that one may then discern the salient differences between them. Only then can one detect the developing pattern of the argument, beginning with the lowest, most primitive form of life and culminating in the highest and most developed life. Both the differences and the development remain invisible to the reader unless the parallels are uncovered, and it is this development which I claim to be the most important point of the whole treatise. In the development from lower to higher souls, the following characteristics are progressively realized until they reach their full development in the divine life of perpetually active thinking. In the transition from nutrition to sensation to thinking, there is a gradual transformation:

- from an actuality involving process (κίνησις) and potentiality to actuality beyond potentiality and process
- from dependence on objects in the external environment to self-sufficient independence from anything outside itself
- from an underlying matter with its own determinate independent nature apart from its receptivity, towards progressively indeterminate receptivity towards its object
- from the destruction of the object in the assimilation to the more and more adequate preservation of the object
- from a vulnerability relative to its objects to a greater capacity for preserving its own nature in the active identification with its object
- from a partial identification between the object and the organism to a complete identity between these terms
- from material activity and dependence on the body to immaterial activity and independence from the body
- from the ability to admit of only a small range of objects to a wider and wider range of objects and of contrariety, becoming more and more universal in its scope
- from assimilating the matter of its object, to assimilating its non-substantial categories, and finally to assimilating the underlying substance of its objects
- from natural necessity requiring its object for survival, to freedom desiring its object in order to live well

Throughout my argument I will be attempting to show how these features are progressively realized as one moves up the series of souls from the nutritive to the sensitive and finally to the intellective.

The argument of the book closely follows the order of Aristotle's exposition in books II and III of the treatise. In the first chapter ("Defining the Soul—The Serial Logic of *De Anima* II.1–3"), I offer a close reading of *De Anima* II.1–3, Aristotle's account of how to grasp the essence of soul in a definition, in order to show how the chapters form a coherently connected dialectical investigation of how one must proceed in the rest of the treatise. Aristotle first offers a definition of soul common to all levels: the basic activity of self-maintenance, necessarily present in all mortal living beings, which is the potentiality for further activities. He then makes clear that defining the soul in this way does not identify the form in each living being that makes it the particular kind of being that it is. Only the highest actuality of the living being truly explains why the being is the way it is—according to the lowest actuality common to all mortal living beings, plants, animals, and humans are indistinguishable. Faced then with the conclusion that there can be no comprehensive account (λόγος) of all souls, Aristotle uncovers that souls are in fact ordered in a series, in which the lower souls are taken up into the higher souls as degrees of potentiality relative to the higher actuality. When beings are organized into such an ordered series of prior and posterior terms, the lower terms are shown to exist for the sake of the higher terms, and the highest term is the ultimate end (τέλος) sought by all the members of the series, which exist within this ultimate term as stages of potentiality in its full actualization. In other words, the highest activity is the final cause and form of all other soul.[5] Further, what is sought at the lower levels is realized with greater success as one moves through the serial ordering. Thus the nature and essence of soul is ultimately found in the soul's thinking activity, which is the final cause of all the souls in the series.

Thus life, and consequently soul, which is the principle and cause of living beings, is an instance of a core-dependent (πρὸς ἕν) equivocal term, where the core meaning lies in the activity of the highest and most developed soul, the thinking soul. This solution shows how moving through the series to the ultimate term both discloses the cause of all the previous kinds of soul and the unifying principle of the various parts of soul within the living being which possesses them all. To confirm my reading of Aristotle's method in *De Anima*, I look at two parallel argumentative structures from *De Caelo* and *Politics* which also begin from the simplest, most immediate appearance through the subsequent terms of the series until the full nature and essence of the object under investigation is disclosed.

In the second chapter ("Unconscious and Stationary Life: Nutritive Soul") I examine *De Anima* II.4 on nutritive soul to bring out what is the character of the most primitive appearance of soul. In order to do so, I show what distinguishes nutritive soul from inanimate beings, and anticipate what nutritive soul lacks—a lack which is subsequently filled in sensitive soul. I emphasize the two structures that Aristotle detects in nutritive activity, one which anticipates the structure of all awareness, and the other which anticipates the treatment of how the soul moves the body. I further argue that the three senses of the soul's causation mentioned by Aristotle in this chapter—efficient, formal, and final—correspond to the three activities governed by nutritive soul—growth, nutrition, and reproduction. Even at this lowest level of soul, there is manifested an unchanging *energeia* beyond change (κίνησις), an impassibility of the organism according to which it maintains its own nature without being overcome by the nourishing object that it assimilates to itself. It is also in II.4 that Aristotle introduces the idea that lower levels of living, in pursuing their own immanent ends, are ultimately seeking the divine mode of life, but only imperfectly, which on my reading of the treatise provides the linchpin of the whole work.

In the third chapter ("Embodied Cognition: Sensitive Soul"), I treat Aristotle's account of sensitive soul in its theoretical mode. Like nutritive soul, sensitive soul realizes itself through assimilation of its object without losing its own nature in this process. As in the previous chapter, Aristotle shows how the soul of sensitive beings acts as efficient, formal, and final cause of the sensitive being. It is in the passive side of sensation, the change (κίνησις) of the organs at the periphery of the sensitive animal treated in II.7–12, that we see how soul is the efficient cause of sensation. Just as growth is not a standard change of quantity but one in which the organism preserves itself through the course of the change through controlled growth and diminution, the change (κίνησις) in the sense organs is a change of quality in which the nature of the organ is preserved and actualized through the course of the change. In III.1–2, Aristotle turns from this consideration of the passive receptivity of the organs to the active awareness underlying all sense organs, which is the formal cause of the sensitive being and the *energeia* at the center of sensation. Finally, I examine his treatment of imagination to show how the production of an image as a by-product of sensation is the final cause of sensation, which in turn becomes the underlying matter for the next highest activity of soul, thinking. This change in the organs, the general awareness of changes in the organs and the production of an image which accompanies this awareness in turn correspond to the threefold division into kinds of sense objects: proper, common, and incidental objects.

In the fourth chapter ("Theoretical Cognition and Divine Life"), I turn to the culminating stage of Aristotle's hierarchy of theoretical cognition, the thinking soul of the human being treated in III.4–6. In active thinking, the soul achieves what was sought imperfectly at all lower levels of soul. I show how the argument follows the same pattern present in the lower levels of soul. III.4 offers an analysis of the receptivity of mind, through the acquisition of the state (ἕξις) of knowledge, corresponding to the receptivity of the five senses. In III.5, corresponding to the treatment of general sensitive awareness in III.1–2, Aristotle treats the active thinking consciousness which brings thinking soul to its full actuality in active contemplation of the truth it knows. Here the efficient, formal, and final causes of intellective soul are united in active thinking. I argue that in his analysis of this highest actuality of soul, one makes the transition from psychology to theology.

When this active thinking is isolated from the receptive aspect of mortal living beings, one has the divine living activity which is the final cause of all the lower levels of ensouled life. I close with an interpretation of the oft-neglected sixth chapter of book III, where Aristotle shows how all the lower activities of the soul are contained and actualized in actively thinking mind in the same way that the various non-substantial categorical attributes of the object grasped by the lower activities are united by the underlying substance which mind thinks.

In the fifth and final chapter ("The Soul That Moves the Body: Mortal Self-Motion and the Circular Motion of the Outermost Sphere"), I treat the second conceptual half of the *De Anima*: the soul's role as cause of movement through space. I argue that the reason this second division of the soul as the cause of locomotion is given such a comparatively short and densely obscure treatment is due to the way it simply repeats the argument about theoretical cognition which Aristotle has just argued for in the first division. Just as Aristotle located the structure of all cognition in the pre-cognitive activity of nutrition, showing how sensitive and intellective awareness simply constitute more adequate and complete articulations of the common structure of all cognition, in his treatment of the desiring soul's movement of the body, he seeks to show how the structure of the soul's locomotive power appears in a primitive way in the stationary activities of nutritive soul. Developing out of this primitive appearance of self-motion, appetitive desire (ἐπιθυμία) and rational desire (βούλησις) constitute progressively complete articulations of this common structure. Aristotle's chief goal in this section is to show how self-movers contain an unmoving aspect, independent of stimuli in their external environment, which ensures the self-mover retains an independence from sensible externality throughout its locomotion. In the analysis of theoretical cognition in III.5, the consideration of a human's active thinking of already acquired knowledge as the highest form of cognitive awareness culminates with an insight into the nature of separate divine activity of thinking divorced from the soul's lower activities, or any potentiality at all. In the same way, the consideration of the human's rational, virtuous practical activity at the summit of the hierarchy of self-motion[6] culminates in a reflection on the perfectly complete, circular self-motion of the divine outermost sphere of the fixed stars, motion which is also an actuality without potentiality and which operates without any of the lower activities of soul. In both cases, this transition from psychology to theology (in III.5's treatment of eternal, immortal thinking and in III.11's analogy between the various forms of motion and the spheres) is as brief as could be, since the in-depth investigation of the nature of divine activity belongs to first philosophy (metaphysics or theology), while psychology belongs to the study of nature. At the same time we catch a glimpse of the divine activity towards which all the activities analyzed in *De Anima* were striving, with various degrees of success, and the human in both cases has been shown to possess this divine actuality in both its theoretical and practical activity in remarkable ways. The human, uniting all the lower living powers within its theoretical and practical thinking activity, is thus the closest mortal approximation of the divine life of pure actuality.

This transition of the study of soul, which is largely a branch of natural philosophy, into theology or first philosophy, raises important questions about the scope of the *De Anima.*[7] The study of soul for Aristotle is the study of the formal principle of living beings. The definition of soul which he articulates ("first actuality of a natural instrumental body") seems to suggest that this investigation will restrict itself to the formal principle of mortal, perishable beings, that is, only those beings which live under the moon.[8] But we know from other treatises that Aristotle's view of living beings includes not only plants, animals, and human beings, but also celestial beings, as well as the prime mover. From the outset of his investigation, Aristotle is carefully ambiguous about the scope of his treatise: "The knowledge [of the soul] seems to contribute greatly to all truth, but above all to [truth about] nature. For the soul is in a way the principle of living beings" (402a4–7).[9] The study of soul will *above all* contribute to our knowledge of nature, that is, material, moving being. But that is not to say that it does not also encompass all being, even immortal, unmoving being.[10] In outlining the puzzle about how to articulate a comprehensive *logos* of all living beings, Aristotle asks whether there must be a separate account for "horse, dog, human, and *god*" (402b7), thus at least introducing the possibility that psychology might at a certain point pass into theology, and that any comprehensive account of the soul as the cause of living activities cannot be complete without reference to divine life.

At the heart of the treatise is the question of whether the soul has any activities which it exercises in itself apart from the body. He refers to these as affections *proper to* the soul (ἴδια πάθη), in contrast to those attributes or activities which can only operate through the conjunction of soul and body. In a treatise devoted to investigating the nature (φύσις) and essence (οὐσία) of the soul, what could manifest these more clearly than the soul operating in itself without reference to anything else? Almost all the activities of the soul are what Aristotle calls "enmattered *logoi*," form as the actualization of some part of the body. But only if there is some activity proper to the soul can there be a living being that exists separately from body and the activities which exist in and through the body (403a10–12). So understanding this question of the independence of certain activities of the soul from the body is importantly connected to understanding whether there might exist either a *thinking* being or a *self-moving* being which does not engage in the nutritive and perceptual activities of soul which are unambiguously and necessarily dependent on their bodies and on objects outside themselves.

The closing puzzle of I.1 thus examines the question of whether the study of soul belongs completely to natural philosophy, which studies both the form and matter of natural beings. If all activities of the soul are inseparable from body, then psychology is firmly embedded in natural philosophy, and anyone who studied some aspect of living being apart from body would be proceeding abstractly, like a mathematician. Only if there are beings characterized by living activities independent of bodies does the first philosopher have an integral role in the study of the soul. In this book, I argue that this role of the metaphysician or theologian is not ancillary to the project of understanding the various kinds of soul and their unity. The nature and essence of the soul *is* mind—a mind which properly speaking is *God*—and all other embodied activities of the soul are reaching out towards this principle, participating in that life to the extent their particular form or nature allows, in the terms Aristotle articulates in *De Anima* II.4 so reminiscent of Plato's *Symposium* (207d).

Thinking as the Essence of Life in Other Aristotelian Treatises

Aristotle's developed views in treatises like *De Anima* are often distinguished from earlier stages in his philosophical development, the earliest of which is identified with Platonism. Yet on the reading I am offering of *De Anima*, the overall conception of the relation between the various living activities remains constant from this early work through to *De Anima*.[11] The *Protrepticus*, an invitation to philosophy by way of an introduction outlining the superiority of the philosophical life over other ways of living, outlines exactly the same analysis of life I am arguing is present in *De Anima*: that the core meaning of life is thinking, that is, the active contemplation which is the sole function of God, but is also intermittently exercised by the human. If, as is generally believed, the *Protrepticus* is an early work,[12] then there is a remarkable consistency in Aristotle's overall biological/psychological philosophy. And regardless of this claim about chronology, the clear expression in a popular style of many of the same points I claim Aristotle is making in *De Anima* offers confirmation of my interpretation.

Aristotle distinguishes between two senses of living, one in reference to the potentiality for a certain living activity, and the other in reference to the actual exercise of this capacity. He illustrates the distinction with the example of perception: one is said to be a living animal when one is only potentially seeing, with eyes shut or while asleep, but also when one is awake, with eyes open, and actively seeing. The same holds for knowing. One is living both when one knows and understands but does not think about the content of one's knowledge, and when one is using this understanding by actively contemplating it. Aristotle argues that in each of these cases, one is said to be living in the stricter sense of the word when one is actively perceiving and knowing in the latter more active senses. Given the potential and actual senses of living in these cases,

> it's clear that "living" will correspondingly be taken in two senses: a waking person must be said to live in the true and proper sense, but sleeping people must be said to live because they are capable of making the transition into the process in virtue of which we say a person is waking and perceiving something.[13]

With reference to any living activity, one is thus said to be more alive in the exercise of the activity than in its unexercised potentiality.

This distinction between being more or less knowing or perceiving is not restricted to the actuality and potentiality of a single specific living activity, but applies also to terms that are ordered in terms of their priority or posteriority:

> For we use "more" not only in the case of excess in things which come under one definition, but also in virtue of priority and posteriority, e.g., we say that health is more a good than the things that conduce to health, and that what is desirable in itself by its own nature is more a good than what produces it. (And yet, as far as the *definition* is concerned, we see that there is no single account predicated of both when we say, both of useful things and of virtue, that each is good.)[14]

Even when the activities do not have the same defining account (λόγος), if they fall in the order of prior and posterior with the posterior existing for the sake of the prior while the prior exists for the sake of itself, then one can say that prior terms offer the stricter sense of the term in question. Applied to living, this would mean that though our definitions of what it means to survive, to perceive, and to think will be different, insofar as they are all living activities and the former exist for the sake of the latter, the latter exhibit more strictly what it means to be living. As Aristotle writes, when a being has several functions or capacities, it is by exercising the best or noblest of its capacities that it is being what it is in the strictest sense. Applied to life and soul, Aristotle draws the following conclusion:

> Now thinking and reasoning are, either alone or most of all, the particular functions of the soul. It is now simple and easy to figure out that the person who thinks correctly *is alive to a higher degree* [italics mine], and that the ones who attain truth to the highest degree live to the highest degree, and that these are the ones who are thinking and contemplating according to the most perfect knowledge.[15]

Thus once one finds the highest kind of living capacity, the actualization of this capacity in its active exercise will be the strictest sense of what it means to live. Yet to be able to say of various activities that some exhibit life in a higher way and some in a lesser way, there must be some common connection by virtue of which they can be compared on the same scale of more and less. Concerning the pleasure which accompanies the exercise of all living activities, Aristotle writes:

> We say the pleasure of living is the pleasure we get from exercising the soul—for that is living in the true sense. If, then, there are several uses of the soul, still the chief of all certainly is that of being wise to the highest degree. It is clear then, that the pleasure that arises from wisdom and contemplation is, necessarily, alone or most of all, the pleasure of living.[16]

The pleasures one takes in living and in thinking are not just different, but the one is the refinement and full development of the pleasure one takes in even the most primitive living activities. It is the same pleasure, but to a higher degree, simply because it is the same activity present at all levels, but according to various degrees of development. And to find what is the ultimate measure of the various stages of development, one must look at the object in question in its fullest development: "The natural purpose is the one which is naturally the last to be completely finished in a process of development."[17] This purpose is the last stage of development of the being, and is that for the sake of which all the earlier stages existed.[18] In this sense, the fully developed nature of the being in question has the most causative powers of all the stages in its development. For just as nutrition exists for the sake of sensation, sensation being in this sense the "cause" of nutrition, thinking is the final cause of both sensation and nutrition. It is also more intelligible than the less developed stages, since what was being sought imperfectly in earlier stages is fully manifested in the culmination of the development. Concerning this greater intelligibility and higher causative power, Aristotle writes:

> The prior is always more intelligible than the posterior, as is that which is better by nature than that which is worse. For knowledge is more concerned with things that are defined and ordered than with their contraries, and more with causes than with effects . . . And things that are prior are more a cause than those that are posterior, for if you take away the former, you take away the things that have their substance from them.[19]

Already in this early treatise, Aristotle makes clear that the various living activities are in fact the same activity only at various levels of clarity and explicitness. Opinion, for instance, is not simply a distinct living activity from knowledge, but is a less successful realization of the same activity manifested in active thinking:

> If true opinion is desirable precisely according to the manner and extent to which it is like wisdom by reason of being true, then if this is found more in wisdom, wisdom is more desirable than opining truly.[20]

What one desires in having true opinions is the very same thing one desires in knowing something, with the difference that what was sought in the former is more completely attained in the latter, which means that the knowing is the measure of the value of true opinion. True opinion is valuable to the extent that it resembles that which it is indirectly seeking to attain.

For the same reason Aristotle writes that mind, though not present in non-human animals, is actually possessed by them obscurely:

> For animals too have some small glimmers of reason and practical wisdom, but are entirely deprived of the intellectual wisdom of observation, and this is present in the gods alone, just as a human being actually falls short of many animals in the accuracy and power of its perception and impulses.[21]

Animals, in the fact that they are defined by their perceptive capacity, manifest obscure traces of the rational activities of humans. And in turn, these are imperfect vestiges of the divine activity of thinking which in this way is the measure or standard by which the worth of all living activities is evaluated.

Finally, in the *Protrepticus* Aristotle argues that since all living activities are ultimately the same living activity at different levels of development and explicitness, what all living beings are ultimately seeking is the activity of thinking:

> Whatever, then, is the virtue of this part (i.e., the best part of the soul—reason and thinking), it must be, *for all beings in general and for us*, the most desirable of all things: for I think one might actually take this position, that we *are* this part, either alone or especially [italics mine].[22]

This is the position Aristotle takes in *De Anima*: that all living beings ultimately seek to be like God, whose activity is perpetually active thinking, an activity which among mortal beings only humans engage in successfully, but which all living activities desire, attaining this goal to varying degrees of success. For this view to be coherent, it must be shown that living activities are not simply distinct from one another, but each manifest the same structure to progressively explicit degrees.

The *Protrepticus* also argues that as one moves from the lowest to the highest living activities, one moves from natural necessity, that is, requiring the object of the activity in order to survive, towards a more rational freedom, requiring the object of the activity not for mere survival but for "living well." As a result, it can seem that the lower activities, like nutrition or touch, are more fundamental and inherently related to life, whereas seeing or thinking, being simply optional, are less essentially connected to living. Nevertheless, Aristotle explicitly repudiates this view:

> For the things that are loved for the sake of something else and without which life is impossible should be called necessities and joint causes, while those that are loved for themselves, even if nothing follows from them, should be called goods in the strict sense.[23]

As we will see in the course of our argument, these higher, more free activities are not only more strictly manifesting goodness, but are also more strictly exhibiting what it means to be alive, while the highest activity of divine thinking requiring nothing outside itself, is the core meaning of life towards which the lower activities all aspire.

Yet if the view I am arguing for were only present in this early popular work and not the Aristotelian treatises which, along with *De Anima*, are agreed to have been written later, it could be argued that I am simply imposing an early, Platonic viewpoint on the more empirical standpoint of Aristotle's developed perspective. There are, however, equally clear indications that this same view can be found in Aristotle's other works as well. Let us look at a handful of the most important passages in this regard.

In *De Caelo*, to describe the immaterial noetic beings beyond the outermost sphere, Aristotle writes that they possess "the best and most self-sufficient of lives [τὴν ἀρίστην . . . ζωὴν καὶ αὐταρκεστάτην],"[24] and that this life exists beyond place, time, affection, and alteration. Of this immortal and divine life, Aristotle writes: "From it derive the being [τὸ εἶναι] and life [τὸ ζῆν] which other things, some more or less articulately [ἀκριβέστερον] but others feebly [ἀμαυρῶς], enjoy."[25] Here is explicitly stated what I take to be the key to interpreting the structure of Aristotle's analysis of soul and living being in *De Anima*. All living beings express a common structure in progressively clearer approximations of the divine life which causes them. Divine thinking is most alive, while nutritive soul is least alive. This is indicated in an important passage from the *History of Animals*, where Aristotle writes,

> Nature proceeds little by little from things lifeless to animal life in such a way that it is impossible to determine the exact line of demarcation, nor on which side thereof an intermediate form should lie. Thus, next after lifeless things comes the plant, and of plants one will differ from another as to the amount of apparent vitality; and, in a word, the whole genus of plants, whilst it is devoid of life as compared with an animal, is endowed with life as compared with other corporeal entities. Indeed, as we just remarked, there is observed in plants a continuous scale of ascent towards the animal . . . And so throughout the entire animal scale there is a graduated differentiation in amount of vitality and in capacity for motion.[26]

Living beings differ from one another based on "the amount of apparent vitality" in each, and the lower sometimes exhibit something of the higher but only indistinctly. There is "a graduated differentiation in amount of vitality," in which plants are least alive, so to speak, and humans the most. The goal of the current analysis of *De Anima* is to give some precision to what could be meant by degrees of being alive.

In *De Caelo*, Aristotle explains that the activity (πρᾶξις) of the stars (which he takes to be alive) must be compared with the activities of plants and animals. There he lays out one of the important differences in the hierarchy of living activities leading towards the perfection of the divine life:

> We must, then, think of the action of the stars as similar to that of animals and plants. For on our earth it is man that has the greatest variety of actions—for there are many goods that man can secure; hence his actions are various and directed to ends beyond them—while the perfectly conditioned has no need of action, since it is itself the end, and actions always requires two terms, end and means. The lower animals have less variety of action than man; and plants perhaps have little action and of one kind only. For either they have but one attainable good (as indeed man has), or, if several, each contributes directly to their ultimate good. One thing then has and enjoys the ultimate good, other things attain to it, one immediately by few steps, another by many, while yet another does not even attempt to secure it but is satisfied to reach a point not far removed from that consummation. Thus, taking health as the end, there will be one thing that always possesses health, others that attain it, one by reducing flesh, another by running and thus reducing flesh, another by taking steps himself to run, thus further increasing the number of movements, while another cannot attain health itself, but only running or reduction of flesh, so that one or other of these is for such a being the end. For while it is clearly best for any being to attain the real end, yet, if that cannot be, the nearer it is to the best the better will be its state.[27]

In this passage, Aristotle distinguishes various levels of being alive. There is God, in whom no change (κίνησις) or practical act (πρᾶξις) exists, being in eternal possession of its own end. In contrast, two other kinds of living being attain this divine end, but only as the result of a process. The first heaven attains this divine end through one act, namely, the perfect circular locomotion in which beginning and end coincide. The other kind of being that also attains this divine end, the human, does so only by the intermediation of several activities, the nutritive and sensitive activities necessary and instrumental for the activity of human thinking. Non-thinking animals engage in fewer activities, and non-sensitive plants engage in only one activity, and neither of these actually attains the end towards which they ultimately strive in seeking the ultimate good proper to their specific kind of living nature.

They are only able to perform activities which in the human are instrumental to attaining the divine end, without themselves attaining this end. There is a hierarchy of life depending on how close a being is to having the capacity to engage in the activity of thinking which characterizes the self-sufficient divine life.[28]

In other passages Aristotle makes clear that different levels of being and living are characterized by their distance from the principle, which determines how adequately each, according to its own mode of being, is able to satisfy the universal desire for the being and life of the divine. In a discussion of the eternity of becoming, Aristotle writes:

> For in all things, as we affirm, nature always strikes after the better. Now being . . . is better than not-being; but not all things can possess being, since they are too far removed from the principle. God therefore adopted the remaining alternative, and fulfilled the perfection of the universe by making coming-to-be uninterrupted; for the greatest possible coherence would thus be secured to existence, because that coming-to-be should itself come-to-be perpetually is the closest approximation of eternal being.[29]

Here we see how Aristotle understands how lower levels of being, in desiring to exist or live according to their own nature, are ultimately seeking to be like the divine, according to the degree their nature and location on the continuous hierarchy of being permits.

But what precisely does each level of ensouled being desire in desiring to be like God? In a passage from *Eudemian Ethics*, Aristotle explains that the desire to be alive is ultimately the desire for cognition, and the soul's desire for cognition is a desire to be determined by its object as fully as possible without losing its own identity in the process. In an absolutely crucial discussion of "what is living according to actuality [ἐνέργεια] and as an end [τέλος],"[30] Aristotle says that to live in this sense is to perceive and to know. He asks what it is that is ultimately desired in a living being's striving to preserve its own life and concludes that it is these very activities of perception and knowledge for oneself (one's own perception and one's own knowing)[31] which make them most desirable. He then identifies even more fundamentally what is desired in this desire to know:

> For we must take two things into consideration, that life is desirable and also that the good is, and thence that it is desirable that such a nature should belong to oneself [ὑπάρχειν] as belongs to them. If,

> then, of such a pair of corresponding series there is always one series of the desirable, and the known and the perceived are in general constituted by their participation in the nature of the determined [κοινωνεῖν τῆς ὡρισμένης φύσεως]; so that to wish to perceive one's self is to wish oneself to be of a certain definite character—since, then, we are not in ourselves [κατ' αὐτούς] possessed of each of such characters, but only by participation in these qualities in perceiving and knowing—for the perceiver becomes perceived in that way and in that respect in which he first perceives, and according to the way in which and the object which he perceives; and the knower becomes known in the same way—therefore it is for this reason that one always desires to live, because one always desires to know; and this is because he himself wishes to be the object known.[32]

Apart from the objects of our characteristic activities, we mortal living beings are indeterminate, mere potencies to become beings with fully determinate natures: unlike the gods, who are determinate in themselves, mortal beings can only be in actuality what they are in relation to something different than themselves—some external object through which it is able to realize its potentialities. In a passage to which I will repeatedly return, Aristotle distinguishes mortal from divine life in precisely this way: while the God's excellent existence means that it does not think anything beyond itself, "with us welfare involves a something beyond us [καθ' ἕτερον], but the deity is his own well-being."[33]

Thus the two sides of the argument which Aristotle asks us to grasp along with him are the nature of the living being and the nature of the object of that being's activity: the animal and its object of perception, the human and its object of perception or knowledge. Both these sides are desirable. Our desire is to realize our potential activities, yet this cannot happen without the presence of the objects of those activities. As belonging to the class of living beings that know, we are potentially all the things we can potentially perceive and know, but only through being determined by the objects do we become actively what we are. In fact, what we ultimately desire is for these two sides to come together as one. We become more fully what we are once we become determinate in our identification with the object of our activities. Given that in the exercise of all of the soul's activities the activity and the object become one, the soul becomes the object of thought, the object of perception, and even the object of nutrition. Yet since the very nature of the living being in question is to be determined by these objects, it does not lose itself in becoming determined by the object, but it fulfills its own nature. I become most fully what I am in becoming the object of nutrition, perception, and thinking. Thus, the desire for cognition, whether it be in the proto-cognitive identification of object and living being in nutrition or the explicitly cognitive activities of perception and thinking, is ultimately a desire to become determined by its objects and hence most actively what it is.[34] Souls are essentially natures with certain powers to receive objects into themselves and be determined by them without simply losing themselves in the process.[35] This is one of the most fundamental analogies uniting all levels of soul, and understanding how one level is more truly alive than another involves understanding the different ways that these organisms become determined by their object while preserving themselves in the process.

The purpose of my interpretation of *De Anima* is to show how that treatise, when properly understood, gives the theoretical foundation for these claims about a hierarchy of degrees of life constituted out of various degrees of approximation to the life of divine thinking which is the full actuality and nature of being alive sought by all lower levels of ensouled beings.

Interpretations of *De Anima*: Ancient and Medieval

My own reading shares a great deal in common with certain ancient readings of *De Anima*, especially their attention to the theological interest of the work and their attempt to identify what is the unifying thread of the work which explains the structure of the whole. Following Iamblichus,[36] grasping this σκοπός (*skopos*), or overall aim of the work, encourages the interpreter to ask of each part of the treatise: what does this have to do with the overarching purpose of the work? As Simplicius notes in his commentary on the *Categories*, one identifies the aim of the treatise so that one can refer everything to this.[37] The Neoplatonists identified this unifying thread (σκοπός) not only for each treatise, but also for the whole philosophy of a thinker. Simplicius identifies this chief philosophical aim for Aristotle as ascending to a One, Ammonius to reach the common cause of all things and to grasp its nature, while for Philiponus Aristotle's goal is to attain knowledge of the creative cause of all things.[38] The general consensus among Neoplatonic commentators on the unifying theme or *skopos* of the *De Anima* is that the main aim of the treatise is to understand the ψυχὴ λογική, the rational soul.

This coincides with my argument that mind is both the unifying activity comprehensive of all lower activities, and that it is the unifying thread binding together the parts of the treatise. My general thesis, that the essence and nature of the life of ensouled beings is mind, which is most perfectly manifested in God's perpetually active thinking, and that all the lower activities of soul are less developed instances of this core sense, is not a new one. Most likely this is how Alexander of Aphrodisias[39]—whose commentary on the *De Anima* is not extant—read the treatise. In *Metaphysics*, Aristotle writes that "waking, perception and thinking are most pleasant, and hopes and memories are so because of their reference to these."[40] Alexander, commenting on this passage, explains that all these activities are pleasant because they are "images and shadows"[41] of thinking activity. I am here arguing that the same is true of all living activities. It is perhaps to Alexander's reading of *De Anima* that Plotinus refers in *Ennead* I.4, *On True Happiness*. In this consideration of whether merely being alive could be identified with genuine happiness, Plotinus writes:

> It has been said more than once that the perfect life and the true life, the essential life, is in the mind [νοῦς] beyond this sphere, and that all other forms of life are incomplete, are phantoms of life, imperfect, not pure, not more truly life than they are its contrary: here let it be said succinctly that since all living things proceed from the one principle but possess life in different degrees, this principle must be the first life and the most complete.

Plotinus himself does not produce a commentary on *De Anima*, and it is not even clear that he himself embraces the view of *De Anima* he describes in this passage, but he does demonstrate here that the view I am here ascribing to Aristotle's *De Anima* was a view embraced by certain ancient philosophers, either as an interpretation of Aristotle or as the truth of the matter: that the essence of life is divine thinking, and that the lives exhibited by lower souls are different degrees of this pure life. Variations of this view became generally embraced among philosophers in the Neoplatonic tradition.[42]

Yet certain independent philosophical interests belonging to Neoplatonism distinguish the ancient commentators from my reading of Aristotle's psychology. Neoplatonism, beginning from the knowledge of the One as first principle of everything other than it, seeks to explain systematically how this principle produces everything in progressive stages beginning with what most closely approximates this primordial unity and moving to what least approximates it. But Aristotle proceeds in exactly the opposite way. He begins from the lowest and most primitive, and moves through progressively more complete living activities. This argument continues until the first principle, that which does not exist for the sake of anything else and which perfectly attains what is sought at the lower levels, is disclosed.[43] Aristotle never attempts to explain how or why the first principle produces what is other than it, but rather assumes the existence of the world and all its distinctions and simply tries to account for how it is governed by this principle. Thus the difference between Aristotle and his Neoplatonic commentators is not that the latter hold to a hierarchical conception of the universe while Aristotle does not, as is sometimes argued,[44] but rather the direction of the analysis of a universe equally hierarchical for both. Further, because the principle for Aristotle does not emerge until the culmination of the investigation, one will misread Aristotle's argument if one assumes the entirety of his view to be present at every instant of the exposition. Several contemporary commentators[45] have stressed the importance of reading each argument within its immediate context, taking into account the developmental character of Aristotle's argumentation. As Burnyeat argues, one cannot, as the ancient commentators generally do, assume the whole of Aristotle's philosophy to be present at every point of his text.[46]

A significant distinction between Aristotle and his Neoplatonic and medieval interpreters lies in the beginning point of their investigation. Beginning with the Hellenistic philosophers after Aristotle there is an assumed beginning with the moral human soul *prior* to nature. The way towards knowledge of soul is *not*, as it is for Plato and Aristotle, through an understanding of nature and its limitations and incompleteness. With the unity of the human soul as an immediate, prior assumption of Neoplatonism, the soul's knowledge of God is through a more immediate and internal route than for Aristotle. One must turn away from nature into the thinking soul in order to discover the principles governing all reality, to return the soul to its origin. Consider the contrasting beginning points of Aristotelian and Neoplatonic psychology: whereas the Neoplatonist begins with soul, turns inward to mind (νοῦς) and discovers the One, Aristotle begins firmly in nature with plants. Aristotle cannot begin with a complete and substantial human soul; this can only be discovered by moving to it through nature. In this sense, Aristotle's conclusion that the human unites within itself the whole of reality, both of lower nature and of divinity, is immediately presupposed as the beginning point in later thinkers. After Plotinus, who discovers the One as the result of an ascent through the various levels of the self, Neoplatonists begin by assuming the One as first principle of all reality as their absolute and unquestioned beginning. Lower, natural forms are no longer stepping-stones on the way to the discovery of God, since the existence or supra-existence of the One is far more certain than anything in nature.

Important consequences result from this difference. In general, Neoplatonic commentators do not pay very much attention to nutritive soul, because it is clearly inseparable from the body. In fact, in many cases commentators speak of the distinction between rational and irrational soul, while identifying nutritive soul as simply the operation of body below the irrational soul of perception and desire.[47] According to the soteriological concerns of Neoplatonic thought, one turns away from nature below the thinking soul in order to return to one's true origin. Blumenthal notes that for the Neoplatonists, the nutritive soul "could be described as φύσις, while ψυχή might be used not only as a term for soul in general, but also more specifically to describe the soul above the level of φύσις."[48] Though integral to Aristotle's own analysis of soul, on this view soul's first appearance is an unfortunate appendage to the real meaning of the work.

In the developmental reading I am proposing, however, Aristotle's analysis of the very first and most primitive appearance of ensouled life is crucial for grasping the work as a whole. For the nature of soul as cause of awareness and self-motion *is* present in this first appearance of life, if only in an unclear and muddled way.[49] This is perhaps the biggest difference between Aristotle and later commentators who read him systematically. Against a systematic reading, the argument of *De Anima* does not begin with an explicit conception of the soul as mind and life as thinking, most fully exhibited in the life of the divine. On this view Aristotle would simply measure the deficiency of each level of soul and life against the perfect standard. I maintain that Aristotle's argument is much more empirical than this. The divine measure of all life emerges as the result and not the presupposition of the argument, and the engine driving the argument is the analysis of what each kind of soul and life is in itself. One investigates each level of soul in itself, holding to the immanent analysis of those phenomena without reference to an external measure, and it is only once one moves to the next highest level of soul that one sees the way that the higher activity more fully satisfies what was being sought at the lower level. In this sense more weight is given to the analysis of each level than if the end point was assumed throughout the investigation. With one notable exception,[50] the fully explicit meaning of life in the divine thinking is not present until this pure activity is disclosed in the analysis of active thinking in III.5 and the perfect circular motion of the outermost sphere in III.11. Ultimately the higher is the measure of the lower, but only after one has analyzed a particular level of soul in itself according to its own standard.

Like the Neoplatonists,[51] Aquinas generally finds a systematic Aristotle in *De Anima*. Throughout the commentary it is assumed that the various arguments are connected, the role of the interpreter being the detection of the sometimes only implicit connections.[52] As Ivo Thomas writes of Aquinas's commentary, "A definite body of doctrine is being inculcated, presented in a predominately deductive form," a form which followed Aristotle's own explanation of demonstrative science in the *Posterior Analytics* and which Aquinas along with other medieval interpreters took to be at least implicitly present in Aristotle's treatises.[53] Yet it is Aquinas's own analysis of the relation between divine life and lower biological examples of ensouled being that is most helpful for grasping the overall argument of *De Anima.*

Medieval writers like Maimonides and Aquinas are deeply concerned with the difference between the way a term such as "life" is predicated of creatures and predicated of God. Against Maimonides's acknowledgment of such positive terms as applying only indirectly to God, where saying God is alive would mean either that God *is not* inanimate or God is the cause of life, Aquinas seeks a more positive understanding of divine names through the relation of *analogy*, a middle ground between univocity and equivocity.

> And in this way some things are said of God and creatures analogically, and not in a purely equivocal nor in a purely univocal sense. For we can name God only from creatures. Hence, whatever is said of God and creatures is said according as there is some relation of the creature to God as to its principle and cause, wherein all the perfections of things pre-exist excellently. Now this mode of community is a mean between pure equivocation and simple univocation. For in analogies the idea is not, as it is in univocals, one and the same; yet it is not totally diverse as in equivocals but the name which is used in a multiple sense signifies various proportions to some one thing.[54]

Maimonides's view, Aquinas argues, conflicts with Aristotle's. Aquinas argues that

> when we say, God is good, the meaning is not, God is the cause of goodness, or, God is not evil; but the meaning is, whatever good we attribute to creatures pre-exists in God, and in a higher way. Hence it does not follow that God is good because he causes goodness; but rather, on the contrary, he causes goodness in things because he is good. As Augustine says, Because He is good, we are.[55]

Aquinas applies the very same analysis to life in Question 18 of the *Prima Pars.* There he defines life by self-movement: "Since a thing is said to live in so far as it operates of itself and is not moved by another, the more perfectly this power is found in anything, the more perfect is the life of that thing."[56] After showing how this is more and more properly realized as one moves through plants, animals, and humans, Aquinas argues that, following Aristotle, it is in God's self-thinking, in no way determined by anything outside itself, that life exists most perfectly. Yet in his *De Anima* commentary, this analysis of life as a core-dependent (πρὸς ἕν) equivocal plays no role. In fact, Aquinas's commentary on *De Anima* inaugurates a prevailing consensus in later interpretations that the Aristotelian God does not enter into the argument of the treatise. Like all Aquinas's Aristotelian commentaries, it is enormously helpful on particular points, but I will try to show that the analysis of living beings that Aquinas derives from Aristotle in his *Summa* is present in *De Anima* in a way that his commentary does not make explicit.

Modern Readings of *De Anima*

In general, modern interpreters of *De Anima* have abandoned a unified reading of the various parts of the treatise. *De Anima* is read by contemporary interpreters either as essentially a treatise on natural philosophy, or biology, with a brief appendix on the independent activities of human mind only loosely connected to the treatment of nutritive and sensitive soul,[57] or as a treatise primarily on philosophy of mind, only loosely connected with the section on plants and nutrition.[58] In both cases, a substantial unifying thread of all the powers of soul is lost, and the theological element of *De Anima* is almost always ignored. Virtually all modern views on both the content and the form and structure of *De Anima* share the perception of Aristotle's psychology as profoundly unsystematic. In the introduction to his edition of *De Anima*, Hicks argues that "the writer's modest aim is by preliminary discussion to settle a few, just a few, fundamental questions as to the nature and attributes of the one principle of life and mind."[59] On this view, Aristotle's treatise is simply a collection of loose ends left over from previous psychological theory which he needs to tie up. Though all commentators recognize the undeniable fact that there is a certain necessary order to the investigation insofar as his treatment of the kinds of soul follow their serial ordering of nutritive, sensitive, and intellective soul, most modern interpreters are hesitant to see in the *De Anima* anything beyond this minimally organized structure. The ancient interpreters' search for a unifying thread (σκοπός) to each work they studied is no longer a pressing concern for most contemporary commentators. As Amélie Rorty writes, due to the fact that *De Anima* contains subjects belonging to metaphysics, biology, psychology, and action theory,

> not surprisingly, contemporary approaches to *De Anima* reflect a range of heterogeneous philosophical preoccupations. The confluence of several lines of investigations that bring scholars to *De Anima* represents the lines of thought that originally formed the work.[60]

Though one might expect this of specialized studies on particular topics found in Aristotle's *De Anima*, even the most important general commentaries on the work do not find a principle of unification of the parts of the treatise.

There are perhaps good philological reasons for resisting any overly unified reading of the treatise. As Martha Nussbaum notes, we can never know with certainty what Aristotle's works looked like prior to the edition of Andronicus, and so the question of whether *De Anima* was "a unitary work,"[61] or whether the text we have was simply a compilation of more or less unconnected pieces, cannot be decided apart from understanding the parts and seeing if they form a coherently ordered whole. For the question about the structure and unity of the treatise is not merely a question of formal composition, but has important implications for the content of Aristotle's views on the soul. If the capacities for nutrition, sensation, locomotion, and thinking are related in some substantial way, perhaps the nature of the object being investigated determines the procedure by which Aristotle structures the treatise. The structure of the being under investigation might just determine the structure of our thinking about it.

Some commentators do seek some kind of unifying principle behind the various living activities investigated in *De Anima*, but deny that divine thinking has anything to do with this connection, or even that Aristotle's psychology contains any theological concern. That there exists an overall teleological structure to Aristotle's cosmos, with the activity of inanimate and animate nature and the heavenly bodies progressively ordered towards an ultimate end, a first principle or the unmoved mover, has been recently dismissed by many commentators as a medieval theistic prejudice imposed upon a much more modest teleology restricted to ends particular and intrinsic to individual things, a view of great consequence in relation to the overall structure and progression of *De Anima*.[62]

Martin Heidegger, in explicit opposition to Thomistic readings of Aristotle, articulates clearly this de-theologizing impulse in interpreting Aristotle in his 1922 essay "Phenomenological Interpretations with Respect to Aristotle: Indication of the Hermeneutical Situation." Setting his own interpretation against medieval readings of Aristotle, Heidegger argues that Aristotle's analysis is phenomenological, in the sense that each phenomenon investigated is measured by its own *internal* standards.[63] This insight is important for distinguishing Aristotle's more empirical method from subsequent Neoplatonic and Scholastic systemizations of his philosophy.[64] Corresponding to this view of Aristotle's unsystematic method is a certain view of philosophy as fundamentally non-theological. If one is going to analyze beings according to their own immanent standards and not measure them according to their relation to some perfect standard, it must remain atheistic, or at least theology must be separated from philosophy. For Heidegger, Aristotle's analysis of living beings begins and terminates in nature, holding fast to the nature of the object investigated according to the inner logic of natural life.[65]

Though such an exclusion of theology from psychology does not belong exclusively to modern interpretations, modern commentators tend to deny that Aristotle's God even makes an appearance in *De Anima*, reading III.5 on the activity of thinking as an analysis restricted to a certain aspect of human thinking. Obviously there can be no explanatory role for divine thinking in *De Anima* if it does not even make an appearance in the treatise. Consequently I will have to show, following certain modern interpreters like M. Frede, Caston, Burnyeat, and Kosman, that Aristotle's divine principle does in fact come into view in this culmination of his treatment of intellect. Further, I argue that divine activity appears not only at the culmination of the theoretical aspect of cognition, but also at a similar point in the argument about self-motion, through a comparison between the self-motion of a rational and virtuous human agent with the circular motion of the whole universe, which Aristotle considers to be a divine body.

In what follows I would like to show that the modern insight into the unsystematic character of Aristotle's procedure does not have to entail either abandoning a strongly unifying thread that holds together the various strands of the argument, or an elimination of Aristotle's theological interest in analyzing the souls of living beings. It is by understanding the analysis of living beings in terms of a core-dependent (πρὸς ἕν) equivocity with divine thinking and circular self-motion as the core nature of being alive, expressed with increasing degrees of clarity as one ascends the series of living beings, that one can do justice to both ancient, medieval, and modern interpretations of Aristotle's *De Anima*, and most importantly, to Aristotle's own thought.

Towards a New Interpretation of *De Anima*

Several recent commentators have pointed towards the way I am suggesting the *De Anima* needs to be read. Charles Kahn suggests the key to understanding Aristotle's analysis of any one of the levels of soul is to put it in the context of a comparison with the other kinds of soul. For many of the observations Aristotle makes about each kind of soul are included in order to contrast with similar features of other levels of soul. Kahn writes:

> If we are to comprehend Aristotle's conception of the sensory soul in its full complexity, we must be prepared to follow it from its roots in the vital physiology of the organism to this flowering in a faculty of critical awareness, including the specifically human awareness of ourselves and of our own existence as thinking, sentient beings. We must, in short, see sense perception within the context of Aristotle's psychology as a whole.[66]

The image of the organism flowering from the most primitive to the most developed level of soul is instructive, for it suggests that rather than looking at a simple variety of souls and their living activities, one is looking at the teleological development of one kind of substance. The flower in its full bloom is the true expression of its nature, which is only unclearly and implicitly present at earlier stages of its development.

Aryeh Kosman writes on the sense in which nutrition, perception, and thinking all involve the same activity at different stages of approximation to divine thinking. In a series of interconnected articles on *De Anima* and other treatises to which the present study is deeply indebted,[67] Kosman has outlined the basis for a unified grasp of the argument of *De Anima* in which theoretical contemplation is "the (divine) full self-manifesting and self-capturing activity of *consciousness* . . . of which the ruder and more incorporate activities of perception and nutrition are equally images, if meaner and less noble."[68] All these living activities are defined

> by their capacity to be open to further determination by virtue of that determinacy of essential being that characterizes them in the first instance as substances . . . For human beings, this openness to further determination is centred on perception and thought, but it is a general feature of human psychic powers as set forth in *De Anima*. The nutritive capacity—the capacity to eat—is a capacity to take in other matter (the power of ingestion) and to transform it into oneself (the power of digestion); thus the *De Anima* begins its discussion of psychic powers with an account of nutrition, and specifically of nutriment, that is, of food. In the same way, the capacity to perceive is a power to take in the sensible forms of the world

> and transform them into consciousness . . . A significantly different story will therefore have to be told about knowing, and particularly about νοῦς, which is the ἀρχή of the perceptive and knowing powers in general, the highest form of consciousness. But the story will be similar in that the knower will become the object known without relinquishing its determinate identity.[69]

This is a crucial similarity which must be traced through the hierarchy of life: that each is a certain mode of assimilating or being determined by one's object without losing one's nature in the process. Kosman's interpretation thus self-consciously takes up Alexander's thesis about the relation of the various living activities. He affirms the "cogency of Alexander's suggestion that νοῦς is in fact the paradigm instance and thus the ἀρχή of the many animate modes of awareness."[70]

Although the details of his account are very different than my own reading, Ronald Polansky expresses very well one of the main tasks of the interpreter of *De Anima* who wishes to grasp the overall structure of the argument. The interpreter must grasp the analogies and disanalogies between the functions of the soul:

> Engaging in multiple functions, soul resembles other things that have functions, and its own functions resemble each other. This suggests that soul enters into many analogous and disanalogous relationships . . . Much of the *De Anima* concentrates on such relationships. For example, the nutritive capacity of soul turns potential food into actual food through the action upon it of heat. The sensible object through a medium acts upon the sense organ so that they become assimilated to the sensible object. Hence, the animal assimilates its food, but the sensible object assimilates the sense to it.[71]

Beyond this analogy of nutrition and sensation, Polansky also emphasizes the importance of rigorously following the analogies and disanalogies between sensation and thought:

> It is not generally sufficiently emphasized that Aristotle presents his account of thought by following up such features of sense-perception . . . What seem extremely dense and ragged discussions (on thinking) show themselves possessed of a straightforward and orderly development through their connections with the previous sections on sense.[72]

It is only through identification of these analogical structures that one can appreciate the true unfolding progression of the argument of *De Anima*. Without recognizing the similarity of structure, the disanalogies are invisible.

John Russon further identifies the main analogy between the various levels of ensouled life:

> All the functions of soul . . . are, I will show, essentially actions whereby the self and the other are in some manner identified. This basic principle derives from *De Generatione et Corruptione*, and we can trace it throughout Aristotle's account of the forms of ensouling to see how it applies; we must see what *kind* of identification is involved, and how the form the identification takes differs with different kinds of soul.[73]

Russon here points out how the basic structure of acting and being affected from *On Generation and Corruption* offers the structure within which the interactions of living activities and their objects will be analyzed. He goes on to give an admirable comparison of these various modes of identification of organism and object through nutrition, perception, and thinking. In the course of this analysis, Russon notes in passing that identifying the common structure of the various activities of soul in this way reveals a very particular logical relation which obtains between them:

> We will now go on to see that this "identification with the other" which defines ψυχή is a πρὸς ἕν equivocal such that ensoulings will become progressively higher in proportion as they are identifications which involve progressively less destruction of one contrary, with νοῦς being the final term in the series in relation to which the lesser forms are defined.[74]

The idea that the relation between the various analogical levels of soul are ultimately unified as a πρὸς ἕν equivocal or "core-dependent homonymy" is given more explicit defense by Christopher Shields in his chapter on *De Anima* in his *Order and Multiplicity: Homonymy in the Philosophy of Aristotle*.[75] Shields writes:

> Although he does not say so explicitly, Aristotle suggests that life is a core-dependent homonym. It is therefore incumbent upon him to specify its core and to explain how its non-core instances stand in appropriate relation to that core.[76]

Shields identifies this core-instance as God's self-thinking. God is not only alive, as is argued in *Metaphysics* XII, but is the source of all life. Shields characterizes what it is about God's thinking that is the core meaning of the homonymy of living in nutrition, perception, and human thinking too weakly in my view—he identifies it as "the notion of an intentional system," or "end-directed behavior," in beings whose ends are not derived from without.[77] I will argue that the core analogical similarity is much more robust than this, but Shields has clearly identified the logical structure and principle of unification of both the various forms of life, and also, as a consequence of this, of the *De Anima*.

While scholars like Kosman, Kahn, Russon, Polansky, and Shields have laid the groundwork for seeing the serial ordering of the soul's nutritive, sensitive, and intellective powers as degrees of actualization of cognition, absolutely no one in the commentary tradition has noticed that this analogy between nutrition, sensation, and thinking also holds true for Aristotle's treatment of the second major division of the soul's power, that is, desire's power to move the body through space. Nor has anyone noticed that in the analysis of the highest level of mortal self-motion, the practical mind's movement of the rationally virtuous agent, there is an appearance of the paradigmatic instance of self-motion, the divine circular motion of the outermost sphere which serves as the measure of all mortal self-motion. While there is a long and distinguished tradition of interpreters who see Aristotle's treatment of active intellect in III.5 as a transition from psychology to theology, it has not been noticed that precisely this same transition from psychology to theology is made in the second conceptual half of the argument. Aristotle's God thus serves as the paradigm of both the theoretical and desiderative activities of living beings, and the anchor of the argument of the whole treatise. So where my treatment of cognition builds upon a small but emerging scholarly trend which sees the importance for the argument of *De Anima* of the analogy between nutrition, sensation, and thinking as modes of assimilative cognition, my demonstration that the same analogies hold for the part of the soul responsible for locomotion is altogether new. Because no one has previously understood Aristotle's chapters on desire and locomotion in this way, the completely systematic character of the treatise has never been properly articulated.

Richard Bodéüs, in the excellent introduction to his masterful edition and translation of *De Anima*, makes reference to a line of interpretation very similar to my own, identifying it as Hegelian and dismissing it as a distortion of Aristotle's intentions in *De Anima*:

> Mind, which Aristotle admits appears to be an incorruptible substance, is situated by him as the final term and, therefore, the summit of the series of the hierarchized capacities of soul. It thus seems, for him, to be the soul *par excellence*, the only one, according to some, which one must take into consideration, even when one is not looking to recenter psychology on the human. The argument goes a long way. For if mind is the highest expression of the soul (Hegel said of "consciousness"), then the *DA* becomes a sort of introduction to metaphysics, necessary for the understanding of Aristotelian theology. This still remains the interpretation defended by certain present-day Hegelians.[78]

Bodéüs goes on to characterize the argument as "specious," since (1) it ignores how Aristotle qualifies the nutritive soul as fundamental, not the intellective, and (2) it ignores the fact that even in his account of thinking, Aristotle, from an empirical perspective, seeks to show how mind is rooted in sensibility.[79]

I will deal with these two criticisms in the course of the argument; here I wish simply to comment briefly on the Hegelian roots of the interpretation I am presenting. Hegel in fact offers a fairly detailed interpretation of *De Anima*, which can be found if one synthesizes the very general treatment of *De Anima* in his *Lectures on the History of Philosophy* with the more detailed analysis of soul and life in his *Encyclopedia*. If one takes Hegel at his word, his own account of the soul in the *Encyclopedia* does not differ in content but only in form and organization from his understanding of Aristotelian psychology as it appears in *De Anima* and the *Parva Naturalia*:

> The books of Aristotle *On the Soul*, along with his discussions of its special aspects and states, are for this reason still the most admirable, perhaps even the sole, work of philosophical value on this topic. The main aim of a philosophy of spirit can only be to reintroduce unity of concept into the cognition of spirit, and so reinterpret the meaning of those Aristotelian books.[80]

Therefore one can turn to this definitive account of Hegel's psychology in the *Encyclopedia* for the specific details of Hegel's reading of those Aristotelian works on psychology.[81]

What is Hegel's reading of *De Anima*, and how does it differ from both the modern, unsystematic view of the treatise, and the older understandings of the work as systematic? Hegel states that, against most Neoplatonic and medieval interpretations, the *De Anima* (like his other treatises) is unsystematic and empirical in method. This means that one does not begin with the completeness of divine thinking, and show how it is revealed in stages through lower forms. The divine actuality of thinking does appear imperfectly in the lower forms, but this complete actuality is the result and not the presupposition of Aristotle's argument. Instead, Aristotle looks at each level of soul independently, and leaves to the reader to grasp how each lower level of soul is taken up into the next highest level, until the divine principle as the pure concept of life appears as the fulfillment of what was sought at all the other levels. As opposed to Neoplatonic or Scholastic philosophy, Aristotle's thought begins from the standpoint of nature and motion as grasped through the senses, studies each kind of being and discovers its nature, and as a *result* of grasping the lower levels of being discovers the human soul, and ultimately, God.[82] The difficulty of interpreting Aristotle, according to Hegel, is that one must see the unified direction of the argument through his grasp of isolated concrete objects: "His teaching must be reduced to universal principles," as he himself "seldom leads it back to abstract thought-determinations."[83]

Though the *De Anima* is not for Hegel a systematic work, this does not mean that he is in agreement with most modern readings of the work. For Hegel, there *are* profound connections between Aristotle's analysis of plant, animal, and human soul and God as a perfect paradigm of life of which the lower levels of organic being are imperfect vestiges,[84] yet Aristotle does not make the connections explicit. These arguments can only be understood through attention to each level and its proximate higher and lower levels in order to grasp the direction of the argument.[85] God or thinking is discovered through analysis of each lower level on its own terms, and then through consideration of how the lower form of soul is a lack in relation to the next highest form of soul, and how the lack is more fully overcome at the next highest level. Since the *De Anima* is "a series of progressive determinations which are not necessarily blended into a whole,"[86] one must attend to the differences of the various souls in order to grasp the direction of the argument as a whole.

Hegel views the *De Anima* as Aristotle's own philosophy of spirit, showing how the concept, subjectivity, freedom, or infinite self-determination emerges out of nature at various levels of explicitness, although all these concepts are un-Aristotelian ways of expressing what is ultimately the Aristotelian divine principle of self-thinking thought. Here are two descriptions in Hegel's *Encyclopedia* of the method demanded in an approach to nature and psychology based upon the concept of freedom:

> Nature is to be viewed as a system of stages, emerging of necessity one from another as its proximate truth, though by no means such that one stage springs *naturally* from the other but only within the terms of the idea [λόγος] which constitutes the basis of nature itself.[87]

> Nature is as such a living whole. The movement through its stages is precisely this: that . . . out of an immediacy and externality which represents its "death" the *idea* of freedom reverts into itself, *in the first instance as the living being* [italics mine], but then also as overcoming this determinateness in which it is only life, and bringing itself to explicit existence as spirit, which is the truth and final end of nature as also the genuine actuality of the idea.[88]

Having arisen out of the study of non-organic nature and external natural necessity in the *Physics* and other natural treatises, *De Anima*'s focus is on ensouled or organic nature, the first stage of nature whose identity is an internal moving principle of life as the activity of assimilation of its object into the self, an assimilation in which a formerly independent and external other assumes a new status as merely a subordinate moment or element ordered to the function and end internal to the organism. Aristotle is seen to move through the lower forms of life as imperfect or inexplicit partial manifestations of God, which is seen in retrospect as the principle animating all the lower stages of life. With the intellective psychic capacity of the human, one makes the transition to pure spirit, liberated from the natural through the appearance of a rational power independent from body. In the movement from plant life to animal life to human life, one sees how freedom or mind is prefigured in nature. Just as there is no absolutely rigid distinction between the physical and the organic (a fact suggested in the Aristotelian idea of the motion of inanimate nature as "incomplete *entelecheia*," *entelecheia* being the principle of soul), there is no rigid distinction between organic nature and mental activity: for this reason Aristotle can, without incoherence, treat plant, animal, and human soul in one treatise. Hegel presents an interpretation of *De Anima* which is often ignored in the tradition of Aristotelian commentary, but which I think should be recovered in light of these recent interpretations of Kahn, Russon, Polansky, Shields, and Kosman.[89]

CHAPTER 1

Defining the Soul—The Serial Logic of *De Anima* II.1–3

Any interpretation of the overall aim and argument of the *De Anima* must be able to reconcile its reading with Aristotle's methodological reflections in that treatise. Unfortunately Aristotle's treatment of how to study the soul in *De Anima* II.1–3 is notoriously difficult to interpret. In general terms, the steps of Aristotle's argument can be broken up in the following way:

- He starts by offering three different permutations of a general definition of soul.
- He then moves on to criticize this definition as being not sufficiently explanatory.
- He begins afresh by looking at the multiplicity of different souls, arriving at a new definition which, paradoxically, seems substantially identical to the general one he criticized and seemed to reject.
- He then appeals to a pyramidal ordering of the various kinds of soul which make any common definition seem "laughable."

Tracing Aristotle's intention through this labyrinthine logic has proved extremely frustrating for those left behind to make sense of these three puzzling chapters, a fact that is clearly demonstrated by the plethora of divergent (and often diametrically opposed) interpretations.[1] The collective interpretative energy expended in trying to grasp what Aristotle is outlining as his method is understandable, for without some clue into his overall approach to the question of soul, discerning the aim and structure of the argument of the *De Anima* as a whole is nearly impossible.

Interpretations of these methodological chapters of *De Anima* fall roughly into four kinds.[2] One view[3] is that the "most common definition" (κοινότατος λόγος) of II.1 adequately grasps the nature of soul, and what follows in II.2 is not a criticism and overcoming of the imperfections of that definition, but rather a proof reconfirming the first definition, this time starting from the effects that are better known to us and moving to the universal definition. Another view[4] is that the opening of II.2 rejects the definition in II.1 not because of its content but because of its form—it does not make explicit the cause of soul. On this view, the definition of soul by its individual activities is shown to be adequate by producing a syllogism whose conclusion at the end of II.2 is the same as the proposed definition from II.1. A third view[5] looks to Aristotle's analysis in II.3 of the serial logic of soul and sees therein a denial that a definition (λόγος) of all soul is even possible, beyond particular definitions of each individual soul. Certain others,[6] acknowledging the importance of the critique of a common definition, yet wanting to preserve the result of the previous two chapters, see no incompatibility between having both the common genus of soul of the first two chapters and the particular definitions of the series existing independently yet complementing each other.

In the reading of II.1–3 that follows, I argue that it is only by showing the connections between the three chapters that one can see how each step of Aristotle's argumentation constitutes an indispensable stage of an emerging view of how to give a definition (λόγος) which captures the essence of all soul.[7] As opposed to the view of many modern interpreters, I want to show that every step of Aristotle's argument in these chapters is coherently connected, that each passage is necessitated by and follows logically from what precedes it. The end of the argument is not already present and explicit from the beginning through each of its steps. Yet this does not mean that the various passages are arbitrarily connected. The stages of the argument are incomplete but important steps leading toward the discovery of the principle and end of the investigation. It is the role of the interpreter to grasp the transitions between the various stages of Aristotle's argumentation, and only once one does this can the overall sense of Aristotle's methodological reflections in these chapters be discerned.

Yet it is not simply the unity of the three chapters which must be discerned. Although it is rarely noted by interpreters, Aristotle moves back and forth between the problem of how to give a proper definition of soul and the problem of the status of the parts of soul and their unity. Even in book I, *aporiai* about finding an explanation which includes all souls[8] directly precede the *aporiai* about the parts of soul.[9] The sections on the parts of the soul have always been thought to be digressions from the main argument on method. Yet understanding Aristotle's intentions in these chapters is not possible until one grasps how his reflections on the unity of the soul's parts do not in fact form digressions from the consideration of the method of definition. They simply form the epistemological and ontological sides of the same question, both of which are only answered once the serial unity of all soul is introduced in II.3.

The purpose of finding a definition (λόγος) of soul is the very same purpose which Aristotle sets out for his treatise as a whole: to reveal the soul's nature (φύσις) and its most fundamental essence (I.1.402a7–8). Aristotle begins with the Platonic approach of grasping what is identical and common in all instances of soul, the universal idea or self-identical genus[10] present in the multiplicity: what Aristotle calls the most common definition (κοινότατος λόγος), one which Aristotle concludes gives a "sketch" of what the soul is. The soul defined in this general form is the first activity of the soul which emerges in its development, the bare activity of self-maintenance which constitutes the minimum requirement for its continued living. In II.2, however, this kind of definition is criticized for only stating the fact *that* soul is without making explicit the cause of *why* it is. One must begin again, moving from what is most unclear in itself but most apparent, to what is most knowable according to reason (λόγος). From this Aristotle moves to look at the variety of different souls. But the most common definition is not simply abandoned at this point for the multiplicity of various souls. Rather, by identifying the first appearance of living being as that without which the animate would be inanimate, it points to where one must begin in investigating the various kinds of soul. What is most common to all souls is actually the most primitive stage of soul's development, the point from which the truly objective approach should begin. Chapter II.2 thus makes clear that the parts of each soul are not independent, but simply instrumental to the realization of one actuality present throughout, and consequently, the soul is not ultimately defined by the various lower parts or potentialities, but by the fullest actuality and realization of this potentiality.

Finally, in II.3, Aristotle shows through the comparison of nutrition in the animal and in the plant that what appeared to be most common and identical in all souls, the capacity for self-nourishment, actually becomes a fundamentally different activity as it occurs in different formal contexts: though an analogy exists between nutrition in the plant and the animal, looking at the two activities as synonymous is a mistake. The logic of the series is discovered by this realization. At each higher level of soul, that which was sought by the activity of the lower becomes matter, instrumental potentiality, existing purely for the sake of the realization of the higher activity; in fact the lower faculties realize themselves more fully within the context of the higher activity of soul. Once we arrive at the human soul and the appearance of intellect as the final term of the series and that for the sake of which the lower faculties exist, we have discovered the "nature" of the soul in and of itself, for "the nature [φύσις] of a thing is its end [τέλος]. For what each thing is when fully developed, we call its nature."[11] All the souls are in turn defined through the final term, for they all exist within it as potential. The account (λόγος) connecting all souls is not something which exists merely in the mind of the philosopher, but in the very object itself. The ontological and epistemological questions thus become one in the solution to both.

This analysis of II.1–3 confirms a recent insight of Christopher Shields into Aristotle's view of life: that for Aristotle in *De Anima*, life—and consequently soul, since it is the principle of life in mortal beings—has the structure of a core-dependent homonymy, in which all kinds of soul are defined in reference to its one central meaning. This focal or core meaning of life is not (as is usually believed)[12] the most common and primitive biological conception of life, its nutritive activities, but rather the highest and most complete sense of life, its intellective activity, which appears first in the human, but belongs most properly to the eternal self-contemplation of God.[13] In Shields's terms, "life" is a core-dependent homonym, whose core is divine contemplation and whose non-core instances (the hierarchy of souls) are derivative from this focal meaning. Certain interpreters have recently brought to the fore the importance throughout the Aristotelian corpus of the core-dependent homonymy (πρὸς ἕν λεγόμενα, *pros hen legomena*) structure, and specifically cases where the various senses of a concept are ordered in an ascending hierarchy. In an important treatment of the serial structure of the *Categories*, Kyle Fraser has clearly shown that the categories of being share the same structure at various degrees of refinement and explicitness, a structure which only becomes clear in the category of substance upon which all the other non-substantial categories depend. In turn, among substances, the full nature of substance is only fully manifest in the divine activity of thinking.[14] That the investigation of life would extend this argumentative structure is natural, since, as Aristotle writes, "being for living things is life" (II.4.415b13).[15] Yet when Fraser refers to the parallel between the serial ordering of the categories and the serial ordering of souls in *De Anima*, he understands substance as the focal meaning of being to be analogous to the nutritive soul of plants as the focal meaning of soul and life. For just as the only one of the categories which can exist independently from the others in the series is substance, so too the only soul which can exist independently of the others is the nutritive soul in plants.[16] I want to correct this view of *De Anima* by bringing it more into agreement with the structure of Fraser's analysis of Aristotle's *Metaphysics*. The nature of life (and of soul as the principle of life) lies in thought, and most perfectly in the uninterrupted thought of God.

To make this point, a careful analysis of *De Anima* II.1–3 is crucial. For those who think that the focal sense of life and soul are the nutritive activities, the most common definition (κοινότατος λόγος) of II.1 is the most adequate account (λόγος), and, though it may or may not need to be argued in another form (i.e., the formulation of soul at the end of II.2), it gives the proper substantive content and nature of the essence of soul. For those who deny that life and soul are best understood by the structure of a serially ordered core-dependent (πρὸς ἕν) relation, the unrelated definitions of each individual kind of soul at II.2.413b12–13 along with the denial of any common definition at II.3.414b25–28 is Aristotle's final word, that the only definitions possible are unrelated definitions of each kind of soul separately. I would like to show, however, through a careful analysis of book II.1–3, that the argument can only be understood as stages along the way to the final view that the nature of soul is found in the ultimate term of the series, thinking, which is the final cause of all the posterior senses and which manifests most clearly the structure of the same living activity which is present at different levels of articulation along the hierarchy. By proceeding this way Aristotle's account of soul finds a middle ground between the pure synonymy of the variety of souls and their unconnected homonymy.

In this way, the argument of II.1–3 answers the puzzle articulated in I.1 about how to know the essence and attributes of soul.[17] Aristotle there outlines a threat of circularity which presents itself: knowing the attributes of a being helps to grasp its essence, while the attributes are only known through the essence to which they belong. This circularity would mean that neither the attributes nor the essence could be known. On the current interpretation, II.1–3 does exhibit a certain circularity, though one that is not vicious and escapes the impasse. The most common definition gives a preliminary grasp of the essence of soul by identifying the genus common to the various kinds of soul. This then makes the attributes or particular powers of soul apparent, so that one can then identify all members in the series of soul. But it is only by understanding the order of the series of souls, and then reaching the summit of this series, that one genuinely fully grasps the nature and essence of soul, by understanding the final and formal cause of soul: mind (νοῦς).[18]

In order to establish this interpretation, I will first look briefly at the most common definition of II.1 in the light of Johannes Hübner's excellent interpretation of that chapter,[19] and I then will offer a closer, line-by-line interpretation of *De Anima* II.2–3, to show how Aristotle both incorporates and then gradually moves beyond this most general account (κοινότατος λόγος) as adequately defining the nature of soul. As a way of confirming this interpretation, I will conclude with some reflections on Aristotle's methodological remarks in *De Caelo* and the *Politics*, showing how what he calls his "regular way of proceeding"[20] is, on my reading, the same in these three works.

De Anima II.1

There are several puzzling questions that arise concerning the status of the most common definition of soul offered in II.1. In what way does the result of his investigation of previous thinkers inform his own new beginning? In book I the previous history leads us to see soul as defined primarily through motion and perception: it is thus surprising to see the soul defined in II.1 as primarily living in a way that even plants and sleeping beings live, unconscious and unmoving. And if this bare living, unconscious and unmoving, is in fact the substance of soul, what status do the subsequent activities have? Put in another way, is thinking merely an abstraction from the fundamental sense of life, or is thinking rather the fullest realization of life? More generally, what is the reason for seeking the most common definition (κοινότατος λόγος) in II.1, and how is it used in what follows in II.2–3? What is the relation of this most common definition in II.1 and the nutritive soul (θρεπτικὴ ψυχή), which, when discussed in II.4, is referred to as the "first and most common power of soul [πρώτη καὶ κοινοτάτη δύναμις ψυχῆς]," that according to which all things have life?[21] For the most common definition is not any one kind of soul, although perhaps it is closest to the nutritive soul of plants. These are questions that cannot be answered with reference to II.1 alone, but should be kept in mind when considering the function of II.1 in the overall argument.

Aristotle opens book II of *De Anima* by proclaiming the analysis of previous opinions on the soul to be closed, signaling a new beginning to the investigation. He formulates two related questions: "Let us return again as if from the beginning, attempting to define what is soul and what would be the most general account of it [τί ἐστι ψυχὴ καὶ τίς ἂν εἴη κοινότατος λόγος αὐτῆς]" (II.1.412a4–6). At the outset it seems that the answer to the first question might be found in the answer to the second: we can best find out what soul is by giving the account that is most inclusive of all soul. If we find what is common to each soul, that in which all members of the genus equally partake, this would quite plausibly give us an account of what is the nature and essence of soul. We will see, however, that as we proceed through chapters II.1–3, the identity of these two questions becomes problematic. The καί linking τί ἐστι ψυχή and κοινότατος λόγος αὐτῆς (that is, the conjunction linking the question "what is the soul" with the question "what is its most common definition") in II.1 first appears epexegetical (the two appear to be equivalent);[22] in II.2 it becomes apparently disjunctive (the two become mutually exclusive); and by II.3, the most common definition is revealed to be a necessary but incomplete moment on the way to establishing Aristotle's further goal of defining the soul through the series.

Aristotle's procedure in II.1 in seeking the most common definition is fundamentally Platonic.[23] Locating the identity of an object of investigation in the universal genus beyond the various *differentiae* which belong to the more particular determinations is a Platonic way of proceeding. One need only look to the *Phaedrus* to get an example of the kind of Platonic method employed by Aristotle in seeking the most common definition at the beginning of book II. In criticizing the structure of Lysias's speech, Socrates insists upon the necessity of beginning every argument with a definition of the essence of the object of discussion.[24] If one does not clearly articulate the essence (οὐσία) of the object, it is possible that the whole discussion might miss the mark, either by talking about what are in reality unrelated or distinct things under the illusory unity of a name, or by allowing one's interlocutor or reader to have in mind their own completely different idea of the object throughout the course of the investigation.[25] To avoid these traps, there must be agreement in the beginning on the essence of the object discussed or investigated.

This demand is eventually thought to be satisfied by the dialectical method outlined by Socrates in the second part of the dialogue.[26] One must first, through synthesis or συναγωγή, capture what is identical in all the multiple appearances of the object by finding the one idea common in all its instances. Having defined the essence identical in all the variety, one must then begin from this common form and divide this unity, through the process of διαίρεσις or division, into its various more particular forms (εἴδη) according to their differences from each other and from the highest form. Thus for Plato, one must identify the perfectly self-identical idea common in all particular instances, and then show this common trait as it is progressively mixed with others in the less ideal sensible appearances of the idea through adding differentia to what is common in the process of dividing (διαίρεσις).

This is precisely the kind of definition sought by Aristotle in his pursuit of the most common definition. Following this Platonic method, Aristotle thus seeks to uncover that which is identical in all soul which distinguishes it from things which have no soul. He divides[27] the category of substance until he separates all beings which are not living bodies,[28] identifying soul as the principle or form of these kinds of beings. Living natural bodies are distinguished from non-living natural bodies by certain activities which they necessarily possess: self-nourishment, growth, and decay (II.1.412a14–15). In terms of understanding the proximity between this most common definition and the nutritive soul, it is important to note that these activities later emerge as characteristic activities of nutritive soul, the first stage of the psychic hierarchy.

Of the three senses of substance (οὐσία) discussed in the central books of the *Metaphysics* (matter, form, and compound), Aristotle concludes his two classificatory divisions by translating these senses into the language of living beings: matter is body, form is soul, and the living body is the compound of both.[29] This produces the first of three slightly different versions of the most common definition: "the soul is substance as form of a natural body having life potentially" (II.1.412a19–20). "Form" is immediately expanded into "*entelecheia*," which in turn is differentiated into two senses.

Aristotle's division of activity into two kinds, one analogous to knowledge (ἐπιστήμη), the other to active thinking (θεωρεῖν), clearly refers to the more general threefold structure of activity as first potentiality, second potentiality/ first actuality, and second actuality which appears in II.5 of *De Anima*. Yet by correlating soul in its most common definition with second potentiality, Aristotle is not saying that soul is a wholly inactive implicit capacity for further activities. Hübner rightly attacks this conception of the definition, and stresses the fact that Aristotle is emphasizing in this most common definition how the soul is *active*.[30] The activity of soul to which he refers is basic organic self-maintenance. Essential in the particular context of this passage is the chronological, developmental relation between knowledge (ἐπιστήμη) and active thinking (θεωρεῖν), that knowledge comes before active reflection upon knowledge in time, with relation to one and the same person.[31] This is indeed the principal feature Aristotle explicitly addresses in the passage in question:

> [*entelecheia*] is said in two ways, on the one hand as knowledge, while on the other as thinking. It is clear that [soul is] just like knowledge. For both sleep and waking are in the belonging to soul, and there is an analogy between waking and thinking, and between sleep and having but not being active. But knowledge is prior with respect to the same person in becoming. Consequently soul is the *first entelecheia* of a natural body having life potentially. (II.1.412a22–28)

Two points mentioned by Hübner are particularly important to note. First, when the soul is identified as *first* activity of the body, analogous to unexercised knowledge, this identification occurs directly following the observation that, in the development of the person, the possession of knowledge about something is chronologically prior to the active thinking about that thing. Thus this activity corresponds to the very first activity which emerges in the soul's development. As I will explain in the conclusion of this chapter, Aristotle's movement through the series of souls from nutritive to intellective is not just an account of the various kinds of soul, but it is an account of the development of intellective soul from its conception to its full development. Thus the most common soul is identified with the soul at its most primitive stage of development (for Hübner, the embryo). It is the emergence of this organic activity in a natural body which distinguishes the living from non-living.

Secondly, Hübner argues convincingly that critics have been misled in understanding the soul in this account to be analogous to a series of potential activities. Rather, the most common characteristic of all soul is a necessarily constant activity through every moment of the living thing's life. For while certain activities cease in sleep, it is wrong to suppose that all activity ceases in sleep. If this were the case, sleep would mean the death of the animal. Rather, when the sensitive activities become latent in sleep, the activities of the nutritive soul persist, and even intensify. In fact, in sleep the animal not only falls back into a more plant-like existence, but also returns to the activity that characterized it in the very first appearance of its life development. The most common definition (κοινότατος λόγος) of soul is thus its most basic activity which cannot go unexercised without the death of the organism, the bare minimal activity required for its continued existence. It is for this reason the most inclusive definition of soul, in that it includes not only every instance of living being, but also every moment of the living existence of each being. This allows us to include as living certain beings and states of beings which must be considered alive: namely, the sleeping animal and the plant. Both of these are intimately connected with the nutritive soul.[32] This connection between nutrition, sleep, and the first appearance of life is elucidated in support of Hübner's interpretation at several points of *Generation of Animals.*

The general definition of soul, as the first activity of an instrumental body, when properly understood, is remarkably close to the definition of the activity of nutritive soul.[33] This proximity poses a certain problem, since Aristotle explicitly states that the most general definition (like the definition of figure) "will harmonize with every case, but will be the proper definition of none" (II.3.414b23–25). Thus the most common definition of soul and the nutritive soul cannot be simply identical. Hübner resolves this difficulty convincingly by pointing out that within nutritive soul, there are activities which do not need to exist constantly and explicitly for its continued existence, such as growth and decay. Thus even within nutritive soul there is a basic constant activity, and then subsequent activities which can either remain latent or be actively expressed. If the "most common definition" (κοινότατος λόγος) were the "proper definition" (ἴδιος λόγος) of the nutritive soul characteristic of plants, then there would be no distinction between first- and second-level *entelecheia* in the nutritive soul, but this is not the case. The basic activity of self-maintenance is thus a structural feature of all ensouled beings, yet the most common definition is not the proper definition of any particular soul, including the nutritive. This feature not only distinguishes the living from the inanimate, but also excludes the eternal circular motion of the heavens, which are without the possibility of any latent activities and thus beyond the distinction of first and second *entelecheia*.

When Aristotle returns to consider the relation of the body and soul (after comparing it with the case of the axe and the eye),[34] he confirms this interpretation of soul as first activity:

> That which has the capacity to live is not the body which has lost its soul, but that which possesses its soul; so seed and fruit are potentially bodies of this kind. The waking activity is like cutting and seeing, while the soul is like the capacity for vision and the potential of the tool. The body is the being in potency. (II.1.412b25–413a2)

Here we have the seed or embryo as the first potentiality prior to the living activity (body), the first actual realization of life and the first activity as soul when sleeping, and the exercise of the activities latent in sleep as the waking state. This is in full accord with another passage from *Generation of Animals*, where the embryo prior to its separation from its parent is merely potential life, while the first activity of actually realized life which occurs in this separation is like the fully explicit nutritive soul characteristic of plants:[35]

> It is plain that the semen and the embryo, while not yet separate, must be assumed to have nutritive soul potentially, but not actually, until (like those embryos that are separated from their mother) it absorbs nourishment and performs the function of the nutritive soul. For at first all such embryos seem to live the life of a plant.[36]

Thus conceiving the most common definition of soul as activity of self-preservation can be fully reconciled with understanding the definition (λόγος) to be identifying the soul with second potentiality/first activity, since this most immediate activity is also a potentiality for exercising whatever the higher "optional" activities of the soul in question might be. The three levels of (1) first potentiality, (2) second potentiality–first activity, (3) second activity correspond in the passage above to (1) the potential body (the unseparated embryo), (2) soul, and (3) the exercise of soul's higher activities. But that which is identical in all souls and which separates it from inanimate or dead beings is importantly not merely the potentiality for subsequent activities, it is itself the concrete activity of basic self-maintenance.

By the end of II.1, we thus have clearly formulated what the soul is in the sense of what is most common to all instances of soul: it is the soul's barest capacity for activity prior to movement and consciousness, existing either in the plant or in the sleeping animal/human.[37] In animals and humans, the sleep of the soul is the suspension of all its higher activities which distinguish it from the plant, since by suspending the most primitive form of sensation, that is, touch, none of the higher activities can be exercised. It is for this reason that sleep and nutrition are so closely related:[38] for sleep is the suspension of all activity in the animal beyond its nutritive activity. Plants, as essentially unconscious, exist prior to the distinction of sleeping and waking, but the activity characteristic of them also characterizes sleeping animal and human soul (thus the most common definition should not be seen as a definition *proper* to the nutritive soul of plants). It is the one activity the cessation of which the animal cannot survive. This most basic function is itself the activity or *entelecheia* of the body, the activity upon which any further activities are dependent. It is the activity responsible for the preservation of the barest fact of living in the organism, and this is true of every level of the psychic hierarchy. This is the unity prior to any of the distinctions belonging to the various kinds of souls. As a definition of soul, it thus merely states the side of universality and identity, without accounting for any of the differences between various kinds of soul.

When one thinks of where one has arrived by the end of the chapter, the result should be extremely surprising. Beyond the question of what is the most common and inclusive definition (κοινότατος λόγος) of soul, the broader question to be answered is *what is the soul?* By the current account, the substance of the soul would be the most basic and primitive vital functions. The plant would be soul in the truest sense, and animals and humans would be most properly soul when asleep, when closest to this fundamental activity characteristic of plants.[39] This is very different from the conclusions which Aristotle draws from his treatment of previous opinions on the soul. There he concluded that the consensus was that soul was primarily defined by awareness, movement, and incorporeality (I.2.405b11–12).[40] Now soul has been defined as that which is prior to any sensation or locomotion, and by the most physical of all psychic processes, the digestion of food and the resulting growth, decay and preservation of the body. Anything beyond this is something added on to this most fundamental sense of living and psychic activity. Can this be Aristotle's answer to the question, what is the essence (οὐσία) of soul? In the following chapter Aristotle offers a criticism of this conclusion as being only provisory, thus redirecting the investigation and orienting it towards a conclusion more in keeping with what he draws positively from his predecessors' conception of soul.

De Anima II.2

Chapter II opens (II.1.413a1–21) with two objections to the previous approach to the question of "what is soul" and how to arrive at its appropriate definition (λόγος). Previously, Aristotle had sought the definition of soul looking directly to its universal account, a definition stating the identity common to all souls beyond their distinction. Aristotle's first objection to this is that it is in violation of his well-known principle about our necessary beginning point: from a beginning with the unclear and most manifest, emerges the clear and most knowable according to reason (λόγος).[41] With this in mind Aristotle says that we must try to come to the question concerning soul from the opposite direction (πάλιν).[42] Previously, we began with the generic, universal definition of soul which distinguished what belongs identically to each soul. From this definition presumably one would move through division or through adding distinctions to the definition of each particular soul. For Aristotle, the formula expressing the essence of soul cannot be grasped immediately through thought. One must begin from the sensible particular, the instance in which the universal principles (ἀρχαί) are present, but only in a very obscure fashion. From the careful analysis of particulars, one can gradually discern with progressive clarity the principles and causes of the sensible instances.

There is, however, profound disagreement among interpreters about what this more unclear but most manifest new beginning point is. It seems obvious to most that Aristotle means that he must now proceed to investigate the various different particular souls, rather than a generic definition of all together. But two questions have caused great interpretative difficulty: first, what is the overall intention and result of this new beginning to which Aristotle now turns? Second, exactly which phenomena does Aristotle have in mind as most manifest to us? As the first question is larger in scope and has more sweeping consequences, let us begin with the second: if we need to start with that which is most unclear (in itself) but most manifest (to us), where does this point us when looking for this new beginning? Answering this question will help shed some light on why Aristotle offered the most common definition of II.1 in the first place. Merely saying that it means we need to move to the concrete, sensible particulars as against the abstract universal determination is too vague, as if Aristotle were merely indeterminately commanding: "Enough with these logical abstractions! Some rigorous empirical investigation of living phenomena must now be done." This interpretation of the new beginning point does not give us any indication of where we should start the investigation. For Aristotle cannot simply begin with any instance of ensouled or living being indiscriminately.

That sensible, mortal living beings are more perceptible (φανερώτερον) to us is clear.[43] More specifically, Aristotle begins with soul as growing, decaying, and nourishing itself—activities which he will eventually associate with the plant soul most properly and characteristically. To those who interpret φανερώτερον as simply "sensibly perceptible," this beginning point is difficult to explain. How are plants more perceptible than animals or humans? How could nutrition and reproduction be more apparent to the senses than sensation itself? There is, admittedly, a weak sense in which growing and eating are more perceptible than sense perception, in which changes to the sense organ are imperceptible. But the plant activity is also more *manifest* to us (as opposed to "perceptible by the senses"), primarily due to the simplicity of its simple nutritive function, unmixed with any higher activities. There is not a multiplicity of hierarchically ordered functions in the plant as there is in the animal and in the human. The unity of the more simple nutritive soul is for this reason more apparent. How the principle is unclear in plants is more obvious.[44] As the author of *On Plants* writes, "Life is found in animals and plants; but while in animals it is clearly manifest, in plants it is hidden and not evident."[45] The tradition defines soul, the principle of life in mortal beings, by motion, awareness, and incorporeality: the plant does not have local motion, has no awareness, and its characteristic activities are the most material and corporeal of all psychic functions. Further, as we now simply have to assert but will need to clarify throughout the course of our investigation, if life is characterized by the principle of *energeia* and *entelecheia*, plant life exhibits this least perfectly and explicitly of all living beings—its activity is most initiated by its surrounding environment rather than by itself, and it least of all preserves itself and its object throughout its activity.

Aristotle then addresses his second criticism of the most common definition in II.1: a properly defining account (τὸν ὁριστικὸν λόγον) should not only show the fact "that" it is (τὸ ὅτι), but must also contain within itself and make manifest the cause (τὴν αἰτίαν) responsible for its existence. In other words, a definition should not be merely descriptive of the phenomena in question, but should also explain what is responsible for the phenomena being the way that they are. Aristotle focuses his critique of merely descriptive accounts by saying that for his contemporaries ("*now*"),[46] definitions are just like conclusions, meaning conclusions of a syllogistic reasoning. A great deal has been made of this mention of syllogistic demonstration. It has been interpreted[47] as meaning that an improper syllogism was used,[48] and now a proper syllogism demonstrating what soul is must be constructed. Yet an objection to this must be made at the outset. First, Aristotle has been seeking to define soul, to find its essence and nature. While definition can be reached through demonstration, that is, through a syllogism in which the middle term states the connection between the other two terms, this is not a syllogism in which the subject term is the object being defined, and in which the proof shows that the essence belongs to this object being defined. Aristotle thus cannot be suggesting that we find a new syllogism to determine a proper definition, one which would demonstrate how a certain essence belongs to soul, as this would clearly violate Aristotle's view that definitions are indemonstrable.[49]

What then does it mean for the descriptive account of II.1 to be like a conclusion, and what should a properly defining account (λόγος) be like instead? And what is the connection between merely revealing the "that" and not the "why," and being like the conclusion of the syllogism? One important characteristic of the relation between the principles of a demonstration and its conclusions is that principles or beginning points are better known than that which they explain, that is, the conclusion. Moving from a definition as conclusion to a definition as premise means to move towards that which is causally prior, more explanatory, and more intelligible.

Let us look briefly at the example Aristotle uses to illustrate the problem with definitions which do not exhibit their cause, but only "that" they exist. He asks us to consider the answer to the question: what is squaring? The first definition he considers,"an equilateral triangle equal to an oblong triangle" (II.2.413a17–18), is an example of the wanting definition. This only expresses the "that" and resembles a conclusion. A proper definition of squaring which contains and manifests the cause is "the discovery of a middle." In his commentary on this passage, Hicks refers the reader to two relevant passages in Euclid. In the first passage at II.14 of the *Elements*, Euclid's goal is to describe a square equal to a given rectilinear figure, and finding the mean of the two sides of the corresponding rectangle gives the length of the side of said square. In the second passage at VI.13, the construction of the side of the square which would be equal to the rectangle is a method used for the sake of discovering the middle.[50] I believe it is the latter proof that Aristotle and his audience have in mind: to say that squaring is finding a square that is equal to a rectangle is right, and perfectly descriptive of the process involved in the operation. Yet it does not specify that for the sake of which the construction exists: discovering the middle term, or the mean proportional. Thus it describes what squaring is, but does not appeal to any higher level of explanatory context for the existence of this operation; it merely gives the conclusion of the operation: a square that is equal to a given rectangle.

In what way is the definition of the soul in II.1 as "first *entelecheia* of a natural instrumental body" guilty of this same inadequacy? How is it like a conclusion, demonstrating the fact *that* soul is, without manifesting the cause? It seems to me that there are two senses in which the most common definition states only the fact and not the cause. First, it does not make manifest the sense in which the soul is the cause of the living being in question, for stating the most primitive activity in any being will not be able to capture why the higher functions proper to it exist. Second, it does not state what is the cause of all soul. Aristotle wants to correct both of these deficiencies by showing both how soul is the cause of each living being, and by revealing what is the nature and final cause of all soul. In the interpretation that follows, I hope to show how II.2 seeks to explain how soul is the cause of life in each living being. This is also a step along the way toward revealing the complete nature of soul as the cause of all lower souls at the end of II.3.

As we saw, this first realization serves to identify the first appearance of life in its most immediate form in distinction from the non-living, soul as it is active when asleep. This shows *that* soul exists: to see if something is living, one need merely check for nourishment, growth, and decay. By describing the criteria of the most common living activity, by which one can determine if each thing is alive and distinguish it from inanimate nature, one can establish *that* it is alive, but not *why* it is alive. Why does the sleeping soul exist? For sleeping alone? Or does the sleeping soul exist for the sake of exercising its waking function? If so, nothing of this cause which would describe that for the sake of which the first *entelecheia* exists is specified in this definition of soul. The first *entelecheia* is like the conclusion, whereas the second *entelecheia*, the full manifestation of what is simply implicit in the first, reveals the cause. It is also more knowable than the first *entelecheia*: "for the activities [ἐνέργειαι] and their exercise [πράξεις] are prior to the powers [δυνάμεων] according to reason [λόγον]" (II.4.415a19–20). The most common definition of soul as first *entelecheia* is a conclusion in the sense of being lesser known and being less explanatory than its cause. The sense of this should become clearer as we discover Aristotle's solution to this deficiency in the definition (λόγος) of soul. For in chapter II.2, we gradually move from defining each soul through its potentiality, to defining each soul by its characteristic activity, not as first *entelecheia* but as second. Then in II.3, this logic is extended from defining each kind of soul to defining soul as a whole: the nature of soul is not revealed in its most implicit and potential state, the nutritive activities that characterize plants and sleeping animals, but in its most explicit and actual state, the active thinking which characterizes the most complete and comprehensive activity of the highest soul: human intellective soul.

After this opening criticism of the most common definition of II.1, Aristotle begins the investigation anew. What is crucial to draw from II.2 is the fact that the result of the chapter in the account of soul as "a certain activity and articulation [λόγος] of such a thing having potency" (II.2.414a27–28) is not a repetition of the content of the earlier most common definition, for first actuality has become the more open-ended "a certain actuality." The argument is indicating that the definition of soul is not located in its most primitive, immediate realization, identical in all souls, but in its final and most developed realization. This way of defining does not say what soul is specifically, but says that the soul of each thing is its characteristic and defining feature, that is, its highest activity and ultimate end. I divide the argument of the rest of the chapter into three fairly distinct yet seamlessly connected stages.

Section I: II.2.413a22–413b13

The goal and result of this section is to define each kind of soul based on its distinguishing characteristic and proper defining activity, thereby establishing the variety of different souls. With the most common definition, souls were all defined as simply living by looking to their most implicit and basic activity, the one activity which must remain after stripping away all other activities for the living being to survive. On this view, there is no principle by which to distinguish between living beings. In contrast, here we have the criterion introduced by which one can determine the different basic categories of living, the activity without which each soul cannot be *that particular kind of soul* that it is. Things are no longer defined by their lowest activity by which they merely remain in existence, but by the lowest characteristic through which they are the kind of soul that they are: for although plants are defined by living, animals are defined as animals through having sensation.

Aristotle lists the multiple senses of life,[51] and observes that we say a thing is living if any one of these meanings belongs to it.[52] At this point the various different living activities appear as a simple assortment with no notion of serial ordering, as if one could have, for example, sense or local movement without nutrition. Yet the serial logic of soul begins faintly emerging immediately once we look at that which simply grows (τὰ φυόμενα—II.2.413a25). Aristotle thus begins with the first activity characteristic of any newly emerged living being, before its nourishment or decay: growth.[53] What is there from the beginning turns out to be what was there in the most common definition of soul: growth, nourishment, and decay.[54] Here what was accomplished with the most common definition is taken up into the new beginning, for the most common sense of soul, the first *entelecheia* of a natural instrumental body, is the objective beginning point of the new investigation into the lowest characteristic activity of the species of soul.[55] In plants this is nutrition, since if one takes away nutrition from the plant, it cannot be a plant: "It is nourished and continues to live, as long as it is able to receive [λαμβάνειν][56] food" (II.2.413a30–31). Take away this capacity, and the plant can no longer be a plant.[57]

Yet while the plant can no longer be itself without its characteristic function, nourishment, and while an animal cannot survive without also having this capacity, an animal is an animal due to a different activity: the capacity to sense. This is what it is to be an animal first of all (πρῶτος): "Living belongs to living things because of this principle [nutrition], but something is an animal because of sensation" (II.2.413b1–2). There are certain other activities that may or may not belong to animals: being moved and changing place (μὴ κινούμενα μηδ' ἀλλάττοντα τόπον; II.2.413b3).[58] These are dependent upon sensation, and without sensation nothing can be an animal. Even within the various senses there exists one primary level without which something cannot be an animal and others which either might or might not exist without affecting the being's belonging to the animal kingdom: touch has the same relation to animals as nutrition to living beings in general.

No longer defining soul by the first *entelecheia* common to all souls, Aristotle at this stage defines each soul by its first and most primitive *proper* activity, the absolute minimum activity each requires to belong to that particular level of soul. The consequence of this new position is that the common definition of soul has thus been broken into various definitions of separate psychic activities whose connection is not yet evident.[59]

Importantly, since it has been established that the definition we are now seeking is the one that gives the cause of soul, Aristotle states plainly that the cause of these activities of soul has not yet been made manifest at this stage of the argument: the λόγος (account) is not yet ὁριστικός, "defining." Consequently, the new criterion laid out at the outset of II.2 has not been fulfilled.[60] We know the fact that nutritive soul defines the plant and sensitive soul defines the animal, but we do not know the reason for the sake of which these activities exist. As we will see, this is because Aristotle has not yet made explicit how the lower activities exist for the sake of the higher activities, and because the ultimate cause for the sake of which each exists has not been discovered: intellective activity.

The result of this argument is that the principle for the definition of the two first divisions of the soul—nutritive and sensitive soul—has been established, and it has been shown that each lower kind of soul is able to exist separately from the higher. Notice that only the sensitive and nutritive souls are here treated, in other words, those activities which form the "parts" of the human intellective soul. In fact Aristotle closes the section by referring to the nutritive soul (θρεπτικόν) as "the *part of the soul* [τὸ μόριον τῆς ψυχῆς] in which even plants partake" (II.2.413b7–8). Yet if the sensitive part can exist apart from the intellective, and the nutritive part separately from both sensitive and intellective, and in general the lower can exist independently of the higher in different species, separated not just in thought (λόγος) but in space, then how could the highest soul which contains them all have any unity at all? What is the relation between whole and parts? This is the question to which Aristotle now passes. What was at first an epistemological question of definition has shown itself to be an ontological question of how the soul is one in its multiple activities.

Section II: II.2.413b13–414a4

The conclusion of the first section introduces the problem addressed in the second, namely if these activities exist simultaneously as separate kinds of soul, existing separately in space, yet are also combined in higher stages of life, is the necessary consequence the Platonic view of the soul's division into independent parts?[61] Aristotle writes:

> Whether each of these (powers of the soul) is a soul or a part, and if a part, whether in this way as being separable in thought alone or also in space, concerning certain of these questions it is not difficult to know, but some questions are difficult. (II.2.413b13–16)

Against the Platonic view of different parts of soul being located independently in different parts of the body, Aristotle cites two examples which show how each level is one in *entelecheia*, while its multiplicity of powers exists in potency (δυνάμει) (II.2.413b18–19). This fact is easier to see in simpler living beings, and Aristotle cites the cases of plants and certain insects.[62]

Though these passages are difficult to interpret because we are not exactly sure what phenomena Aristotle was observing, the conclusion drawn from them seems clear. The *entelecheia* proper to plants, as we saw from the last section, was nutritive soul, the bare activity of life. When divided, the plants discussed by Aristotle continue to live, thus the whole characteristic *entelecheia* is present and governing every part of the body:[63] the whole soul is principle of all the parts, which are potential, and thus instrumental in the service of the dominant *entelecheia*. Since the plant has only one activity, only its various physical parts are potential, and Aristotle's observation here indicates that all the parts are principally governed by their defining activity. He goes on to cite the case of the insect, which, when cut into pieces, appears to manifest sensation and movement in the newly formed independent parts. What this example adds to the last is we have in this animal a more complex combination of powers or "parts" of the soul. Yet the relation of the determining, characteristic form of the insect to its lower, subordinate powers is the same as the plant to its various parts. That is, the characteristic activities which make the insect an animal, its sensation and movement, determine all its parts and lower powers. Thus the parts of the soul are not separable except in thought (as there is certainly a difference, for example, in what it is to be sensation and what it is to be nutrition), but are all instrumental and ordered to the primary and proper *entelecheia*.

In contrast to the result of the previous section, where the horse and the dog would be indifferently classified as animals based on their minimum species-defining characteristic, here each being is defined by its highest, more distinguishing activity, by which each different kind within a certain species of soul (plant, animal, human) is differentiated, that by which it is the particular kind of animal it is. Aristotle concludes this section by stating that "this makes the difference between animals" (II.2.413b33–414a1). Importantly, we still have only the fact *that* each of these various kinds of living beings exist, as defined by their higher, most particularly characteristic activity. Aristotle reminds us again that with this step in the argument, a sufficiently causal explanation for these differences between animals has not been reached: "On account of which cause this is so, must be examined later" (II.2.414a1).

Section III: II.2.414a5–28

This leads to the last section of the argument, where the soul is redefined as the distinguishing activity (*energeia*) of each thing. This marks a huge transition in the argument and constitutes a step beyond the most common definition of soul which has never been properly grasped by commentators.

The passage is dense and obscure, so we must proceed carefully and follow each step of the argumentation.

Aristotle takes up the argument from II.2.413b11–12, where soul was defined in terms of each kind of soul, by being nutritive, sensitive, discursive, or by moving. He specifies that "that by which we live" and "that by which we sense" have two senses, just as that by which we know. The case of knowing thus serves as the paradigm for this new distinction introduced. Aristotle writes of these two senses: "We say on the one hand knowing and on the other hand the soul, for we say that we know by each of these" (II.2.414a5–6). Having given an example from the side of the soul, Aristotle cites the same example from the side of the body with relation to health: "Similarly in one sense that by which we are healthy is by health, in another sense it is by a certain part of the body or by the whole body" (II.2.414a7–8). Aristotle associates the first sense in each example (knowledge and health), with the shape, form, *logos*, and *energeia* of the recipient (this is Aristotle's first use of *energeia* rather than *entelecheia*, and we will return to the significance of this terminological shift in a moment). This second sense in both examples (soul and the part or whole of the body) is the recipient of the former activity, that which is capable of knowledge and health. The side of the recipient is further defined as matter and the underlying, that which is acted upon (πάσχοντος), or that which is ordered (διατιθέμενος). The first, the activity of the agent (ποιητικόν [vs. the patient or πάσχοντος]), occurs in that which is receiving the activity.

It may appear somewhat startling that when Aristotle considers the two senses of "that by which we know," he identifies the fully realized form with ἐπιστήμη (knowledge), and the matter with *soul*.[64] How can the soul be matter? Soul is not matter in any absolute sense, but does here serve as the matter of knowing. Aristotle demonstrates here the flexibility and context-sensitivity in his use of the form-matter distinction.[65] Matter is a category of thought which simply means "the underlying," the context of a determinate capacity to receive further determination by its coordinate form.[66] It is to illustrate this flexibility that we were offered an example of form and matter both from the side of soul (knowledge) and the side of body (health).

The meaning of this entire passage depends on the next two lines: "And the soul is that by which we live and perceive and reason firstly [πρώτως]—that is a certain λόγος and form, but not the matter and the underlying [τὸ ὑποκείμενον]" (II.2.414a12–14). At this point, interpreters, perhaps misled by associating this πρώτως (firstly) with the πρώτη ἐντελέχεια (first activity) of the most common definition, take this to be nothing more than a reiteration in different terms of the sense of the first definition of soul, "the first *entelecheia* of a natural instrumental body."[67] Yet Aristotle is here denying precisely that definition. The first *entelecheia*, although it is itself a certain activity and realization, is the dormant capacity for further determination, the soul when asleep. It is that which underlies the higher activities, of which it is merely potency. Here we discover that the first *entelecheia* is, in the language employed in this passage, the matter of the second *entelecheia*. The primary, ruling sense of soul, Aristotle is here stating (against the previous definition), is not the matter, but the form: not the first, but the second *entelecheia*. It is for this reason that it made perfect sense at II.2.414a9–10 for Aristotle to switch into the language of *energeia*, in the sense of activity's full exercise, as against the potential implicit and unexercised sense of *entelecheia*. We are no longer talking about soul as *entelecheia* which can be seen either as possession of the capacity for an activity or the exercise of the activity itself. Here reference is being made only to the actual activity: this is the primary, governing (πρῶτος) sense of *entelecheia*.

Notice the difference between the final definition in II.1 ("the first *entelecheia* of a natural instrumental body") and the final formulation of II.2 ("a certain *entelecheia* and *logos* of that which has a certain capacity"). The first definition identifies soul as something common to all; if this definition had been proved adequate, how to approach defining the nature of soul would be clear. But with this revised definition, what defines each soul is its highest *entelecheia*, and this is different for each kind of soul. How to proceed to give a unified account of soul inclusive of this diversity has thus become obscure.

This conclusion has significant consequences beyond the relation of the parts or powers in the soul, extending to the question of the nature of the soul itself. Under the first definition of soul in II.1, one would have said that soul in its primary sense is the plant soul, or the animal/human soul as sleeping: soul as merely living prior to thought and movement. But if soul is the form and *entelecheia* of all potency, then the governing sense of soul and its true nature lie no longer in nutrition, but in soul's most complete and developed manifestation, that is, thinking.

De Anima II.3

At the end of chapter 2, we are left with a serious problem in terms of defining soul: if the definition of soul is in fact wholly particular to the *entelecheia* proper to each kind of living being, then there can be no account of what soul is, only what particular souls are. It is the possibility mentioned by Aristotle in the opening chapter of the treatise: "whether there is one account [λόγος] of soul, such as of the living being, or whether there is a different account for each particular, such as an account of horse, of dog, of man, and of god. The universal living being would either be nothing or be posterior" (I.1.402b5–8). In fact we learn in chapter II.3 that what seemed identical in all living beings, the nutritive soul, is actually transformed according to the higher formal context within which it occurs, so that even what seemed to be common and identical in all instances of soul is not always merely the same. The chapter offers an attempt to overcome the possibility of no unified account (λόγος) of soul through the unity characteristic of an ordered series. The ordered series also explains the unity of the soul and its parts. Only once we realize how the particular kinds of soul are ordered in a serial hierarchy of priority and posteriority can we see how a unified account of soul can be found which goes beyond a mere description of soul to both showing how each soul in particular is a cause and giving the cause of all soul.

Aristotle starts by recapitulating the conclusion of the previous section, that different kinds of soul are distinguished by having a different number of living activities (nourishment, appetite, sensation, movement in space, thought). They have either only one of these capacities (the plant), all the capacities (the human) or some of the capacities (all animals in between). The differences in the number of properties possessed by a particular kind of living being grounds the variety of life.

Aristotle follows these preliminary objections with a concrete examination of why the most common definition, in which one tried to define soul as if it were something said synonymously (συνώνυμα or καθ' ἕν λεγόμενα), is both inadequate and inaccurate. Before looking at how he definitively undermines the possibility of the synonymy of life and of the most common definition that genuinely reveals the essence, nature, and cause of all soul, let us briefly recall the problem with this most common definition, this time through reference to a definition of soul in another context criticized by Aristotle for the very same deficiency which plagued this general account. In the *Topics*, in a discussion of falsely applying one common term to phenomena which are in fact equivocal, Aristotle makes the following criticism of the definition of life offered by Dionysius:

> If, then, the definition applies in a like manner to the whole range of the homonym, it does not define any one of the objects described by the term. This is what happens to Dionysius' definition of life when stated as a movement of a creature sustained by nutriment, congenitally present with it; for this is found in plants as much as in animals, whereas life seems to be not one kind of thing only, but one thing in animals and another in plants.[68]

A common definition is inadequate if it assimilates two different phenomena to the same idea, when with respect to that very idea they differ. Of course individuals within a species will have differences among each other, but this does not mean that the species is predicated of them synonymously, for Socrates and Callias are both the same with respect to "what it is to be human."[69] The differences do not occur at the level of the species. But if every single ensouled being must eat, grow, and decay, why can't one predicate the nutritive soul of all living beings?

At II.3.414b1, Aristotle sets out to explain why there is nothing said synonymously of all living beings by showing how the nutritive power, though present in all mortal living beings, is different according to the context of the higher power of soul which defines the living being. He begins his argument by defining plants as having *only* the nutritive power (τὸ θρεπτικόν). This makes a plant a plant and distinguishes it from all other kinds of living being, which on top of this faculty also have the power of sensation (τὸ αἰσθητικόν). Having the power of sensation necessarily means that one has the sense of touch, since it is the most necessary of all the senses without which the others cannot inhere in the living being; though, like the nutritive soul which can exist without sensation, touch can exist without any of the higher senses. Touch involves sensation of pleasure and pain. This presence of touch necessarily implies desire,[70] which divides Platonically into appetite (ἐπιθυμία), spirit (θυμός), and rational wish (βούλησις), since touch and the sensation of pleasure and pain imply appetite (ἐπιθυμία) (that Aristotle employs the Platonic tripartite division of the soul is significant for the critique of his "Platonic" most common definition, as we will see in a moment).

This whole complex of interrelated concepts is essentially related to nutrition in animals, since touch is the sensation proper to food. Food is made up of the four elements, which have the essential tangible qualities of hot, dry, wet, and cold, which are the qualities proper to the sense of touch. The senses possessed by higher animals have nothing to do with nutrition (and touch is not inherently related to their sensible qualities, odors, sounds, or colors). Only touch and the one sense which is itself a form of touch—taste—have to do with nutrition.[71] An animal's relation to nutrition, the sensation of hunger and thirst, is simply the most primitive form of desire (ἐπιθυμία) for those objects proper to the sense of touch: hunger is desire for the hot and the dry, thirst for the cold and the wet, while for those animals with taste in addition to touch, both are a desire for the seasoning of each.

What is essential to make explicit in this passage is that the nutritive soul is not simply identical in plants and animals, but is determined by whatever their distinguishing activity is.[72] Aristotle would say that it is precisely because Plato ignores the equivocity of life that he ends up wrongly ascribing appetitive desire (ἐπιθυμία) and sensation to plants:[73] observing what constitutes the animal relation to nourishment, along with the fact that being nourished does not belong uniquely to animals but also to plants, Plato simply transposes the animal relation to nourishment to plant life, without noticing how certain activities which are peculiar to animals alter the meaning of nourishment for plants whose being is most properly defined by this activity.

Aristotle does not make the logic of the series any more explicit at this point, saying that he must "be more clear about these things later" (II.3.414b14). The only point necessary for the purpose of establishing the homonymy of the most common sense of life has been made through the identification of sensation and appetite in animals and its transformative effects on the essence of the animal's nutritive capacities in comparison with this same capacity in plants. When he goes on to list the higher faculties in this context (II.3.414b17–19), he is deepening the point by foreshadowing in a precise way the structure of desire: for imagination is still unclear, but will be associated with the second kind of desire, spirit (θυμός), and will further alter the animal's relation to nutrition, as will the capacity for movement (allowing hunting and gathering). With the appearance of reasoning capacity and intellect, the structure of desire becomes the third and highest category of desire, rational desire (βούλησις). Aristotle closes the passage by suggesting that by moving this way through the series, one not only discovers the highest, most complete intellective soul of the human, but that which is even more valuable and honorable than the intellective soul of man: the eternal intellective activity that is the life of God: "in addition to these movement through space belongs to some, and to others belong discursive thinking [τὸ διανοητικόν] and mind [νοῦς], i.e., to humans if there is some other being similar or even superior to humans" (II.3 414b16–19).

Aristotle once again makes a shift in argument from a discussion of parts of the soul to the method of definition. Having shown in the previous argument how the lower activities which exist independently in lower souls are ordered, transformed, and more fully realized when integrated as potencies that are instrumental to the higher *entelecheia*, and that it is wrong to think that the activity at a lower level is identical to the same function within a higher formal context, Aristotle concludes that "it is clear that the account of soul is one in the same way as the account of figure" (II.3.414b20–21). The analogy made here between the serial logic of figure and soul and the explanation that follows it is absolutely determinative for our understanding of Aristotle's method in the *De Anima*. Since this crux of the argument is open to so many different opposing readings, it is worthwhile to cite the passage at length:

> It is then clear that the account of soul and of figure would be one in the same way. For as in the latter case there is no figure beyond the triangle and the others in the series, in the latter case there is no soul beyond the ones we have mentioned. There could emerge a common account [κοινὸς λόγος] in the case of figures, which will harmonize with each one, but will be proper to none of them. Therefore it is ridiculous to seek a common account [κοινὸν λόγον], both in the case of these examples and others, which will be the proper account of no one of the beings, nor will exist in relation to a particular [οἰκεῖον] and undivided form [εἶδος], leaving such an account behind. (II.3.414b20–28)

Having undermined in the argument leading up to this point the possibility of something identical in each soul, this unity cannot exist beyond the terms in the series. Thus if there is an account of all souls, it must fulfill the two conditions expressed here as lacking in the laughable *logos*: it must (1) itself be an account proper (ἴδιος) to a certain kind of soul, and (2) such an account must express the unity of all the instances of the concept at least "in relation to a particular [οἰκεῖον][74] and undivided form [εἶδος]." If the souls were not hierarchically connected, they would have no connection at all, and the unity of the common name would be purely arbitrary. Ontologically the soul's parts would simply fall apart; epistemologically no objectively unifying account could be formulated. Thus the adequate universal cannot simply be something self-identical beyond all relation to particularity: it must itself be a particular, while comprehending the other particulars within itself. Thus if all instances of soul are going to be referred to one account, this must itself be the account of an actually existing soul. But how can one among many particulars be a comprehensive account connecting all instances?

The key is what is particular to the relation between serially ordered terms: in both the case of figure[75] and soul, "the prior always exists in the posterior of the series in potency" (II.3.414b29–30). We know from what has preceded that to be potential relative to a higher actuality means to be the underlying matter to the higher determining form, and to have an essence which is instrumental to the realization of the higher end. In the context of plants, the nutritive soul is the determining form to which the plant's body is merely instrumental. But in the higher context of the sensitive soul, the nutritive soul itself becomes instrumental, existing for the sake of fulfilling the higher sensitive activities. Further, within the context of these higher activities, the lower powers are not canceled but preserved and stabilized within the higher activity.

In the light of the logic of serial unity, Aristotle gives us the key of how one needs to proceed, and therefore the key of how we are to read the rest of the treatise:

> Thus one must inquire according to each particular, "what is the soul of each?" for example: what is the soul of the plant? or of the human? or of the animal? But one must examine on account of what cause [διὰ τίνα δ' αἰτίαν] they are thusly in the series. (II.3.414b32–415a1)

There is thus a twofold movement in the argument. By asking what each individual kind of soul is, one is looking for the final cause inherent to its characteristic mode of living as separate from the higher activities. This captures the fact *that* this soul exists. But the question of cause which has framed Aristotle's argument since II.2 is only resolved by looking at the question in terms of the subsequent term in the series. After looking at the nutritive soul as separate in plants, by looking at the animal we can see nutritive activity existing not for itself, but for the sake of the higher realization of sense awareness. The cause of the nutritive turns out to be the sensitive, and in general, the higher gives us the reason for the lower. One moves up through the various activities of soul, from the nutritive to the sensitive, from the lowest sense of touch to the higher senses of smell, hearing, and vision, through locomotion, imagination, discursive reason, until one reaches the final term of the series, mind (νοῦς) and its active contemplation. The answer to the question about cause is not fully answered until one reaches that which does not exist for the sake of realizing a higher, more complete and inclusive activity, but which exists completely for itself.[76] At this point everything that was being sought at the lower levels is fully realized. In the human, all these activities are combined, and all are instrumental for the realization of the function which properly characterizes the human from other mortal souls, contemplative activity.

There is thus one account (λόγος) of soul, yet this is not a general account (κοινὸς λόγος). The definition of the most complete term in the series is what gives us the focal definition of soul, because it possesses all the other kinds of soul in potentiality within its actuality, and because it is that for the sake of which all the others exist. Thus by giving the proper account (ἴδιος λόγος) of the most complete term of the series, you are giving the nature of all soul. It is the account of all soul, but is also a proper account of soul in its most developed form. To think either that Aristotle is here abandoning the question of the nature of soul, the essence of soul, beyond a series of particular definitions, as if each kind of living was homonymous, or to think that this nature is revealed most truly by the most common definition from the first stage of the argument, as if living were simply synonymous, is to miss the whole purpose of the treatise, and to wholly misunderstand what Aristotle means by a *logos* that is explanatory and not merely descriptive.

The serial logic described here by Aristotle thus opens a middle way between the pure synonymy of the most common definition and the pure homonymy of unconnected definitions of particular souls. For the logic of the series is a particular instance of the relationship between things which are core-dependent (πρὸς ἕν λεγόμενα) homonymy—entities which are all related to one thing.[77] The central meaning is not an abstraction beyond the particulars, but is itself a particular member of the series. What it is to live for each kind of soul is different, and in this sense, life is said homonymously at each level. Yet with the appearance of the final term of the series (here the thinking soul), the cause of each sense of living can be grasped, because thinking soul includes each of the lower senses of living within its own higher living activity. It is by grasping what it means to be living for intellective soul that we can understand what it means to be living for nutritive and sensitive soul.[78] These can only be understood once we discover the complete and fully explicit nature of soul. At this point each sense of living can be understood relative to this most complete sense of living: thought thinking itself. We better understand each lower term of the series of souls in light of discovering the most complete and comprehensive activity of soul. For if the activity of life is at every level *entelecheia*, possessing one's end within itself, this will become most clear once we move to that which can fulfill itself without requiring some being outside itself.

An important objection might be made to this explanation of how one gives a properly explanatory account (λόγος), one which discloses the cause of the phenomenon beyond mere description: how can one give the cause of something's existence, for example the nutritive soul, in something beyond the thing, the sensitive or ultimately the intellective soul? In the *Posterior Analytics*, Aristotle is clear that, according to his understanding of causation, the cause of a substance is not something other than the thing itself (in contrast with processes like eclipses and thunder, where the cause *is* other than the thing itself). Rather the cause is the entity itself, under the description which reveals its intrinsic (καθ' αὐτό) predicates. The "why it is" is simply the form of the thing in question.[79] This cannot be denied, yet there is a peculiarity in the case of entities which are ordered serially. It is only in things which are ordered in a series that one can answer a "why?" question with something other than the object investigated. For what is higher in the series is not truly other. What is being investigated is the soul: both the higher and lower are souls, and in fact the lower exists as a part in potentiality in what is higher, in which they both belong to the same thing. Moving from the nutritive soul up through the series of souls is not simply discovering a hierarchy of different beings in nature, discovering the essence of plants, then animals, then humans. We are moving to discover the nature of soul itself, in relation to itself beyond its bodily affections.

The definition of soul as first actuality, if taken as it is commonly understood as a way of distinguishing it from a further second actuality, does not truly apply at the first level of nutritive soul, which is *perpetually* active without the potentiality of sleep. Kosman argues for this traditional understanding of the definition, writing that soul is defined as a first grade of activity, "a capacity for active functioning that may or may not be realized, a power that may or may not be actively exercised; the soul is, as he puts it, the principle of both sleeping and waking life."[80] The fact that this definition of soul does not easily apply to soul as thinking is often noticed, but it is rarely noted that the definition is problematic at the other end of the hierarchy of life. Each soul is defined not through its "first" actuality, since one cannot define perceptive soul by what it is actively doing when asleep, or define thinking soul as it is found in the neonate before it is even able to think anything. Thus each soul is defined by its highest actuality. But soul is present in the first actuality at each level, corresponding to the actuality of nutrition, for this is what distinguishes a living being from a dead or non-living being, the actuality of self-nourishment. For one must acknowledge soul to be present even when other activities are merely latent, in the sleeping perceiver and in the wholly unknowing neonate—though at this point one is only *potentially* perceiving and *potentially* knowing, one is nevertheless actually alive and self-preserving.

What this demonstrates is that the whole progress of the *De Anima* is in fact a development out of soul in its first actuality, to a second actuality of active perception, and a third actuality of active knowledge. Each level of actuality is the potentiality for the subsequent actuality, or as Aristotle says in his analogy with figure, "The prior always exists in potentiality in the series" (II.3.414b29–30), such that the actuality of nutrition is the potentiality of perception, and the actuality of perception is the potentiality of thinking. In this sense, thinking is the actuality of the whole series. One sees how, as illustrated in the chart below, the first actuality of soul as self-nourishing in fact corresponds to the pure potentiality of the thinking soul as ignorance and the potentiality of perception in sleep. The level indicated in bold is the basic self-preserving activity of nutritive soul (see table 1).

Thus the *De Anima* is about identifying the various levels of the actualization of living substance, not just identifying independent faculties. The method of the book is to define soul first in its immediate, simplest manifestation, and show how from out of this the soul unfolds to its fullest actuality. One defines a thing through its actuality, not its potentiality:

TABLE 1. Powers of the Soul and the Three Levels of Potentiality and Actuality

NUTRITION	PERCEPTION	THINKING
Actuality	Actuality	Actuality 2
	Potentiality	Actuality 1/Potentiality 2
		Potentiality 1

The argument in this light describes an unfolding of soul from its most implicit and primitive beginning to the development of its complete nature.[81] The nutritive was characterized as the sleep of the soul, a sleep in which the higher activities are implicit. The sensitive in turn was characterized as the waking of soul, which constitutes the activation of the senses, yet without having learned from these senses. Beyond mere sensitive waking, contemplation culminates the internalization of what was apprehended as external through the senses, moving from sensible learning to the active contemplation which fulfills it. In the highest form of intellective soul, all the lower souls are united and fulfilled. Thus it is in moving from the most common and simple activity of soul up through the series until one reaches the final term for the sake of which each level exists and which exists purely for the sake of itself that one has discovered the cause of all levels and the nature of soul in itself. Thus Aristotle concludes that this investigation of the hierarchical series is the true method: "that the account [λόγος] concerning each of these is also the most proper account of the soul, it is clear" (II.3.415a12–13).

Throughout the section on method, Aristotle repeatedly defers any answer to the question of the separation of thinking from the body (II.1.413a8–10; II.2.413b24–27; II.3.415a11–12). While human thinking is a realization of the potentiality of the body as instrumental to its learning and coming to itself, there might be, Aristotle repeatedly says, a form of intellect wholly apart from any dependence or relation to body. This is not the point at which the status of divine intellect in *De Anima* can be resolved, but let us briefly recall a passage from the opening chapter of *De Anima* to suggest how this question might be settled. Aristotle formulates the purpose of the treatise in the following form: "We seek to know and to investigate both the nature [φύσιν] and the essence [οὐσίαν] of the soul, and then the attributes concerning it. Of these attributes some seem to be affections proper to the soul, but others seem to belong to the living animal because of it" (I.1.402a7–10). We have seen, at least in a preliminary way, that the nature and essence of soul is thinking. Yet, as Aristotle argues, the common account (λόγος) cannot be a universal beyond any particular instance. Yet thinking is perfectly and perpetually realized in the thinking of God as the nature and essence of life to which all forms of soul are related. Having discovered this nature, we look into both those attributes or affections which are proper to it (thinking), and those attributes or affection which are bodily, but exist *because* of this nature—namely, nutrition, sensation, desire, locomotion, imagination—which, we have seen, all exist for the sake of their final cause, thinking.[82]

This view must be grounded in the substantive treatment of the series of soul in what follows these methodological chapters. It is important to keep in mind that in discussing the series, and the movement from plant to sensitive soul in this chapter, we have not really begun the analysis. We have just observed certain features about the movement that allowed us to discover the method for finding an account (λόγος) of soul which reveals its cause, nature, and essence. The actual work is left to do and it starts with II.4, but Aristotle has determined how he will proceed, and has given his readers the key to following the argument which follows.[83] But if this view is true, we can see how Aristotle denies an abstract universal of soul identical in all the souls which participate in it, but he does not reject the idea of an ideal, paradigmatic living activity, which posterior living activities approximate to varying degrees.

Method in *Politics* and *De Caelo*

As a way of confirming this interpretation of Aristotle's method in *De Anima*, it is enlightening to compare how Aristotle appears on this interpretation to proceed in *De Anima* with how he proceeds in certain other treatises, especially his study of the state in the *Politics* and his study of bodies in *De Caelo*, each of which shed light on his account in *De Anima*.

Consider first how Aristotle proceeds in the introduction to the *Politics*. He looks at the city (πόλις) as a species of association (κοινωνία), thus placing the investigation of the the city-state or πόλις in the context of a broader investigation of associations. Although every type of association seeks a certain good, the city has a special status among the various other types of association: the dominant (κυριωτάτη) sense of association or κοινωνία is the one that seeks the most sovereign object and which comprehends all the other species of association within itself.[84] At this level, the association reaches the stage of being "nearly or quite self-sufficient,"[85] requiring no higher form beyond itself. In *De Anima*, the intellective soul of the human will be seen to seek the most sovereign object, and this highest soul of the human contains within itself the nutritive and sensitive faculties, which it uses for the realization of its highest and most proper end, thinking. It is the dominant sense of life, satisfying that which is sought vainly at subordinate levels of life.[86]

He criticizes those who think that there is some identical nature in each form of association (κοινωνία) by which they are all called an association, as if they were differentiated merely by degree rather than by species. There is no such thing as the association or κοινωνία-in-itself, but only the more and less comprehensive instances of association. This is the same criticism that Aristotle makes of his most common definition (κοινότατος λόγος) in *De Anima*: one errs if one thinks that the question "what is it" is answered by identifying something identical in all the instances separate from its external differences.[87]

That this kind of differentiation is not true, Aristotle proposes to show *according to his regular method* (κατὰ τὴν ὑφηγημένην μέθοδον).[88] By this method one divides (διαιρεῖν) the whole until one reaches the uncompounded elements. Yet these elements do not lie in some arbitrary order, where one could then begin the investigation with any one of them. One must begin the investigation by looking at the things growing from the beginning (ἐξ ἀρχῆς τὰ πράγματα φυόμενα).[89] It is worthwhile to make a brief digression at this point to show how the serial logic of soul in *De Anima* is, just as much as the method described here in the *Politics*, an account of the unfolding of soul from its first appearance to its most developed form. Moving from the nutritive faculty to the sensitive and the intellective soul is not simply an ascent through the various forms of life in plants, animals, and humans. These constitute separate parts of nature, but are also all moments of the development and growth of the soul from its first appearance to its most complete manifestation. Aristotle is thus also disclosing the unfolding of the substance from its initial, most implicit state to the full development of its capacities: this is why, as already mentioned, Aristotle begins anew at II.2.413a25 by looking at soul as growing (τὰ φυόμενα). For the movement through the stages of soul also traces the development of the highest soul, the human, from fetus to adult.

In the first place, Aristotle identifies the first emergence of life in the fetus with the mode of being characteristic of nutritive soul. In *Generation of Animals*, Aristotle makes several remarks about the plant-like existence of the fetus and its relation to the uterus. When seed and the female matter come together and consolidate in conception, separating from the parents and coming together to make living being, the fruit of the conception (the κύημα) acts like a sown seed. Growing an umbilical cord of blood vessels which acts as the root by which it draws nourishment,[90] the fetus takes on the life of a plant: "It absorbs nourishment and performs the function of the nutritive soul . . . all such embryos seem to live the life of a plant [φυτοῦ βίον]."[91] For Aristotle, the first principle of the animal, the heart (the principle of growth belonging to the nutritive activity)[92] is formed within the mother, and the whole later ordering of the body is contained in this beginning.[93] Like the plant, the fetus is not locomotive, and its earth is the mother's uterus until it is born and becomes a potentially locomotive animal.[94] Until then, it is not locomotive but necessarily dependent upon an external object to which it is fastened like a plant to the earth, without which it could not nourish itself and would soon die.[95] Wholly passive in its nutritive activities, its food (like the plant's) is already processed and in liquid form when it enters its body.[96]

Second, Aristotle identifies the child with the animal and its sensitive, non-intellective soul. As we have seen, sleep is the activity of the nutritive soul at the level of the sensitive being: all the activities by which it is defined as sensitive go into a latent state, with only the nutritive faculties remaining. Aristotle writes that once the baby is born, though it is a waking, sensitive animal, it closely resembles a plant in its activities due to the fact that it sleeps so much: "As soon then as the offspring of all animals are born, especially those born imperfect, they are in the habit of sleeping, because they continue sleeping also within the mother when they first acquire sensation."[97] It is precisely because the focus of the newborn's activities are primarily nutritive, and more specifically, growth, that its activities, primarily sleeping, are so close to those of plants.[98] These first stages are like an intermediate stage (a μεταξύ) between their plant-like, purely nutritive sleeping existence in the uterus, and their full existence as sensitive animals. Thus the movement of animals from the beginning is from a sleeping state to a waking state, and animals "wake up more as they grow older,"[99] developing from the nutritive state to the sensitive state.

Once children outgrow this primarily nutritive state, they are not fully developed intellectual souls, but are predominantly animal and sensitive: "In children may be observed the traces and seeds of what will one day be settled habits, though psychologically a child hardly differs for the time being from an animal."[100] Importantly, what differentiates this earlier sensitive stage from their fully developed intellective nature is the degree of independence of their soul from their body: in the young, "their psychical principle is corporeal and impeded in its motions."[101] Only once the adult emerges does the soul become what it is most fully, the third stage of intellective soul, which has the greatest amount of independence of soul from the bodily.

Thus the development of the hierarchy of souls is an account of the growth of the highest soul from the moment of its appearance until it attains its complete existence. It is crucial to understand how Aristotle understands the relation of the moments of this development. In the order of temporal development, the nutritive activities are prior. But this does not mean it is prior in nature or thought (λόγος); in fact, the opposite is true.

> Now the order of development and the order of substance (οὐσία) are always the inverse of each other. For that which is posterior in the order of development is antecedent in the order of nature . . . In order of time, then, the material and the generative process must necessarily be anterior; but in logical order (τῷ λόγῳ) the substance (οὐσίαν) and the form (μορφήν) of each being precedes the material.[102]

The nature (φύσις) or essence (οὐσία) of the living thing is not most revealed in its initial, most primitive stages, but in the final stage of its development,[103] in thinking, just as life belongs more properly and explicitly to the animal in its waking, sensitive activities than in its merely nutritive, sleeping activity: "For life most of all appertains to wakefulness, on account of sensation."[104] For the prior stages in the development become merely instrumental to the fulfillment of the later stages once these emerge, much like the materials of a house (bricks and stones), which, though they exist prior to the house in its development, are posterior to the house as their cause or that for the sake of which they exist.[105]

Beginning one's investigation of the series from its first, most primitive appearance and tracing its growth thus overcomes a merely subjective beginning point arbitrarily imposed by the investigator, allowing one to observe the development of the thing out of itself according to its own logic. In the *Politics*, Aristotle follows the unfolding of the most primitive forms of association (κοινωνία) into the full development of the city (πόλις). The various stages of the unfolding of the city as the most complete community (κοινωνία) are viewed as parts of this complete whole.[106] On our own account, this is precisely how Aristotle proceeds in *De Anima* II.1–3. By finding that which is common to all instances of soul in II.1, Aristotle begins his investigation by identifying the point where life first emerges out of inanimate nature, the most immediate form of living, the wholly simple and uncompounded life. He moves from this immediate form of nutritive soul and follows the unfolding or growth until he reaches the most complete and comprehensive form of soul, intellection.

Aristotle draws several consequences from the serial order of association or κοινωνία which are worth keeping in mind when looking at the *De Anima*:

> And therefore, if the earlier forms of society [κοινωνίαι] are natural, so is the state [πόλις], for it is the end [τέλος] of them, and the nature [φύσις] of a thing is its end. For what each thing is when fully developed, we call its nature,[107] whether we are speaking of a man, a horse, or a family. Besides, the final cause and end of a thing is the best, and to be self-sufficing [αὐτάρκεια] is the end and the best.[108]

Because the self-complete, autonomous community (κοινωνία) grows naturally out of the first immediate appearance of partnership in the household, the family and the state are not opposed to each other as nature (φύσις) to convention (νομός). The state is the natural development and end of all associations. If one asked the question: what is the essence (οὐσία) and nature (φύσις) of association (κοινωνία), Aristotle's answer would be "the city [πόλις]." The kind of autonomy manifested in the city is what is sought imperfectly by all the various forms of association, and in this sense it is the cause of the lower forms. Thus Aristotle says, "The city [πόλις] is by nature clearly prior to the family and to the individual, since the whole is of necessity prior to the part."[109] The last term of the series is prior to the first as its principle and cause, that for the sake of which the lower forms exist.

The serial logic in *De Anima* is exactly analogous. Just as Aristotle's goal is to show how the city is not merely conventional (governed by custom or νομός) but also natural, he seeks to show in the *De Anima* that thought is not opposed to the lower forms of life (nutrition and sensation), but that it is the most comprehensive activity of life and emerges out of the most primordial form of life as its fulfillment. When Aristotle asks at the beginning of the treatise "what is the nature and essence of the soul?" the answer he ultimately gives is "thinking," the final term of the series of souls. Thinking is not a secondary attribute of the essence of life as nutrition and reproduction, or of soul as it is when asleep, but it is the fulfillment of these lower functions and the cause for the sake of which they are what they are. This becomes clearest in the most developed and comprehensive soul, that of the human, where all functions exist as instrumental to the activity of thought, and within the context of thinking soul each lower function is more completely realized.

Just as the *Politics* treats the question of the city (πόλις) as the paradigmatic and most comprehensive species of association (κοινωνία), the *De Caelo* treats the question of bodies as the most paradigmatic and comprehensive species of magnitude (μεγέθη).[110] The body is that which can be divisible in all ways, whereas the line is divisible only in one way, and the surface in two ways (just as the plant possesses one activity, the animal two, and the human all three). The body thus comprehends the line and the surface within itself. Aristotle writes that "beyond these three there is no other magnitude,"[111] just as in the *De Anima* he argues that there is nothing beyond the lower appearances of soul and the perfection and completion belonging to the thinking soul. It is worth citing at length the passage in which Aristotle describes the relation between the three species of magnitude and the way one passes from one species to the next:

> One thing, however, is clear. We cannot pass beyond [μετάβασις] body to a further kind [γένος], as we passed from length to surface, and from surface to body. For if we could, it would cease to be true that body is complete magnitude. We could pass beyond [ἔκβασιν] it only in virtue of a defect in it [κατὰ τὴν ἔλλειψιν] and that which is complete cannot be defective, since it extends in every direction.[112]

This account of the method for defining the terms in a series offers a precious hint which helps us grasp exactly how Aristotle proceeds during the remaining argument of *De Anima*. Every level of the object investigated is studied according to its own mode of being, and one passes to the next level because of an imperfection or a lack of ability to fulfill what is sought at the lower level. One moves to the next appearance of the object, which incorporates the lower end within itself as its potential or matter, instrumental to its own higher end in which what is sought at the lower level is more adequately attained. Yet this chain of explanations and appeal to higher causes does not proceed to infinity, but is concluded by the term in which what is sought by the lower forms is satisfactorily attained. Once one reaches the term of the series, that which exists for the sake of itself and not for the sake of any further term, one has discovered the nature and essence of the genus as a whole.

One final feature must be noted about the analogy between the serial arguments in *Politics, De Caelo,* and *De Anima*. In each series, the final term is merely a relative completeness, the absolute paradigm of which is only to be found in divine activity. The source of the limitation of its completeness is always the same: that which is mortal always remains in relation to something other than itself, rendering its completeness and comprehensiveness merely finite. In *De Caelo*, despite the completeness of the body with relation to the other species of magnitude, bodies remain limited in relation to other bodies.[113] This imperfection is not relative to some abstract ideal of completeness, but to the divine completeness and perfection manifest in the body of the whole universe, outside of which exists nothing that limits it: for its circular shape is prior to all other figures.[114] In the *Politics*, the self-sufficiency (αὐταρκεία) achieved in the city is qualified as existing ὡς ἔπος εἰπεῖν (so to speak, almost).[115] This qualification indicates that the political self-sufficiency (αὐταρκεία) is limited in relation to the self-sufficiency of divine contemplation as described in the last book of the *Nicomachean Ethics*.[116]

Conclusion

In Plato's dialectical method one begins by finding the perfectly united ideal, which is common in all particulars, and then through division arrives at the progressively mixed and degraded forms of this ideal, its multiple sensible appearances. For Aristotle, in contrast, what is common is not the highest, but remains merely the beginning point. The most common definition (κοινότατος λόγος) is preserved within the investigation not as the definition of the essence and nature of soul, but as providing the beginning point for the investigation into soul's nature and essence: the nutritive soul, common to all mortal living beings. For when Aristotle moves to his investigations of the series in II.4, it is in exactly the terms of the most common definition of II.1 that the nutritive activity is described: "For the nutritive soul belongs even to the others, and it is the first and most common power of the soul [καὶ πρώτη καὶ κοινοτάτη δύναμίς ἐστι ψυχῆς], according to which life belongs to all" (II.4.415a23–5). One thus looks at this common activity in all instances, and moves upward towards the ideal activity which is prior to, and the cause and explanation of, the lower. By showing the unresolved tension between what is sought and what is actually achieved at each level, one moves through progressively comprehensive forms until one reaches the paradigm instance of the activity in question. Each higher level is the cause of the lower, and the highest activity of intellect is the nature and cause of all posterior souls. Thus ultimately, the movement from II.1 to II.3 is one which begins by soul according to the implicit potentiality (δύναμις) of first *entelecheia*, and moves through the three chapters towards defining it by the fully explicit *energeia* of its most complete reality. This is confirmed at the end of II.3, where Aristotle encapsulates the result of the previous three chapters before he moves to the necessity of beginning the investigation of each activity through the object of this *energeia* (II.3.415a1ff.). The most common definition does not stand as the account of the nature and essence of soul, yet neither do the individual definitions of soul. Nor is the solution to take these two together as separate yet complementary sides of the true account of soul. The logic of the series outlines how this question is to be resolved: the nature of the soul is in fact the final term of the series, but the individual, incomplete parts of the complete soul are preserved in the ascent as instrumentally necessary for the final term of thinking in the mortal living being. In this way Aristotle finds a middle ground between the synonymy of the various souls, and their unconnected homonymy.

CHAPTER 2

Unconscious and Stationary Life: Nutritive Soul

Introduction

The role of Aristotle's analysis of the nutritive soul and the vital activities characteristic of plants in the argument of *De Anima* is often overlooked by commentators.[1] This is to some extent understandable. His treatment of nutrition occupies only one chapter, as opposed to the much longer considerations of perception, thought, and desire. Further, the *De Anima* is frequently discussed within the context of questions in contemporary philosophy of mind, and of all the elements in Aristotle's psychology, plant life and nutrition most clearly fall outside the interest of this branch of philosophy. Aristotle's analysis of nutritive soul falls more within the scope of a speculative philosophy of nature, of the type which has been generally abandoned by contemporary philosophy in favor of leaving such questions to the natural, more empirically oriented sciences of botany, chemistry, and biology.

Yet not taking Aristotle's reflections upon plant life into account in analyzing the *De Anima* of course transgresses his expressed admonition to his contemporaries, who, when contemplating soul, "seem only to investigate concerning human soul" (I.1.402b3–5). Obviously Aristotle believed that certain errors which plague other views of soul arise from ignoring a more comprehensive view which includes the activities of other living beings, namely animals and plants. Accordingly, some essential features of what Aristotle attempts to communicate about the nature of living, ensouled beings are missed if one does not pay close attention to nutrition, growth, and reproduction. More precisely, if one is to grasp the overall direction of the argument in the treatise, proper attention needs to be paid to what distinguishes the πρώτη ψυχή (first soul) and its nutritive activity from non-living natural being below and the sensitive activity of animals above. No one has ever, to my knowledge, done a systematic analysis of the importance of nutrition in Aristotle's psychology. This is the goal of the present chapter: identifying what the nutritive soul is, how it works, and its relation to the higher activities of soul.

In what follows, two related but distinct objects are to be investigated. First, I lay the groundwork for understanding the argument of the *De Anima* as a whole by articulating the nature of the first and most primitive appearance of soul, that is, the nutritive soul. Second, I explain how this nutritive soul works in plants, which have only that kind of soul, as opposed to how nutritive soul operates in various kinds of animals. I take two interpretative liberties which will hopefully create more clarity than confusion. Though I rely primarily on *De Anima* II.4, the brevity and compactness of Aristotle's argument in this chapter demands that one look to his analysis of nutritive soul and plant life in his other works to complement and confirm the argument there. Second, I take the liberty of going back and forth between the discussion of features which are characteristic of nutritive soul in distinction from the higher powers, and features which are characteristic of plants in distinction from animals. There is clearly not a perfect overlap, since many significant differences between plants and animals have to do precisely with the way they perform their nutritive activities. By looking at these activities in plants in distinction from animals, we can come better to discern the general character of nutritive soul, since it is in plants that this principle exists in isolation without the transformative effect of the higher formal context.

De Anima II.4

From the argument up to this chapter, we have discovered that what the soul *is* is primarily grasped through understanding the active exercise of its function rather than its merely latent potency for this activity. Aristotle now brings the argument one step further, stating that prior to the activities, one must consider their objects (ἀντικείμενα).[2] ἀντικείμενα, although correctly translated as "objects" in this context, also carries the sense of things which are external and lie opposed to the soul, things facing the soul, its antitheses. As we will see, rising up the hierarchy of the soul's activities, its objects (ἀντικείμενα) become less and less antithetical. In this first level of soul, however, the activity is initiated only through the presence of the external object, and cannot be initiated by itself alone. More generally, what is made clear in Aristotle's preliminary comments to this chapter is that the activities of soul are inherently relational,[3] dependent on their object to be most fully what they are. Neither human thinking, nor perception, nor nutrition can be active without the presence of their respective objects, nor can they be understood apart from this relationship.[4] It is when any of the moments of the process of acting and being acted upon are isolated from the whole that the activity is not properly understood.[5]

Though all mortal psychic activities always maintain some relation to an object as source or trigger of the activity, as one moves up the hierarchy of these activities, both the degree to which the object is external and the degree to which the object rather than the organism acts as the initiating trigger of the activity is reduced. For this reason, the fact that to proceed objectively—that is, according to the actual development of the activity in question—we must begin with the objects (ἀντικείμενα) of the activities is especially demanded here by the fact that we are starting from life and soul not in its innermost nature, but from its first and most immediate appearance in the nutritive activity most characteristic of plants. The same is perhaps true of perception, but less so with imagination, and even less so with the intellective soul of humans (which does however retain some passivity and externality through the receptive side of mind or νοῦς).

Thus Aristotle states that we must begin the investigation into the hierarchy of psychic activities by considering the object of the most common and immediate appearance of life: food. Another result of this way of proceeding is that inanimate nature, as the object of plant nourishment, is incorporated into the hierarchy of nature as instrumentally necessary for the existence of the simplest forms of life. In considering only the activities of living soul, we have already seen how each level of life becomes instrumental to the end of the next highest activity on the hierarchy. As Aristotle makes clear in the *Politics*, this hierarchical relation of instrumentality that holds between the levels of life can also be glimpsed through the food chain:

> After the birth of animals, plants exist for their sake, and that the other animals exist for the sake of man, the tame for use and food, the wild, if not all, at least the greater part of them for food, and for the provision of clothing and various instruments. Now if nature makes nothing incomplete, and nothing in vain, the inference must be that she has made all animals (living beings) for the sake of man.[6]

In turn, food for plants, the composite of inanimate elements,[7] is here brought into this hierarchy of instrumentality, and thus also given a certain relation to the final end of all living and being. As Aristotle says later on in this chapter, "Food is related to the ensouled being, and not accidentally [κατὰ συμβεβηκός] . . . It is not able to exist when deprived of food" (II.4.416b10–11; 19–20). *De Anima* is a treatise on animate existence, yet from the beginning of his analysis of the hierarchy of animate existence, the investigation of ensouled, living being is connected with inanimate being, for, as he says a bit later, "All natural bodies are instruments of the soul"

(II.4.415b18–19). Thus in much the same way that nutritive soul exists as a potentiality for the sake of the higher activity of the sensitive soul (and so on up the hierarchy of life), the inanimate world of composite and non-composite inanimate bodies, as well as the elements out of which they are composed, are all ultimately potencies existing for the sake of living activities.[8] Of course, this is not only the case in terms of the use of the inanimate as nourishment for the animate, but goes, as we shall see, far more deeply into the material constitution of plants and animals: the elements must all have a certain nature in order for the various activities of living beings to be possible (the food chain is merely an external sign pointing towards this ontological priority of the higher over the lower). But by beginning his investigation of life through a consideration of how the inanimate is instrumentally necessary as food for animate being, the whole of inanimate nature, which is beyond the scope of the treatise, is brought into relation with the argument that follows.[9]

After these preliminary methodological considerations, Aristotle's account of nutritive soul in II.4 falls into what I see as four important divisions.

1. In one of the most important passages for discerning the movement of the argument as a whole, Aristotle explains how each kind of natural activity is a certain approximation or participation in the most complete and continuous divine activity.
2. He then moves on to what might appear to be a digression on the three ways in which soul is the cause responsible for living beings: as formal, final, and efficient cause. (I will attempt to show that this is not a digression, and that in fact these three modes of causality correspond to the three activities of nutritive soul: nutrition, reproduction, and growth.)
3. Aristotle then gives an analysis of eating and digestion, showing them to have a structure which nutrition shares in common with sensation and thinking, a structure which originates in the general theory of action and passion in *On Generation and Corruption* I.7. He settles a dispute between two possible accounts of how nutrition works: that like is nourished by like, and that contrary is nourished by contrary. The former theory errs by not being able to account for the obvious change that occurs through digestion, while the latter theory errs by not acknowledging the sense in which the activity of nutrition is an *energeia* beyond mere process or κίνησις. In order to resolve this dispute Aristotle outlines (admittedly not very explicitly) the three-level theory of potentiality and actuality which becomes so central to the

analysis of perception and thinking, a model which includes both kinds of transition: change or κίνησις, which involves the destruction of one contrary by another, and *energeia*, which involves the preservation and fulfillment of what the living being already is beyond process. In this way, nutritive soul, while incapable of awareness, anticipates the structure of all cognition—in this sense nutrition is *proto-cognitive.*

4. Finally, Aristotle offers a second model (wholly compatible with the first) for understanding the interaction between the four factors in nutrition: nutritive soul (that which feeds), vital heat and food (the two sides of the instrument by which the soul feeds the body), and the body (that which is fed). While the former structure anticipated the structure of cognition, this structure anticipates the side of soul responsible for the animal's self-movement through space analyzed at III.9–11. In this way, nutritive soul, while incapable of causing locomotion, is *proto-kinetic.* Understanding this fourfold model is also important for understanding the connection and difference between nutritive soul and the higher levels of soul.

After going through these four stages of the argument, I shall consider more generally some ways in which the nutritive soul is lacking in relation to the higher levels of soul, deficiencies which impel the argument of *De Anima* forward to these higher levels so that what is being sought at the lower levels can be more adequately attained.

The Natural Activities of Soul and Divine Participation

In one of the most important passages of the whole treatise, Aristotle then considers the ontological and theological significance of reproduction. "Making another just like itself [τὸ ποιῆσαι ἕτερον οἷον αὐτό]" is the most natural (φυσικώτατον) of all functions for living beings, meaning that it is the end for the sake of which all living beings will ultimately strive, unless somehow prevented from attaining it. Because of its central place in the current argument, I cite the passage in its entirety:

> For the most natural of the functions for living beings, insofar as they are complete and neither are deprived of something nor have spontaneous generation, is to make another just like itself, an animal making an animal, a plant making a plant, in order that they may participate in the eternal and the divine as much as they are capable. For all desire [ὀρέγεται] this, on account of which they do such things which they do according to nature. But this "on account

> of which" is twofold, meaning both that for the sake of which [*genitive*], and that for the benefit of which [*dative*]. And since it is not able to have a share in the eternal and the divine through continuity of existence, because it is not possible for corruptible things to remain one and the same in number, it partakes in this, inasmuch as each is able to participate in it, some more and some less. And it does not itself remain but one like itself, not one in number, but one in species. (II.4.415a26–415b8)[10]

Let us begin with this distinction between the two senses of the expression "that for the sake of which." The genitive sense appears to mean the ultimate end of the being in question, that which it would ideally ultimately attain but from which it falls short—in this case, the eternal perseverance of divine being. The dative sense appears rather to be referring to the immediate well-being of the individual in question: its immanent end. The first, more ultimate end is thus a relation to something beyond itself, while the second, more immediate end is an immanent self-relation of the organism. The "distance"[11] between the two constitute what Aristotle, in the *De Caelo* passage we discussed in chapter 2, called the lack (ἔλλειψιν) which impels one beyond a certain level of being to the next highest level, in order to discern how this higher level more adequately satisfies what is ultimately sought in the lower. These two senses of acting "for the sake of" correspond with Aristotle's initial designation of self-nutrition and reproduction as the objects of study for nutritive soul. Self-nourishment exists most directly for the benefit of the individual, in order that it may continue to survive as an individual, whereas reproduction exists for the sake of something beyond itself, here the continuity and preservation of the species. Of course these are not unrelated, since the preservation of the species is only possible on the condition that certain individuals preserve themselves until they can reproduce themselves. Both exist for the preservation and perseverance of life through time, and while nourishment is necessary to maintain the individual that would reproduce the species, the reproduction of the species more adequately approximates divine eternity than individual self-preservation.

What is it exactly that all desire?[12] The "this" (ἐκείνου) after which all things strive is unfortunately left somewhat indeterminate in the text. As Jonathan Lear writes, "We have not worked our way into Aristotle's world until we understand how in the most basic life activities, reproduction, an organism, insofar as its nature allows, partakes of the divine."[13] It seems to me that the "this" after which all things strive could plausibly refer to one of three things, differing in the degree of generality of Aristotle's claim. Either all things desire specifically "to make another like themselves,"[14] or more generally, "to exist eternally, remaining one in number," or most generally, "to participate[15] in the eternal and the divine as much as they are able." These do not, in fact, need to be opposed readings, since the desire to reproduce one's species is an instance of attempting to remain one and the same through time, which is in turn an instance of the more general desire to imitate the divine activity in all its acts. Yet I suggest the most plausible interpretation is the more general one: what is desired is to partake as much as is possible for such a being in the eternal and divine mode of being, that is, thinking. Otherwise, it is difficult to see how the other two options, reproduction and self-preservation, could admit of more and less in the way Aristotle mentions in the passage. And it would be wrong to restrict this feature only to reproduction, since it is the goal of any activity that is in accordance with nature (κατὰ φύσιν).

This is clear from the passage in the *Eudemian Ethics* we already considered:

> It is clear that perceiving and knowing (are life in the sense of activity and end) . . . And perceiving for oneself and knowing for oneself is the most desirable for each—and on account of this there is an inborn desire in all things for life [τοῦ ζῆν. . . ἔμφυτος ἡ ὄρεξις], for it is necessary to posit that living is a certain knowledge.[16]

Here Aristotle makes the striking claim that even bare living—which would include nutrition—is a certain kind of knowing, and that our desire for self-preservation is thus fundamentally a desire for the awareness present in sense-perception but most of all in knowledge. Of course, this does not mean that plants are consciously seeking knowledge while falling short, but even their unconscious impulse towards self-preservation, and their identification of themselves with an external object in nutrition, is a primitive realization of the universal desire in all things to be like the divine pure thinking.

That human thinking should be included among such activities according to nature is also made clear from the famous opening line of the *Metaphysics*: "All men by nature [φύσει] desire [ὀρέγονται] to know." Sensible pleasures beyond nutritive functions should also be included among these natural activities which seek to partake of the divine. Consider the following passage from *Nicomachean Ethics* VII on the implicit unity of the apparently disparate kinds of pleasures, similar in many ways to the passage currently under consideration:

> But since no one nature or state either is or is thought the best for all, neither do all pursue the same pleasure; yet all pursue pleasure.

> And perhaps they actually pursue not the pleasure they think they pursue nor that which they would say they pursue, but the same pleasure [see VII.14.1154b26 for the description of God's activity as the highest pleasure]: for all things have by nature something divine in them.[17]

As Francisco Gonzalez writes: "What Aristotle seems to mean here is that there is one activity which is most truly pleasurable and that in pursuing lower pleasures all living things are really striving towards this higher pleasure."[18] All things in seeking the end which is immanent to their own nature ultimately seek, to various degrees of success, the best and most complete activity. Thus, the reproduction of the species directly under consideration in our *De Anima* passage is just one form of natural activity in which living things partake in the divine mode of living which most of all remains what it is throughout its activity. Aristotle speaks of this desire as existing not only in the lowest level of animate life, but even in the motion of the inanimate elements, whose eternal cyclical transformations indicate a desire to be perpetually active in imitation of divine actuality.[19] This desire to remain oneself is but one aspect of the more general fact that all beings are seeking to participate in the divine eternal activity of thinking. That each being does this to the degree which it is capable of doing, some to a greater and some to a lesser extent, indicates a hierarchy of different degrees of success in the satisfaction of this desire. We must therefore see, first of all, if, moving up the hierarchy of living activities, plants through their nutritive activities remain more one and the same than inanimate beings, animals and their perceptual activities more than nutritive, and human thinking activity more than the sensitive. Further, we must see if there are other activities which characterize the divine activity that emerge gradually by degrees through the hierarchy of life.

It is important to see the inadequacy of the imitation of the divine activity found in the reproduction of the species. This can be partially grasped through the very difference between remaining one and the same in number, and remaining one and the same in form (εἶδος). As Aristotle writes in *On Generation and Corruption*, "Men and animals do not return upon themselves [ἀνακάμπτουσιν εἰς αὐτοὺς] so that the same individual comes-to-be a second time (for though your coming-to-be presupposes your father's, his coming-to-be does not presuppose yours) . . . This coming to be seems to constitute a rectilinear sequence."[20] Viewed from the perspective of the collective identity of the species, reproduction involves an eternal circular return upon the same beginning which approximates the circular motion of the heavenly bodies. Yet this same activity of returning upon oneself is not accomplished with regards to one and the same individual, which never returns back upon itself, but rather begins at one point and ends in another, limited at both ends.

Further, for plants, the particular way in which the divine nature is imitated is continuity not principally through the particular identity of the individual (although there is some of this in the self-preserving activity of nutrition), but rather in the collective identity of the species. At the level of collective preservation, all living beings (plants, animals, humans) are equal—each species of living being successfully preserves its kind, and in this respect there is no more or less.[21] Only once the most primitive awareness emerges in the sensitive activity of animals do we get imitation of divine eternity as a particular identity, distinct from the collective species. Once there is subjective awareness in the living being, its activities are able more effectively to preserve itself as this particular individual, one and the same in number. We will address this greater degree of individual preservation in animals with subjective awareness in our treatment of sensitive soul.

As a result of this discussion, it is unclear exactly how the nutritive soul is the cause of the organism's activities, rather than the external object. This compels Aristotle to make explicit more fully how nutritive soul ultimately is the formal, final, and efficient cause of its activities. Thus we now turn to this central passage at II.4.415a26–415b7.

The Three Activities of Nutritive Soul and Its Threefold Causation

In what might seem to be a digression from the argument, Aristotle moves on to discuss the ways in which the soul is cause (αἰτία) and principle (ἀρχή) (II.4.415b8ff.).[22] But following the previous argument, it is clear why Aristotle must now establish how, even at this first level of soul, the soul is the cause and source of its activities in these three senses. First, the activity of nourishment is initiated from without by the food, so that the efficient cause of nutrition can appear external to the organism. Second, since divine eternity is that for the sake of which the soul ultimately acts, the final cause can also appear to lie beyond the living being. Third, in terms of the formal cause, the organism's goal of self-preservation is not reached at the level of its own immanent form, but only at the level of the species beyond the individual. In these three ways living beings may appear from the preceding argument to have their cause and end outside of themselves.

There is the additional problem concerning the source of motion in plants (and some primitive animals) that they do not seem to have motion at all, being necessarily fixed in one place. The soul has already been identified as the cause and principle of living beings, but it is not yet clear how soul can be cause in any of the three non-material senses: formal, final, or efficient cause. Aristotle must therefore clarify, before examining the nutritive activity of plants, the ways in which the cause of living beings and their activities is not primarily external, as it is in inanimate nature. This passage on the soul as *cause* is used to distinguish the plant and its living activity as the first appearance of soul and life from the incomplete activity of natural, inanimate motions. To do so, in the face of the apparent externality of both the object of food and the eternal activity of the divine as perpetually active being, he must explain how the nutritive soul as internal principle and cause of the living being is both final and efficient cause of its various activities.

Aristotle states that the soul is the cause of the activity of living things in the three non-material senses: the soul is cause as that whence the motion originates (efficient cause), the "for the sake of which" it exists (final cause), and as the essence or οὐσία of the living body (formal cause). These three senses of causation are merely three aspects of the soul's responsibility for the being of the living organism. The soul is the substance, essence, or definition of the being of the plant or animal, what it is to be the particular kind of living being in question, that which makes it this kind of being and not that one: this is how soul is the *formal* cause of the living body. As defining all the characteristic activities and functions of the living being, it is also the ultimate end, since it provides the purpose (τέλος) of all its bodily parts, making them instruments serving the ends defined by the soul as the essence of that living being: this is how soul is the *final* cause of the living body. Finally, by giving a determinate nature to the living being, the soul ensures that change in the living being does not happen in an indiscriminate manner, but as structured according to the limits prescribed by this nature: this is soul as the *efficient* cause of the living body. It is crucial to note, both in order to grasp how soul is the cause in these three ways, and what this "digression" has to do with the rest of Aristotle's account of nutritive soul in II.4, the way in which soul as cause in these three senses is intimately related to the powers of nutritive soul analyzed in what follows.

For Aristotle, nutritive soul is responsible for three activities, and he outlines how these activities work in *De Anima* II.4. These activities are self-nourishment, growth, and reproduction.[23] What has gone unnoticed by commentators is the connection between the three kinds of causation and these three powers of soul. Nourishment is the preservation of the living being as an individual thing and substance (τόδε τι καὶ οὐσία), while growth is the change or κίνησις in relation to quantity which exists even in plants which neither sense nor move.[24] Aristotle identifies reproduction as the ultimate end or τέλος of the nutritive soul, that for the sake of which other nutritive activities exist (see II.4.416b24–25). Thus the soul causes self-nourishment, growth, and reproduction as the formal, efficient, and final cause.

According to the primary division of the soul's powers discussed above, that between awareness and motion, the *energeia* of nutrition, the basic self-maintenance and preservation of life in the living being, should be thought of as a type of proto-awareness, in the sense that it shares a common structure with perception and thought, that is, taking in and being determined by its object, without losing (but rather realizing) its own nature in the process. Growth, on the other hand, falls on the side of soul's change (κίνησις), and it is the most primitive form of such change, prior to both ἀλλοίωσις (alteration) and κίνησις κατὰ τόπον (locomotion). This explains how plants do in fact share, if only in a primitive sense, in these two distinguishing characteristics of soul: awareness and motion. As the cause of its essence (οὐσία) and the perseverance of this essence, soul as the cause of nutrition is the *formal* cause of this nutritive level of life. As the cause of quantitative change in the living being, soul as cause of growth is the *efficient* cause of this nutritive level of life. And both the formal cause and efficient cause, Aristotle argues, ultimately exist for the sake of the ultimate end of nutritive soul, so that soul as the cause of reproduction of the species is the final cause of nutritive life.

Let us look in detail at each of the nutritive soul's activities.

Nutrition and formal cause. Soul as formal cause, as the essence (οὐσία) of the living being, is soul as the cause of nutrition, which is precisely described as the preservation of the essence of the living being as an individual (τόδε τι), the maintaining of its nature in existence. This essence includes the overall shape of the whole including its parts. The form and substance of the living being constitute the unmoving center of its being which persists underneath all its changes. The activity of the soul both determines what the soul is, and preserves this essential nature throughout its existence. It is nutrition that is chiefly responsible for this individual self-preservation of the center of the living thing's being. An example of this self-maintenance is the activity of holding together the living being and preventing it from being torn apart:[25] "In addition to these things, what is it that holds together the fire and earth [i.e., the material constituents of its body] which are carried in opposite directions? For it will be torn asunder, unless there is something preventing this" (II.4.416a6–8). Nutrition is a function directed toward maintaining the life of the being. As Aristotle says, "The cause of being for all things is the essence (οὐσία), but being for living beings is living" (II.4.415b12–14). It follows that basic self-maintenance and self-preservation of life is the preservation of οὐσία (the substance and form of the being). Thus soul as the cause of nutritive activity is the formal cause of its life.

Yet one might ask: how is this most material of activities—the ingestion and digestion of food—related to the form of the living being at all? Nutrition of all soul's activities is the most closely related to the body or the matter of the living being. But Aristotle writes that "although food is akin to the matter, that which is fed is the figure—i.e., the form—taken along with the matter."[26] While it might seem like the activity of nutrition affects only the matter or body of the living being, in fact it is the incarnate form or the ensouled body which is kept in existence.

For Aristotle, nutrition is the use of food for the preservation of the vital heat of the organism. Living is associated with a certain vital heat,[27] and nutrition is described as the maintenance of this basic heat intimately associated with the form of the being in question. The preservation of the essence (οὐσία) is achieved by nutrition in that the vital heat, centered in the heart or the analogous part, must be maintained within the living being in order for it to persist as living. We can understand more clearly what this preservation of its essence is by looking at what happens in death, the failure of this preservation. For death is the organism's failure to nourish its heat. For both natural death from itself (μάναρσις) and violent death from without (σβέσις), there is a common explanation: "Either of these ways in which fire ceases to be may be brought about by the same cause, for, when there is a deficiency in nutriment and the warmth can obtain no maintenance, the fire fails."[28] Food *nourishes* insofar as it conserves this central psychic power, corporeally manifest in the heat of the living being. Aristotle uses the analogy of a hearth fire[29] to explain what happens in nutrition: fuel must be added to the central source of heat and essence (οὐσία) to keep it burning and to keep the living being alive (in animals this is the heart, which acts as "the source of the creature's essential nature").[30] The food acts as fuel to be burned (τὸ καυστόν) in order to maintain the vital heat of the organism. In this way, it is through nutrition that the essence of the being is preserved.

Importantly, in this explanation of nutrition through the analogy with fueling the hearth fire, the fire is both the agent of the activity, and that which is fed and preserved. Nutrition is thus not an ordinary *change*, for the heat in nutrition is used precisely to preserve the source of this heat. The source produces that by which it is itself maintained: in this way the beginning (ἀρχή) and the end (τέλος) are united. Vital heat is produced to be used in nutrition in order for this very vital heat to be maintained. In general, nutrition relates to the living being as essence (οὐσία), and this is never changed by nutrition, only preserved as it already was.[31] Like any *energeia*, nutrition as basic self-maintenance (as opposed to the preparatory process of breaking down and concocting the food) does not take up time, since one is never on the way to self-maintenance. The activity is necessarily complete in every moment, or else the living being would die. For this reason this activity cannot admit of the more or the less, since one either is or is not being maintained alive. There is a process with stages further and closer from the end result in terms of the ingestion and transformation of the food, but not in the nourishing itself.[32]

Growth and efficient cause. If nutrition is related to preserving the form or unchanging center of the living being, growth is rather related to maintaining stability in its changing periphery, that is, the various *parts*[33] of the organism. The actual activities are one and the same—both self-nourishment and growth involve the transformation of food into itself—but what it means to be nourished and what it means to grow are different.[34] While nutrition was about the preservation of the being's substance, the ensouled body has the capacity for growth (αὐξητικόν) insofar as it is a certain quantity. The one happens to the living being considered as substance and separately existing individual, the other happen to the same being considered as a quantity (μέγεθος).[35]

The activity of nutrition, we have seen, constitutes an *energeia*, in which the subject of the activity preserves itself as unaffected and unchanged. Yet the plant does not remain unchanged and unaffected insofar as it *grows*. The living being as nutritive has only this one kind of animate change—quantitative change, or growth and diminution. Aristotle's analysis of growth in the chapter resolves the problem of how nutritive soul is the efficient cause, or cause of change (κίνησις), in the living being, when plants, which have only nutritive soul, are fixed in place and thus have no locomotion. Aristotle makes clear that though change of place is the chief sense of change, it is not the *only* kind of change. Soul is equally the cause of the change (κίνησις) involved in sensation, which, in Aristotle's frequent comment about sensation (αἴσθησις), "seems to be a certain alteration [τις ἀλλοίωσις]" (a phrase often used by Aristotle to indicate the kind of process involved in sensation, without reducing sensation to merely this process). And even in those living beings without sensation or locomotion, soul is still the cause from which change originates, since the growth and diminution essentially related to nutrition is the most primitive kind of change. This is not to say, of course, that a plant, possessing only nutritive soul, cannot be changed qualitatively (ἀλλοίωσις) or have its location moved (κίνησις κατὰ τόπον). Of course one can heat a plant or move it from one place to another. But this change will not have as its cause and principle the soul of the being, but rather an external cause. It will be an ordinary change (κίνησις).

In contrast, the growth of a living being is structured by a λόγος (ratio) and a πέρας (limit). This is in contrast to the growth of one of the inanimate bodies—fire, in the example Aristotle cites—as there is no internal limit to the size of a fire. As long as there continues to be food or fuel for an inanimate being, it can grow indefinitely. Growth of a living being is structured by a proportion determined through the soul of the being: "For the growth of fire goes to the unlimited, as long as there is fuel to be burned [τὸ καυστόν], but of things combined by nature there is a limit and a proportion [πέρας καὶ λόγος] to the quantity and growth. These belong to the soul, but not to fire, and to λόγος, but not to matter" (II.4.416a15–18). The growth is limited in the sense that a living being will not be able to extend its quantitative bulk infinitely, but rather each kind of being has a certain maximum bulk beyond which it cannot go. If it exceeds the limit of this proportion, it is destroyed.[36] Further, the growth is also structured by a proportion or a ratio (λόγος) which is maintained through the change of quantity.

Not only is this growth governed by a certain limit and proportion, but it is initiated from within. Unlike an inanimate, elemental body, which moves towards a natural location outside of itself, as determined by the spatial orientation of the universe as a whole, the ensouled body grows according to its own internally determined spatial orientation. This point comes out in Aristotle's criticism of Empedocles's theory of growth:

> Empedocles did not state this rightly, positing that growth in plants laying down their roots downwards happens on account of earth being carried in this way according to nature, and growing upwards on account of fire in a similar way. For he grasps neither up or down rightly. For up and down are not the same for all things as for the universe, but the head of animals is like the roots of plants, if it is necessary to say that instruments are different and the same by their functions. (II.4.415b28–416a5)

Growth is in relation to the various parts of living beings, and these parts are what they are by virtue of their ability to carry out the functions determined by the form or soul of the living being. It is in accordance with these requirements that the growth of an organism is structured, and not in accordance with the properties of the constitutive matter apart from its formal determination. Aristotle puts the same point thusly in *On Generation and Corruption* I.5:

> Now, that any and every part should grow—and grow by the accession of something—is possible in respect of form, but not in respect

> of matter. For we must think of the process as being like what happens when a man measures water with the same measure; for what comes-to-be is always different. And it is in this sense that the matter of the flesh grows, some flowing out and some flowing in; not in the sense that fresh matter accedes to every particle of it. There is, however, an accession to every part of its figure or form.[37]

The overall proportion of the body grows when fed. While there is change of size, the proportion of the whole is preserved. If it were simply the matter apart from this overall proportion which grew, one could have one part continually growing and all the rest remaining just as they are. The matter is always changing, yet it is the shape or form that ultimately grows, and in this way characteristic of animate growth: by preserving its overall proportion throughout the course of the change in quantity.

◆ ◆ ◆

Before moving on to examine reproduction as the final cause of nutritive soul, it is important for my argument to clarify precisely the relation between nutrition and growth, since I want ultimately to argue that this relationship prefigures the relationship in perception between the general awareness of the common sense to the qualified sense of alteration which goes on in the five sense organs.

Nutrition and growth make up one and the same process: taking in food and assimilating it to its body through digestion.[38] In a formulation that Aristotle does not use here but which I believe is implicit, they are one *in number*. Yet their essence is not the same. This latter fact Aristotle makes explicit: "But being for food and for the capacity to grow are not the same. For it is insofar as it is a certain quantity that the ensouled being is capable of growth, but there is nourishment for it insofar as it is an individual [τόδε τι] and a substance [οὐσία]" (II.4.416b11–13). Though growth and nourishment refer to the very same process, each refers to this process under a different categorial description of the ensouled being, viewed either as a substance or as a certain quantity. Nutrition is thus a preservation and maintenance of the very center of its being, its basic life and existence as this particular kind of being. Here there is no change (κίνησις) throughout the activity, at least not with reference to the living being. (There is change to the object of food, through the destruction of its form and transformation into blood.) It is through the use of heat on food that the living being returns upon itself to preserve the heat required for its persistence as the individual being that it is. This circular movement out of itself and back upon itself characterizes the self-preserving character of *energeia.* In contrast to these features of nutrition, growth is the very first kind of change (κίνησις)—change with respect to quantity—on Aristotle's hierarchy of motions. Here there is change: the quantity at the beginning of the movement is not the same as the quantity at the end of the movement of either growing or diminution. The previous quantity is not preserved through the activity, but is destroyed by the resulting quantity. Yet this growth differs importantly from inanimate growth by virtue of soul's presence as the efficient cause: for while inanimate beings like fire can grow without limit or internal regulation, animate growth is structured through an internal limit (πέρας) and proportion (λόγος). While nutrition thus concerns the unchanging center of the nutritive living being, growth is concerned with change at the periphery of the being, in relation to its parts. The center is not separate from the parts however, and thus the changes in the parts are limited by the unchanging essence of the center, which permeates the whole.

This relationship between the preservation of the unchanging center of the being in nutrition and the structured change of the quantitative parts in growth is best grasped through Aristotle's mathematical image for grasping the relationship between the common awareness and individual senses in III.2:

> But it is just as that which some call the point [στιγμήν], which exists both as one and as two, and in this last sense (considered as two) it is divisible. And insofar as it is indivisible, that which judges is one and simultaneous, but insofar as it is divisible, it uses the same mark twice and simultaneously. Insofar as it uses the limit as two, it judges two things, and these are separated just as a separate instrument. But insofar as it is one, it acts as one and simultaneously. (III.2.427a9–16)

This passage is very difficult, and our full interpretation of it will have to wait for our interpretation of perception. Yet for the purposes of understanding the relationship between nutrition and growth, I believe that the logical structure of the passage is quite illuminating. The point is one in relation itself, yet viewed as the limit of two lines extending outward from itself, it is two: it is the principle (ἀρχή) of both, without losing its indivisibility with regards to itself. Nutrition, as an unchanging *energeia*, is indivisible. The life of the being and its corresponding heat are preserved without change in and through the activity of nutrition. Yet this *energeia* viewed in relation to the living being as a divisible quantity acts as the principle of its changing parts, just as the point is the principle (ἀρχή) of two distinct lines. As principle it exerts a certain power over each part, yet it does not remain indivisibly identical in each: for the line has a result which is different than the beginning. Similarly, the change in growth has the soul and its corresponding heat as its principle and its efficient cause, whose inner *logos* and limit (πέρας) regulate the change, but the change is not a return upon itself in which the beginning and end are identical: in other words, the change is rectilinear, as opposed to the circular activity of nutritive self-maintenance.

Reproduction and final cause. Nutritive soul, Aristotle states in this section on the causative power of soul, acts also as the final cause, the "for-the-sake-of-which" of the nutritive living being. Aristotle clearly identifies *reproduction* as the final cause of nutritive soul. In an aside toward the end of II.4, he explains how because the ultimate end or goal of nutritive soul is the generation of another like itself, and since all things should be named by their end (τέλος), this first soul would be more aptly called reproductive (γεννητική) rather than nutritive (θρεπτική) (II.4.416b23–25). Since the nutritive soul of plants obviously also has a self-nourishing and a growing function, this can only mean that these lower functions ultimately exist for the sake of its ultimate end (τέλος), and thus can be reduced to it as purely instrumental for this end. In fact, Aristotle often reduces the formal and final cause of nutritive soul to the final cause. He even occasionally states that plants have only one function: reproduction.[39]

Reproduction, unlike nutrition and growth, which are for the benefit of the individual, involves the preservation of the living being's form beyond its individual existence. In the "making of another like itself [τὸ ποιῆσαι ἕτερον οἷον αὐτό]," there is a persistence or remaining (διαμένειν) throughout time of the being, but only in something which resembles it. Crucially for our account, at the level of nutritive soul the final cause lies *outside* the individual. Nutrition and growth exist for the good of the individual being, yet the goal for the sake of which they exist is not fulfilled relative to this individual. This is a deficiency in plants that is remedied at higher levels of soul's activity.

◆ ◆ ◆

One final consideration concerning nutrition, reproduction, and growth before we examine the structure of nutritive activity: what constitutes the unity of the three activities which characterize nutritive soul? The unity of the various modes of perception and thinking are not so difficult to see, but what do nutrition, growth, and reproduction share in common such that they belong to one level of soul? The connection between the growth of the living being and its nourishment is perhaps more obvious, since Aristotle is explicit about this unity (see *DA* II.4.416a15–18), but what does reproduction have to do with these two activities? In fact, there are important and substantive connections between these three activities both at the level of formal and material description.

Aristotle writes that all the activities of nutritive soul are distinguished from the other powers of soul—perceptive and thinking soul—through their connection to the activity of nutrition.[40] For Aristotle, in animals the heart is the common principle (ἀρχή) of all these activities, while food is their common material instrument. In fact, the matter of nutrition and growth are the same,[41] that is, blood. Further, the difference between the material for growth and nutrition and the material for reproduction (the menstrual blood and semen)[42] is simply the degree of concoction of the useful residue[43] from nutrition. The first stage of concoction of useful residue is used for self-maintenance, the next is for growth, and the third and last for reproduction.[44] The matter of all three activities is generated through taking food into itself and concocting to varying degrees.

Beyond this material connection, self-nourishment, growth, and reproduction can also be reduced to the same ultimate purpose: the preservation of the being in some way or another. The closest thing to a definition of the living being in II.4 stresses this self-preserving aspect of nutritive soul: "Therefore this principle [ἀρχή] of soul is a power of preserving that which possesses it as such" (II.4.416b17–19). The living being uses food in order to "preserve [σώζει] its essence [οὐσίαν]," to maintain its essence in existence. It cannot remain what it is without the presence of food, and thus its innermost essence is essentially related to this external object, without which it ceases to be what it is. Growth, in turn, despite the fact that it involves change, is the preservation of a certain *logos* or proportion throughout the living being throughout its changes in quantity.[45] The power of reproduction is the power of informing matter so as to produce another like oneself, thus preserving the existence of the individual's species-form.[46] A general statement of nutritive soul's nature which includes all three of its activities would be the preservation of a living being's nature through time.

The Proto-Cognitive, Proto-Locomotive Structures of Nutritive Activity

De Anima II.4 concludes with an outline of two distinct structures which govern nutritive activity. The first structure outlined at 416a21–416b9 explains how the organism breaks down the nature of its food, which is initially different from it, and then, having made the food identical with itself, assimilates it to its own body. This structure is common to the cognitive activities analyzed in *De Anima*, sensation and thinking. The second structure, at 416b20–29, outlines a fourfold distinction between that which feeds, that which is fed, and two senses of the bodily instrument by which the soul causes the body to be fed. This structure is common to the general structure of locomotion articulated in III.10 at 433b13–27. In both cases, it is through first detecting the common structure of cognition on the one hand and locomotion on the other even in the pre-conscious and stationary activity of nutrition, and then identifying the differences between this common structure at every level of soul, that the overall argument of *De Anima* can be grasped.

The Proto-Cognitive Structure of Nutrition: The "Like by Like" versus "Unlike by Unlike" Debate

When one pays heed to the role of nutritive activities in the argument, the common activity of all levels of soul becomes especially clear: the soul makes the living being one with its objects; it identifies itself with some object that is other than itself.[47] This is equally true, though in importantly different ways, for nutrition, perception, and thinking. It has been noted by many interpreters[48] that in the primary division of distinguishing traits of the soul, awareness and motion, both sense perception and thinking fall under the general heading of "awareness." They are each forms of cognition, ways of grasping truths about the world. Yet I think this reduction of perception and thinking to the general term "cognition" should be reduced one further level down the hierarchy of soul's activities, based on the overall structure of Aristotle's argument. Even more fundamentally and precisely than being a "means of getting information from the world,"[49] perception and thinking are ways that the living being becomes determined by its object, assimilating it and making itself identical to it. When stated in this way, we see that while the taking in of food and identification of the food with its own body is not literally *cognition*, it should be viewed as sharing a common structure with these cognitive activities and as a consequence as a *proto*-cognitive function of soul. This becomes clearer as we look at how precise the analogy is between the way Aristotle structures the moments of nutrition and the way he structures perception and thinking.

Further, this identification with its object is not the destruction or overcoming of the living being's nature by the nature of the object. Rather, animate being is able to assimilate the object to itself without losing its own identity. Not only does it not *lose* its own identity in the course of its active interaction with its objects: it in fact becomes its own nature *more fully* as a result of its taking into itself the nature of its object, which allows it to grow, preserve itself, and attain its own nature. Thus the identification of the living being with its food happens on its own terms, so to speak. It remains what it is through the course of the activity, or, to use the language that Artistotle uses throughout the *De Anima*, it *preserves* itself in its identification with its object. One must first discern this parallel between the functions and activities of each level of soul in *De Anima* in order to discern the importance of the differences between how this unification of living being and its object is accomplished.

Aristotle distinguishes several moments in the activity of self-nutrition, the significance of which can only be fully grasped in light of his general treatment of acting and being acted upon (ποιεῖν and πάσχειν) in *On Generation and Corruption* I.7 (where he outlines the debate about whether things are affected by their likes or by their contraries),[50] and his categorizations of actuality and potentiality in *De Anima* in the chapter immediately following this treatment of nutrition. In this absolutely central passage of II.5, Aristotle uses the various senses in which someone can be "knowing," and in which an object can "be known," in order to distinguish three stages of actuality and potentiality as follows:

1. The very first sense of potential knower is one in which someone is said to be knowing by virtue of merely belonging to the class of things which know and have knowledge, based on the as-yet undeveloped potentiality of their underlying nature (their matter). At this stage he is not *actually* knowing at all: he has learned nothing and is thus ignorant (the contrary of knowing). This stage is a pure potency, and the person is a knower only by virtue of the kind of being he is, belonging to the class of beings which are able to know.
2. The second form of potency is, in contrast to the first, at the same time an actuality: having learned some truths, someone is said to be knowing when he possesses the knowledge, even when he is not actively contemplating what he knows. One could say here that he actually knows in that he possesses the knowledge (it is a state of possessing or a ἕξις), but that he is not *actively* knowing, that is, thinking what he knows. The actual possession of knowledge is simultaneously an actuality and a potentiality for active thinking.
3. The fullest actuality of someone knowing is someone who is actively thinking that which they know. This is, Aristotle says, the most appropriate and ruling (κυρίως) sense of what it means to know. Here the knower is no longer potentially a knower of A, but is knowing A in its most active and actual sense.

Importantly, the transition from potentiality #1 to potentiality #2, in which the ignorant person through learning becomes a knower, involves a change of quality (ἀλλοίωσις) and change (μεταβολή) of disposition from its contrary. This change is towards its contrary, and thus it constitutes the destruction (φθορά) of the original potentiality (i.e., the ignorance is destroyed by learning and becoming knowledgeable). It is not ordinary alteration *tout court*, however, since it is not simply towards the privation of the original state (ἐπὶ τὰς στερητικὰς διαθέσεις), but is a realization of its nature or a progress (ἐπίδοσις) towards *itself*, through the acquisition of its natural state of possession (ἕξις). The transition from potentiality #2 to actuality #2, in contrast, involves no such destruction of the first moment, but rather its preservation (σωτηρία). The one who knows, in his transition to active reflection upon his knowledge, does not destroy the knowledge, but most fully realizes it. The schema is depicted in table 2.

TABLE 2. Sensation and the Three Levels of Potentiality and Actuality

SENSE			OBJECT	
1a. 1st potentiality →	2a. 2nd potentiality/ 1st actuality →	3. 2nd actuality	← 2b. 2nd potentiality/ 1st actuality	← 1b. 1st potentiality
Man does not yet know, but is a knower potentially in virtue of belonging to the class of knowers, prior to any actual knowing.	Man is a knower actually in virtue of actually possessing knowledge of A, but only potentially knowing in that he is not actively exercising this capacity.	Man is a knower actively in that he is actively thinking what he knows./ The object is known actively in that it is actively being thought. In this second actuality, subject and object are identical.	The object is actually known in that it has been learned and is possessed within the soul, but is only potentially known in that it is not being actively contemplated.	The object is known potentially in virtue of belonging to the class of knowable objects, prior to having been actually learned.

Kosman has usefully illustrated how this three-level schema of potentiality and actuality maps on to sensation, through the example of hearing.[51] While we will have to return to the question of the structure of hearing and sensation in general once we move on to Aristotle's treatment of sensation (αἴσθησις) in the next chapter, I refer now to Kosman's schematization because it will help bring out what is the structure of nutrition for Aristotle by comparison. Table 3 roughly approximates Kosman's diagram.[52]

TABLE 3. Hearing and the Three Levels of Potentiality and Actuality

SENSE		SENSE = OBJECT	OBJECT	
1st potentiality →	1st actuality (2nd potentiality) →	2nd actuality	← 1st actuality (2nd potentiality)	← 1st potentiality
Ear →	Power of hearing →	Active hearing = active sounding	← Audible (capable of being heard, i.e., sounding bell)	← Bell (unsounding, prior to being struck)
αἰσθητήριον →	αἰσθητικόν →	αἴσθησις	← αἰσθητόν (2)	← αἰσθητόν (1)

Aristotle does not discuss the various moments of nutritive activity according to this schema, at least not explicitly so. But by comparing the contexts of his discussion of nutrition and his discussion in II.5 of this three-level theory of potentiality and actuality in relation to sensation, the parallel becomes evident. In the discussion of both the three-level theory of potentiality and actuality and the discussion of the various moments in nutrition, the analysis comes up in the context of a discussion of whether the activity is one between opposites (unlike by unlike), or rather between terms which are identical (like by like).[53] The solution in all cases is the same, that viewed as first potentialities, the subject and the object are contraries, while viewed as first actualities, the activity is of like by like. Or, in other words, "It is therefore, on the one hand, as if it is affected by its like, but on the other hand as if by its unlike, just as we said. For as unlike is affected, but having been affected it is like" (II.5.417a18–20).[54]

Commentators have not noticed the parallel structure between perception and nutrition and the way that each activity is a way in which the living being takes in the external object in order to become identical with it, because they have not been properly attentive to the way the debate between "like-by-like" and "contrary-by-contrary" theorists of affecting and being affected from *On Generation and Corruption* I.7 structures Aristotle's treatment of nutrition as much as it does his treatment of perception.[55] Burnyeat has brought out effectively how the argument of *On Generation and Corruption* I.7, which treats "being affected" and "acting on" in relation to basic, ordinary change,[56] undergoes subtle but important changes when it is echoed in the treatment of that special kind of alteration that is perception. The same thing is true of the argument as it is deployed in relation to nutrition, which differs from both ordinary alteration and perceptive alteration.

Aristotle settles the debate between those who say that like can only be affected by like and those who say something can only be affected by a contrary by pointing out that both must be true for "acting on" and "being affected" to happen. This is because, if there is to be any affection, the agent and patient must have some respect in which they are identical—they must belong to the same genus—while also having some respect in which they are contrary to one another—they must differ in species.[57] In the case of nutrition, the "generic" identity corresponds to the fact that the object of food and the living being are constituted out of the same matter: they must be *materially* identical in order for there to be a nutritive relationship in the first place. This material identity is required for the food to be potentially nourishing: it must be potentially the same matter as that out of which the body is made, and to be potentially flesh or bone means that it is constituted out of the same elements as the body of the organism. As Aristotle states later on in the treatise, "All of them are fed by what they are constituted from."[58] Yet prior to the concoction of the food, the food and the living body are specifically different in the sense that the form which determines the matter of each is different. In order for the assimilation to be complete, this specific difference must be broken down through the concoction of the food by vital heat, which breaks down the form—of egg or cheese for example—and gives it the form of the living body.[59]

The nature of nutrition becomes clearer in contrasting it with ordinary "acting on" and "being affected." Aristotle writes of this latter process:

> We can now understand why fire heats and the cold thing cools, and in general why the active thing assimilates to itself the patient. For agent and patient are contrary to one another, and coming-to-be is the process into the contrary; hence the patient must change into the agent, since it is only thus that coming-to-be will be a process into the contrary.[60]

Thus the object which is changed begins with some characteristic that is contrary to a characteristic in some other being, and this other being—playing the role of agent—passes on the characteristic to the changing object by destroying the original characteristic and replacing it with a new one. Fire, as the agent of change, changes a cold thing (the patient of the change), into a hot thing. In contrast with nutrition, it is important to note here that (1) the agent is not the changing object but rather the object which initiates the change; and (2) the changing object is wholly receptive: it does not bestow its own characteristic on another, but simply receives a new characteristic (the agent's) from without through being assimilated to the agent in respect to this already actualized characteristic. We must keep these features of acting and being affected in mind to understand how the process of change is radically transformed at the first level of ensouled action and passion.

In determining what the real relationship between the food and the fed (τροφή and τρεφόμενος) is, as in his discussions of acting on and being affected in *On Generation and Corruption* I.7 and of perception in *De Anima* II.5, Aristotle seeks a middle ground between identity and contrariety theorists of nutrition. He writes:

> Some say that like is fed by like, just as it is increased by like, but it seems to some others exactly the opposite, just as we said, that contrary is fed by contrary, since like is unaffected [ἀπαθοῦς] by like, but the food changes and is digested. And change [μεταβολή] for all things is to the opposite or intermediate. (II.4.416a29–34)

To understand what is guiding Aristotle's discussion of nutrition in this dialectical treatment, we must understand precisely why it is that both those who hold nutrition is of "like by like" and of "contrary by contrary" understand nutrition in that way, and why for Aristotle they are both right and both wrong. This is because the activity of nutrition involves both a moment of change (κίνησις)—a process from contrary to contrary in which the beginning point (undigested food) is lost in the result (the body of the living being)—and a moment of *energeia*—in which the beginning point remains itself, unmoved (ἀκίνητος) and unaffected (ἀπαθής),[61] which therefore involves a transition not between contraries, but between like terms. The relation of food to that which is fed in nutrition in this respect is like the relation of the building material to the carpenter: in the process of building, the matter undergoes a change (κίνησις) by which it is transformed into something which it previously was not, while the carpenter remains unaffected and unchanged in the activity, the only transition being to activity from idleness (εἰς ἐνέργειαν ἐξ ἀργίας). By focusing on one or the other aspect of nutrition, previous theorists of nutrition could not grasp both these sides: Aristotle seeks to think how there can be in nutrition both self-maintaining *energeia* (on the side of the organism) and change or κίνησις (on the side of the object) by carefully distinguishing the constituent moments of what happens when a living being eats.

Let us look more closely at the passage on contrariety and identity in nutrition. Aristotle opens the discussion of the idea that contrary is fed by contrary by contrasting the relationship of food and the fed with some other relationships of contraries:

> But it seems that food is a contrary to a contrary, not every contrary to every contrary, but as many of the contraries that have not only their generation from one another, but also growth. For many things are generated from one another, but not all are quantities, such as health from illness. But not even those things seem to be food for one another in the same way, but water is food for fire, while fire does not feed water. These [i.e., contraries] seem to be most of all food and the thing fed among the simple bodies [i.e., the elements]. (II.4.416a21–29)

There are thus two prerequisites for a relation between contraries to be considered a relationship of feeding and fed: the contraries must be capable of growth from one another, and (as follows from this) they must be quantities. By the fact that the terms must both be quantities, contrary qualities like health and sickness cannot grow or be nourished by one another. Thus Aristotle shifts to a consideration of whether growth and feeding occur primarily in the simplest bodies, the four elements. Yet not even all the changes between elements seem to involve growth. Of the three kinds of change—growth, alteration, and locomotion—nutrition is essentially associated with growth, and this is the kind of change essential to the nutritive soul. This kind of change must belong to something if it is to nourish itself. This means that the relation between the contrary terms of food and object fed cannot be simply one of coming-into-existence (γένεσις), such as when air comes to be out of water. One might think that because the volume is increased in vaporization of water that this change is growth. But this change differs importantly from growth, and hence cannot be a relationship of feeding and fed. In the change of water to air, the end result does not preexist the change, and thus it is not the growth of air but the coming-to-be of air.[62] In contrast, Aristotle writes that "growth is an increase, and diminution is a lessening, of the magnitude *which is there already*—that, indeed, is why the growing thing must possess some magnitude."[63] Thus two contraries must actually exist as quantities prior to any change that could be called growth: that which will grow and that which will be transformed into and added to the growing thing. Not only must the quantitative thing growing preexist the change (along with that which is added to it to increase it), but "that which grows or alters persists in its identity through the altering and through the growing or diminishing, though the quality (in alteration) and the quantity (in growth) do not remain the same."[64]

Having narrowed down the terms which are involved in growth to material, elemental changes, Aristotle makes clear that growth generally occurs only between certain elements, and even then only in one direction: water feeds fire,[65] but not vice versa. As opposed to health coming to be from illness, where both terms are not simultaneously present prior to the change, in nutrition and growth one begins with two unlike quantities—the food (water) and the warm living body (fire)—one of which, the body, persists through the interaction and transforms the other, the food, into itself, such that it remains the same thing only with more quantitative bulk. Water and fire, which are the extreme contrary elements—since cold and moist share no quality in common with hot and dry—appear to be principally the material terms involved in growth and hence nutrition.[66] Here Aristotle is talking about an elemental, inanimate relationship, yet his choice of elements is extremely significant to the discussion of how nutrition works. These elements (fire and water) are also the material involved in the living activity of nourishment: it is the heat—or fire[67]—of the body which is fed by the water, or more generally, something watery.[68] Aristotle's example of fire and water is therefore significant, since the food, primarily water and earth, is what feeds the living being by virtue of its vital *heat*, its inner fire.[69] The same unidirectional relationship that holds between the contrary elements therefore holds for food and that which is fed: "Food is affected by that which is fed, but this is not affected by the food" (II.4.416a34–35).[70] In general, this affection is concoction, the action of heat on a passive matter, or a "mastering" of the constituent moisture,[71] making a new uniform substance by eliminating what is foreign to it.[72] Nourishment is a particular example of concoction.[73] The undigested food is taken into the stomach, and the action of heating produces a vapor which enters the vessels, becomes blood, and travels to the heart[74]—this is the useful residue—leaving behind a dry and useless, excremental residue.[75] This is also how nourishment in the animal works, for it is not just anything that can nourish the body, but blood.

Aristotle resolves this conflict between identity and contrariety theorists of nutrition in the way he universally resolves this relation: by distinguishing three distinct moments of nutrition—in this case, ingestion, digestion, and self-nourishment:[76]

> Whether the food is the last thing added or the first makes a difference. But if both [are food], but the one is undigested and the

> other is digested, one might speak of food in both ways [i.e., like-by-like and contrary-by-contrary]. If it is undigested, contrary is fed by contrary; but if digested, then like is fed by like. Therefore it appears that both in a certain way speak rightly and not rightly. (II.4.416b3–9)

Before we analyze this passage, two observations must be made. First, in this *De Anima* passage, the distinction between first potentiality and second potentiality exists *only* on the side of the object. For the nutritive heat in the living being cannot become merely potential, but must be perpetually active in order for the organism to survive. Though I will be drawing on other treatises to show a corresponding distinction between potentiality and actuality on the side of the organism, it is significant that in II.4 Aristotle does not bring these points out explicitly. Second, the process of digestion is distinct from the activity of nutrition, growth, and reproduction. It is what happens prior to these activities to prepare the food and make these activities possible. This externality of digestion from the proper activities of nutritive soul can be seen by the fact that in plants, digestion of the food happens outside the organism by means of heat in the environment. This is important, because when one moves to perception, this external activity is more deeply internalized, and the perpetual activity on the side of the organism is differentiated into the potentiality of the sleeping animal and the actuality of the waking animal.

Now let us return to the passage at hand. In a first moment, there is the ingestion of food: receiving the nutritive object into itself prior to the identification of object and living body. The mouth (or analogously, the roots in plants) takes the object from outside and draws it into that which is capable of receiving objects of food, that is, the stomach, whose function is to "receive the incoming food [δέχασθαι τὴν εἰσελθοῦσαν τροφήν]."[77] At this stage the food is undigested. Aristotle calls this the "first" food. It has the potential to nourish by virtue of its matter, that is, its elemental composition, but not yet by virtue of what it is considered as its own form (cheese, bread, etc.). At this point it is only *potentially* nourishing, and the food (water-earth mixture) and the body's heat are contraries. The transition of the "first" food into the "last" food through the agency of the vital heat constitutes an ordinary change, one in which an object is destroyed as a result of the transformation which takes up time. The food in its own identity no longer exists after digestion, as it has been transformed into blood, the matter of the body.

In its second potentiality/first actuality, food in its last form *has been* digested (πεπεμμένη)[78] but has not yet actually nourished the living being: in contrast to the first food or first potentiality, the last, digested food *actually* possesses the capacity to nourish. Thus it has been transformed into the nourishing blood by heat, which extracts the essential moisture from the water-earth combination, which is the essentially nourishing component of the original food. The living body then feeds on its like, the blood produced through digestion, in order to maintain itself in its being. The transition from the first actuality (actually potentially nourishing) to second actuality (nourishing the body and thus preserving its life and existence) does not involve change (κίνησις) in which the beginning of the change is destroyed by the end of the change.

In terms of nutrition, it seems that the moments of the activity break down in the following way according to the threefold schema of potentiality and actuality that we outlined earlier (see table 4).

TABLE 4. Nutrition and the Three Levels of Potentiality and Actuality

SENSE			OBJECT	
1st potentiality →	2nd potentiality/ 1st actuality →	2nd actuality	← 2nd potentiality/ 1st actuality	← 1st potentiality
The part that receives the undigested food from outside (τὸ δεκτικόν) →	Vital heat/θρεπτικὴ ψυχή →	Actual nourishment/being nourished	← Digested food (πεπεμμένη) (the "last" food, i.e., blood)	← Undigested (ἄπεπτος) food (the "first" food)

Several aspects of this breakdown of nutrition are worth noting. In contrast with the ordinary acting on-being affected structure outlined in *On Generation and Corruption* I.7, the object which initiates the activity, in this case the food, is not the one which preserves its characteristic and passes it on to the patient. It is rather the affected being which transforms its food into itself. This is what I referred to as being affected "on its own terms." The living being which nourishes itself does not just receive its determination from outside, but receives its object and controls the change which then follows. This contrast brings out how the living organism, in contrast to inanimate beings, is affected in certain ways by objects in its environment which are structured by its nature and soul, and which serve to preserve and realize this nature rather than being overcome or overpowered by the interaction.

To anticipate an important difference between nutrition and sensation, compare Aristotle's account of the structure of the various aspects of sensation, using vision as the paradigm. Moving from nutrition to vision, three new elements in the activity emerge. First, there is a distinction in what is external to the living being between the object and the medium, the one which remains the same and the other which is affected or changed, whereas in nutrition one simply has the object of the activity, the food. Second, there is a distinction in the living being itself between the center of its awareness and the periphery—its heart and its external sense organs—the one which remains unchanged, the other which is altered, where in nutrition there is simply the vital heat, but no peripheral instrument set apart from the center of the nutritive instrument.

Finally, Aristotle introduces—at least in the two highest senses—a third factor beyond either the object or the activity but which is necessary for the two sides to be united. In vision, this is a source of light, fire or the upper bodies, which activates the potential of light to be seen and the potential of the eye to see. There is no explicit analogue of this factor beyond the distinction of subject and object in chapter II.4 on nutrition. It is not clear, however, that this means this third factor beyond subject and object is absent in the structure of the nutritive soul's activities. In *On Generation and Corruption* II.10–11, Aristotle considers the role of the sun's movement in generation, and he finds that its approach and retreat are responsible for the activity and non-activity of its capacity for nutrition, growth, and reproduction.[79] The sun's circular motion, derived from the circular rotation of the outermost sphere, is the cause of the always repeating cycle of seasons, which in turn determines the cycle of life and death in sublunar beings.[80] Aristotle also refers to the sun as partly responsible for the reproduction of the species, stating in the *Physics* that "it takes a man *and the sun* to generate man."[81] Further, Aristotle makes clear that the heat in the plant's environment, both in the heated earth and the heated environing air, along with the heat from its food, is sufficient to keep the plant alive, since it does not have something like the heart in animals which generates heat from within.[82] This heat from the environment is presumably from the sun.[83] What this suggests is that the sun, which acts as the cause of seeing and being seen, might also be in nutrition the cause of feeding and being fed, growth, and reproduction. This fills out nicely a similarity between Aristotle and Plato which I think is crucial for grasping the argument of *De Anima*, namely, Aristotle's nearly wholehearted acceptance of Plato's analogy in the *Republic* between the sun as the principle uniting vision and the visible, and the divine first principle as uniting thinking and the objects of thought. For Plato not only makes the sun's light the cause of perception, but he makes its heat the cause of coming to be and the passing away of natural beings:

> "The sun, I presume you will say, not only furnishes to visibles the power of visibility but it also provides for their generation and growth and nurture though it is not itself in generation." "Of course." "In like manner, then, you are to say that the objects of knowledge not only receive from the presence of the good their being known, but their very existence and essence is derived to them from it, though the good itself is not essence but still transcends essence in dignity and surpassing power."[84]

Though there is no indication of it in *De Anima* II.4 or anywhere else in that treatise, it seems plausible, based on Aristotle's comments about the causal effect of the sun on all coming to be and passing away in *On Generation and Corruption* II.10, that he thought that the sun was a principle of nutritive soul, just as he understands it to be a principle of perceptive soul analogous to the way active mind (νοῦς) is a principle of intellective soul (two points which *are* clearly Aristotle's view in *De Anima*).[85]

Once we move to perception, we will have to recall the structure of nutrition elaborated here and contrast it with what goes on in the analogous moments of the animal's perceptive relation to the world. For the moment, let us turn to the second nutritive structure, which connects the pre-locomotive activity of nutrition to the various forms of self-motion in animals and humans.

The Proto-Locomotive Structure of Nutrition

At the end of II.4, Aristotle outlines a fourfold structure of what happens in nutrition. At first Aristotle identifies three factors in nutrition:

> And there are three things: that which is fed [τὸ τρεφόμενον], that by which it is fed [ᾧ τρέφεται], and that which feeds [τὸ τρέφον]. That which feeds is the first soul, while that which is fed is the body which has this soul, and that by which it is fed is the food. (II.4.416b21–23)

Then, through an analogy of the factors in nutrition with a pilot steering a boat, a fourth factor of nutrition is invoked, the heat used by the soul to effect its functions:

> But "that by which it is fed [ᾧ τρέφεται]" is twofold, just like "that by which it steers [ᾧ κυβερνᾷ]": there is both the hand and the

> rudder, the latter[86] both moving [τὸ κινοῦν] and being moved [τὸ κινούμενον], the former only moving [τὸ δὲ κινοῦν μόνον]. And it is necessary for all food to have the capacity to be digested [δύνασθαι πέττεσθαι], and heat [τὸ θερμόν] does the work of digestion [ἐργάζεται . . . τὴν πέψιν]. Consequently every ensouled being has heat. (II.4.416b25–29)

One could fill out the steering/feeding analogy as follows. The nutritive soul in nutrition is analogous to the pilot in steering: both are the first movers which remain unmoved (or only incidentally moved) throughout the course of the change or motion. The body which is being fed in nutrition is like the boat which is being steered—it is not changing anything in nutrition, rather it is only being changed. The food is, like the rudder, both moved and moving. It is moved by the soul and its heat, and it in turn affects the body which is nourished by it, just as the rudder is moved by the pilot's hand, and in turn moves the entire boat.

All this is fairly clear in Aristotle's comparison of nutrition and piloting a boat. Yet properly understanding the status of the hand and vital heat in this analogy is complicated by a manuscript controversy in the above passage at 416b27: "the one moving and being moved [τὸ μὲν κινοῦν καὶ κινούμενον], the other only moving [τὸ δὲ κινοῦν μόνον]." It is disputed whether the last words of this sentence should read τὸ κινοῦν μόνον, τὸ κινούμενον μόνον, or simply τὸ κινούμενον. Against Rodier and Ross, I am following the overwhelming majority of the manuscripts which read τὸ κινοῦν μόνον, a reading which is also supported by most of the ancient commentators (except Philoponus). On the κινούμενον reading I am denying, a scribe misread κινούμενον for κινούνμονον, a mistake that would be easy enough to make: this would mean that the hand moves (the rudder) and is moved (by the pilot), while the rudder is simply moved (by the hand), just as the heat is moved or controlled (by the nutritive soul) while it also moves or affects the object of food, which in turn is moved but moves nothing. This version of the text and the understanding it implies is shown in table 5.

TABLE 5. The Analogy of Piloting a Ship (1)

τὸ κινοῦν	τὸ κινοῦν καὶ κινούμενον	τὸ κινούμενον
pilot	hand	rudder
nutritive soul	heat	food

Notice that on this view there is a wide ontological divide between the soul and its heat: the former only moves, while the latter is both moved and moves. On this view heat is simply a material instrument for the soul. Yet Gad Freudenthal has cast serious doubt on this reading of vital heat in his excellent book *Aristotle's Theory of Material Substance*. In this extremely illuminating study, Freudenthal attempts to show that "Aristotle construes vital heat itself as capable of informing matter"; it possesses an "informing power"[87] which allows it to effect all the operations for which nutritive soul is responsible: self-preservation (the material persistence of the individual), growth (the regulated quantitative increase of the individual), and reproduction of the species (persistence of the species by producing another like itself). Heat thus becomes the material analogue of nutritive soul, responsible for the performance of all its activities. Aristotle makes explicit this tight equivalence between soul and heat in several passages.[88] Vital heat is the material vehicle for the execution of the various functions of nutritive soul, since it possesses all the necessary potentialities to carry out these activities.[89]

Freudenthal does not look very deeply to the passage currently under consideration, though it seems to me the truth of his thesis stands or falls on how one most plausibly understands the analogy of heat and hand. For the interpreter who makes the current revision of the text and abandons the majority of manuscript evidence, there are some serious problems which must be answered. First of all, this interpretation loses one of the terms of Aristotle's analysis of nutrition: the body, that which is fed (τὸ τρεφόμενον). This is the purely passive moment of nutrition: the body does not affect anything in the process of being nourished; it is the recipient of the activity as a whole. The body, to fill out the analogy with the steering of the ship, corresponds to the ship being steered (τὸ κυβερνόμενον), or, in terms of the language of change or κίνησις, it is τὸ κινούμενον (that which is moved). And what is the body moved or changed by? Precisely the food which has been transformed into blood, just as the ship is moved by the rudder. For what is the purpose of the rudder, if not to be the last moving cause of the ship? Yet on this alternate reading of the text, the rudder moves nothing. The pilot, for all his hard work at moving the rudder with his hand, regrettably works in vain, since the rudder has no effect on anything beyond itself.

Aristotle argues that both heat and food, like hand and rudder, are instrumental to the activity in question. Yet there remains an important distinction which should be preserved between an instrument in the sense of an integral part of the user (the hand) and a tool independent of that user (the rudder).

But surely the alternate reading is right to want to argue that the heat is not simply moving, but is also moved? But this loses the whole point of the self-preserving activity of self-nutrition we have already outlined. For the body nourishes itself by means of heat precisely to maintain that heat as it was. The vital heat which is the agent of nutrition does not change in the sense of a process with a beginning different from the end result: being alive simply corresponds to a certain heat in the body, and one uses this vital heat for nutrition and digestion precisely in order to maintain the level of heat needed for survival. Thus there is no change (κίνησις) in the sense of process from something to something different. And when the beginning point and end point of the activity are the same, one can say that the heat is unmoving (ἀκίνητος), although this does not mean it is inert, or simply unchanged.

Thus in my own construal of this passage, the analogy breaks down as in table 6.

TABLE 6. The Analogy of Piloting a Ship (2)

τὸ κινοῦν	τὸ κινοῦν	τὸ κινοῦν καὶ κινούμενον	τὸ κινούμενον
pilot	hand	rudder	ship
nutritive soul	heat	food	body
τὸ τρέφον	ᾧ τρέφεται		τὸ τρεφόμενον

Nutritive soul is the unmoved formal activity in nutrition, while the material analogue of this form, the matter which has the properties necessary to perform the activities characteristic of nutritive soul, is the vital heat, which is τὸ κινοῦν μόνον. The object of food is changed by the heat through concoction and transformed into the material of the body (blood)—and this final nourishment in turn changes or affects the body through contributing to its preservation and growth.

This entire structure of τὸ τρέφον, ᾧ τρέφεται, and τὸ τρεφόμενον is itself modeled on the general structure of motion articulated in the *Physics* (VIII.7 and V.1). Within the *De Anima*, although it has gone generally unnoticed, this analysis of nutrition articulates a structure which undeniably anticipates Aristotle's analysis of locomotion in III.10 at 433b13–27.[90] As with the common structure between nutrition and cognition, it is the subtle differences between the levels just as much as the similarities which must be grasped to understand the direction of the argument. I will treat the development of this common structure from nutrition to locomotion in detail in my treatment of how the soul moves the body through space in chapter 5. For the moment I simply indicate the general direction of the movement from nutritive to locomotive soul. What is simple and undifferentiated in the more primitive activity of nutrition becomes internally differentiated in the more complex activity of locomotion, both within the soul and within the bodily instrument of the soul. Because the locomotive soul is distinguished into unmoved and moved aspects where the nutritive soul is simply an unmoved mover, and because the locomotive soul's bodily instrument (the heart) is similarly differentiated in this way as opposed to the simple presence of heat, the animal is able to initiate its motion from itself, while nutritive soul is comparatively outwardly initiated and unable to move the organism. I conclude the treatment of nutrition by indicating certain important features of nutrition which will become especially significant in tracing the development of soul from nutrition to thought.

What Nutrition Lacks Relative to the Higher Activities of Soul

The nutritive soul of the plant manifests a surprising degree of sophistication: without any sensitive awareness, it is nevertheless able to distinguish between what should and should not be taken into itself, and then transform this object into its own body. It preserves and perpetuates its form, both in itself and in its species, in the face of being affected by objects in its environment. But what about the plant dictates that it does not have even the most primitive sensible awareness? In order to grasp the progression of Aristotle's argument from nutrition to perception, and to see how we move closer to understanding the soul in itself in this progression, one must properly understand what are the deficiencies of plants and their merely nutritive activity which are remedied at the level of living beings which nourish themselves *and* perceive the world, namely animals. Damian Murphy[91] asks exactly the right question in this regard: why can plants not perceive? Both plants and animals are affected by sensible qualities, yet plants, like inanimate beings, are "unconscious of being affected."[92] What exactly do plants lack that animals possess such that the former cannot perceive the world and the latter can?

For Aristotle, there are three principal differences between perceiving and non-perceiving living beings which explain why plants cannot perceive:

1. They can't receive form without matter (II.12.424a17–19; II.12.424b1–3; III.12.434a27–30).
2. They do not have a mean (II.12.424b1; III.13.435a22–23).
3. They are simple or uncompounded, consisting only (or predominately) of earth (III.12.434a27–30; III.12.434b9–11; III.13.435a11–25).

Although a fuller grasp of these deficiencies in plants will depend upon our treatment of Aristotle's account of perception, we must get some preliminary sense of how it is that plants lack these features possessed by animals.

Receiving the Form without the Matter

In his general summary of sense perception in *De Anima* II.12, Aristotle defines perception as the capacity to receive sensible forms without matter. It seems to me this can only be properly understood in contrast with how objects are received in nutrition. Consider nutritive activity in the light of the image used by Aristotle to explain what happens in perception: the signet ring and the wax. To clarify what is meant by defining perception as the capacity to receive sensible forms without the matter, Aristotle writes that it works just as "the wax receives the mark of the signet ring without the iron or gold, and it takes the gold or bronze mark, but not considered as gold or bronze" (II.12.424a19–21).

If perception is analogous to taking the outer shape or form of the signet ring (the sensible forms—flavors, colors, sounds, etc.) while leaving the ring itself, the piece of bronze, iron, or gold outside, then in nutrition the whole ring, the composite of matter and form, is assimilated, but the outer mark or signet of the ring is destroyed in the process: the form-matter composite is ingested, but here it is merely insofar as it is gold, bronze, or iron matter that the object is assimilated. Plants *do* take in the form-matter composite, but the form of their food is accidental and irrelevant to nutrition. In one sense it is not as if the form of food is irrelevant to nutritive activity: it matters what the identity of the object is, since not everything can be an object of food for anything, and only a certain range of objects is potentially food for any particular kind of living being. But the highest determining form of the food does not matter in nutrition, except in the most elemental sense: the form of the object understood as bread, olive, milk does not matter, since this aspect of the food is only nutritive insofar as it is destroyed. What is essential in these objects is the ultimate matter out of which they are composed, whether earth, water, air, or fire, and which basic qualities these possess. For food is nutriment insofar as it has dry, moist, hot, and cold properties[93] which belong to it as earth and water, not as milk or bread. Therefore it is the object of food as elemental and material that nourishes, just as it is the body of the living being as elemental that is nourished and grows. As long as the food is at least partially made up by the same matter as the matter of blood, the process of digestion will separate out and evacuate the inessential part which is not potentially the body of the living being, and use what remains as essential.

This contrast between nutrition which assimilates the matter-form composite into itself and perception which merely assimilates the sensible quality or form while leaving the matter underlying this form outside itself suggests a certain reading of what it means to be "receptive of sensible forms without matter." It is in the light of this contrast between nutrition and perception that Sorabji understands this formulation: plants in their nutritive activity need to take the foreign matter into themselves, while perceiving animals leave this foreign matter outside.[94] On this reading, Aristotle's explanation of perception draws its meaning out of a direct contrast not with how plants are qualitatively altered, but rather through a contrast between the activity of nutrition and the activity of perception. I want to affirm that this is a crucial aspect of Aristotle's overall argument at this point, but to see how this is so we must first deal with a crucial objection to this view articulated by Damian Murphy.

Murphy astutely objects to this understanding of the capacity to receive forms without the matter in that "it is not clear why the fact that plants must receive foreign matter together with sensible forms should prevent perception."[95] He argues that being "receptive of form without the matter" is not a reference back to what goes on in nutrition, but rather merely an argument against those philosophers who held a materialist-emanationist view of perception. Further, since plants are in fact sensibly altered by tangible forms like heat and cold, it is difficult to explain why these alterations are not *perceived* alterations simply because nutrition takes in the matter of the object. Murphy writes:

> So let us posit a plant which is first cold and later hot. From the standpoint of everyday thinking, that plant has undergone ordinary alteration and has received the form of the hot. Since, again from the standpoint of everyday thinking, there is no reason to suspect that in all such alterations a plant must have received external hot matter, we can conclude that on (at least some) such occasions the plant receives forms without receiving matter. But Aristotle is here saying that the reason why plants do not perceive is that they *do not* receive forms without receiving matter.[96]

This is an instructive objection to the idea that Aristotle, by defining perception as reception of form without matter, is pointing towards a dis-analogy between nutrition and perception. While it is true that matter is assimilated in nutrition, when we are attempting to determine why plants do not perceive, or why they are not qualitatively altered in a perceptive way, this nutritive assimilation of the object is irrelevant. What is more important is to examine cases in which plants *are* qualitatively altered, when they receive the form of an object without its matter (such as when they are heated by fire—receiving the form of heat—without taking the fire itself into themselves), and determine what is different between this non-perceptive assimilation and an animal's perceptive assimilation of sensible form without the matter.

What is important about this observation is that it underlines how the three principal kinds of change—growth (change of quantity), alteration (change of quality), and locomotion (change of place)—can occur in all beings, not merely in living beings. An inanimate object can grow, be altered, and be moved. Yet these three kinds of change occur differently in their ensouled versions: nutrition, perception, and self-movement. Hence, as we saw, a living being grows very differently than an inanimate being, since its growth is structured by the soul which provides a certain ratio or proportion limiting and controlling its growth. What we see here is that plants, although their growth is special due to the presence of soul, are qualitatively altered just like any other being, since they do not have a soul which controls and limits qualitative alteration the way their nutritive soul structured their growth.

In ignoring how II.12 is defining perception through a comparison with nutrition, interpreters have missed the thrust of Aristotle's argument. In particular, the passage at II.12.424a24ff. which treats the relation between the first sense organ (the heart) and the power of perception, suffers from this neglect. Aristotle writes:

> The first sense organ is that in which such a power [i.e., perception] resides. And they are the same, but their being is different. For that which is perceiving is a certain quantity [μέγεθος].[97] But this is not the being of the capacity to perceive, nor is sensation a quantity [μέγεθος], but rather a certain ratio [λόγος] and power [δύναμις] of this organ. (II.12.424a24–28)[98]

Why bring up quantity at this point in the discussion? I think this can only be understood as yet another way of distinguishing nutrition and growth, which are essentially related to the quantitative bulk of food and the organism's body, from perception. When the parts of the animal grow, after all, this has to do with the very same parts which are used by the animal in perception. But perception (αἴσθησις) is not essentially related to the perceiving part as a quantity (μέγεθος), but rather as a certain non-quantitative proportion (λόγος) which exists in these parts. Without yet getting into details about what this qualitative mean in perception is, we can see what distinguishes it from the "limit and proportion of quantity and growth [πέρας καὶ λόγος μεγέθους τε καὶ αὐξήσεως]" (II.4.416a17), the structured proportion discussed in the chapter on nutrition which governs ensouled nutritive growth: it is the proportion (λόγος) of *quality*, not of *quantity*. Thus one of the reasons plants do not perceive is because they do not have this proportion or range relative to the objects of perception, which are always qualities. They have a structuring proportion only in relation to nutritive soul and growth, since they do not have a sensitive soul.

Thus if nutrition is about assimilating and identifying with objects understood as quantities and as elemental matter, perception in contrast is about assimilating and identifying itself not with underlying matter, but with the qualities understood as the sensible forms of these objects. Therefore Murphy rightly notes that it would be wrong to say (with Sorabji and Everson) that plants can only receive sensible forms together with foreign matter, making their self-nourishing activity the only way in which they can be affected by the world. Sorabji and Everson take the plant's nutritive relation and overgeneralize it to cover every possible way a plant could be affected. As Murphy points out, a plant can be affected qualitatively without taking matter into itself. Yet the difference remains that this qualitative change is not a specifically ensouled change, it is not governed by the nutritive soul of the plant, and therefore a plant is qualitatively altered just like any inanimate being is affected by sensible forms of an external object.

Although the conclusions drawn by Sorabji are problematic, he is certainly on the right track in understanding the definition of perception as a capacity to receive forms without matter in the light of a comparison with nutrition, which is a capacity to receive matter into itself through breaking down its form and transforming it into its own body. From the difference between nutrition's reception of matter and destruction of form and sensation's reception of form without matter, one can learn much about the deficiencies of plants relative to animals which preclude plants from having any awareness. But it is crucial to understand that though nutritive activities are the only ways in which plants are affected in an *ensouled* way—with all changes being informed, structured, and controlled by the soul—it is not as if all possible changes which occur in plants happen in the way these nutritive changes do: by taking in foreign matter. Rather, any other kind of change will happen in plants just as they happen in inanimate beings: as ordinary alterations.

Plants as Having No Mean

In the same chapter that Aristotle defines perception in contrast to nutrition as "reception of form without the matter," Aristotle also stresses the fact that animals perceive on account of having a mean (μεσότητα) which plants lack:

> And why in the world do plants not perceive, having a certain part of the soul and being affected in a certain way by objects of touch? For indeed the plant is cooled and heated. The reason is not having a mean [μεσότητα], nor even such a principle to receive forms of the sense objects, but only to be affected with the matter. (II.12.424a32–424b3)[99]

Without getting into the details of how exactly the mean works in sensation, in order to understand what it means for a plant not to have a mean, we can give a preliminary account of why a mean is needed for sensation to be possible. The mean is a mode of indeterminacy, of having one's nature not too precisely associated with any particular sensible quality. In nutrition, the body is only nourished insofar as the food has been transformed into material completely identical with itself. It has none of the indeterminacy of sensation, since its own bodily nature is fixed, and any object which is nourishing must have the capacity to be transformed into this fixed bodily constitution. In sensation, the sensible form can be assimilated so long as it is within a certain qualitative range allowed by the organ. This allows the organism to admit a wider range of objects in sensation as compared to nutrition, and also means that the object does not have to be destroyed in order to be assimilated.[100]

This sensible mean must be neutral in relation to the range of qualities it is able to admit while remaining itself and preserving its function. In that which does not have a sensible mean, the particular sense quality is intimately associated with the nature of the being in question. Changing this quality means the end of the being in question. Yet the senses are means in being essentially related to their objects, without having the determinate identity of any particular one of these objects. For example, in vision, the eye is capable of receiving color because it is a colorless transparent being, essentially related to colors without being any particular color; in hearing, the inner air of the ear is not a sound, but is capable of taking on sounds (II.7.418b26–27). As Aristotle puts it, a sense is able to be receptive of a wide range of objects within a certain genus because it is in itself potentially all of them without being actually any of them. If something in its very nature is actually one of its objects, it is not able to take on other objects in that genus without losing its nature. The sense is not a *pure* potentiality—it is constituted out of actual air or water and thus has their determinate properties—but it is purely potential relative to its proper objects. This indeterminacy is a property of the very material out of which the media and organs of sensation in the higher, distance senses (vision, hearing, smell) are constituted: air and water are less determinate and more receptive of other forms than earth.[101] Since the matter is in its very nature indeterminate within a certain range, the matter is not "affected" so long as the sense object occurs within that range.

Yet it is not only these higher senses that are means: even the lowest sense of touch is receptive of its objects due to being a mean. Yet like plants, the organ of touch is constituted predominantly out of earth, the least indeterminate of the elements.[102] And unlike the other senses, which do not possess in actuality any of the sensible qualities they are able to receive, the organ of touch (the heart) does have a certain hotness, coldness, dryness, or moistness. How then is the sense of touch able to be neutral relative to the variety of tangible objects it must be able to receive? It is thus most important to distinguish why the non-perceptive plant does not have the most basic sense of touch, especially since the objects of nutrition and of touch are the same: "All animals are fed by the dry or the wet, the hot or the cold, and touch is the sense that apprehends these" (II.3.414b7–9).[103] They are both affected by these sense objects,[104] yet one is affected perceptively and the other is not. How does an animal's having a sensible mean explain this difference?

Concerning the neutrality of the senses as means between the extremes on the range of objects apprehended by that sense, Aristotle writes that "in relation to touch it is neither hot nor cold" (II.11.424a9–10). This is not by being something that has no temperature, in the way that the matter of vision has no color, but rather by having an organ which is between the extremes of cold and hot on the scale of temperature. But how can the sense of touch perceive other temperatures if it is itself of a certain temperature? There is a demand that if some sensible difference is going to be *perceived* by the organism, there must be some stable standard beyond the physical change to its body against which the alteration can be measured. If the being is affected but nothing remains constant beyond the change, there is nothing in the living being by which it could be aware of the difference between the initial state and the affected state.

Thus the sense of mean for touch is slightly different than for the higher senses. What distinguishes touch from plants is precisely the fact that it does have some constant temperature beyond the affections which occur at its periphery. As Bodéüs writes, plants are characterized by a "lack of constant internal thermal regulation."[105] This controls the warmth of the body, even when it is affected by the sensible qualities of objects, performing two related tasks: maintaining a constant measure against which differences can be measured, and bringing the body back to a certain normal temperature after any affection (just as the nature of the eye as transparent will always regain its neutrality and potentiality since it is transparent by nature). Thus touch is able to be a mean relative to tangible extremes because of the greater distinction between center and periphery in the animal, namely the differentiation between the heart as the center of perception and its organs. The heart regulates the heat in all parts of the body, while itself remaining relatively constant through the changes to the organs. It is this distinction between a controlling center and a controlled periphery which plants lack, and it is for this reason that they are non-perceptually heated and cooled.

The Simplicity of Plants

This lack of differentiation between center and periphery in plants compared to animals points towards a more general feature of plants: they are less differentiated than higher living beings. Aristotle returns often to the fact that plants are able to live even when divided (I.4.409a8; I.5.411b19; II.2.413b17).[106] This fact reveals something essential about plants, and the lower animals such as insects: they do not possess a very great degree of differentiation of parts,[107] with the result that one part is able to take over the function of another part if they are separated. This is in large part due to the simplicity of their form, which has relatively few functions as compared to higher living beings: "Plants, again, inasmuch as they are without locomotion, present no great variety in their heterogeneous parts. For, where the functions are but few, few also are the organs required to effect them."[108] What follows from this is that in such simple beings, the form and its underlying matter are only difficult to distinguish due to their proximity. Fundamental to the question of surviving bodily division is the fact that the *principle* of the living being is not very differentiated from that of which it *is* the principle (i.e., the *principled*). In fact, Aristotle writes that "the principle [ἀρχή] potentially belonging to [the plant] is present in every part."[109] In the animal, there is a heart which is the principle of its life and all its activities, and then the other parts which are ruled and ordered by this central part. The part which is analogous to the heart in plants is "intermediate between the root and the stem,"[110] but obviously this is not as distinct and differentiated a part as the heart in blooded animals. In the animal, the heart is akin to the fleshly form and principle of the living being, while the parts are the material ordered and subservient to this form. Thus in plants, what this lack of structural differentiation indicates is a lack of distinction between the form and matter in the plant, or the function from the instrumental parts which subserve this function. Since the "principle" or form is equally present everywhere in the body of the plant, when one part is separated, everything required for its functions and its continued survival is present. The animal, in contrast, can survive without many of its instrumental parts, but without the heart it has no possibility of survival. And various functions of the highly differentiated animal cannot be accomplished without the specific part that enables them: loss of the eye will mean that vision is impossible, since the function is not able to be taken over by some other instrumental part, and likewise for the other senses.

This lack of differentiation between the formal and material aspects of the plant is equally manifest in respect to the manner in which it generates and is generated. For in the plant, the distinction between male and female has not yet occurred; the plant seed is a unity of the male and female matter prior to their differentiation: as Aristotle says, "Animals seem almost to be like divided plants."[111] For Aristotle, these are respectively the formal and material aspects of the animals' generation: while the female matter in generation (the καταμήνια) provides the body and bulk (ὄγκον) of the future animal, the male sperm is the making cause (δημιουργόν) and active principle of motion in generation. Although when the distinction of male and female has not occurred in something it makes no sense to identify it as female,[112] there is a sense in which Aristotle views the plant as more female than male, since in animals it is the female which provides the nutritive soul, while the male causes the sensitive soul.

Another way in which the plant has as undifferentiated what is distinguished in animals is the lack of distinction in plants between waking and sleeping. If male and female principles in generation are intimately related to the form/matter distinction, the waking/sleep distinction refers to the actuality/potentiality distinction in Aristotle's thought. The lack of distinction between sleeping and waking means that in the plant, potential and actual exercise of its activities are not clearly distinguished.

It would be wrong to say that the plant is asleep, for both sleeping and waking are states of the sensitive part of soul, in which plants have no part. But there is a certain analogy between the sleep of animals and the activity of plants, insofar as sleep is the inactivity of that which distinguishes plants from animals: the common sense which enables all the senses. When this part is rendered inactive, so are all the activities which distinguish higher living beings from plants: intellect, perception, and locomotion. The animal becomes "like a plant," rooted in one place, non-thinking and non-perceiving. Even in terms of the position of its body, the upper parts are brought into the same position as the lower parts and the animal loses its erect stature in its reclined position.[113]

Once these higher functions retreat into latency, the animal becomes more plant-like, with the body concentrating its activities in fulfillment of its nutritive functions. Aristotle remarks that the functions of nutritive soul, particularly self-nourishment and growth, are intensified in sleep (surely owing to the fact that the body is occupied with accomplishing the higher activities while awake).[114] This intimate relation between sleep and nutrition is further confirmed by the fact that sleepiness is brought on most of all after ingestion of food, that sleep is deepest after food,[115] and that the return to the waking state occurs primarily once the activity of digestion is complete and the body has thus been restored and prepared for further exercise of its higher functions.[116] Plants, though in truth existing prior to the differentiation of waking and sleeping, exist in a mode analogous to perpetual sleep. This state is described as a fettering, imprisonment, or arrest (δεσμός, ἀκινησία) in contrast to which waking corresponds to a freeing or release.[117]

There is great significance to the fact that the distinction of sleep and waking is not yet differentiated at the point of nutritive soul. There is no rest for nutritive activity without the death of the animal, and thus its self-nourishment is a constant striving. On the one hand, the continuity of this activity is quite different from another continuous activity, the self-thinking of God. The continuous activity of the plant or animal's self-nourishment is always a striving to appropriate what is different and external to the organism, whereas divine thinking (and thinking in general, including human thinking) is, as we will see, a relation to itself, not a relation to some object outside of itself. Thus this activity requires no effort and does not wear itself out, but is rather characterized by the leisure and pleasure of complete self-possession.[118] Yet the plant and animal in nourishment always stand in a relation to something outside which they lack but require to persist in being. It involves therefore, constant effort and striving. On the other hand, nutritive activity in this respect is also different from perception. Both require effort because they are seeking what is outside of themselves, food and the sensible object, but the perceptive animal is equipped with the differentiation of waking and sleeping, which is the inactivity of the sensible part, so that it does not wear itself out in its effort. Without this distinction of rest and activity, the plant is condemned to continuous striving throughout the course of its life for objects outside of itself, without the ability to rest within itself in sleep.

The Destruction of Nutritive Objects versus the Preservation of Sense Objects

One of the things that are remarkable about the first appearance of life in nutritive soul is the way that the living being is able to assimilate and be affected by its objects while retaining its own nature, without being overcome by the form of the object which it assimilates to itself. Yet while in nutrition the living being remains the same in the result of the activity, the object of the activity is necessarily destroyed. There is therefore in nutrition a moment of ordinary alteration, characteristic of inanimate change. In a discussion of whether it is the body of the living being or the food which grows, Aristotle writes that "the substance of the one [i.e., living body] remains unchanged, but the substance of the other (namely, of the food) does not."[119] Further, as we have already seen in *De Anima* II.4, Aristotle makes clear: "The food is affected by the thing being fed, but this is not affected by the food, just as the person building is not affected by the material, but the material is affected by him. But the builder changes only from idleness to activity" (II.4.416a35–416b3). In order for the soul to nourish the body, the object it assimilates is not able to remain what it is, but must be broken down and changed into the body's own matter, ultimately into blood. For nutritive soul, the object of food has purely instrumental being, rather than having some being in and of itself which must be preserved in the course of its activity. Nutritive soul only ever encounters *itself* in relating to its objects; there is nothing for it which is different from itself. Its unity with its environment is thus immediate and undifferentiated: immediate in the sense that, unlike in sensation, there is no *medium* separating the direct contact between body and food, and undifferentiated in the sense that for nutritive soul there is nothing other than itself: there is no moment in nutrition where the soul distinguishes itself over and against its environment (that is to say, it has no *awareness*, no consciousness of there being an object that is different than itself). In sensation, we are aware of the way in which we are affected by an object, but at the same time the quality by which we are affected is known to belong to an object other than ourselves.

As we saw in our treatment of the *Eudemian Ethics*,[120] the desire for life is a desire for consciousness, defined as the desire to be determined by an object. This desire is not wholly fulfilled in nutrition. Though the organism is determined by its object, in nutrition the living being is not determined by its object as it is in itself, but rather only according to the nature of the living being at the expense of the nature of the object, which is merely matter serving the form of the living being.

What partly accounts for the object being affected and destroyed by the living body is the demand of immediate direct contact for the purposes of nutrition. We will see that what allows for the preservation of the object at the level of perception is the presence of a medium between object and organ of perception, which allows for the continuity required for material alterations without requiring the immediate destruction of contraries.

Another reason why the plant in nutrition never encounters an object as different and distinct from itself is that this identification with an object as other demands some kind of distinction within itself between a part that can be affected by the object and a part which remains the same. In sense awareness, the distinction between the center of awareness in the heart and the sense organs at the periphery allows for this sense of an object as actually other than itself. But the only distinction in nutrition is between the organism's heat and its object. It must therefore be immediately transformed into its own being.

In the progression from nutritive soul to sensitive soul, we can infer certain demands on the soul. First, the object through which the soul is active and accomplishes its ends should also remain itself through the course of the soul's activity. Second, the soul should not be determined by an object merely in terms of the matter of that object. Rather, the soul should be determined by the form of the object as it is in itself, while simultaneously retaining its own nature. The soul seeks to hold itself in a relation to its objects as they exist in and of themselves. This cannot be accomplished in nutrition: one needs to move beyond the nutritive relation to objects in order for such a preservation of the object as it is in itself to begin to be accomplished.

This point can be clarified through an analogy with a similar argument in the *Ethics.* Aristotle there famously distinguishes three kinds of friendship, two degenerate forms and one ideal form: utility friendship, friendships of pleasure, and virtue friendship. The friendship of utility and pleasure are judged to be imperfect in relation to the virtuous friendship for the following reason:

> Those who love for the sake of utility love for the sake of what is good for *themselves*, and those who love for the sake of pleasure do so for the sake of what is pleasant to *themselves*, and not in so far as the other is the person loved but in so far as he is useful or pleasant. And thus these friendships are only incidental; for it is not as being the man he is that the loved person is loved, but as providing some good or pleasure.[121]

The relation to the object of love and friendship is not an identification based on what the person is in and of himself, but only an instrumental relationship based on the needs of the subject. The innermost being or nature of the object is completely accidental to the relationship, what determines that the connection lies only within the characteristics of the subject. This is just like the situation of the living being in nutrition. The plant does not identify itself to the object of nutrition as the being which the object has in itself, but rather as the being which the object has in relation to the needs and desire of the organism. It is a relationship of pure utility for itself—the being or form of its object in itself is accidental to the relationship. Therein lies the subordinate status of the nutritive relation.[122] As one moves up the hierarchy of friendship and of nutritive activities alike, the desire to be identified with the object as it is in itself is progressively realized.

One of the crucial differences between perception and nutrition that accounts for the fact that the object is destroyed in nutrition but preserved in perception is the presence of a medium in sensation as opposed to the immediate contact between food and organism in nutrition. For nutrition to occur, there must be immediate contact between the nutritive heat and the object of food. If something were to come between them, the transformation of food into the body of the organism would be impossible. The contact required in nutrition ties nutrition to the lowest of the senses, touch. Yet even in touch, Aristotle argues, a medium separating the organ from the object plays an indispensable role in perception. The medium plays a double role in perception: it both separates and connects the organism and its object. As separating them, it preserves a distinction between the object and the organism; as connecting them, it permits their identification. In nutrition, since there is no medium but rather direct contact between the transforming nutritive heat and the food, the identification cannot simultaneously preserve distinction. The only way the identification of the organism's body and the nourishment can occur is through destruction of the difference—through immediately transforming food into itself. As opposed to nutrition, the perceptive relation to an object requires that the object remain what it is through the course of the activity: if I were to use up and break down the green of the leaves I am seeing, I couldn't see their green at all. The object must remain what it is in order for me to assimilate its sensible form, and it is therefore the separating function of the medium which permits this perceptive relation.

Self-Sufficiency (αὐτάρκεια): Degrees of Dependence and Independence in Plants

As one moves through the activities characteristic of each kind of higher soul, we will see that the living being progressively contains more and more of what it needs within itself. The hierarchy of life in this way is a progression towards becoming truly self-sufficient (αὐτάρκης), where its activities are self-initiated (ἐπ'αὐτό). As we will see, sensation is "able to be exercised whenever one likes, unless something from outside prevents it" (II.5.417a27–8),[123] though even sensation is not truly self-initiated compared to thinking—unlike thinking, it is necessary for there to be a sense object outside itself. Nutrition, however, is far more determined by necessity than either thinking or perceiving. For nutrition must perpetually be in activity for the living being to survive: it is wholly beyond any choice or possible potentiality or latency in its activity.[124] This is precisely why the nutritive soul is left out of ethical considerations: ethics has to do with what is "up to us," or within our control to change, but the nutritive soul is not able to act or not act: since this basic self-maintenance cannot sink into latency and consequently must remain perpetually active, it is wholly prior to any volition.[125]

This is a complicated matter, however, for in a certain respect, the lowest forms of being might appear in many ways more self-sufficient (αὐτάρκης) than the higher. For one, nutritive activities can happen independently of the higher activities, though the reverse is not true (at least for mortal beings). Further, in plants, male and female are together in a completely undifferentiated mode. While the male and female in animals must look outside of itself to complete its ability to fulfill the highest purpose of its nutritive soul, that is, to produce another such as itself, the plant contains everything it needs for this within itself.[126] This same apparent completeness could be seen in the lack of dependence upon the external of an oviparous animal during its gestation. Within the egg is contained both the beginning of the animal, and the nutriment.[127]

This indicates a very interesting progression in the argument and in the hierarchy of life. What first appears as an undifferentiated, undistinguished whole becomes clearly distinguished and differentiated, only to become united again at the highest level. For in thinking, one is no longer relating to an external object, since the "matter" of thinking—the appearances or images (φαντάσματα)—exist within the human, and at the highest level, the divine has nothing outside of itself to which it could relate externally, both at the level of the body of the world outside of which there is no further matter, and at the level of the unmoved mover whose life is nothing but a self-thinking.

One respect in which plants are more determined from without is that the time in which plant reproduction occurs is completely governed by the seasons, that is, by the changes in the surrounding environment.[128] This is true generally of changes in plants in comparison with animals: their changes are more determined by external facts such as the time of the year and the corresponding changes in environment than their own internal time and development. Aristotle illustrates this through the analogy of balding in the human and the loss of leaves in plants. The loss of leaves happens according to the annual environmental change of the season, but the leaves grow back once the new cycle of seasons begins, and the cycle repeats itself annually throughout the course of the plant's life. The human, on the other hand, has its "seasons" measured by its own internal development, not by some external environmental cycle. The period of the human life is not cyclical, but linear: the ages of human life from birth to death are analogously related to spring, summer, autumn, and winter.[129]

This difference between an organism being determined wholly from without and its being determined predominantly from within occurs, not surprisingly, on a sliding scale, with the most external relationship existing in plants and the most internal in humans. Animals are more externally determined in their patterns of change than humans. More primitive animals change colors according to the seasons like the leaves on trees, he observes, and this external determination is observable in behavior such as seasonal mating and hibernation during winter. This hierarchy of living beings characterized by external determination at the bottom and internal determination at the top show that, though *entelecheia* or possession of one's end, cause, and principle within oneself is characteristic of all living beings, the degree to which this causation is internal differs according to the complexity of the organism and its place in the hierarchy of life. Aristotle explains this distinction of degree of having one's principle within by the amount of internal vital heat in each being.

The vital heat required for all life, that material factor which distinguishes the living from the non-living, is in the plant also derived from without in the form of heat from the sun,[130] whereas the heart is a principle of heat in the center of the animal: "What the heat in animals produces from their nutriment, the heat of the warm season in the environment puts together and combines by concoction out of the sea-water and the earth."[131]

But if the process of nutrition requires heat, whence the heat involved in plant nutrition? The plant has no heart, the principle of vital heat in the animal, and the part which is analogous to the heart in the plant, the principle (ἀρχή) which begins as the bud and in the developed plant is located "between stem and root,"[132] is not generative of heat. Rather than being heat internal to the animal, the food of the plant is concocted outside of itself in the surrounding earth by the warmth of the sun and its effect on the surrounding air in its immediate environment.[133] Thus the heat required for life which is centered in the heart for animals is located outside the plant in its environment, both in the earth in which it is rooted and the warmed air surrounding it. Ultimately, the source of this environmental heat is itself located in a principle beyond the immediate environment, that is, the sun.[134]

The passivity and relative lack of independence in plants is also clearly seen by comparing how plants and animals nourish themselves. When one compares the merely nutritive soul of the plant with higher living beings which possess higher activities, it becomes apparent that though the plant has an internal cause and end in a way that differentiates it in very significant ways from inanimate nature, the plant is the most passive and externally determined of all living beings. First of all, the plant lacks the internal heat which the animal requires for the active transformation of food into its own body. This heat is responsible for the concoction of the food which transforms the foreign object of nutrition into material for its own body. For this reason, food must be digested or transformed into itself from without, and in fact Aristotle talks about what is ingested by the plant as "already digested."[135] While the animal must take in the object and then extract what is essential by separating out the inessential from that object for its own nourishment, this process has already been done by the plant's environment.

It is for this reason that, unlike animals, the plant produces no useless residue, but rather every bit which it ingests is used in the production of its ultimate end: the fruit and seed towards which all its activity is directed.[136] Consequently, Aristotle looks at the plant's surrounding earth in which it lives as analogous to its stomach, the part which exists inside the animal for the purpose of breaking down the object of nutrition and transforming it into itself: "In animals the stomach and intestines represent the ground from which the nutriment is to be taken."[137] Here is an example of a principle which is external in plants which will become internalized as one moves up the hierarchy of life: the "stomachal sac is as it were an *internal substitute for earth*."[138] One consequence of this internalization of the function played by earth in the plant's surrounding environment is the autonomy which this gives the living being. Because of this internalization, it is no longer necessary for them to be fixed in place in order to survive: "All animals which move about may contain within themselves nourishment enough to make them *independent* when they move from one place to another."[139]

One final sign of the greater degree of internalization of cause and principle in living beings, as we saw, was the fact that the spatial orientation of the organism—up and down, front and back, left and right—is not determined from without by the cosmos as a whole, but rather from within based on the function of the living being. For the elements, their directionality is determined from without according to their natural location. In contrast, once one moves to the first, most primitive appearance of life, up and down for the plant does not correspond to up and down absolutely, as it is determined by the cosmos or the whole, but rather these directions are determined by the activities of the plant: "up" in a living being is defined by the location of that part which ingests the food, while "down" is defined by that part which releases the residue or fruit of the nutritive activity. For plants therefore, the roots are "up" and the bloom is "down," the exact inverse of cosmological spatial orientation. It is as one ascends the hierarchy of living beings that this objective spatial orientation is reinstituted.

◆ ◆ ◆

Having thus uncovered the structure of nutritive activity and the ways that it is superior to inanimate being, along with some of the deficiencies belonging to plants in relation to higher beings, we now pass to a study of Aristotle's account of perception in *De Anima*, in order to uncover its similarities with nutrition, as well as the ways in which it more deeply satisfies what nutrition strives towards but only imperfectly attains.

CHAPTER 3

Embodied Cognition: Sensitive Soul

Through our analysis of nutritive soul, we have seen the philosophical significance for Aristotle of the power by which soul maintains itself, grows, and eventually produces another living body. We now move on to the next highest activity of soul—sensation—where we will see the higher end for which animal bodies are used, bodies which nutritive soul produces and equips with the five sense organs required to be aware of the world around them. In other words, we will see how the final purpose of nutritive soul becomes merely instrumental matter for the fulfillment of the final end of the next highest level of soul: assimilating the outside world perceptually. In this chapter, I want to show how the characteristics by which the nutritive activity of living beings is distinguished from inanimate nature are more deeply exhibited in the activity of sensation: the sensitive being involves less standard change (κίνησις) in the exercise of its activity; its activity is further internalized; it is itself less determinate and consequently able to receive a wider range of objects while preserving itself without losing its own nature; and its assimilative activity is less material than in the analogous assimilation of nutritive soul.

Aristotle opens his treatment of perception with an introductory chapter on the various senses of potentiality and being affected, which, through an analysis of three levels of potentiality and actuality characteristic of knowing, introduces distinctions that implicitly differentiate perception from nutrition, which lies below it, and thinking, which lies above it.

In perception one has for the first time, on the side of the organism, the distinction between potentiality and actuality:

> But since we speak of perceiving in two senses—for we say a hearer and a seer hears and sees, both if it happens to be asleep, and if it is already actively perceiving—one must then say "perception" in two senses, one as potential, the other as actual. Similarly also the sense object[1] is spoken of in two ways, in potency and in actuality. (II.5.417a9–14)

As we saw in the last chapter, the object of nutrition was already distinguishable into potentially and actually nourishing (undigested and digested food). But nutrition itself could not fall into potency, or the organism would die: this basic self-maintenance is in active exercise perpetually throughout its life from generation to death. To see the difference between sensation and nutrition here, it is important to recall the distinction between the digestive and nutritive activities of nutritive soul. Any potentiality in the organism belongs to that by which the object is transformed—the digestive activity[2]—and not the nutritive activity itself.[3] But the distinction between waking and sleeping shows that the organism can cease actively perceiving without ceasing to exist altogether. In this way one moves to a less necessary activity, given that sensation can be inactive without the destruction of the animal. Though sensation will prove to be necessary for its self-preservation, the level of natural necessity in the transition from nutrition to sensation is reduced.

But this distinction between potentiality and actuality in the organism is not as differentiated as it is for the thinking soul. Aristotle's introduction to the treatment of perception in II.5 largely consists of a comparison between the three levels of potentiality and actuality in thinking to analogous distinctions in sense. In thinking, besides the distinction between potentially exercising one's knowledge and actively exercising it by thinking about it—θεωρεῖν—there is also a transition, distinct from the aforementioned transition, between an empty, ignorant, purely receptive mind that has not yet learned, and a mind which has lost this ignorance through learning and become a possessor of knowledge. In other words, the active moment of awareness of the received object and the passive moment where the object is received are distinct in knowing. This is not the case for perception, whose receptive and active moments are undifferentiated. There is no difference between when the organism assimilates and identifies itself with its object, and when it focuses its conscious awareness on itself as determined by the object. In thinking, to which Aristotle contrasts perception on this point, one can first receive an object into the mind through learning, and then in a distinct moment the mind can reflect upon this settled disposition, making the moments of passive receptivity and active awareness more clearly distinguishable. This clarity and greater differentiation in the case of knowing is the reason why Aristotle uses the example of knowing to explain sensation: its higher degree of differentiation allows the less differentiated but closely parallel activity of sensation to be grasped with more clarity.

This lack of differentiation accounts for one of the great difficulties with understanding the chapters on perception: the passive and active aspects of perception occur inseparably together. This is asserted by Aristotle at the beginning of his analysis of the senses of potentiality and actuality in a statement that has remained cryptic to interpreters: "First, let us speak of being affected [πάσχειν] and being moved [κινεῖσθαι], and being active [ἐνεργεῖν] as the same being" (II.5.417a14–16). In sensation the process of being affected and changed is the same as actively perceiving. Nevertheless, Aristotle does focus on the passive and active sides of sensation in two distinct stages in the argument. In his treatment of the five senses from II.7–11 as well as his conclusion to this examination, Aristotle treats the passive, receptive side of sensation: its being affected (πάσχειν) or being moved (κινεῖσθαι)—this is the material side of perception, what goes on at the periphery of the sensitive organism in its organs.[4] This is what Aristotle sometimes calls the αἴσθημα (*aisthema*), the being affected (πάθος) of the organ by the object, apart from the communication of this affection to the seat of general awareness.[5] II.12 acts as a transition toward his treatment of the active side of sensation in the first two chapters of book III.

Of particular interest in the contrast between nutrition and perception are the different kinds of change (κίνησις) which characterize the transitions between the three levels of potentiality and actuality outlined in II.5. I take there to be three kinds of "being affected" or "alteration" which we must grasp in order to discern how perception involves an important stage in the progression from change (κίνησις) to *energeia*.

First, there is standard alteration, the kind explained in *Physics* III.1–3, characteristic of all natural beings including the inanimate.[6] This kind of change involves the destruction of one quality by another, and is a transition from something to its privation (τήν τε ἐπὶ τὰς στερητικὰς διαθέσεις; II.5.417b15–16).

Second, there is what I will call nonstandard or qualified alteration #1, where, as with ordinary alteration, the initial quality is destroyed, yet with the qualification that the transition from one quality to the next is not simply towards the privation of what the being was, but is rather a development towards its natural state (ἕξις) and realization of its full nature.[7] This kind of change (κίνησις) is similar to standard alteration but is importantly unlike it in the sense that despite the destruction of the beginning of the change, it involves a certain preservation and realization of what the being already was to begin with. Aristotle illustrates this transition by the example of the boy who has not yet learned something but has the ability to be taught and possess this knowledge. It is the transition between something which is potentially doing or being something by virtue of its matter and belonging to a certain class which is characterized by being able to do or be that thing, to that which actually possesses the capacity to actively exercise it. He writes of this transition, as a way to distinguish it from ordinary alteration, that it "either ought not be called 'being affected [πάσχειν],' just as we said, or else there are two ways of being altered, the one a change towards the privative state [τήν τε ἐπὶ τὰς στερητικὰς διαθέσεις] and the other a change towards the states of possession [ἕξεις] and the nature" (II.5.417b15–17). Thus this sense of alteration and being affected is a qualified one, sharing something in common both with ordinary alteration and the transition from first actuality to second actuality.[8]

Third, there is what we can call nonstandard or qualified alteration #2. This transition is closest to full *energeia*: there is no destruction of the first quality by the second, but what the being is at the beginning of the transition is completely preserved in the result, the only change being one from potentiality to activity. This transition, illustrated by Aristotle through the example of someone possessing knowledge of writing and speaking without exercising it who then begins actively exercising this knowledge by putting it into use, "either is not a being altered (for it is a progression to itself and to its *entelecheia*), or it is another kind [γένος or genus] of being altered" (II.5.417b6–7).

One may object that the first kind of transition, nonstandard alteration #1 between a first potentiality and a second potentiality, is deemed irrelevant in the case of perception by Aristotle when he writes that "the first change of the sense capacity [αἰσθητικοῦ] is caused by the generating man (the father), and whenever [the baby] is born, it already has perceiving just as [unexercised] knowledge [ἐπιστήμη]" (II.5.417b16–18). In sensation, the first transition has thus already occurred when the animal is born: it already possesses the capacity to perceive, which needs only to be activated through interaction with an object of sense. In order to prevent readers from too closely identifying the example of knowledge with perception, Aristotle is explaining how the capacity to perceive objects, unlike the capacity to think objects, does not need to be taught, but is the possession of the baby from birth. But this does not mean the two senses of potentiality and the senses of transition or change from each which we distinguish by means of the knowledge example do not apply to the analysis of sensation, and in fact Aristotle will use it in subsequent chapters on the individual senses. When an indeterminate, merely potential receptive organ is determined by its object and becomes like it, this is clearly not "a certain kind of being affected" (πάσχειν τι) in the ultimate sense of the mere transition from inactive possession to active exercise—this reception of the sensible form qualifies not as a destruction of the organ but rather a realization of its nature, which is precisely defined by its receptivity to sensible forms within its coordinate genus of objects. To say that this reception of sensible form is simply an instance of non-standard alteration #2 is to say that, like the individual with knowledge (ἐπιστήμη), the sensitive being already contains within it the sensible forms in actuality, and these forms require only active awareness of them. This is obviously not the case with perception: the organ is like the empty mind of the child, which must be filled by being determined by an object of perception and receiving its sensible form.

The first transition in sensation, an example of nonstandard alteration or being affected #1, is the alteration that occurs through the transformation of the organ which becomes like the object of sense with respect to the sensible quality. This is a qualified sense of alteration for two reasons. First, since it is the very nature of the sense organ to take on such qualities, it is not just any destruction of a previously possessed quality—though the transition of the organ from being unlike the sense object to being like it is a destruction (φθορά)—but it is also a realization of its nature as taking on the sensible forms of external objects: the receptive organ by assimilating its object is, after all, becoming itself more fully. Second, just as animate growth controlled by nutritive soul is not like just any quantitative change (κίνησις) but is one which preserves a certain proportion (λόγος) throughout the course of the change,[9] ensouled, perceptive alteration is also one in which a certain proportion is preserved through the course of the change: the quality may change but only within a certain controlled, determinate range. The second transition is simply the resulting transition of the sense—the capacity to see or hear—from inactively exercising itself to actively exercising itself. This is a case of nonstandard alteration #2, where the already affected organ and the sense object become one in the fully active sense awareness. This does not represent a temporal progression but rather a conceptual schematization of the simultaneously occurring moments of perception. Note that the transition involved in nonstandard alteration #1—just like the transition in ordinary alteration—is between unlike terms (with the proper qualification in the case of nonstandard alteration, that it is moving towards its nature, which it thus possesses in some respect prior to the change), while the transition in alteration #2 is between like terms. Therefore Aristotle resolves the debate between those who view perception as like by like and perception as contrary by contrary in the same way he resolved the debate concerning nutrition: "Thus it is not the same when it is being affected, but it becomes like its object once it has been affected, and is such as what acts on it" (II.5.418a5–6).

Yet there is an important difference to notice. Nutrition as we saw works quite differently in terms of these three kinds of alteration. Whereas perception involves no ordinary, unqualified alteration, the first moment of the nutritive process does: the destruction of food is an ordinary alteration of food, since there is no sense that the object realizes its full nature in being broken down and digested—it has its own proper nature and ends independently of acting as nourishment for another. The first moment of sensation, in contrast, is an example of a nonstandard change (κίνησις) #1. As the argument moves up the hierarchy from nutrition to perception, it makes an important transition away from change (κίνησις) to *energeia* by leaving behind ordinary alteration from the activity (this is simply another side of the fact that in perception, in contrast with nutrition, the object is preserved rather than destroyed).

The non-standard change (κίνησις) #1 involved in the sense organ changing from being unlike its object to being like its object does have an analogue in nutrition, namely the structured growth of the ensouled being: there is in each of these a real change (κίνησις) where the beginning of the change is destroyed by the result of the change, but one which is a realization of the nature of the being in question, and one which is actually controlled and structured by the soul of the living being.

Sensation is to be further distinguished from nutrition in that the change (κίνησις) involved in its activity is internalized in comparison with what happens at this lowest level of living activity. Recall that in order to answer the question "is like fed by like or is contrary fed by contrary?" Aristotle's solution was that the food prior to being digested was different from the living being, while after digestion the object and organism were the same. This transformation however occurs *outside* the activity, and in the nutrition of plants, completely outside the organism. The same question arises at the level of sensation: is like perceived by like, or is unlike perceived by unlike? Aristotle's solution is almost perfectly analogous: "It is unlike while it is affected, but having been affected it is the same" (II.5.417a18–20; see also II.5.418a5–6). At first the quality of the sense object and the sense organ, though potentially the same, are actually different. After the organ has been affected, however, they are like each other in sharing that sense quality.[10] The distinction between food that is undigested (ἄπεπτος) and food that is digested (πεπεμμένη) corresponds with the distinction between the organ that is unaffected and the organ that has been affected (πεπονθός). This anticipates the distinction between the mind that has learned and been affected by its object, and the mind that actively thinks that content, which Aristotle compares to the matter which has already been affected (τὴν ὕλην πέπονθεν) and craft knowledge (τέχνη) respectively (III.5 430a10–14). In both cases Aristotle applies the general principle that the acting (ποίησις) and the being affected (πάθος) are identified *in that which is acted upon.* But notice the crucial difference. In nutrition, the one transition occurs wholly on the side of the object outside the organism. As a result the object is changed through the course of the activity, whereas the organism remains the same. In sensation, this distinction between the organism and its object is internalized through a differentiation in the organism between its sensitive periphery—the five sense organs—and the perceiving center of the organism, which Aristotle locates in the heart. In this way it is the periphery of the organism that is altered—while the seat of sensitive awareness remains stable through the change.

Because of this internalization of the change (κίνησις), the object of perception is preserved in its own nature through the identification with the sensitive animal, while the object of nutrition is destroyed in its assimilation and identification. Though there is change in the sense organ—before being affected the eye does not appear red, afterwards it does, hence its original quality is destroyed (if only temporarily) by being affected—this change is importantly different from what happens to the food in nutrition. Whereas the food has its own independent nature quite apart from its capacity to be nourishing to a living being, a nature which it loses when it is broken down and transformed into the body of the organism, the sense organ is essentially defined by its potentiality to become its objects. In having its own quality temporarily altered and receiving the quality of its object,[11] the alteration which occurs is, as Aristotle characterizes it, one which moves "towards its positive states of possession [ἕξεις] and nature" (II.5.417b16). The change which occurs in the food, on the other hand, more closely resembles standard inanimate change in being a change "towards the privative state [ἐπὶ τὰς στερητικὰς διαθέσεις]"—that is, a change to a contrary quality which is not at the same time a self-realization of the nature of the thing. Thus the transition from nutrition to sensation is a move away from change (κίνησις) in its usual sense.

The reason that the sensitive assimilation is able to preserve its object, while the nutritive assimilation is not, is related to the more differentiated character of perception. In nutrition, it was the object itself which underwent the transformation by the nutritive heat of the organism. In perception, because there is a receptive periphery distinguished from the active center of sensation, it is these receptive parts of the body which are acted upon, and that which initiates the change (κίνησις), that is, the sense object, need not itself be moved: it is preserved in its own self-identity. This restores the reversal of acting (ποιεῖν) and being acted upon (πάσχειν) that occurred in the transition from inanimate change to nutritive activity, where that which is affected (the living being that is nourished) is actually that which passes on its own quality to that which acts (the food).[12] In sensation, the object is clearly the agent and the sense organ the patient, yet without losing how the organism preserves itself in its being affected by its object in the nutritive relation. The sensitive animal is able to be affected and altered without losing its own determinate qualitative character in the process.

In what follows I will argue that in II.7–12 Aristotle explains the soul's role as the *efficient* cause of sensation through his analysis of the passively receptive and material role of the sensitive body parts at the periphery of the organism, that is, the sense organs and their assimilation of the proper objects of sense.[13] In III.1–2 he looks at soul in its role as the *formal* cause of sensation, through his exposition of the active principle of general awareness materially located at the center of the animal, which grasps the common objects of sense. Finally, he closes his analysis of sensation with his chapter on imagination, which (I argue) he views as the *final* cause of sensation, that is, producing the potential object for thinking. It is by virtue of imagination that the possibility for the third class of sense objects—incidental sense objects—is grasped. On this reading the structure of Aristotle's argument is far more organized than has been previously recognized, and the parallels with his treatment of nutrition and thinking more pronounced.

The Alteration of the Sense Organs and the Receptive Periphery of the Organism—Sensitive Soul as Efficient Cause

In each of the chapters devoted to the individual special senses and sense organs in II.7–11—vision, hearing, smell, taste, and touch—Aristotle addresses two main questions about each sense:

1. What are the main components in an instance of sensation for that sense—the organ, the medium, the object—and what must be true of each of those components?
2. What necessary conditions or processes must take place in relation to these components in order for the object to be actually perceptible, the medium to be actually able to transmit its object, and the organ to be actually able to receive the sensible form? This is much like the question of what must occur to the food in order for it to be assimilated to the self-nourishing living being, in that it is not a question of what happens in the exercise of the activity in question, but rather a question of what processes prepare the terms of the activity for the identity of object and organism in their active exercise.

Aristotle's treatment of each of the five proper senses is very detailed, and it is not always immediately evident why he is being so exhaustive in his analysis. I would argue that in his treatment of the five senses, Aristotle is showing that the five senses are themselves to be located on the emerging hierarchy of psychic activities, with touch as the lowest, most obscure and closest to nutrition of all the senses, and vision as the highest, clearest and closest to thinking, with taste, smell, and hearing lying in between.[14] The question "why is this detail included in his analysis of this sense?" can often be answered by recognizing that Aristotle is attempting to establish this hierarchical relationship between the senses.[15] But in what follows I will simply focus on some of the most salient features *common* to all the five senses before looking at Aristotle's own summary of these chapters in II.12.

The "ingredients" of a perceptual event, as we noted in the last chapter, are more differentiated than the corresponding ingredients of nutrition. In sensation one has the underlying perceived object and its sensible form, the medium between the object and the organ, and the organ, distinguished into its formal aspect (its capacity to see, hear, etc.) and its underlying material aspect (the eye, ear, etc.). Further, all of the senses except touch involve what later I call an "agent cause," a condition which is required for perception to occur in each case: a source of light (vision), a striking of the object (hearing), inhalation (smell), or liquefaction (taste). Whereas nutrition involved the immediate contact between the nutritive heat and its food, one has in perception a further differentiation both on the side of the object and on the side of the organism. On the side of the object or what is other than the organism, there is the distinction between the object having the sensible form, and the intervening medium in the surrounding environment through which this object is communicated to the organ. Though not immediately evident, Aristotle argues at length for the need of a medium for all five senses, present even in the contact senses in the outer flesh which mediates the sense object to an internal organ located near the heart. Without this medium both separating and connecting the object from the organism, no sensation can occur.[16] The object, medium, and organ must be in continuity with each other: the sensible form in each case is defined as that which has the capacity to move the medium, and the medium in turn moves the sense organ and communicates the sensible form of the object to be received (II.8.420a3–7). The consequence of the introduction of a medium into the relation of organism and its object in perception (in contrast with nutrition) is that the object is better preserved and assimilated by the organism without any interaction with its underlying matter. Normally an object can only produce an affection when agent and patient are in direct mutual contact.[17]

The intervening medium enables the kind of connection between object and organism which would exist through direct contact, while allowing the object to be an unmoved mover. The medium thus separates and protects the object of sense from the destruction facing the object of food, while also connecting the organism with this object. After all, were the medium not present, replaced by a void between perceiver and perceived, sensation would be just as impossible as if one were to put the object right up to the organ.

On the side of the organism, a similar differentiation also occurs between the perceptive center of the organism (the heart as the seat of sensitive awareness) and its peripheral parts, or organs, which receive the sensible form from outside. The center of the organism which connects all the perceptive parts at the periphery does not yet come into view in book II, as the focus is restricted to the perceptive parts, so we will postpone our analysis of this perceptive center until the next section. Crucially, there must be material continuity between the medium and the organ—they share the same quality by virtue of which they are receptive of the relevant sensible quality. The medium for vision is water or air by virtue of their transparency, and the eye is also constituted from a watery transparent material. The medium for hearing, primarily air but also water, is also the matter of the inner air of the ear (II.8.420a3–6). The intervening air of the medium is thus made to be sensible, and this in turn makes sensible the inner air of the ear, which by itself remains unmoved (ἀκίνητος).

The precise material composition of medium and organ, both of which must be receptive of the sensible form of the object, is not accidental. In order to be receptive of the quality in question, this material must be indeterminate relative to the determination it can potentially receive. For example, the transparent which can receive colors is itself colorless, and the air that receives sound is itself silent.[18] If they were to be determinate relative to the genus of objects which they can potentially receive (i.e., if they were *actually* colored or resonant rather than being merely potentially so), this would create interference with the reception of the object and would not reveal the sensible form to the perceiver as it is in itself. Think, for example, of how one sees through a colored lens and how this prevents one from perceiving other colors as they are in themselves. Aristotle gives the example of someone who has a ringing in their ear:

> But a sign of whether one hears or not is the constant ringing of the ears, just like a horn. For here the air in the ears is always moved by its own proper motion. Sound, however, is the sound of something else and not a sound proper [to the organ]. On

> account of this they say that we hear by the empty and resonant [ἠχοῦντι], because we hear by that which has air enclosed within it. (II.8.420a15–19)[19]

Since they are material, neither the medium nor the organ can be wholly indeterminate. For neither air nor water, the chief sensible media for the distance senses, are without determination, as they are defined by the possession of certain sensible qualities. But relative to the kinds of qualities they are capable of receiving for each sense, these must be as far as possible without determinate qualities to accomplish a successful instance of perception. Aristotle argues that water and air are receptive of color, sound, and odor, precisely because they are colorless, soundless, and odorless. This is because these elements are "indeterminate and do not remain [ἀόριστα καὶ οὐ μένει]" (II.12.424b15);[20] their nature is such as to easily take on further determination and become something else without losing their own nature.[21]

Aristotle's analysis of the organ of taste makes these points clearer:

> It is necessary for the organ perceptive of the tasteable to be neither moist in actuality nor incapable of becoming moist. For taste is affected in a certain way by the object of taste, *qua* object of taste. It is necessary therefore for the organ of taste, i.e., that which is able to be moistened while being preserved [σωζόμενον] but is not moist, to be moistened. A sign of this is that the tongue is unable to perceive when dry or excessively wet. (II.10.422a34–422b5)

This passage illustrates nicely the structure of sensation's receptivity: the organ must be unlike the object but potentially like it, that is, its nature must be capable of becoming like it. Yet the organ must preserve its own nature in becoming like its object through being affected by it; that is to say, it must not lose itself in being determined by its object.[22] If it had its own determinate quality in the same genus essential to its nature prior to the assimilation of the determination of its object, this quality proper to it would be destroyed in its own nature.

Yet even with this indeterminacy, its receptivity is not without limits. It can only preserve its nature within a certain range of contrariety, beyond which its ability to receive is paralyzed or destroyed. Touch is the most determinate mode of indeterminate receptivity.[23] While the organ does possess the tangible qualities it receives in actuality (it does have a temperature, a certain moisture, etc.), this is only as a mean or middle state between the extremes that it can receive—it is neither hot nor cold but intermediate.[24]

Thus it still has this neutrality relative to its objects which makes it able to receive the full range of contrariety within the genus of its proper object. This is what Aristotle later calls the μέσον κριτικόν (II.11.424a6) or μεσότητα (II.12.424b1), a neutral mean between extremes, which, on account of this neutrality, is receptive to being affected by both extremes.

Concerning the object of sense (αἰσθητόν), each sense is receptive not just of some particular determination, but of a whole range of qualities within an underlying genus, that is, within the range of colors, sounds, odors, flavors, and the tangible qualities defining bodies. Each sense has a certain limited universality, in each case being receptive to a range between extremes: all colors are visible; all odors are smellable; and so on (II.9.421b3–8). It seems that this range of objects in Aristotle's account is in fact twofold. On the one hand Aristotle explains that vision is of the visible and the invisible, hearing of both sound and silence, smell of the odorous and odorless, taste of the flavored and unflavored, touch of the tangible and intangible, where the privative term means "barely perceptible,"[25] either through being too intense or too weak (II.9.421b3–8; II.10.422a20–34; II.11.424a10–15), or even the imperceptible, since it is by hearing that one judges something to be wholly silent. On the other hand, each sense is defined by a primary contrariety or set of contraries which serve as the extremes within which all its objects fall: black/white, high/low, sweet/bitter, and hot/cold-moist/dry: each sense is able to receive the primary contraries and their various combinations which lie between them (II.11.422b23–33).[26]

The meaning of the openness to determination by a wide range of objects between extremes must be viewed in contrast to the assimilation of food by the nutritive soul. Here the body of the living being has a specific, determinate nature, and to assimilate food to itself the object must be transformed into exactly that nature. It cannot remain what it is but must be transformed into blood. In sensation, because the organs are themselves of an indeterminate nature neutral to the objects it can potentially receive, the sensitive body can admit of a far wider range between contraries. But because this receptivity is bodily and does have a determinate character of its own, this receptivity is not limitless, but is destroyed when one goes beyond the extremes (ὑπερβολαί) established by the ratio determining what it can become.

These sensible forms, the qualities proper to each class of proper sense, are the productive cause—they are ποιητικόν—of the active sensation.[27] Sensation is never self-initiated, but demands the object along with certain external accompanying conditions for a transition to its active exercise. For although in the transition from nutrition to perception the affection (πάσχειν) of the object was internalized in the peripheral sense organs, the original object remains outside, as does the intervening medium through which it appears to the animal.

Having looked at the central points in Aristotle's treatment of the proper senses, let us now pass to the general conclusions he draws to close his reflection on the receptive parts at the periphery of the sensitive organism in chapter II.12.

Several points about this crucial chapter have been misunderstood because commentators do not acknowledge precisely enough what aspect of sensation Aristotle is analyzing at this point in the argument, that is, how he is simply summarizing the passively receptive aspect of sensation at the periphery of the organism, and that nothing about the active center or principle of awareness in sensation emerges until book III. The chapter is devoted to an analysis of the relation between the formal and material aspects (i.e., the αἴσθησις as a sense capacity and its respective organ) of the first actuality of each of the five senses. This object of investigation had already been raised by Aristotle in the context of his methodological discussion of II.1, thinking about the relation between the first actuality or form and the material potentiality of the perceiving parts: "If the eye [ὀφθαλμός] were a living being, its soul would be its vision [ὄψις]. For this is its essence according to its reason [οὐσία . . . κατὰ τὸν λόγον]. And the eye is the matter of vision, which if it is lost there is no eye, except homonymously" (II.1.412b18–21). Thus there are three levels of potentiality and actuality relative to the special sense organs and their capacity. The eye is the matter or potentiality for vision, vision is the form or soul of the eye, the first actualization of this material potentiality. Beyond this first actuality, seeing is the full, second actualization of the capacity of seeing (see II.1.412b27–413a2). This is the form and the matter for each proper sense—the capacity and its coordinate organ.

The first point common to his treatment of all five proper senses is his definition of each sense (αἴσθησις) as "that which is able to receive [τὸ δεκτικὸν] sensible forms without the matter" (II.12.424a17–19). As with the capacity for self-nourishment, the capacity for perceiving the world is described as an assimilation of the object and identification of the organism with the object. Yet perception's assimilation of its object is distinguished from nutrition through the fact that it assimilates sensible form without matter, whereas nutrition might be defined as "reception of the matter without the form." In one sense this formula "receiving form without matter" is quite straightforward: while in nutrition the entire object is taken into the organism and transformed into its own body, here the object is left outside, and the sensible form is assimilated without this object. The material stuff out of which the food is constituted in nutrition is taken in, and in sensation left out. But as always with Aristotle, matter is a relative term, relative, that is, to the determining form in each particular case. As Kosman states, "Matter is a principle of indeterminacy relative to some actual being."[28] But here matter should be understood not so much as its constitutive stuff, but rather as the object which underlies the various sensible forms or predicates. In sensation, the underlying object, or the "remote object of perception," is left outside the assimilation. The sensible forms—which are the sensible qualities like red, bitter, hot, and so on—are the immediate objects of perception with which the organ becomes identified.[29] So while in nutrition one takes the entire apple and assimilates it to oneself, though only as having such and such a matter potentially identical with the matter of the living body, in perception one receives the sensible form of red or sweet-smelling without the matter, which is not so much the underlying material components of the apple (though this is also true), but more the apple itself which is the underlying object of the formal determinations "red" and "sweet-smelling."

This is illustrated through the example which Aristotle employs:

> For example, the wax receives the impression of the seal without the iron and gold, it receives the gold or bronze seal, but not as gold or bronze. Similarly also the sense is affected by that which has the color or flavor or sound, but this is not said as each of those objects, but as this particular determination, and according to the form [λόγος]. (II.12.424a19–24)

The analogy with wax[30] should be interpreted to confirm that the expression "without the matter" (II.12.424a18–19) means "without the object underlying the sensible predicates" and not "without the material stuff." For the seal is simply bronze, gold, or iron with the added determination of a certain shape: the wax receives this formal determination without the underlying object of this determining quality. Though this illustration can be deceiving because bronze and gold are also "material stuff," Aristotle's explanation makes clear which sense of "matter" he intends. For the sense is affected "by that which has the color or flavor or sound [ὑπὸ τοῦ ἔχοντος χρῶμα]" (II.12.424a22–23), not under the description of that object itself, but only by the object as having this or that sensible qualitative determination. What is important to see here is that the underlying object is the object of perception, though the sense is only directly affected by the sensible form determining that object. As Kosman states, the remote object of perception, though not immediately perceived and left out of the identification between perceiver and perceived, is the *ultimate* object of perception, "that toward which the awareness is finally directed . . . it is distinct from the perceptual form that is the vehicle of our gaining awareness of it, and . . . in the economy of perception, it is where ultimate importance lies."[31] Only in this way can one see how (1) the object grasped in perception and in the object grasped in thought are ultimately the same object, and (2) the identification of object and knower and organism is more complete in thinking than in this partial identification through sensation.

Thus when one perceives the red of the apple, the directly perceived object is the sensible form—the red—and the underlying object—the apple—is left outside the assimilation. But we do not ultimately perceive redness floating in the void—but the redness of the apple. This relation to the whole object in perception, we will see, emerges through incidental perception, where one can indeed perceive something like "apple." But importantly, in incidental perception, what is perceived incidentally—the apple—is itself a predicate of what is directly perceived—the red. It is only in thinking that one ultimately grasps the object directly, as that which underlies the attributes, instead of the attributes underlying the object. We will discuss this in more detail in our treatment of incidental perception, but for the time being, in order to see the deficiency or lack in perception, it is important to recognize that what perception of a proper object leaves out is precisely what perception ultimately seeks to grasp: "The end of an act of perception is not merely to perceive an immediate object, but to perceive that the relevant matter is characterized by that object."[32]

From this perspective, though there is something gained in the progression from nutrition to perception, namely the preservation of the object in the assimilation, there is something lost which will only be recovered fully in thinking, namely, the fact that the object is not properly the comprehensive whole in sensation but only its sensible qualitative predicates. Nutrition, in taking in the underlying object, is in one respect a more comprehensive identification of organism and object. But because the determining form of the object in nutrition is broken down, the preservation of the form of the perceived object through leaving it outside of the assimilation eventually allows for an assimilation in thought of the substantial form underlying all predicates which preserves what the object is rather than destroying it. Thus, perception is a less comprehensive assimilation which ultimately makes possible a more comprehensive one.

This power to receive sensible forms is located in the extended body, that is, in the five sense organs. Aristotle refers to each of these organs as the "first sense organ [αἰσθητήριον πρῶτον]" (II.12.424a24), meaning the first organ to receive the affection of the object.[33] But the sense itself, meaning the power of each organ, is not itself a body, but a certain λόγος (*logos*) and power of each body part. It is the form of each organ, and each organ is the matter of each sense. Though what Aristotle means exactly by *logos* here remains opaque, if translated as "ratio" it likely means the ratio of the extremes which it can perceive; hence when one exceeds these extremes defined in the *logos*, this capacity to perceive is destroyed. But if translated as the essence, definition, or function of the organ, then *logos* is the *reason* for the transparent eye jelly in the eye being the way it is: so that it may receive colors—that is its definition or reason for existing. This is what Aristotle means in the already cited passage in which he characterizes vision as the hypothetical soul of the eye in that it is "the essence [οὐσία] of the eye in the sense of its definition [κατὰ τὸν λόγον]" (II.1.412b19–20). It seems to me that from the argument in II.12, both these meanings of *logos* are implied. The capacity to perceive, which is the form of each organ, is thus not a body, yet it cannot be separated from a body of which it is the realization. It is the informing and defining activity of that part of the body which makes it what it is. And it is also the blending of the extremes that it can receive into a ratio defining the limits of its receptivity.

The way Aristotle describes the relation of sense faculty to each respective sense organ and the qualitative change which occurs in sensation should be read alongside Aristotle's account of the quantitative change (κίνησις) of the self-nourishing body in growth. The matter of this growing activity, namely, the nutritive fire or heat, is an ancillary cause of the effect, but only insofar as it is structured by the nutritive soul, a "limit [πέρας] and a proportion [λόγος] of the size and growth" (II.4.416a17), evoking the λόγος τις καὶ δύναμις here in II.12. The relation here between nutritive soul and its heat is exactly that of the sense capacity, which is identified as a proportion (λόγος) and power (δύναμις), and its organ, identified as an extended body (μέγεθος).

Aristotle then explains how the form of each of the five modes of sensible receptivity cannot admit of an infinite range of sensible qualities while preserving itself. Extremely intense sense objects can destroy the λόγος understood as a ratio defining the range of what it can perceive—this proportion (λόγος) constitutes its power to receive further sensible determinations. Aristotle gives further determination to this idea of a controlling ratio or proportion in each organ which allows the organ to be receptive of a wide range of determinations without losing its own nature by defining it as a mean (μεσότητα) as discussed above. Being itself neutral or in the middle of the extremes that it is capable of receiving, the determination of the organ allows for it to become affected by determinations in both directions of its defined range, up to the limit defined in this ratio of extremes. Similarly, under normal conditions the proportion (λόγος) of the nutritive soul holds together the contrary elements like fire and earth within the same body. But there are certain extremes beyond which the nutritive soul will no longer be able to admit of further growth. And whereas an inanimate body like fire can grow without limit, exceeding the quantitative proportion (λόγος) of the nutritive soul can destroy its λόγος altogether, along with the power for self-maintenance which it provides. Thus where the nutritive soul is responsible for a controlled quantitative change (κίνησις) in the body through growth without losing its own nature and function, the sensitive soul present in various modes in each of the five senses is responsible for structuring the qualitative affections of these organs without allowing their nature and function to be lost. If this analogy holds, then one should view this proportion or range (λόγος) present in each of the organs, determining their functioning and preserving their nature while allowing them to be determined and *altered* by their object, as the efficient cause of sensation—that which controls change in the form of perceptual alteration in the sensitive being. The difference is that the primary mode of change controlled by nutritive soul was the quantitative change of growth, the primary mode of change controlled by sensitive soul is the qualitative change of alteration (ἀλλοίωσις).

The last section of II.12 (424b3ff.) ends with a puzzle which forms the basis of Aristotle's exposition of active, general awareness in III.1–2. It concerns the distinction between what appears to be two kinds of affection by a sense object: perceptively and non-perceptively aware affections. He thus opens the question of what perception is *beyond* the something's becoming affected by receiving the sensible form without its underlying object. Air can become smelly, a screen can have color projected onto it, yet despite their being affected we would not say that this air or the screen perceive or become aware of these sensible forms. But up until this point in the treatment of perception in *De Anima* we do not have the basis for distinguishing between perceptive and non-perceptive affections of something by sensible form. Aristotle thus concludes his explanation of how the proper sense organs are affected by their respective sense objects by asking the question: "What then is smelling beyond a certain being affected [τὸ πάσχειν τι]? Or is smelling perceiving [αἰσθάνεσθαι], while the air being affected rather becomes perceptible?" (II.12.424b16–18). This marks the transition between the account of the proper senses, which explain how it is that the periphery of the organism is receptive of sensible forms. But while remaining at the periphery of the sensitive animal no satisfactory answer can be given to this question of the difference between the affection of sensed and non-sensed sensible forms. Book III thus moves on to the properly cognitive aspect of perceptual activity, that by which we are not simply affected by sensible forms in a stream of environmental stimuli, but are consciously aware of these affections. In order to do this, Aristotle must move from his treatment of the proper senses to an explanation of the sensitive awareness common to all five proper senses. Further, at the end of book II, there is no center to the perceptive being; each sense is its own world, apprehending its own discrete sphere of being without any community between them. Aristotle must further show how these discrete modes of receptivity are connected in one animal.[34]

Book III thus takes up this question of what lies *beyond* the five senses in perception by virtue of which the affection of the organs leads to an awareness of the affections of the organs. This takes the form of an examination of whether there is a sixth sense beyond the five by virtue of which the animal senses its being affected by its objects. The conclusion of this extremely obscure argument (III.1.424b22–425a13) is that the investigation of the proper sensibles is complete, that there are neither any sense objects in the world nor any sense organs in the sensitive animals which are missing. Having completed this analysis of the receptive parts at the periphery of the organism and the passive, material moment of sensation, Aristotle can move on to an examination of the formal side of perception, the general awareness common to all the senses that makes the affection of the organs by the objects of sense *perceived* affections, that by virtue of which the affected animal does not become merely perceptible, but *perceiving*.

The Awareness Common to All Senses—Sensitive Soul as Formal Cause[35]

In response to this question of what sensation is *beyond* being affected, III.1–2 treats "all aspects of perception which go beyond the separate operation of the special senses."[36] Undeniably these chapters "are of a much looser literary texture, dealing with a variety of miscellaneous questions."[37] In these chapters, Aristotle formulates various questions about what there is in sensation that lies beyond the operation of the passive receptivity of the separate proper senses—which include questions concerning the power by which we perceive the common objects like motion, rest, shape, magnitude and number, the power by which we perceive the proper objects of one proper sense by another proper sense, the power by which we sense that we see and hear, and the power by which we distinguish the qualities proper to different proper senses as distinct. These questions, taken together, are intended to disclose the active moment of awareness common to all sensation. Each of these questions is raised by Aristotle not so much for its intrinsic interest—he does not solve either in any clear and obvious way—but they are used in order to show the need for the principle of general awareness in the sensitive being. These various paths to this general principle of all sensation are required because this inner principle of active general awareness is so difficult to apprehend in an analysis of sensation, whose passive, outward-directed moment is so much clearer.[38] Grasping the active center of sensation is further complicated by the fact that, in Aristotle's view, it is not even separate from the external passive receptivity of the organs. The principle disclosed in III.1–2 is not to be taken as a discrete power from the account of the proper senses in book II, but as the principle of active awareness present in the functioning of each of the proper senses which distinguishes their receptivity from that of non-sensitive affections.

To understand Aristotle's argument about common sensation, it seems to me crucial to recognize the peculiar manner by which he proceeds in III.1–2. He does not lay down some settled doctrine concerning this power, but rather gradually makes explicit various problems with sensation which simply cannot be solved through the proper senses alone, and suggests how a sensitive power common to all the senses can solve these various impasses.[39] What becomes gradually clear (or at least relatively clear) is that there exists a general awareness of all the proper senses in conjunction with one another, which is, however, nothing above and beyond (παρά) them. It is what Brunschwig calls "the shared activity of the senses, or their synergy."[40] There are various sensitive powers we seem to possess, but which remain inexplicable in the view of sensation we have at the end of II.12. With each new puzzle the need for a common sensitive power becomes more clearly manifest. Exactly how the common sense works as a solution to each puzzle is not made absolutely clear in *De Anima*, though in most cases Aristotle states his view less allusively in the treatises which make up *Parva Naturalia.* I shall focus on the *De Anima*'s gradual disclosure of the common sense through these puzzles, invoking the later clarifications only for added confirmation of the interpretation.

The awareness common to all the proper senses is disclosed in several discrete but interconnected stages.

Stage 1

True to the method he outlined in II.4, Aristotle brings up this common power of sensation through a reflection on the object of this power, the common sense objects. Having introduced the common objects in the context of the threefold division of sense objects, he then postpones his investigation of the capacity which apprehends these objects until after he examines the proper senses and their objects. But it is already suggested that some common sense must exist by the classification of these common objects as being perceived essentially (καθ' αὑτά), like the proper objects, and not incidentally (κατὰ συμβεβηκός), as the incidental objects.[41] Since these common objects are perceived incidentally by each proper sense but not incidentally *tout court*, this suggests there must be some sensitive power which perceives motion, rest, magnitude, number, and shape directly.[42]

Stage 2

Aristotle closes his investigation of the proper senses with the question: what is there beyond each of these proper senses besides being affected (II.12.424b17)? Is there some power by which the sensitive being is aware that it is affected by the sense object? This question introduces the treatment of the principle (ἀρχή) of sensation in III.1–2, devoted to finding the active and formal element of sensation beyond the passive affection of the organs in their reception of form without matter.

Stage 3

As a first stage of answering this question, Aristotle attempts to establish that since all possible objects are sensed by the five senses, there are no proper senses besides the five he has analyzed in II.7–11. This establishes that whatever general awareness does exist, it will not be a mode of perception separate from the five proper senses (III.1.424b22–425a13).

Stage 4

Following from this conclusion about there being no sense perception beyond the five senses (although he will subsequently establish the conclusion independently of the above argument), Aristotle goes back to the common objects, and establishes that there can be no special sense organ for them. Then through contrasting two different perceptual phenomena, he points in two ways towards the necessity of a power common to all five senses:

First, hypothetically, *if* there were a proper sense for the common sensibles, the common objects would be perceived the way one sense grasps the proper object of another sense, illustrated through the example of seeing something sweet.[43] Aristotle thus establishes the distinction between the way we perceive common objects and the way we perceive proper objects of one proper sense by another proper sense. The common sensibles, though incidental to the proper senses as distinct from one another,[44] are essential (καθ' αὑτά) objects of the sensitive power common to the five proper senses (αἴσθησιν κοινήν). This is the first appearance of such a common power of sensation.

Second, our perception of proper objects of one sense by a different proper sense is further distinguished from incidental perception *tout court*, that is, how we perceive the son of Cleon only incidentally to our vision of white. Though both are sensations incidental to the proper sense that is active in each of them, the phenomenon of perceiving objects of one proper sense by another is possible because beyond the functioning of each sense as separate, there is also the functioning of the five senses *as one* (ᾗ μία; III.1.425a31). The implicit assumption is that in order for us to be conscious of a unity of distinct sensible qualities within one object belonging to distinct senses, the senses themselves must be united in the perceiver, and they must also function as one.[45] In standard instances of incidental perception, in contrast, this unity of the sensitive organism is not presupposed, since the incidentally perceived term does not have its origin in one of the five proper senses.

Thus both of these phenomena—perception of the common sensibles and perception of a proper object by the proper sense of a different proper object—are explained in terms of all the senses acting as one unified power in conjunction with one another.[46] Aristotle closes this stage of the argument through the observation that one possible purpose of having a multiplicity of senses is to allow us to distinguish more clearly between the proper objects of each sense and the common objects and the conceptual clarity which results (III.1.425b4–11).

Stage 5

Aristotle then goes on to formulate puzzles (ἀπορίαι) about the nature of the power by which we perceive that which we see and hear. Kosman has given what is in my view an authoritative treatment of this section of the argument in his "Perceiving That We Perceive: *On the Soul* III, 2," so I can refer the reader to his article while simply restating those findings which are pertinent for our present purposes. Against the interpretation of many commentators, in this passage Aristotle is not analyzing reflective self-consciousness, that is, our conscious reflection upon our acts of perception. Rather, he is explicitly attending to the question with which he left off at the end of II.12: what is seeing or hearing or smelling beyond being affected? What is the difference between the unaware affection of a non-sensitive being and an aware affection of a sensitive one? By virtue of what are seeing, hearing, smelling, tasting, and touching modes of awareness? In other words, Aristotle's object in III.2 is to draw attention to the principle of "apperceptive awareness."[47] Aristotle first excludes the possibility (already implicitly rejected in III.1) that it is by some other power distinct from the five senses that we are aware of how the organs of the five senses are affected by their objects, arguing that this conception forces the meta-sense to have *both* color and the eye's seeing as its object, while also falling into an infinite regress of principles of awareness. The conclusion which follows is that it is by the proper sense itself, by seeing or hearing themselves, that we are aware. Yet this leads to the following paradox at III.2.425b17–20: "But this involves an *aporia*. For if to perceive by sight is to see, if it is color or what has color that is seen, if that which sees is itself seen, then that which first sees[48] will have color." In other words, if we ascribe to the seeing eye both the function of being affected by receiving the object perceived *and* the awareness of this receptivity, then the consequence will follow that since what is seen is color, the first passive aspect of seeing, which is the object of the second apperceptive aspect of seeing, will be colored.

Aristotle diffuses this objection with two arguments:

First, not *all* seeing is of color. That there is a certain awareness in vision *beyond* actively being affected by a colored object is made clear by Aristotle through the following phenomenon described at III.2.425b20–23: "It is clear however that perceiving by vision is not simply one. For even when we do not see, we discern by vision both darkness and light, but not in the same way" (III.2.425b20–23). Hence even when the eye is not affected by some object in darkness (for as we know, light must be present in order to see), it is by vision that we discern that we see nothing. Thus one of the extremes in the range of what can be perceived—the privative extreme—suggests an awareness beyond the organ's affection, for, as we saw, the organ cannot be affected in the dark, yet somehow vision also perceives darkness. We can draw the conclusion that there is some aspect of vision beyond simply being affected by color in the lit transparent medium, a visual awareness in some sense active even without this passive aspect of vision.[49]

Second, since, as Aristotle articulated at length at 425b26–426a26 that in active sensation (i.e., second actuality), the perceiver and objects perceived are one and the same, though their being is different, it is acceptable to say that in being aware of perception, one is simultaneously also aware of the object of perception, or that "that which first sees [i.e., the eyeball] will have color" (III.2.425b19–20). Since the activity of the object being perceived is one with the perceiving sense, it is true that at the moment of active sensation, the eye is colored, only in this sense that perceiver and perceived are identical—the organism's hearing (ἄκουσιν) and the object's sounding (ψόφησιν) "are one and the same, though the being of each is not the same" (III.2.425b26–7). This identity of the object's acting (ποίησις) and the ear's being acted upon (πάθος) occur together in the ear (following the general principle that the identity of acting [ποιεῖν] and being acted upon [πάσχειν] always happens in the passive term). Therefore since the perceiving organ is identical with the perceived sensible form in active perception, sensation's awareness of itself and its object are one and the same event: the perception of the object is always at the same time a perception of oneself as affected by the object, that is, a self-perceiving. The result of this consideration of apperceptive awareness is that there is an awareness of the affection of the organ by the object accompanying all instances of perception, but that this awareness is not something separate from each perceiving organ.[50] As Kosman concludes, though the argument proves that there is awareness accompanying the affection of the organ by the object, "there is nothing *in addition* to the qualified mode of being affected [πάσχειν τι] which *constitutes* the awareness of perception."[51]

Stage 6

Having analyzed the unity of perceived object and perceiver in the complete actuality of sensing, Aristotle moves on (III.2.426a27–b7) to consider this identity in actual sense in one particular instance of perception: when the object perceived is a harmonious blend of two (or more) qualities within the same sensory range. Andrew Barker has offered an excellent interpretation of Aristotle's argument in this section, which had previously remained opaque to ancient and modern commentators alike.[52] Aristotle argues that since a musical concord or harmony or blended harmony of various notes (in which the constituent notes disappear as separate into the blend) is a musical sound, and the musical sound and hearing are one in the full actuality of hearing, then since the concord is a ratio, the hearing itself is a ratio. Yet the hearing of this concord is destroyed if one of the component parts becomes excessively loud (thus overwhelming the other element) or excessively quiet (thus being overwhelmed by the other element). Aristotle generalizes this conclusion about hearing musical concords to complex objects of the other senses being overwhelmed when one element of the concord overpowers the other. Although the unmixed and pure elements in a non-blended ratio are still pleasurable to hear as distinct (as in a discord), when they are blended into one in a mixture this is more pleasant.

Though this section does not contribute anything directly to our understanding of the common power of sensation, this analysis of what happens when multiple objects within the range of one proper sense are perceived as one becomes the basis upon which Aristotle will examine, in the last section of III.2, what happens when multiple objects of *distinct* proper senses are apprehended as one and the same object, a phenomenon which does contribute to our apprehension of common sensation. That this is the import of this section of the argument becomes clear later on in *De Anima* (III.7.431a20–431b1), when Aristotle, in reference to the question of how the common sense unites the sensation of sweet and hot in order to distinguish between them, asks:

> What is the difference whether one wonders how one discerns objects which are not of the same kind [τὰ μὴ ὁμογενῆ] or contraries (of the same kind), such as white and black? Let C stand to D just as A (white) stands to B (black). The relation produced by alternation will also hold. If C and D belong to one thing, they will be just like A and B, which are one and the same but their being is not the same: it is just this way with C and D. And it is the same account even if A is sweet and B is black. (III.7.431a24–431b1)

The argument is clear: grasping distinct objects within one underlying genus is exactly like grasping distinct objects in different genera if there is a common awareness underlying the five senses. Thus Aristotle has explained how a harmony of objects within the same class of proper objects is perceived, to show how the same apprehension of a blend of qualities is possible even when the qualities belong to distinct proper senses.[53]

Stage 7

Aristotle opens this last section with a remark that summarizes the result of the previous section on the variety of sense objects within the range of each proper sense. He states that each sense is of the underlying sense object (τοῦ ὑποκειμένου αἰσθητοῦ). In sensation, what underlies sense is precisely the quality that is the proper object of a proper sense: the flavor, sound, color, and so on.[54] Each proper sense and its corresponding sense organ thus discriminates the various differences within this underlying sense object (the primary contraries of each sense object and the range of qualities between them).

Yet it is not only objects blended from distinct sensible forms from within the range of a single proper sense that we perceive, but we also perceive objects with multiple qualities which are the proper objects of *distinct* senses. How then are these conjunctions of qualities both perceived together and distinguished from one another, Aristotle asks. When we are experiencing something as simultaneously white and sweet, how are we able to perceive both these qualities as distinct, by what power do we perceive that they differ (III.2.426b12–14)?[55] What is it that discriminates sense objects belonging to different proper senses from each other? Aristotle holds fast to the fact that, as against Plato,[56] this discriminating power must itself be a perceptual and not an intellectual power, since the objects in question are objects of perception.

Aristotle then goes on to eliminate certain possible candidates for this perceptual power which integrates our awareness of objects from distinct senses:

1. Common to all the sense organs is their flesh, which is sensitive to tangible objects. But flesh cannot be the common organ of all the senses, or else each of the senses would require contact with their object. Since the three highest senses work at a distance without contact with their object, this cannot be the locus of the common power we are seeking to identify (III.2.426b15–17).
2. But this activity of discriminating objects of distinct senses as distinct cannot be performed by the senses if they are simply distinct from one another, unless some connection underlies them. If this hypothesis were true and one judged the objects of distinct senses to be different by the distinct senses themselves, Aristotle argues that this would be just as if you and I were perceiving objects at the same time. Since clearly one cannot discern whether objects are different or the same when they are perceived by completely distinct perceivers, we should conclude that the same impossibility would apply to judgments by two unconnected and discrete senses. The conclusion: there must be some sense awareness common to the senses by virtue of which the distinction between the objects of distinct senses is made (III.2.426b17–23).
3. It is not that each of the senses is perceived at separate points in time, as if one first perceived white and then sweet in succession. As Aristotle says, it is not simply that we *now* say there is a difference, but also that one says there is a difference *now*. But this latter kind of judgment requires simultaneous perception of both terms of the comparison. Thus there is a demand that the perception of distinct proper objects be undivided, at least with respect to time (III.2.426b23–29).
4. Further, if the perceiver is *simply* one, it is not possible that it should be moved in the same undivided respect and in the same undivided moment of time by contrary (bitter and sweet) or even distinct (sweet and white) movements. We have already

> shown (in point 3 above) that the perception does not occur at different times. Therefore it must be if these distinct qualities are perceived simultaneously and by the same power that there be *some* respect in which this power is divided and affected in different respects, and some respect in which the sense power is one and the same throughout. (III.2.426b29–427a2)

Aristotle then states a solution to the problem which avoids all of the above difficulties and synthesizes his analysis of the passively receptive external aspect of sensation and the active internal aspect:

> Is that which discriminates indivisible and inseparable in number, but separated in being? Is it then, in a certain way, that the divisible perceives divided things, but as indivisible? For it is divisible in being, but indivisible in place and number. (III.2.427a2–5)

The sensitive being is divided into five distinct regions of sensation, and these perceive the proper objects as distinct and divided from one another, yet one can also view the organism from the perspective of the awareness which unifies the five senses. As opposed to the two perceiving individuals, two distinct senses in the same individual ultimately belong to one and the same interconnected and unified perceiver.

But Aristotle immediately raises one final objection to this solution:

> Or is this impossible? For the same and indivisible thing may be contraries potentially, but not in being, but in actively being *divisible*, but it is not able to *be* white and black simultaneously, nor even to be affected by the forms of these, if such are sensing [αἴσθησις] and thinking [νόησις]. (III.2.427a5–9)

Aristotle thus reasserts that something which is genuinely one can only be contrary predicates in potency, though it can only actively be one of these qualities. But this succession is not the simultaneous phenomenon currently under investigation, but rather the simultaneous perception of distinct properties. But recall the analogy that Aristotle draws between the relation of vision to the eye and the relation of the sensitive soul to the whole body (II.1.412b17ff.). The body and its distinct perceiving parts constitute the matter for the general sensitive awareness, the potentiality of which the sensitive awareness throughout the organism is the actuality, implicitly answering the objection Aristotle raises.

He then suggests the ultimate resolution to this through a mathematical analogy, that of a point connecting two lines:

> But just as that which some call a point [στιγμήν], which is one and two, in this same way it [i.e., the seat of awareness] is also divisible. [Considering it] as [something] indivisible, the power of sensation that discriminates [τὸ κρῖνόν] is one and simultaneous, but [considering it] as [something] divisible, it uses the same symbol [i.e., in the diagram of a point at the intersection of two lines] twice at the same time. Insofar then as it [i.e., the power of sensation that discriminates] treats the limit [i.e., any line's end point] as two, it discriminates two things [i.e., two distinct lines], and they are separate as discriminated by something separate [i.e., by the proper sense]. But insofar as it discriminates by one power, it discriminates one thing all at the same time. (III.2.427a9–14)

The point, by definition indivisible, represents the unifying center of sensation, the general principle of awareness that all the proper senses share as parts of a perceptive whole.[57] It is through this unifying form of the five proper senses that one gets a unified object in sensation and not atomic sense qualities—by virtue of this common sensitive power the information from each sense in relation to the information from the other senses. Yet as the end point of two lines, the point is double, and in this way it is the end point for each of the five senses—in this respect it is as multiple as the five senses, since each of the five senses ultimately can only be affected perceptively insofar as they are integrated with the center of sensation.[58] Notice that in the image of the point which is the end point of two lines, the point is a part of each of the lines. For it is the eye alone that sees color, but this eye which has the power to see should not be conceived as existing separately from the seat of awareness, but as one with this center, and the same holds for each of the other senses. Obviously an eye or nose separated from the integrated whole of sensation is not able to perceive anything, but once it is integrated, they alone are exactly the kinds of parts which have the capacity to perceive colors and odors. Thus vision happens in the eye and hearing happens in the ear, so long as these organs are understood as being integrated into the sensitive organism as a whole. In III.7 Aristotle discusses the process by which "the air makes the eye such and such, and this makes another term such: similarly with hearing. But the ultimate end is one, and a single mean,[59] although the being for this is multiple" (III.7.431a17–19). In order for any of the proper senses to be complete, its affection at the periphery must be communicated to the center. It is at that point that the eye sees.

The relation between the general, or common, awareness of the sentient being and its sense organs receptive of proper objects should thus be conceived on the relation of active form, informing all its parts, and instrumental matter through which this form realizes its functions.[60] As Aristotle writes in his chapter on active mind:

> Since just as in all nature there is something which is the matter relative to each genus (which is all those things in potency), and another which is the cause and the agent by making all things (for example the way a craft [τέχνη] is related to its matter), it is necessary for these differences also to exist in the soul. (III.5.430a10–14)

For it is this general awareness which makes the affected organs—the underlying matter of the perceiving animal—into instances of perception. But just as form is in general not *separate* from matter, general awareness is not separate from the organs which constitute the individual modes of this awareness.

I mention this passage from III.5 on thinking because of an important parallel we shall see once we treat this section in the following chapter. Just as the treatment of sensation first investigates the passive, receptive, or "material" aspect of sensation through an exposition of the five senses and their organs, and then moves on to the active principle of awareness by which these affected organs are actual instances of sensation, Aristotle will treat the passive and receptive or material side of mind (νοῦς) in III.4 before looking at the active principle by which these received objects are actually thought in III.5. We have already seen this structure prefigured at the level of nutritive soul in the distinction between growth (soul as efficient cause) and nutrition (soul as formal cause). Just as Aristotle in sensation first treats the change (κίνησις) occurring at the external periphery of the organism and then treats the active awareness which is the form of sense perception, in nutrition he treats growth as the change (κίνησις) which occurs at the periphery of the organism and nutrition as the activity which maintains its form and center.

Aristotle closes this chapter by stating that he has completed his discussion "concerning the principle by which we say an animal to be able to perceive" (III.2.427a14–16). This is what has been disclosed through our various investigative paths, the principle (ἀρχή) of all sensation or principle of awareness by which the animal's sensible affections are to be distinguished from sensible affections of *non*-perceptive beings. This last line does not merely indicate that the treatment of sensation is now complete,[61] but rather summarizes for the reader what the achievement of the past two tortuously argued chapters has been: to uncover the ruling principle of all sensitive awareness, the active, formal side of the sensitive animal.[62]

I have argued here that there are two relatively distinct stages to Aristotle's argument: a treatment of the passive, receptive side of sensation from the perspective of the periphery of the organism or the five proper senses with which the sensitive animal takes in objects from outside, and then a treatment of the active internal center of the sensitive animal. We have already seen this at the level of nutrition through the distinction between the organism as growing and the organism as self-nourishing. We will see this further at the level of thinking through treating thought as wholly indeterminate and receptive in III.4, to thought as active in III.5. It is in order to distinguish these material and formal aspects of sensitive living being that Aristotle employed the "methodological fiction"[63] of treating the function of the proper senses as self-complete and independent of one another and arguing as if the totality of their activity consisted in being passively determined by the sensible form of the underlying object.[64] The several obscurities and ambiguities of Aristotle's tortuous exposition stem from the fact that these moments that he is distinguishing are conceptual aspects of an absolutely unified and indivisible sensitive activity.

Imagination (φαντασία) and Incidental Perception—Sensitive Soul as Final Cause[65]

After closing his treatment of the principle (ἀρχή) of perception, Aristotle does not move directly to the next taxonomically separate division of soul (i.e., thinking), but rather to a chapter analyzing imagination (φαντασία, *phantasia*). The placement of this chapter in the otherwise straightforwardly structured progression from II.4 on nutrition through II.7-III.2 on perception and III.4–6 on theoretical thinking can appear puzzling, as is the reason why Aristotle even deems it necessary to analyze the power by which images or appearances are generated in us when so many other important cognitive activities are barely mentioned in *De Anima* (opinion, memory, discursive thinking, etc.). In this section we must discern the reason for devoting an entire chapter to *phantasia* at this point in the argument. III.3 is a difficult chapter and involves many interpretative ambiguities which lie outside the scope of our argument. We must simply clarify why the transition from thinking to sensation cannot be made without a basic understanding of the nature of *phantasia*.[66] I argue that with the section on imagination (*phantasia*), Aristotle concludes his treatment of sensation by identifying the final cause of sensitive soul, that is, generating the potential object for thinking, and explaining what is necessary for incidental perception, the third and last category of sense object. *Phantasia* in this chapter forms a bridge which both separates and connects perception and thinking, closing his treatment of the former and opening his treatment of the latter.

It is important to understand the view of the relation between sensation and thinking criticized by Aristotle in III.3 to grasp his own view of the relation and its mediation by *phantasia*. Aristotle proceeds to show, against the view which he sees as prevalent in his predecessors, that there is a thinking power absolutely distinct from perception, a power which he argues is (1) not bodily, and (2) not governed by a naive materialist interpretation of the demand that like be known by like.

According to this view Aristotle opposes, we think sensible objects in the world by being materially affected by them in parts of the body identical to the objects of thought. Thinking would then be just as dependent as sensation on being stimulated from without by an external object. The three passages from his predecessors cited by Aristotle all make reference to this view of thinking. The first Empedocles passage argues that wisdom (μῆτις) is relative to some object present in the surroundings (πρὸς παρεόν). The second, in its original context, has to do with how thinking depends on changes in the body, drawing the conclusion that one's thoughts are always changing in accordance with bodily affections. This in turn introduces the problem that if thinking were truly grounded in such bodily changes as it is in perception, the stability associated with thinking would be impossible in the face of the constant flux of our body's changes and affections. Finally, in the passage cited from Homer, the disposition of one's mind is assumed to be dependent upon one's external circumstances.[67]

Aristotle must show, against these views, that there is an activity of soul that is distinct from perception in several ways. Unlike perception, it must neither depend upon an external object, nor upon stimulation from one's immediate environment, nor upon changes occurring in the body. This thinking activity would be genuinely distinct from perception and thus suitable as an object of study on its own. To show this, Aristotle must establish how these views of thinking as identical to perception in these fundamental respects are untenable. Aristotle argues for the rejection of these views by showing that conceiving of thinking as a bodily process and as directly caused by a stimulus from the immediate environment leads to two possible conclusions, neither of which can explain the possibility of error. The second conclusion, that error is contact of the unlike with the unlike, is quickly shown to be impossible through an elegant argument about knowledge of contraries (III.3.427b4–6). The refutation of the first, that "all appearances are true [πάντα τὰ φαινόμενα εἶναι ἀληθῆ]," is taken to be self-evidently wrong, but it is also the implicit task of the whole chapter on *phantasia*, that power by which appearances (φαινόμενα) are presented to us, to show how while some appearances (φαινόμενα or φαντάσματα) are true, some are false. As Caston argues,[68] having rejected these views for this reason, Aristotle must show that his own view of perception and thinking *can* explain the possibility of error.

Against these pre-Platonic views of thinking, Aristotle's treatment of *phantasia* makes several points which are crucial for the transition from sensation to thinking in the unfolding argument, points which both show how there is something distinct from perception called thinking, and making possible certain attributes of thinking that Aristotle will defend in subsequent chapters. As Aristotle makes explicit, he cannot properly discuss thinking until he has analyzed *phantasia*, since all modes of (at least) discursive thinking depend on *phantasia* (III.3.427b27–29). Images or appearances (I use the two terms interchangeably to translate φάντασμα, phantasma) are what underlie the intelligible forms which are the proper objects of thinking, and thus much about the thinking capacity can be determined through understanding the nature of our relation to the appearance out of which the objects of thought are discriminated.

The exposition of *phantasia* in III.3 thus serves several important functions in the development from sensation to thinking.

Function 1

The first appeal made to *phantasia* serves the purpose of distinguishing, against previous thinkers, thinking from perception.[69] Sensation (αἴσθησις) is distinguished from thinking (νοεῖν) based on the fact that (a) sensation occurs in all animals, thinking only in some, and (b) sensation (i.e., of proper sensibles) is always right, whereas discursive thinking (διανοεῖσθαι) admits of falsity. Importantly, it is at this point in the chapter that the concept of *phantasia* is first introduced, to *explain*[70] these distinctions. That is, if there is a power which depends on sensation and which itself is depended upon by thinking, this would explain why sense is universally possessed by all animals while thinking is not. And if this power can in turn explain falsity, then we can understand why perception of proper objects admits of no falsity, while all modes of discursive thinking do (as do the other objects of perception, i.e., common and incidental). Thus Aristotle writes: "For imagination is different from both sensation and thinking [διανοίας]. It does not occur without sensation, and without it there is no thinking [ὑπόληψις]" (III.3.427b14–16). In this way, *phantasia* is introduced to explain the difference between perception and thinking, the necessary truth and presence of the former in all animals, and the possible falsity and presence of the latter exclusively in animals with reason (λόγος).

Function 2

Unlike sensation, which is always a relation to an external object, thinking is wholly a self-relation, completely independent from the world outside the soul and needing nothing outside itself to occur. The image or appearance, which exists internally apart from any external stimulus, thus allows for this transition towards greater autonomy from the external environment in thought. Thinking, Aristotle argues in the chapters following III.3, is separate, unmixed, impassible, yet this would be impossible were it to take the object of perception immediately as its object. For an embodied being, this separation from the external world of sense is only possible if it can take as its objects appearances (φαντάσματα) which exist independently of the sensitive impulses from which they were originally derived.

Function 3

Directly related to this independence of *phantasia* from the external environment is a consequent spontaneity and capacity to be self-initiated in its activity, given that there is nothing outside the organism on which its activity is dependent. *Phantasia*, Aristotle argues, is "an affection that is up to us, whenever we want" (III.3.427b17–20). This is in fact the very same way Aristotle differentiates sensation from thinking: only thinking can be exercised by us when we wish (II.5.417a27–8), and this would not be possible if that which underlies the object of thinking, the image or appearance, were not also spontaneously called up by us.

Function 4

Further, as opposed to sensation or opinion, one can have an image or appearance before oneself without automatically believing the appearance to be true, that is, one can either believe or withhold belief in the truth of any particular appearance. This allows thinking, and even other images, to correct perceptual deceptions (III.3.427b21–26). The appearance thus acts as both source of error but also what is required to correct perceptual error: as Frede argues, "The disadvantage of inaccuracy turns then into an advantage."[71] And as a result of not necessarily believing it to be true, one is also not automatically emotionally affected by that appearance—like spectators looking at a painting—this disinterested stance affords a critical distance from one's object required for theorizing about it beyond a merely practical attitude.[72]

Function 5

Although it is separate from sensation, the appearance (φάντασμα) maintains a relation to the sense objects from which it is derived.[73] In this way, when mind thinks images or appearances, there is a mediated relation to the externality of the sensible world. Thus Aristotle appeals to *phantasia* to avoid an unbridgeable gulf (χωρισμός) between the sensible and intelligible, with thinking grasping intellectual objects and sense grasping sensible objects unrelated to the intelligible ones.[74] Though Aristotle views the sphere of sensible objects and of intelligible objects as distinct, one thinks the essences of the very same objects whose sensible characteristics were perceived by the senses. Only through *phantasia* can this connection be explained psychologically in terms of how one can move from the sensible to the intelligible.[75]

Function 6

In contrast to perception, which is bound to the presence of an object and thus fleeting, the image or appearance arrests this flux of purely present sensation by virtue of its remaining or persisting in the individual in the absence of any sensation of the object. This stability is necessary in order to be able to think the universal in the particularity of sensation.[76] For the persistence of images allows many particulars to be considered together, and, as Bodéüs writes, "the only good way of warding off the snare of images is to take them all into consideration, to multiply the φαντάσματα [images or appearances]."[77]

Function 7

Against any doctrine for which all appearances or images are true, Aristotle seeks to show that appearances (φαντάσματα) all admit of falsity. If they did not, there would be no need for a thinking relation to an object. As it is, perception is only infallible in relation to present sensible *qualities*: once one moves to other categorical distinctions within incidental objects—quantitative distinctions among the common objects as well as the underlying substance of a thing, along with other categories, perception is no longer infallibly reliable and requires the activity of mind (νοῦς). The dependence of incidental objects on *phantasia* thus explains how error is possible in all modes of cognition besides proper perception and mind's thinking of essence. Further, in sensation, the sensible quality which is the proper object and building block of all sensation underlies all categories of being in the object, and therein lies much of the unreliability of common and incidental perception: both the common objects and incidental objects are only incidentally related to the sensible qualities that underlie them in the object of sense. By contrast, in thinking it is substance which underlies all distinctions, thus restoring the proper categorical structure to the object and explaining the necessary inherence of its other categorical distinctions within it.

Grasping how *phantasia* makes these transitions from sensation to thinking possible is important for understanding the argument of III.3 and its relation to the ongoing argument of *De Anima*. Understanding the nature of *phantasia*—"what it is and why it exists" (III.3.429a8–9)[78]—is necessary, Aristotle argues, for understanding thinking. Implicit here is the fact that only as much about *phantasia* need be included in *De Anima* as is needed to explain thinking in the subsequent chapters (this I suspect is the principle of inclusion in III.3, which leaves out many features of *phantasia* discussed in the *Parva Naturalia*). Thinking requires that *phantasia* be clarified, Aristotle says, because thinking occurs through imagination and discursive thinking. The mind never reflects on a sense object directly, but only mediately through the appearance (φάντασμα) produced in the soul by sensation, as we will see in what follows (III.3.427b27–29). Thus, before turning to thinking, it is necessary to determine the status of *phantasia*, that power (δύναμις) or state of possession (ἕξις) "according to which appearances [φαντάσματα] happen for us" (III.3.428a1–2).

Since it is a power (δύναμις)[79] by which we can discriminate objects both truly and falsely, Aristotle seeks to distinguish it from all other powers falling under this description. For Aristotle, these include sensation (αἴσθησις), opinion (δόξα), knowledge (ἐπιστήμη), and thought (νοῦς).[80] Employing the same strategies of differentiating capacities as in the last section, Aristotle concludes that *phantasia* must be a power distinct from all of them or any combination of them. So what then is *phantasia* on Aristotle's own account?[81] Aristotle gives his own extremely condensed account of *phantasia* at III.3.428b10ff.

The link between imagination and sensation here is crucial. Given how imagination can occur independently of any active sensation or even potential sensation when the animal is asleep, it is clear that imagination is not sensation. Yet its causal origin still lies in active sensation, of which it is a by-product. Hence imagination can only happen in living beings with sensation. Further, its objects are of the same kind as the objects of sensation, in that the distinctions grasped by *phantasia* are the very same ones grasped in sense perception. It is in every way just like a sensation (whether proper, common, or incidental), with the only difference being that it is no longer connected to the presence of an external object. As Caston writes, "A phantasma has the same content as a sensory stimulation with the same causal powers."[82] In its origin, the appearance (φάντασμα) is just like the sensitive change (κίνησις) of which it is a by-product. Yet while the perception lasts only as long as the object is present and being actively perceived, the image or appearance persists and remains afterwards, and subsequently assumes an independence of its original sensitive cause. It can then affect (or not affect) our sensitive awareness in just the same way as an object of perception would, only without the need of any stimulus from an external object. Yet this appearance (φάντασμα) need not remain identical in the content it communicates to the original sensation, but can change just like any object of perception can change over time.[83] Therefore, it need not be exactly like an actual perception, but it must have the same powers that would characterize a potential object of perception.

After having defined *phantasia* in this way, Aristotle makes a remark which I believe commentators have not fully appreciated. He writes: "In accordance with this [i.e., *phantasia*], the being which has imagination both does [ποιεῖν] and suffers [πάσχειν] many things, which are able to be both true and false" (III.3.428b16–17). The appearance (φάντασμα) that is produced as a side effect of active sensation is determinative of how the animal both acts and is acted upon. This distinction between acting (ποιεῖν) and being acted upon (πάσχειν) here has a very precise sense, I suggest, corresponding to the two major divisions which characterize soul as the cause of awareness (including both perception and thinking), on the one hand, and motion, on the other.[84] This is the distinction between practical and cognitive activity, distinguished later in the *De Anima* as the corresponding genera of the good and the bad (relative to action) and the true and the false (having nothing to do with action) (III.7.431b10–11). This distinction was made at the very outset of III.3, in terms of, on the one hand, thinking (νοεῖν), discriminating (κρίνειν), and perceiving (αἰσθάνεσθαι), under the common category of the way the soul discriminates and knows beings, and its movement in space, on the other.[85] Aristotle thus concludes his chapter on imagination with a mention of the ways in which the appearance (φάντασμα) can determine both this cognitive side of the animal which is conscious of beings (in section III.3.428b17–429a4), and the practical side of the soul which acts (in lines III.3.429a4–8). In relation to the role of images in this practical side of mind (νοῦς), Aristotle writes:

> And because of their persisting and being similar to the sensations, many animals act [πράττει] according to them, some on account of

> not having mind [νοῦς], like the beasts, and others on account of temporarily lacking mind because of an affection, sickness or sleep, like men. (III.3.429a4–8)

Here we see how images or appearances, in being like the objects of sense except for being wholly internal, act as motivating objects independently of the immediate affects of sensible objects in one's external environment. Understanding the role of appearances (φαντάσματα) in action, however, must be postponed until my study of animal self-motion in chapter 5. What is crucial for our present purpose is the way that the being is also analogously affected in its receptive mode, that is, in its cognition of the world. Aristotle points out that the imaginative change which is the by-product of sensation occurs in three different ways according to the three kinds of sense objects.

Aristotle argues that the object of perception (proper, incidental, and common) and the appearance (φάντασμα) each produces are distinct in all cases ("the movement made by the activity of the sensation [i.e., by these three senses] will differ"; III.3.428b25–27). In this section, Aristotle's chief goal is to establish that the being with imagination can be affected by both a false and a true appearance (φάντασμα),[86] that is, that all appearances (φαντάσματα) admit of falsity. Since such an appearance is a by-product of an active sensation, there are different kinds of appearances according to the kind of perception that produced them: proper, common, or incidental. Aristotle must show that the appearance produced by proper perception—a perception which is always true—can be false, if only once the sense object is no longer actively present and perceived. So the fact that the "proper" appearance is always true when the sense object from which it originates is being actively perceived is accidental to the proper appearance, which in itself is not necessarily true.[87]

Having dealt with proper sense objects in II.7–12 and common sense and its objects in III.1–2, Aristotle moves on to his investigation of imagination without ever giving any substantial exposition of incidental perception, that by which we can have immediate, non-inferential perception of the whole object. These are, however, related to *phantasia* in a more intimate and precise way than the objects of the proper and common senses, in that the incidental objects are unique among the three kinds in requiring an appearance (φάντασμα) in the constitution of the object.[88] The proper objects of sense are necessarily related to their respective sense organs; the common sense objects, though incidental to the qualities perceived by the proper senses which must accompany them, are somehow necessarily related to the general, common awareness located in the heart. Thus the perceptive synthesis of white and motion perceived through the common sense is a synthesis of two terms which are each intrinsic (καθ' αὑτά) objects. Yet the term synthesized with these in incidental perception is intrinsic (καθ' αὑτά) to no aspect of sensation, either the organs or the general awareness centered in the heart. Thus the immediate object of incidental perception is not directly perceived.[89] But this has misled many commentators to think that incidental perception is an intellectual product, not genuinely an instance of perception. Yet this contradicts what Aristotle plainly says about incidental *perception* in the scarce references he makes to this sensitive phenomenon. The only way to maintain that incidental perception is genuinely a perceptual experience, while acknowledging that the perceived term is not the direct result of an affection of either the organs or the common sense, is by acknowledging that this object that is perceived incidentally to a proper object is an image within the soul.

Therefore, as Cashdollar remarks, "the second term of the percept has to have been a stored image which is spontaneously associated with the properly perceived first term."[90] An image like "man" or "son of Cleon" can only occur as the compound of various other images which must have their ultimate origin in the direct or intrinsic (καθ' αὑτά) perception of proper and common objects. Thus when one sees Socrates, one is seeing whatever proper and common objects (white, moving, this size) spontaneously associated[91] with a compound appearance (φάντασμα) derived from other persisting appearances (φαντάσματα) themselves ultimately derived from previous sense experience. This image is almost like a perceptive lens through which the intrinsic (καθ' αὑτά) objects are perceived such that one sees them as a man or Socrates or whatever. As Aristotle says, in accordance with images the one possessing them is affected in many ways (III.3.428b16–17), and it is in accordance with the image of the compound term in the incidental object that one perceives the white as a man or Socrates. One is perceiving man as an attribute (συμβεβηκός) of the directly perceived object—white, loud, perfumed, being in motion, of a certain size, and so on.[92] If this uniquely important dependence of incidental perception on *phantasia* is true, we see that Aristotle's treatment of the three kinds of sensible objects introduced in II.6 determines the structure of what follows: he discusses the cause of the apprehension of proper sense objects in II.7–12, of common sense objects in III.1–2, and then of incidental objects in III.3.

Once one arrives at incidental objects of sense, the whole categorical structure of being is brought into perception: one can thus perceive not only qualitative and quantitative objects of the intrinsic (καθ' αὑτά) sense, but even the unified object to which these directly sensed objects belong (man, son of

Diares, son of Cleon). In fact, as Cashdollar convincingly shows, "the category to which the second term belongs thus seems not to be a crucial matter in incidental perception,"[93] so one can incidentally perceive an object under any of the categories. But in the fact that it can perceive something under the category of substance (οὐσία) (as is the case in his examples of perceiving a man, the son of Cleon and the son of Diares), it perceives incidentally what is the proper object of thought. In doing so, one makes the transition to thinking in order to correct the fallibility and upside-down categorical structure of incidental perception. For when I perceive Socrates, I perceive this substance as predicated of the underlying object of perception, the sensible *qualities* of the proper senses. In thinking, however, this predicative inversion will be turned right side up, and it is the attributes of substance, which are inherently dependent on substance, which will be shown to be predicated of the substance, which alone of the categories has independence. The proper objects of sensation, of which sensation is infallible, are the underlying building blocks for the other fallible objects of sensation, whereas the fallible modes of thinking are the building blocks for the accomplishment of their ultimate end, the infallible noetic grasp of indivisibles or essences.[94] The transition to thinking is necessary to stabilize our perception of substances as only incidentally related to the infallible grasp of sensible qualities by restoring to the various aspects of an object the proper order of predication.[95]

There is one final important structural correspondence between nutrition and perception that comes out of Aristotle's treatment of imagination and is crucial for grasping the unfolding argument. Recall that the final cause of nutrition, that for the sake of which it most ultimately exists, is reproduction. Aristotle defines this as the telos of nutritive soul, "to generate another like itself [τὸ γεννῆσαι οἷον αὐτό]" (II.4.416b24).[96] Earlier in the chapter, Aristotle explains how nutritive soul strives for the eternal mode of being of God, failing at the level of the individual but succeeding in a way through the eternal reproduction and preservation of its species through reproduction: "to make another like itself [τὸ ποιῆσαι ἕτερον οἷον αὐτό]" (II.4.415a28). Aristotle defines this successive eternity of the reproductive activity as "not itself persisting but something like itself [διαμένει οὐκ αὐτὸ ἀλλ' οἷον αὐτό], not one in number but one in form," as opposed to the divine immortality which "persists one and the same in number" (II.4.415b2–7). The self-maintaining activities of nutrition are responsible for individual persistence from generation to destruction of the individual, whereas reproduction, striving for the divine eternity, is not for the benefit of the individual, but the persistence of the species beyond the individual. These are the two senses of final cause identified by Aristotle in this chapter (II.4.415b20ff.).

The language of the chapter on imagination suggests a similar role for imagination relative to sensitive soul as the one Aristotle describes for reproduction relative to nutritive soul. Just as reproduction is nutritive soul's production of something else distinct from but similar to itself, the phantasm is what the activity of sensation produces as both distinct from itself but similar to itself. Appearances (φαντάσματα) are characterized as "remaining and existing similarly to the sensations [τὸ ἐμμένειν καὶ ὁμοίας εἶναι ταῖς αἰσθήσεσι]" (III.3.429a4–5) which initially produce them. While *phantasia* is not the same as sensation (III.3.428a5–16; III.3.428b25–27), the appearance (φάντασμα) produced is *like* sensation (III.3.428b14).

The final cause of sensation could thus be said to be "producing something other but like itself," that is producing an appearance (φάντασμα), which then becomes the underlying matter of the intelligible form grasped by thought in its proximately higher activity of soul. The operation of thought does not come directly out of the sense object and actual perception, but out of coming to learn the essences of things through discerning the forms in the appearances (φαντάσματα). In thinking beings, sensation thus exists for the sake of making thinking possible, which is a truer and more stable relation to the objects it perceives at the level of sensation. At the same time, imagination does not *always* serve as matter for the next highest activity of soul, for it exists also in animals which have no reason. There the image is an end in itself, used to guide the animal unreflectively through the world, just as reproduction in plants, which have no sensation, does not become the matter for a sensitive capacity which develops out of the embryo, but simply serves the perpetuation of that lower mode of nutritive being. This corresponds to the distinction Aristotle makes at III.10.433b29 and III.11.434a5–10 between rational *phantasia* (φαντασία λογιστική) and perceptual *phantasia* (φαντασία αἰσθητική).[97] The former is able to discern the object of thought (νοητόν) in the images, whereas the purely sensitive imagination of the latter never arrives at these objects of thought or the essences (οὐσίαι) of its object, but from its images only further images are produced. Rational *phantasia* (φαντασία λογιστική) is the production of images for an end beyond itself (as instrumental to thinking), whereas perceptual *phantasia* (φαντασία αἰσθητική) contributes only to the continued functioning of its own level of cognition.

What is significant about this parallel between reproduction and imagination[98] is it suggests how, just as nutritive soul was shown to be cause and first principle of the merely living body as its efficient, formal, and final cause, the sensitive soul is, as one would expect, also cause in these three senses. In nutrition, soul as efficient cause ensured that the quantitative change occurring at the periphery of the plant in the growth of its parts was controlled and preserved a *logos* throughout the process, while in sensation soul as efficient cause is the mean which preserves a certain *logos* in the sense organs throughout their alteration. In nutrition, soul is the formal cause as self-nourishing, that which preserves and maintains the unity and nature of the individual. In sensation, this is the principle (ἀρχή) of sensation, the general awareness beyond the mere affection of the organs which unites its disparate sensitive parts into one sensitive consciousness and defines the soul as being sensitive and not merely sensible. Finally, just as the final cause of nutrition was reproduction, thus generating the matter which will underlie subsequent higher activities (i.e., the body produced by nutritive soul is the potentiality for the capacity to perceive), in sensation the soul produces images which will be the matter required for the exercise of the higher capacity of thinking: hence the final cause of sensation, that for the sake of which it ultimately exists, is producing something other than itself that will make thinking possible.[99]

Conclusion

A substantial part of the recent secondary literature on *De Anima* has focused on certain problems concerning Aristotle's view of sensation, which should not be surprising in view of the disproportionate space Aristotle allots to the question in *De Anima*.[100] Obviously there are many difficult puzzles about Aristotle's concept of sensation which I have left far from resolved. Leaving aside the thorny question about functionalism in Aristotle's view of perception,[101] I have simply tried to bring out the analogies and differences between sensation and nutrition, points which cannot be properly appreciated until the overall structure of his treatment of sensation in II.5–III.3 is discerned.

Kahn argues that the treatment of the center of sensation as general awareness is treated separately in book III along with imagination because "the broader conception of the sense faculty, including memory and imagination, would have obscured the sharp features of parallelism and contrast between sense and intellect which are so important for the argument of that treatise."[102] Against this view I have argued in this chapter for a different view of why Aristotle separates proper sensation from common sensation, and common sensation from incidental sensation and imagination. This separation is rather intended to *reinforce* both the parallelism and the differences, not only between sensation and thinking, but also between sensation and nutrition, and this in a very precise way.

CHAPTER 4

Theoretical Cognition and Divine Life

Agreeing with his philosophical predecessors, Aristotle argues that a basic division defines the soul: it is the cause of awareness and the cause of motion. His treatment of the first side of this division, cognition or awareness, culminates in his analysis of thinking in III.4–6. It is at this point that the argument finally discloses that towards which all the lower activities of soul were striving; what was implicitly present at these lower levels at this point becomes fully explicit. He shows that this activity of thinking exists outside of time and beyond all change (κίνησις), is independent of all externality and thus wholly self-sufficient, immaterial, completely universal in its receptivity, free of all natural necessity, wholly self-initiating, being most completely identical with its object. In thinking one reaches the activity which best preserves both its object and itself in their identification. In plants defined by nutrition and animals defined by sensation, the full actuality which they seek in actualizing their lower activities, even when successful, falls short of the full divine actuality ultimately desired.

In contrast, in the thinking human, the full realization of human nature in active thinking involves the very same activity in which God engages. Thus the lack which characterizes all the lower kinds of living beings by separating their immanent from their ultimately desired end is overcome in human rationality. Yet even the human does not perfectly realize the final cause of all living beings; its thinking is only intermittent, and dependent in important ways on the embodied activities of nutrition and sensation. The argument of these chapters shows that it is God's eternal thinking which is the final cause towards which all mortal living beings are striving. These chapters thus disclose the ultimate end for the sake of which the lower activities exist—active thinking. For just as nutrition is the potentiality for grasping the world sensitively, here sensation is shown to exist for the sake of thinking, and is thus fulfilled and contained within its more developed actuality. In this chapter I attempt to show how thinking culminates the hierarchy of living activities leading up to it. At the end of III.4–6 devoted to the topic of thinking, many of the puzzles with which Aristotle opens the *De Anima* are solved in a way that is not directly evident in most interpretations of these chapters.

There is something incredibly daunting, bordering on hubristic, in adding yet another interpretation of Aristotle's enigmatic chapters on thinking to the panoply of radically conflicting interpretations beginning as far back as Theophrastus. Yet it is my hope that the logical structure I have been arguing for can shed some new light on these chapters, giving determination to what, apart from the context of the treatise as a whole, can be read in innumerable conflicting ways.[1]

Franz Brentano, in the introduction to his own treatment of Aristotle's psychology devoted to previous interpretations of νοῦς ποιητικός (*nous poietikos*), notes how "it seems that not even Aristotle's immediate disciples agreed in their conception of the active intellect." For Theophrastus understands this mind to belong to the human, while Eudemus[2] identifies this active intellect with God, thus laying the boundaries for future interpretative disputes to be waged. Brentano concludes from this conflict that, if this debate emerged even between those who had direct contact with the philosopher, "it would also be certain that we must ever give up hope for a well-founded exegesis. But such a contradiction does not exist. We shall see later how the passages from Eudemus and Theophrastus can be brought into perfect agreement."[3] Although my view differs greatly from Brentano's own solution, it is in this direction that I think the principal interpretative division can be reconciled. There is a genuine sense in which both sides are right. I argue that the material mind discussed in III.5 is simply first actuality mind: mind that has learned or become the objects it knows. *Nous poietikos* is the active awareness of second-actuality thinking, the transparent active consciousness which both actualizes the potentiality of knowledge (ἐπιστήμη), and *is* that very activity. Then having isolated this completely active moment of thinking, Aristotle concludes that, being the most honorable kind of living activity there is, this must be the nature of God's activity. In this way human activity in its moments of active contemplation is the same in kind as divine activity of thinking, or, at the very least, it approximates this activity more than any other activity of mortal beings.

In what follows I treat only the theoretical intellect as analyzed by Aristotle in *De Anima* III.4–6.[4] III.4 is about the passive, receptive side of mind (νοῦς) and the actualization of first potentiality mind to second potentiality/first actuality, corresponding to II.7–12 about the receptivity of the five senses. Here Aristotle is explaining how one acquires the state (ἕξις) of knowledge (ἐπιστήμη) in which mind receives and becomes its object. III.5 is primarily about the side of active awareness in all thinking, corresponding to the general common awareness present in all sensation treated gradually disclosed in III.1–2.[5] It is this that effects the transition in thinking from first actuality/second potentiality—the perfect intellectual habit of knowledge (ἐπιστήμη)—to second actuality, the active contemplation of this settled knowledge.[6] Finally, in III.6 Aristotle reflects upon the relation of this active contemplation of essence (οὐσία) to the other modes of cognition, and shows how all these are contained within thinking in the same way that the various distinctions which these lower cognitive activities grasp are held within the unity of the essence (οὐσία) of the object which mind thinks.

In the previous section we looked at the chapter on imagination as the culmination of Aristotle's treatment of sensation. But as *phantasia* serves as a bridge between sense and thought, III.3 should also be viewed as the opening of his treatment of thinking. Following the methodological principle outlined by Aristotle in II.4, one should begin the explanation of an activity by an explanation of its object. In III.3, by examination of the nature of appearances (φαντάσματα), Aristotle discloses the underlying matter of the object of thought. Recall in Aristotle's analysis of sensation that on the side of the object there exist two senses of being potentially perceptible. The underlying object, the unsounding bell, was a potentiality for being heard, just as a colored object in the dark had a potentiality for being seen. A further sense of potentiality was identified once the bell had been sounded or the object illuminated: these were now actually perceptible, needing only a seeing eye or a hearing ear to become actually perceived. This same kind of double potentiality exists in the object of thought.

An object of thought in the most primitive form of potentiality is the image in the soul, corresponding to the unsounded bell or the object in darkness. It is through reflection upon these images, through learning and induction (ἐπαγωγή), that an actual object of thought, the intelligible form or essence of a thing, emerges in the mind. Hence, as Aristotle writes, "the thinking capacity thinks the forms in the images" (III.7.431b2). The potential object of thought is not the sense object in the external world, but the images which originated as a by-product of this sensation. Aristotle writes that "for the discursively thinking soul [τῇ δὲ διανοητικῇ ψυχῇ] the images are like the perceptions [αἰσθήματα]" (III.7.431a14–15). The images are the underlying matter for the object of thought, yet they themselves have no underlying matter, no external object which initiates them, as they exist in the soul: "The images are just like the perceptions, except without matter" (III.8.432a9–10).

In the opening chapter of *De Anima*, in a discussion of whether one should begin with a grasp of the essence in order to know the attributes of an object, or whether one should rather begin with these attributes in order to know the essence, Aristotle writes that although knowing the essence of an object is of great value for knowing its attributes,

> conversely the attributes contribute a great part towards knowing the essence [τί ἐστιν]. For when we are disposed [ἔχωμεν] to give an account [ἀποδιδόναι] of the attributes *in accordance with imagination* [κατὰ τὴν φαντασίαν], of all of them or most of them, then we are also best disposed to speak concerning the essence [οὐσία]. (I.1.402b21–25)

It seems that here Aristotle is giving an implicit account of the process of induction (ἐπαγωγή), "proving the universal through the particular's being clear."[7] One knows the accidents of the thing according to *phantasia* as that which grasps the incidental attributes of a thing; as a result one can arrive at a grasp of the essence (οὐσία) which underlies these attributes. It is in this way that the mind makes explicit out of the potential images of thought the essence (οὐσία or τί ἐστι) of the thing which is the actual object of thought, just as one actualizes the potentiality for sounding in a bell by striking it, thus making the auditory sensible form of the thing actually perceptible.

On the side of the object, there is the threefold articulation of potentiality and actuality (table 7).[8] On the side of the thinker, there is a corresponding structure with which we acquainted through the argument of II.5 (table 8).

TABLE 7. Imagination, Thought, and the Three Levels of Potentiality and Actuality

Image →	Essence or οὐσία of object →	Essence or οὐσία actively being thought
1st potentiality →	2nd potentiality/ 1st actuality →	2nd actuality
	Transition 1: learning through ἐπαγωγή	**Transition 2:** νοῦς ποιητικός

TABLE 8. Mind and the Three Levels of Potentiality and Actuality

Potential νοῦς ignorant →	νοῦς having learned, possessing ἐπιστήμη/ not actively thinking what it knows →	νοῦς actively thinking about its knowledge
1st potentiality →	2nd potentiality/1st actuality →	2nd actuality
	Transition 1: learning through ἐπαγωγή	**Transition 2:** νοῦς ποιητικός

In this chapter I undertake to unravel exactly what is involved in the interaction of these three stages with one another. What is crucial to take from this schema at this point is simply that the image which was the result of sensation now constitutes the first potentiality or matter of the object for wholly potential mind (νοῦς), which is nothing before it learns from reflection upon these images what the essence of its object is. While the object of sense is taken into thinking through the fact that its potential object is derived from and akin to its source in sensation, thinking is a relation to an object no longer external to the soul, an even deeper internalization of living activity than the internalization we identified in the transition from nutrition to sensation.

De Anima III.4—Receptive Mind (νοῦς) and the Transition from First Potentiality to First Actuality

We can now pass to *De Anima* III.4, the first chapter of the treatise devoted completely to thinking. Aristotle opens this treatment of thinking in *De Anima* III.4 by explaining the principal questions which need to be addressed:

> Concerning the part of the soul by which the soul knows [γινώσκει] and thinks [φρονεῖ]—whether it is separable, or not separable in extension but only in reason—one must examine what is its distinguishing characteristic [διαφοράν], and how thinking happens. (III.4.429a10–13)

The manner of Aristotle's presentation of these three questions suggests that the second and third question about mind's chief differentia and how thinking works serve the ultimate purpose of answering the first question about whether and how thinking is separable. Aristotle has made reference to the question of how mind is separate several times in the chapters leading up to his treatment of mind, in each instance postponing the question until a later point of the investigation. In these passages, there are two distinct conceptions of the separability of mind at play, but I hope to show how they are integrally related to one another. First there is the question, relative to the thought of an individual human thinker, of whether thinking is independent from the body. Second, there is the question of ontological independence—whether or not there is any being whose thinking exists independently of the lower activities of soul, namely, nutrition and perception.

In *De Anima* I.4, Aristotle writes:

> It *seems* that the mind is born in us as a certain substance, and not to be destroyed. It would be destroyed most of all by the feebleness of old age, but now perhaps it is just like what happens to the sense organs. For if an old man were to get eyes of a certain kind, he would see just like a young man. Thus old age is not due to an affection of the soul, but to that in which the soul exists, as in drunkenness and disease. Thus thinking and contemplating decays when some other thing within is destroyed, but it is itself impassible [ἀπαθές]. Discursive thinking [διανοεῖσθαι], loving and hating are affections not of that [i.e., mind], but rather of the one possessing mind, as possessing it. Therefore when this is destroyed, one neither remembers[9] nor loves. For they were not a part of this [i.e., mind], but of the common, which has departed [ἀπόλωλεν]. But perhaps mind [νοῦς] is something more divine and is unaffected [ἀπαθές]. (I.4.408b18–29)

Here we have a question about the first sense of mind's independence mentioned: is there a mode of soul's activity which does not involve the body being affected? Aristotle already suggests a certain answer to this puzzle about the relation of mind to the rest of the human being: the mind itself is impassible, but due to its dependence on various bodily processes, is not able to actively exercise itself when the body of the rational living being deteriorates—without this necessarily compromising mind's impassibility. This is a question about whether mind is separate from the bodily activities of the human individual.

Based on this passage it would seem that the question of mind's separate existence for Aristotle is primarily a question about human thinking and whether this thinking is dependent upon bodily processes. Yet in the next passage we will consider, he brings into view the second sense of separability we have mentioned. At II.2.413b24–27, Aristotle writes: "About the intellect and the contemplative ability it is not yet clear, but it seems as if it were a different kind of soul and that this alone can be separated, just as the eternal from the perishable" (II.2.413b24–27). This passage, as Caston notes, occurs in a discussion of "the distribution of powers across different types of living thing."[10] Aristotle shows in *De Anima* that the nutritive soul can exist apart from all other living powers in plants, while perception, although it cannot exist separately from nutritive activities which grow and preserve its perceptive body, can exist separately from thinking in non-rational animals. The question here is: is there a being which thinks independently of the other powers? Clearly with the human we have an instance of a thinking being which necessarily also eats and perceives. But is it possible that thinking instantiates itself in a being apart from the other powers in the same way that nutrition instantiates itself apart from the others in plants? If so, this being would be distinguished from all mortal living beings—plants, animals, and humans—by the eternal nature of its life, and would constitute "a different kind of soul." As Caston rightly remarks, "The reference to a different *kind* suggests that Aristotle is thinking taxonomically here, of a broad group that includes species which live by intellect alone, like God (and perhaps the movers of the celestial spheres—cf. *Eth. Nic.* 6.7.1141a3–b2)."[11] Throughout the book Aristotle has used this criterion, whether there is a species that exists having one power but not another to establish that the two powers are in fact distinct.[12]

So which of these two senses of separability concerns Aristotle in the opening lines of his treatment of thinking in III.4? Caston argues that taxonomical separability is the only sense of separability of psychic powers with which Aristotle is concerned in *De Anima*: "Aristotle is thus concerned in *De anima* with the way *types* overlap and diverge in their extension, and not what occurs within a given token."[13] Thus for Caston questions about whether the mind of the individual (the token) is separable from his body are irrelevant to *De Anima*. But in view of the passage from I.4, this cannot be completely right, since there Aristotle clearly opens the question of whether human thinking is an affection of the soul and body, or just the soul: this is a question about what happens in the token, the individual thinker. Caston overstates things in isolating this one sense of taxonomical separability in *De Anima*, most likely to cut off the possibility of the interpretation of III.5 that he opposes, that the chapter is concerned primarily with the individual human and whether his soul is immortal after separation from the body in death.

But perhaps one does not have to decide for one or the other sense of separation. It does seem that if thinking is taxonomically separable, then thinking must be an activity which functions in some sense independently of body. An unembodied separate thinker is inconceivable if the very essence of thinking is to be a certain kind of actualization of a body, as with perception. Following the treatment of perception, it would be absurd to ask whether there is a being which perceives but is not self-nourishing, given that perceiving cannot be understood apart from the affections of the body which constitute it. But if the two questions are interrelated, which has the explanatory priority? Is it that we will be able to tell whether thinking is separate from body once we determine whether there is an instance of thinking which occurs without body? Or is it that we will see that there is something that exists as pure intellect apart from any bodily affections if we can establish that thinking in embodied beings is not dependent upon body? Aristotle seems to answer this question in a crucial passage concerning the question of whether any of the affections (πάθη) of soul are proper to it apart from the body in the opening chapter of *De Anima*:

> There is a puzzle also concerning the affections [πάθη] of the soul, whether they are all shared also with that which has a soul [i.e., the body] or whether there is something among them peculiar to soul. It is necessary for this to be grasped, but it is not easy. It appears of most of them nothing is affected or acts without body, such as being angry, courageous, desiring and generally perceiving. This would seem most of all proper to thinking [i.e., being an affection proper to soul apart from body]. But if this is a certain *phantasia* or does not exist without *phantasia*, it would not be possible for even this to be without body. If there is a certain one among the functions and affections of the soul which is proper to it, then this would be able to be separated. If there is nothing proper to the soul, then it would not be separate [χωριστή], but just as to the straight, as straight, many things belong, such as touching a bronze sphere at a point, it would not however touch the sphere if separated. It is inseparable, if indeed it exists always with some body. (I.1.403a3–16)

We will have to return to this passage several times throughout our examination of thinking, but what is here crucial to note is that the question of whether our thinking functions independently of body is here explicitly connected with the taxonomical question of whether thinking is able to exist separately from the bodily activities in a being, or whether thinking is simply distinguishable in definition but not in being. And the question of whether mind (νοῦς) is taxonomically separate is viewed here as established if one can show, in an investigation of embodied human thinking, that thinking in some way happens independently of body. Aristotle in fact offers the criterion by which this question can be judged: is thought distinct from imagination—which belongs to the sensitive body—and even if it is distinct, can it function without images or appearances? We have seen already from III.3 that thinking and imagination are distinct—so Aristotle has left to make explicit whether there is a mode of thinking that acts independently of images, and independently of anything else in the body. If not, then Aristotle argues thinking would be analogous to the case of the line, which, when its essence is separated from the material instantiation of the line, does not even have the powers belonging to it by this essence or definition, such as touching a sphere at a point on its circumference. If this holds for thought, no thinking could even occur if the mind were separated from the body, the source of the images thought requires.

Thus in this passage the two senses of separability are intimately related in the following way: if the former is untrue, that is, if thinking is in principle wedded to the body as its actualization and not separate from body, then the theoretical possibility of a mind (νοῦς) without the other activities of the body will be eliminated. Showing the possibility of the first sense of separability is a prerequisite for establishing the second sense.

I hope to show this is precisely how Aristotle proceeds in III.4–5. Through an investigation into embodied human thinking, we look to see in what ways thinking can be said to be an activity of the soul in itself apart from any involvement with body. Mind is identified as incorporeal, but in order to receive its objects, it must employ the images or appearances in the body. Beyond even this dependence on images lies νοῦς ποιητικός (active mind), which is neither bodily nor dependent upon images to be active. Once he discovers how this is true for human thinking, Aristotle then identifies this highest living activity in mortal living beings with the living activity of God, in whom thought exists separately from the rest of the activities of the living being, "as the eternal from the perishable." As we know from other Aristotelian texts, Aristotle argues that there is in fact an instance of thinking activity apart from the lower activities of the soul, namely in the thinking activity of God, while in humans thinking occurs alongside the perceptive and nutritive powers. But the chapters on thinking in *De Anima* do not assume this conclusion, but rather set out to discover it. Grasping this point is of the utmost importance for understanding the argument of III.4–5. Aristotle examines human thinking[14]—the part of the soul by which it knows and thinks—to see whether thinking involves the kind of separability from the body necessary for thinking to have taxonomical separability. For if the activity of thinking is by definition inseparable from the body, it will never be able to occur separately from nutritive and perceptive powers, required for the maintenance and preservation of any living body.

Thus, in order to settle this question of separability, Aristotle informs us that he will examine two questions about thinking: what distinguishes thinking from the other activities of soul, and what exactly goes on when one thinks. As most commentators remark, III.4 then breaks up rather neatly into three sections. In the first section (III.3.428b13-III.4.429b9), Aristotle seeks to answer the question about what thinking soul's primary differentia is, through an extended comparison between certain characteristics of thinking and perceiving. In the second section, (III.4.429b10–22), Aristotle continues this contrast with perception through an examination of the objects of each, deducing further characteristics about mind and its thinking from the nature of the objects of thought. In the third section of the chapter (III.4.429b22–430a9), Aristotle raises certain puzzles (ἀπορίαι) concerning thinking that arise from what has been established about mind in the first two sections, puzzles which are only completely solved through the explanation of the active aspect of conscious awareness in the subsequent chapter.

Section 1: What Distinguishes Thinking?

Just as perception was understood through an implicit comparison with nutritive activity, and nutrition understood through the schema governing inanimate acting and being affected, including inanimate change in *On Generation and Corruption* I.7, thinking is in turn understood through an extended comparison and contrast with perception: "If thinking is like perceiving, either it is a certain kind of being affected [πάσχειν τι] by the object of thought, or some other such thing" (III.4.429a13–15). Insofar as someone who does not know some object can come to know it, this implies that thinking can be affected some way by that object of thought. Thinking must involve some affection in the transition from not thinking an object to thinking it or not knowing something to knowing it. But then Aristotle introduces an equally important condition for thinking which, if we had not read his treatment of perception explaining the sense in which the sensitive being remains unaffected despite the alteration of its affection by the object, might appear to conflict with this idea of receptivity: that mind (νοῦς) must be unaffected (ἀπαθές). "It is necessary for the mind to be unaffected [ἀπαθές], but able to receive the form and to be like it in potency but not to be it, and just as the sense capacity relates to the objects of sense, in a similar way the mind relates to the objects of thought" (III.4.429a15–18). That mind must be impassible—as is made fully explicit at III.4.429a29 with his contrast between the unaffectedness (ἀπάθεια) of perception and thinking—is deduced from the fact that "thinking is like perceiving." Perception too is this combination of becoming affected by the object, while wholly remaining itself in the face of assimilating this other object, that is, being unaffected (ἀπαθές). Recall that even nutrition was defined by a certain resistance to being affected (ἀπάθεια): a maintenance of a certain proportion governing the quantitative change (κίνησις) of its growth, as well as the preservation of its own material determination in the face of the initially foreign matter of its food.[15] In perception, this mode of impassibility (ἀπάθεια) was made up of a certain ratio of the material elements of the organ—that is, a mean—which is particularly receptive of a certain class of sensible qualities precisely because its material composition is neutral to the extremes of the range. This *logos* of the material constituents of the organ is the cause of their being receptive while preserving their own determinate nature.

How are both these aspects, receptivity and impassibility, brought together in thinking? In sensation, each organ is only required to be receptive of a certain range of contraries within a common genus: colors, sounds, and so on. The neutrality or determinacy it exhibits is thus restricted in scope: the eye need only be constituted out of something colorless yet receptive of color, the inner air of the ear need only be constituted out of something silent yet receptive of sound. The objects of thinking, however, are clearly not restricted to any such particular genus: I can think about what it is to be red, loud, hot, as well as what it is to be a plant, a horse, or a god. All beings can be grasped in thought, and consequently, its indeterminacy cannot be restricted to a particular field as with the organs of sensation. Aristotle writes: "It is necessary therefore, since the mind thinks all things, for it to be unmixed [ἀμιγῆ], just as Anaxagoras said, in order that it may rule, that is, in order that it may know" (III.4.429a18–20).[16] If mind is going to be receptive of all kinds of beings, it cannot be mixed with any particular kind of formal determination: this formal determination would then connect it with certain kinds of determinations, but would exclude other kinds of determinations from being assimilated in thinking, either through lack of any common underlying basis for interaction, or through contrariety and opposition to that determination. As transparent, for example, something can receive a certain range of colors, but is wholly closed off to the objects of the other four senses, as well as to the intelligible forms of all things, because of its determinate nature. Further, if the transparent is mixed with any color, certain colors will be excluded from being received. The sense of being unmixed in Aristotle's argument is that the mind's receptivity cannot be a formal determination of an independently determined underlying matter, the way the transparent is a characteristic necessarily present in some body like air or water, each of which has its own set of formal determinations accidental to their transparency. Mind's receptivity is just what it is without being combined with other predicates which are either accidental to this receptivity or opposed to some other formal determination. For, as Aristotle writes, "exhibiting itself alongside [παρεμφαινόμενον] [the object], the foreign prevents and obstructs [the reception of that object]" (III.4.429a20–21).

Having stripped away all formal determinations to make mind all-receptive through being wholly indeterminate, Aristotle thus concludes that mind as receptive has no nature (φύσιν) at all besides "that it is potential"

(III.4.429a22). Specifying that this is ensouled (and thus embodied mind)—"what is called the mind of the soul [καλούμενος τῆς ψυχῆς νοῦς]" (III.4.429a22)—Aristotle explains this notion of having no nature besides potentiality as being "not one of the beings in actuality prior to thinking [οὐθέν ἐστιν ἐνέργειᾳ τῶν ὄντων πρὶν νοεῖν]" (III.4.429a24). Whereas sensation involves the activity of something which has some determinate existence and formal characteristic prior to being active, thinking has no underlying determinate being independently of the object which it thinks. While the transparent in vision is restricted to color, mind is a wholly universal transparency through which all essence can appear.

The independent formal characteristics in the potency underlying the activity of perception belong to the fact that what underlies the activity is a body. For the matter of perceptible bodies is always bound up with a particular contrary.[17] The organs which are the instrumental bodies of the senses are made of elements which have associated with them a certain determinate range of sensible qualities. Thus the complete absence of any formal determination in the mind means that it must be distinct from the body. If mind were a body, Aristotle argues, it would necessarily have a certain quality which either excludes objects opposed to or unrelated to itself by remaining its own determinate self, or would be overcome by its object and lose its own nature. By being nothing prior to its becoming determinate, the mind is better able to receive *all* being, and is also better able to preserve itself in this assimilation, since it does not have its own proper determination which it loses in becoming its object. The nature of the change in sensitive receptivity and intellectual receptivity is different—the one's qualitative determination is altered, whereas the other simply becomes determinate from a complete indeterminacy.

To illustrate sensation and thinking's distinct modes of impassibility (ἀπάθεια) or remaining unaffected while receiving determination from an object, Aristotle notes the limits of sensitive receptivity, grounded in the determinate form of its receptive indeterminacy, as exhibited through its already mentioned vulnerability to extreme sense objects (τοῦ σφόδρα αἰσθητοῦ). This vulnerability of the sense organs was explained by Aristotle in II.12 by the fact that the capacity was defined by a certain ratio (λόγος) of its extended bodily constituents, which can be disturbed if too intensely opposed by the determinations of the object of sense (II.12.424a29ff.). The opposite occurs in thinking, Aristotle remarks, as the thinking of intense objects of thought, meaning more explanatory and universal principles,[18] make one more able to think more particular objects, not less.[19] And as Aristotle writes elsewhere, "We can contemplate truth more continuously than we can *do* anything."[20]

Aristotle concludes from this difference that "the capacity for sensation does not exist without body, but the mind is separate [χωριστός]" (III.4.429b4–5). This is not to say, of course, that thinking does not occur in an embodied living being, that is, it is not yet a claim about the taxonomical separability of thought. For although the mind which receives its objects is not bodily, it requires the body for the images underlying its object. Aristotle argues rather that the potentiality of mind of which active thinking is the actualization is not bodily. Aristotle has thus established, through the demand that we explain mind's ability to think all things and the fact that it is not destroyed or impaired by thinking excessively intelligible objects, that the receptivity of mind is not a body or even the actualization of a body.

This greater indeterminacy than in any other living activity is a crucial point in the full explanation of why thinking is a higher living activity than the others, but of itself it is not able to explain the exalted status Aristotle accords to thinking. If the argument is moving towards discovering the highest living activity, this nothingness or receptivity with no determinate nature whatsoever is obviously an inadequate end point. As Aristotle writes in the *Metaphysics*, "If it thinks nothing, what is there here of dignity? It is just like one who sleeps."[21] The receptivity of mind (νοῦς) is an important aspect of its nature, but until it becomes both determinate and active, the investigation must continue.

Aristotle then further establishes this conclusion concerning thought's separation from yet another angle: an examination of the nature of thought's objects, which will further confirm thought's independence from body, as well as give some further clarification about the relation between thought and perception. But before we move to the second section of III.4, we must explain Aristotle's comments at III.4.429b5 that directly follow his conclusion about the separateness of thinking, for they give us important indications of exactly what aspect of thought Aristotle is analyzing in III.4, and what aspect he is not. He writes:

> Whenever mind has in this way become each of its objects as an active knower [ἐπιστήμων . . . ὁ κατ' ἐνέργειαν] is said to be its objects (and this occurs whenever he is able to be active by himself), he is even then still in a way [a knower] potentially, though not in the same way as prior to learning and discovering. And the mind is able then to think itself. (III.4.429b5–9)[22]

The receptivity of mind as purely potential is the transition from the first potentiality of knowing (the infant human being prior to learning anything) to the first actuality/second potentiality of knowing, in which, as Aristotle here explains, the mind has learned or discovered and thus become its objects. In other words, the form in the sensible image has been understood and internalized, this object can be actively thought at will, since the relation has completely become a self-relation, free of any relation to an object external to the mind.[23] This mind is still only potential, since the object is not being actively contemplated, but it is also *actually* its objects. When the mind thus becomes wholly active in the contemplation of its latent knowledge, the mind is interchangeably thinking its object and itself, just as the apperceptive awareness of sensation was seen to be indifferently aware of itself as affected and the object which acts upon it. All active thinking is a self-thinking. But the question of the nature of this transition from actual knowledge to active thinking of that knowledge is not yet breached. III.4 and its analysis of mind (νοῦς) as receptive focus on the transition from first potentiality to second potentiality/first actuality, describing the process of discovering knowledge from a prior state of ignorance, where the mind becomes its objects, but where the mind is not yet actively thinking itself as determined by these objects.

Compare this to the analysis of sensation. This study of how the mind becomes its objects, apart from the awareness of these objects, or in other words, the passive and receptive side of mind (νοῦς), corresponds to the analysis of the five sense organs culminating in II.12. These chapters, as we have seen, are devoted to the passive reception of sensible form at the periphery of the sensitive organism, in its distinct sense organs. Aristotle closes book II with the question, "What is smelling beyond a certain being affected?" (II.12.424b16–17). He then moves on in III.1–2 to an investigation of the apperceptive aspect of all sensation: our awareness of being affected by a sensible object ("perceiving that we see and that we hear"), shared in common by all five proper senses. I have argued that the difficulty of these chapters is that the distinction between being affected and being aware of this affection is a purely theoretical one, which never occurs in distinct stages in sensation. These are rather the material and formal aspects of one activity, wholly inseparable in the activity of perception, making it very difficult to isolate this active apperceptive moment from the affection of the organ by the object.

Kosman argues against this interpretation of mind according to which the learned state (ἕξις) of knowledge (ἐπιστήμη) involves an identity of subject and object. He writes:

> It is only in complete second actuality that subject and object are identical. Consider again perception; it is not the two related powers of *aisthetikon* and *aistheton*, the perceptual and perceptible, that

> are identical, any more than are the sense organ and the sensible entity. It is only in the full actuality of *aisthesis*, the perceiving-and-being-perceived, which, although distinguishable as two beings, is one identical actuality. Isn't the same true in the case of thinking with respect to *nous* and *noeton*? My mind is not identical to the world's intelligibility—*until, that is, it thinks it.*[24]

I would say instead: "until that is, it *knows* it." Relying on the exact correspondence of thinking with sensation as Kosman does seems problematic. For in perception, object and subject remain external to one another in first actuality—the sounding bell and healthy, waking ear in separate rooms, for example. But in our III.4 passage, Aristotle argues that the first actuality of knower and object known are the same: the mind has become its objects. Because Kosman wants to deny, on this faulty analogy with perception, that in first actuality knowledge (ἐπιστήμη) there is identity of mind and object, he is forced to offer a stretched interpretation of Aristotle's otherwise straightforward remark at the end if III.4: "For theoretical knowledge and the object of knowledge are the same [ἡ γὰρ ἐπιστήμη ἡ θεωρητικὴ καὶ τὸ οὕτως ἐπιστητὸν τὸ αὐτό ἐστιν]" (III.4.430a4–5). Kosman is forced to understand this knowledge (ἐπιστήμη), because it is qualified as theoretical or contemplative (θεωρητική), as completely active second actuality θεωρεῖν.[25] The much more natural way of taking the expression "contemplative intellect" is in contrast with the practical intellect that Aristotle analyzes in III.7–11. Kosman's interpretation also blurs the subject of III.4 and III.5, against Kosman's own sound admonition to the contrary,[26] bringing in an analysis of fully active mind (III.5) into Aristotle's analysis of how mind receives its objects in the first place (III.4). It is precisely because the mind in first-actuality knowledge (ἐπιστήμη) has become its objects that active thinking is mind thinking itself, and not some object outside itself, thus being able to exercise this activity whenever it wants.[27]

This leads us to the explanation in this passage of how thinking achieves a far greater self-sufficiency or freedom from the external than sensation. Recall in his introduction to sensation, Aristotle asked

> why there is no sensation of the senses themselves, and why they produce no sensation without external objects, since there is within them fire and earth and the other elements, of which there is sensation either in themselves, or as accidents of these. It is thus clear that the sense capacity is not in activity, but only in potency. Therefore it is just like fuel, which does not burn itself by itself [αὐτὸ καθ'

> αὐτό][28] without something able to burn it. For it would burn itself, and it would require nothing actively being fire. (II.5.417a2–9)

The senses are not self-activating: both the passive and active aspects of sensation (since they are inseparable) require the presence of an external object. The senses do not perceive themselves apart from the present affection of the respective organ by the object. Mind too does not perceive itself apart from its objects, but it has become a settled identity between itself and its object, thus dissolving the soul's bond to what is other than it, even the difference between the intelligible form and the image, in order to be active. The mind in this state of first actuality is able think "itself by itself [αὐτὸ καθ' αὐτό]," and since it contains everything within itself necessary to become active, it is, as Aristotle says, able to think itself whenever it wants. There are no external restraints imposed upon the mind's active thinking.

Section 2: Thinking Defined by Its Objects

In light of Aristotle's treatment of perception and the vast scope of perception's objects, the reader of *De Anima* is left with the question: what is left for mind to think? Perception not only grasps all possible sensible qualities which constitute the proper objects of each sense, but the common sense also grasps motion and its privation, rest, as well as various quantitative aspects of beings, like number, shape, magnitude, and unity. Finally, incidental perception perceives all other categories of beings besides the intrinsic (καθ' αὐτά) objects of the special senses and the common senses, through what Cashdollar aptly calls "perceptive predication,"[29] perceiving some attribute as predicated incidentally of an intrinsic (καθ' αὐτά) perceived object. All perceptible beings are to be included in this last category. Aristotle gives the examples of perceiving the son of Diares (II.6.418a20–21) (or the son of Cleon [III.1.425a24–26]) by perceiving that the white thing is the son of Diares, or more generally perceiving that the white is this or something else (III.3.428b21–22). This kind of perception thus includes virtually every kind of object which could be conceived, as I can perceive that the wet is water, that the white is flesh, that the white is a human, that the white is Socrates, that the white is sitting, fast, asleep, and so on. All the categories including substance are in this way included in the domain of sensible perception. Given that distinct activities require distinct objects, what then is left for thought to grasp? It is to this question that Aristotle turns at III.4.429b10.

This question is rendered more pressing by the fact that we must not merely discover a sphere of objects proper to thinking, but explain how thinking "thinks all things [πάντα νοεῖ]" (III.4.429a18), as was argued at the beginning of III.4. If indeed the powers of the soul are distinguished by their objects, and perception grasps all sensible qualities along with this vast array of other kinds of being as its common and incidental objects, how can this claim about thinking be right? How can it be true that mind thinks all things when it seems that sensation grasps virtually all things also? How must one distinguish and relate the objects of sense and the objects of mind?

The question is of particular importance for psychology, because an activity is determined by the nature of its object. Aristotle explicitly states at the end of the argument that the relation between essence and concrete individual will be analogous to the relation of intellect which grasps essence to the concrete individual perceived by sensation. So Hicks rightly notes that in this section Aristotle "appears to be discussing the question, are sense and intellect different or are they the same faculty in two different attitudes?"[30]

Continuing the contrast between sensation and thinking, Aristotle contrasts the objects of each of these two activities, which, though distinct, are importantly related. As examples, Aristotle explains how it is through perception that one grasps magnitude, water, or flesh. Magnitude (μέγεθος) is perceived by the common sense, whereas as water and flesh are incidental sense objects (the difference being that water is elemental and thus most strictly defined by its tangible qualities, whereas flesh is a homoiomerous or materially uniform substance composed of the elemental bodies). Within these categories of sense objects, however, Aristotle makes the crucial distinction that will open up a sphere of intelligible objects and allow thinking to think all things. For "magnitude is other than the being of magnitude, and water is other than the being water" (III.4.429b10–11).[31] Using the example of flesh, Aristotle argues (somewhat enigmatically) that one discriminates the being of a thing and the thing itself "either by a different [power] or by something disposed otherwise [ἢ ἄλλῳ ἢ ἄλλως ἔχοντι]" (III.4.429b12–13). For flesh is a form in matter or "a this in a that [τόδε ἐν τῷδε]" (III.4.429b14), just like Aristotle's famous example of "snub" as a certain curvature or shape in a nose. In the cases of these examples from among common and incidental objects, either there are two powers, one which grasps the concrete object, and another which grasps the essence of that object, or else these powers are in reality one power disposed in two different ways.[32]

Aristotle then moves on to the third category of sensible object, the proper object of the special sense, by looking at how heat and cold are grasped. Recall that although the common sense objects were classified as intrinsic (καθ' αὑτά) objects proper to the awareness common to all the senses, Aristotle specified that it is the proper objects of each sense which are most strictly objects of sense: "Of the per se sense objects the proper objects are most strictly [κυρίως] sense objects, and it is with reference to these that the essence [οὐσία] of each sense is disposed by nature [πέφυκεν]" (II.6.418a24–5). Thus hot and cold, the proper objects of touch, are properly discriminated by the sense capacity, as are the other tangible qualities or "those beings of which flesh is a certain ratio [λόγος τις]" (III.4.429b15–16). These basic sensible forms which constitute the proper objects of each particular sense are most truly grasped by sense perception. (It is an interesting question—though it is not addressed at this point in the argument—whether the essences of the proper sense objects discriminated by each corresponding sense are grasped in thought, whether one grasps in thinking the being of hot or the being of red.) But flesh, which is perceived as incidental to these proper objects (that the hot or cold is flesh), is grasped in its essence or form by thinking. What is the relation between that which discriminates the concrete sensible instance of flesh and that which grasps the essence of flesh?

Aristotle expands on his earlier perplexing formulation—that it is perceived either by something different or by something disposed differently—with an equally opaque analogy: "One discriminates the being of flesh by something different [i.e., than the sense capacity which grasps hot and cold], either by something separate [χωριστῷ] or as that which is bent relates to itself whenever it is straightened" (III.4.429b16–18). Certain points can be clearly taken from Aristotle's analogy, which is meant to clarify the relation between the thinking and the sensibility of the human and can be seen as a response to those strains of Plato's thought which take our senses and our thinking to be opposed to each other as becoming is opposed to being and as particularity is opposed to universality. Given that in the previous section mind was seen to be incorporeal in contrast to perception, this analogy is meant as an alternative to conceiving thought which grasps essences and perception which grasps concrete particulars as *simply* distinct, a conclusion which would lead to difficult questions about what constitutes the unity of the opposed individual parts. As Hamlyn writes, this "latter alternative tends to suggest that the intellect by which one judges essences, 'what it is to be an F,' is not after all utterly distinct from the senses."[33] But what is the connection suggested by this mathematical analogy of a crumpled or bent line being straightened out?

What Aristotle means here can be clarified by a similar remark made earlier in I.5, in a discussion of whether the soul needs to be composed of all the elements in order to know:

> For one part or another of the contraries is sufficient to discriminate both itself and its opposite. In fact it is by the straight that we know both the straight and the crooked. For the carpenter's rule is

> the judge for both, but the crooked is neither the judge of itself or the straight. (I.5.411a3–7)[34]

One can take a straight rule and judge whether something is straight or crooked, but with a crooked rule one can neither judge whether a line is straight nor whether it is crooked. Grasping the positive form allows one to judge both itself and the privation of this form. What does this idea have to do with our current passage on the relation between intellect and sensation? Sensation here is like the crooked or bent line, thought to the same line, but now straightened out. From Aristotle's remarks above, we see that sensation is not able to judge the truth of thinking or even of sensation itself, while thinking is able to measure both the truth of sensations and of thought itself. This image suggests that the objects of each activity are the same, while thinking simply has an authoritative grasp of what sensation discriminates imperfectly. But how is this the case if, as Aristotle writes earlier in the treatise, "active sensation is of the particular, but knowledge [ἐπιστήμη] is of universals" (II.6.417b22–23).

Recall, however, that elsewhere Aristotle argues that perception is of the universal, if only unclearly.[35] In incidental perception, one immediately perceives the whole object, yet as an accident perceptually predicated of the directly perceived quality. The transition from sense to thinking and the relation between the two is compared to the straightening of a bent line, I suggest, because the proper categorical structure is restored to the object: one now perceives the attributes as predicated of the underlying object, with the consequence that the true conceptual connection between underlying essence and attributes can be apprehended, rather than the inverted case of the objects being predicated of the qualities, where all connections will appear merely accidental. In straightening the line, one is grasping the very same objects, but in such a way that what is grasped in sensation can actually be judged as adequate or inadequate relative to a genuine standard.

Hence sensation and thinking are ultimately about the same objects, but thinking grasps the essence of them, while sensation grasps the concrete particular. This is true for natural objects as much as it is true of mathematical objects.[36] The conclusion of the section bears upon the central question of whether mind (νοῦς) exists separately from body: "Therefore generally just as the objects [τὰ πράγματα] are separable from matter, in the same way are the [activities] of the mind" (III.4.429b21–22). What does this tell us about the relation between mind and sense? Just as what is thought—the essences of things—are immanent in their concrete particulars as their actuality, our thinking capacity is not merely separate from our sensitive capacity, but is connected to it as potentiality is connected to actuality. There are not two worlds of sensible beings and ideas, just as there are not two selves divided between sensibility and thinking. The line when bent and when straightened is one and the same: the sensitive-rational being has one soul whose sensibility is the material potentiality for its thinking activity—which is authoritative over both and can judge the adequacy of sensible experience and intellectual thoughts.

Section III: Some Puzzles about "How Does Thinking Happen Anyway?"

As a response to the second of the two tasks that Aristotle lays out at the outset of III.4—answering "how does thinking happen anyway?"—Aristotle raises two difficulties:

> If mind [νοῦς] is simple and impassible and has nothing in common with anything, just as Anaxagoras says, how will it think, if thinking is a certain kind of being affected [πάσχειν τι]? For it is insofar as there is something common to both that there appears to be acting and being acted upon. (III.4.429b22–25)

Given that thinking is a certain kind of being affected, the same problem recurs which we find in *On Generation and Corruption*'s treatment of acting (ποιεῖν) and being acted upon (πάσχειν) in general, a problem which recurred concerning nutrition in II.4, perception in II.5, and now thinking in III.4: is like affected by like or contrary by contrary? Since Aristotle has affirmed these Anaxagorean features of mind—particularly being wholly unaffected (ἀπαθές) and sharing no common determination with anything in its complete indeterminacy—certain dis-analogies present a problem with how thinking works along the same lines. Aristotle cites Democritus in *On Generation and Corruption* to elaborate the difficulty with this idea of acting (ποιεῖν) and being acted upon (πάσχειν) between wholly different terms: "It is not possible that others, i.e., differents, should suffer action from one another: on the contrary, even if two things, being others, do act in some way on one another, this happens to them not *qua* others but *qua* possessing an identical property."[37] Thus we must find what thinking shares in common with its object which makes affection of the mind by the object possible. Recall the general principle about action and passion in *On Generation and Corruption*:

> Since only those things which either involve a contrariety or are contraries—and not any things selected at random—are such as to suffer action and to act, agent and patient must be like (i.e., identical) in kind and yet unlike (i.e., contrary) in species. (For by nature

> body is affected by body, flavour by flavour, colour by colour, and so in general what belongs to any kind by a member of the same kind—the reason being that contraries are in every case within a single identical kind, and it is contraries which reciprocally act and suffer action.)[38]

How this principle works in perception is relatively clear compared to thinking. Both the medium and organ are able to be affected by the sensible form because they are continuous with one another and belong to the same genus as the sensible quality, though they are a different species or particular determination of that genus. The flesh through which touch is sensed is composed of the various elements which touch can perceive and is a ratio of the various qualities which define them; though it may not be that particular quality, it is constituted out of the same genus (tangible body) as its objects. In seeing, this commonality with the object is slightly more complex. One may ask how the transparent in air or water is able to receive color when it is said to be colorless. Recall how Aristotle attempts to dispel this by arguing that the light is "in a way [οἷον]" (II.7.418b11) the color of the transparent: transparency thus belongs to the same genus as the colors of which it is receptive. As such, a lit transparent medium or organ can be affected by color, since it belongs to the genus of colors but is itself no particular color.

But the mind has been shown in the first part of the chapter, following Anaxagoras, to be nothing prior to thinking some object, sharing nothing in common with anything else in the world. This opens the question: if mind does not belong to a common genus with the objects of thought, then how is it able to be affected by its object at all? One of the conditions for something being receptive of some determination is that it have some determinate nature defined by its receptivity towards that class of beings. But if mind is nothing in itself, could it be just as well receptive of sensible forms, or any kind of being at all? This is obviously not Aristotle's view: in III.8 he writes that "the stone is not in the soul but its form" (III.8.431b29–432a1). The mind's indeterminate receptivity must be relative only to the objects of thinking, intelligible forms, through belonging to some genus common to its objects. In what way does the mind belong to the same genus as is object, since this is a necessary condition of its being affected by its object?

This puzzle (ἀπορία) thus opens up the second puzzle Aristotle raises: is the mind itself thinkable (νοητός)? This would seem to be the minimal commonality required for thinking to assimilate its objects based on the first puzzle—if both mind and its objects are thinkable, this could constitute the common genus within which acting (ποιεῖν) and being acted upon (πάσχειν) is possible. Further, that the mind is an object of thought was already suggested at III.4.429b9, in reference to how mind, once it has become its object in knowledge (ἐπιστήμη), can then actively think what it understands, and in thinking this object the mind is thinking itself. Hamlyn correctly notes that this puzzle is "the problem of self-consciousness raised analogously for the senses in III.2."[39] While there is no formulation concerning the conscious awareness in thinking explicitly and exactly parallel to the formulation "perceiving that one sees or hears" or "seeing that one sees"—nowhere in Aristotle do we find the locution "thinking that one thinks" (νοοῖμεν ὅτι νοοῦμεν)[40]—this same phenomenon is clearly at issue in the question of mind being thinkable. Just as the opening of III.2 investigated various possible ways this apperceptive aspect of sensation might work, Aristotle here investigates various ways that mind could be considered thinkable (νοητός). Aristotle presents two ways in which mind can be thinkable (both of which he ultimately rejects):

1. If mind is not thinkable through another—i.e., if it is thinkable apart from its objects[41] and if being thinkable is the same in every instance, then there is mind in all things for them to be thinkable. Yet this leads us to the surprising conclusion that all things think. The distinction between what is intelligible and what thinks is wholly collapsed.
2. There is something mixed with mind that makes mind thinkable, which is the same thing that makes (ποιεῖ) anything else thinkable. Yet it would seem that this option contradicts the unmixed nature of mind established earlier in the chapter.

Aristotle then suggests his solution to dissolve the first puzzle:

> Or "being affected by something common" has been defined earlier, that mind [νοῦς] is in a way potentially the objects of thought, but nothing in actuality, before it thinks. Thus in potency it is just like in a writing tablet in which there is nothing written, which corresponds with the mind. (III.4.429b29–430a)[42]

Aristotle is making reference to his discussion of the sense of being affected in the transition from potential mind to knowledge (ἐπιστήμη) in II.5, where he wrote:

> And the one learning and grasping understanding [μανθάνον καὶ λαμβάνον ἐπιστήμην] from being so potentially by the agency of a being in actuality (i.e., one actually understanding) and one able to

> teach, one either must not refer to as "being affected [πάσχειν]," as was said, or there are two ways of being altered [ἀλλοιώσεως], the change from a privative state and the change towards its positive state of possession [ἕξις] and nature [φύσιν]. (II.5.417b12–16)

The potential object of understanding and the potentially understanding mind are thus connected by that for which they are a potency: understanding and being understood. Though it is true that mind has absolutely no determination prior to thinking, and in this way is wholly different from all objects of thought, its very nature is to assimilate and be affected by the objects of thought. This, for Aristotle, satisfies the criterion of commonality required for the very special kind of being affected (πάσχειν) under discussion here: that which leads the passive part of the interaction towards the settled disposition which is its nature. Potential mind and the potential object of thought are connected through the activity of understanding of which they are potentialities. This is the sense of the analogy with the writing tablet, which, though wholly empty, is not a potentiality for just anything (it is not receptive of stones or food), but rather a determinate potentially for the letters that are potentially written upon it.

Aristotle then goes on to explain the sense in which the mind should be understood to be thought:

> And the mind itself is thought just like the objects of thought. For in the case of things without matter the thinker and that which is thought are the same. For contemplative understanding [ἐπιστήμη θεωρητική] and the object of understanding [ἐπιστητόν] are the same. (III.4.430a2–5)

In the state of possession (ἕξις) called knowledge (ἐπιστήμη), the mind has become the object it understands. It is thus the mind which now consists of this actual understanding that will be the object of active contemplation. Mind is thus not completely thinkable on its own, that is, prior to becoming any objects of thought as the pure potentiality prior to learning. The objects of understanding existing within the acquired state (ἕξις) of mind are essences of objects which have been abstracted from the appearances (φαντάσματα) (themselves derived from the sense object that originally produces it) and exist in the mind without matter. The mind then, in actively contemplating what it knows, thinks itself and its objects indifferently. The first actuality of the object understood (ἐπιστητόν) is the same as the first actuality of understanding (ἐπιστήμη); active thinking consciousness will be consciousness of both. So, as Aristotle says, "the mind is thinkable just like the objects of thought" (III.4.430a2–3).

The earlier proposed explanation of the mind's thinkability, that mind (νοῦς) as the essence of what makes something thinkable (νοητός) is present in all things as the cause of their intelligibility, makes all things think and collapses the distinction between what thinks and what is merely intelligible. This explanation is equally dispelled by Aristotle's solution to the problem.[43] It might appear to someone that as the mind is determined by the forms it has become, this is just like the way sensible objects are determined by their intelligible form, since intelligible objects are contained by sensible objects (III.8.432a3–9). But the mind is said to be the same as its objects in knowing (ἐπιστήμη) (i.e., the essences of each thing) *only* as abstracted from their matter. It is then that they are thinkable like the mind to which they are identical. These essences or forms immanent in the underlying objects are not actually thinkable but only potentially thinkable, but they must first produce images through being sensibly perceived, and the form of these objects must then be abstracted from the image and grasped by the first-actuality understanding before they are *actually* thinkable. This preserves the distinction between the essence of an object as the form and cause of its being immanent to its matter, and this form abstracted from that matter as it exists in the understanding. Aristotle writes:

> In things which have matter each of the objects of thought is only potential. Therefore mind [νοῦς] will not belong to these, for it is *without matter* that mind is the potentiality of such things, and being thought *will* belong to this [i.e., the identity of object and mind in first-actuality knowledge (ἐπιστήμη)]. (III.4.430a6–9)

Based on this identity of object and mind in first-actuality knowing (ἐπιστήμη), a new puzzle arises: "But one must examine the cause of not always thinking" (III.4.430a5–6). Mind as first actuality has now internalized its relation to any object outside of itself. It is no longer dependent on either the object of sense or even the sensible image from which the form was abstracted.[44] It is thus wholly a self-relation.[45] It can now think whenever it wants, spontaneously, as it has full possession of its objects; in fact, it is immediately identical with its objects.[46] What explains the fact that the mind is not always thinking about what it knows and understands? In other words, what is the cause of the potentiality of first-actuality understanding? Polansky[47] and Kosman[48] remark rightly, against the previous consensus among contemporary commentators,[49] that this is the question taken up in III.5 on νοῦς ποιητικός (active intellect), that aspect of thinking which explains the distinction between the first and second actuality of mind. For, as Aristotle makes clear in the introduction to his treatment of perception, it is the external objects of each sense which are "the producers of the actuality [τὰ ποιητικὰ τῆς ἐνεργείας]" (II.6.417b20)[50] of each sense.[51] But in the case of thinking, where the objects have become internalized and identified with the mind, the question emerges: what are the productive causes (ποιητικά) of thinking, responsible for bringing the state of possession (ἕξις) of mind as knowing to the full activity of consciousness? Aristotle has already stated the general principle that "all things are affected and moved by something able to produce that is already in actuality" (II.5.417a17–18). If some such further element of the mind is not identified, it would seem on the analogy of sense and thought that the mind should always be in exercise, since its objects are within and already identified with the mind. In seeking the explanation of why the mind possessing knowledge (ἐπιστήμη) sometimes thinks and sometimes does not, Aristotle discovers an intellect which *is* always thinking, or, as he puts it in direct contrast with the human mind, "does not sometimes think and sometimes not think" (III.5.430a22).

Let us go outside the *De Anima* and into an important passage from *On Memory and Recollection* for one final remark on this first-actuality knowing (ἐπιστήμη), the settled knowledge of the one who understands. This unexercised understanding is preserved by *memory* when it is not being thought: "Whenever one has knowledge [ἐπιστήμην] or perception apart from the objects, he thus remembers [μέμνηται]."[52] Memory is not only of the images of sense experiences which become the material for inductive thinking (ἐπαγωγή). There is an epistemic memory that remembers "that we have learned or actively thought."[53] There is memory of intellectual objects (τὸν νοητόν), and crucially for the chapters now under investigation in *De Anima*, "memory, *even of intelligible objects*, involves an image."[54] As such, the settled understanding of mind as knowledge (ἐπιστήμη), though it is not itself a body, is not wholly separate from body in its dependence on appearances (φαντάσματα), since this memory is of images or appearances, and these appearances belong essentially to the center of sensation, located in the heart as the seat of common perception (κοινὴ αἴσθησις).[55] Aristotle qualifies the dependence by making clear that thinking is of *phantasia* only incidentally,[56] just as the geometer who has an understanding of geometry uses drawings to explain and make his knowledge explicit, fully aware that the objects of which he speaks are not the drawings but the objects of thought beyond these to which they refer. What is crucial to note about mind as unexercised knowledge (ἐπιστήμη) is that it is *memory* and thus relies on the images and consequently the sensitive body. According to the standard laid out by Aristotle in the first chapter of *De Anima* (I.1.403a8–10), this kind of mind cannot be considered to be separate, since although it is not a body, it cannot exist without images which are themselves bodily affection. If what has been described about mind to this point were an exhaustive account of the nature and operation of the mind, there could be no thinking being which thinks independently of the bodily activities of soul, that is, nutrition and perception. But, as we know, Aristotle argues there is more to mind than the first actuality of its unexercised understanding. It is to this further aspect of mind that we now pass.

De Anima III.5—The Second Actuality of Human Thinking and Divine Mind (νοῦς)

There is no Aristotelian text (perhaps no philosophical text in the whole tradition) as ambiguous and obscure as *De Anima* III.5, an ambiguity which has been the cause of a head-spinning variety of conflicting interpretations. The large majority of these interpretations since Aquinas follow him in understanding Aristotle to be explaining human intellect with no reference to divine intellect. Victor Caston has very persuasively put this consensus into question in his recent article "Aristotle's Two Intellects, A Modest Proposal." Caston argues about III.5 that Aristotle's

> concern here—as at the climax of his other great works, such as the *Metaphysics*, the *Nicomachean* and the *Eudemian Ethics*—is the difference between the human and the divine. The intellect in question is nothing but its essence (a22–23), which is just actuality (a18), and it functions without interruption (a22) for eternity (a23)—characteristics ascribed only to God, who is unique (1074a35–7) . . . In *De Anima* 3.5, Aristotle is simply putting human psychology in a cosmic perspective . . . in an important respect the second intellect does not belong to human psychology at all, but rather theology.[57]

It seems to me undeniable that the divine comes into view in III.5, for exactly the reason Caston points out—the characteristics shared by the intellect described by Aristotle there are clearly identical with the attributes of the divine intellect he discusses in the *Nicomachean* and *Eudemian Ethics* and book XII of the *Metaphysics*. I want to argue, however, that Caston's argument is too extreme in its separation of Aristotle's theological argument from his psychological argument. Analogously to the *Metaphysics*, Aristotle here discovers what is the most divine aspect of all living activities, the active aspect of human thinking, and because it is the highest he subsequently identifies this activity with the divine.

Kosman argues for the same argumentative structure in *Metaphysics* XII:

> What this suggests is that we need to understand Aristotle's attribution of thinking to the divine in the light of what is essentially a reverse attribution: the attribution of divinity to thinking. That claim that God thinks turns out to mean that since the activity of thought is divine, it may therefore be the clearest icon we have of the being of the divine principle whose essential nature is activity, and on which depend heaven and earth. We say that God thinks because we want to understand the self-directed pure activity that is the activity of the divine, and thinking is the best way to do so, since it most powerfully figures this activity.[58]

To build upon Caston's excellent analysis, I think a fuller interpretation of III.5 needs to put further emphasis on the puzzle at the end of III.4 as the immediate context of III.5; to compare the structure of the analysis of perception into passive and active aspects to this transition between III.4 and III.5 on thinking; and to analyze more rigorously and completely how all the details of Aristotle's analysis of the role of light in vision in II.7 help clarify his explanation of thinking in III.5—in particular the distinction between light and the source of light made in II.7—an analysis which shows that Aristotle's argument is even closer to Plato's allegory of the sun at *Republic* 509b than has previously been supposed.

The structure of III.5 is thus as follows: in the first part Aristotle identifies the active, formal awareness in all thinking to help solve certain puzzles about thinking in III.4. He then goes on to identify this aspect—when it is separated—with the divine activity. Although ultimately the divine activity is the exemplary and explanatory principle of all lower forms of living being, in the structure of the argument Aristotle proceeds by identifying the divine on the basis of discovering the most honorable mortal living activity. It is this activity, separate from all the other living activities necessarily associated with active thinking in human beings, which Aristotle identifies with the activity of the divine.

The previous chapter has addressed that aspect of mind which is receptive of intelligible forms or essences through learning. Once these essences exist in the mind as knowledge (ἐπιστήμη), the transition between this potentiality of being thought and actively thinking these objects must be explained, and as we saw in particular, it must be explained why this object within the mind is not always being thought. Further, certain aspects of what mind (νοῦς) has been shown to be are difficult to explain if one considers only this receptive aspect of mind. For example, it is impassible (ἀπαθές) in only a very qualified sense: having no determination prior to thinking, it does not lose its own determination in becoming its object, and its being affected is a deeper realization of its own nature. But a change *does* occur: what was originally indeterminate becomes identical, as with, for example the essence of being human. Nothingness becomes something, ignorance becomes knowledge.

The chapter opens by inferring from the fact that in all of nature there is a distinction between material and formal aspects, that this must also be true in the soul—presumably because soul is the principle of natural, living beings.[59] This distinction exists in nature, the soul is an instance of a natural being, therefore such a distinction must also apply to the soul.[60]

What is the nature of this general distinction that exists in all natural things? Aristotle identifies the one side as the matter with respect to each kind (ὕλη ἑκάστῳ γένει); this is all the determinations in potency.[61] The qualification here "with respect to each kind [ἑκάστῳ γένει]" indicates that we are talking about the underlying matter relative to the particular kind of being in question, meaning that this material aspect is the potentiality for becoming all things that the particular kind of being in question has the capacity to become. On the other side is what he calls the cause (τὸ αἴτιον) and that which has the capacity to make (ποιητικόν), by virtue of making all things (τῷ ποιεῖν πάντα). Again, the qualification "with respect to each kind [ἑκάστῳ γένει]" applies to this formal aspect of every natural being, meaning that it is responsible for producing all the determinations characteristic of that particular kind of being. This distinction between material and formal aspects is not made specifically in reference to mind or soul, but rather is merely a reference to the material and formal aspects of *every* being in nature.

Aristotle makes reference to two analogies to elaborate his argument in III.5: art (τέχνη) and light (φῶς). The analogy with art (τέχνη) is invoked not in relation to mind in particular, but to this universal distinction in nature between the formal and material aspect of a being, while the analogy with light is used to illustrate how this distinction functions within mind—we will thus postpone our discussion of light for a moment. τέχνη (techne) refers to the expertise, the knowledge which *produces* this form in this matter. It is therefore productive (ποιητικός). Art (τέχνη) is being used, as is often the case with Aristotle, as a figure to help clarify nature, since what always occurs together in a natural being occurs separately and in distinct moments in the production of an artificial object. Art (the medical art, for example) is both the knowledge of the form which the matter has the capacity to become (in the medical art, health),[62] and an understanding of the means required if this form is to be realized in this particular matter.[63] Finally, this form (e.g., health) is that for the sake of which the art is employed. Thus in the analogy with art (τέχνη), one has a productive cause in which formal, efficient, and final causes are united. The same will be true of active thinking: it is the efficient cause, the form, and the final cause of the mind. But in contrast with the example of an art (τέχνη) (and also in contrast with the activities of nutrition and perception), mind has no *independently* existing underlying subject receptive of its formal determinations. For as we have seen, mind is *nothing* prior to thinking. Mind thus exhibits a complete unity of the four causes.

Aristotle then asks us to apply this form/matter distinction to the question at hand: what mind is and how thinking works?

> And there is, on the one hand, a mind [i.e., as was already described in III.4] in virtue of becoming all things, and mind by virtue of making all things, just like a certain state [ἕξις] like light. For in a certain way light makes colors in potentiality into colors in activity. (III.5.430a14–17)

Here Aristotle is in effect saying: "we have already discussed the material side of mind, which is the capacity to become all things by virtue of being affected by the object of thought. The actuality of this material mind is knowledge [ἐπιστήμη]. Let us now turn to mind in the sense of that which makes these objects actually thought. In order to think about this active, formal side of mind, recall our comments about light in II.7." To understand what the active aspect of mind is, how it is related to mind as receptive and how it is related to mind as separate in divine thinking, one must rigorously follow how the analogy with light works by comparing II.7 and III.5. Doing so will help bring out more clearly Aristotle's conception of the nature of mind, and also make more sense of why Aristotle included the details he did in his examination of the role of light in seeing.

Light is the *energeia* of a characteristic of certain substances, which Aristotle calls the transparent (διαφανῆ), meaning that through which something appears. The transparent is the external medium of vision, that through which the colored object appears to the eye. One of the difficulties in understanding the analogy between mind and light comes out of a crucial dis-anology between them: light is simply the medium of seeing, while the mind is the very thing that does the thinking. There is no real medium in thinking, as there is for all five senses, even touch.[64] There is a good reason for this: thinking is not a relation to an object outside of itself: it is a self-relation, when mind thinks its objects it is thinking itself. There is nothing through which the objects must appear to the mind *besides the mind*. In other words, the mind is itself the medium of thinking. It is, in a sense, an intelligible transparency in which objects of thought appear to thinking, much like the transparent in water, air, many solid objects, and the eternal body above through which sun, moon, stars, and planets appear to us. The mind prior to this distinction between potentiality and activity, is analogous to the transparent (διαφανῆ).

This association of mind with the transparent is apt. The objects of vision, colors, are defined as what overlies that which is in itself visible, and being in itself visible is glossed as having in itself the cause of its visibility.[65] This is to distinguish color from the transparent, which is visible, but not in itself or absolutely, but only on account of another color appearing through it. Nothing is seen in the transparent unless it is conveying the color of some object, whereas the object has its color (if only potentially) in itself, apart from any other conditions required for this color to be seen. For this reason, the transparent is both without any color of its own (ἄχρουν), while somewhat figuratively its transparency *is* its color.

Now consider mind: it too is not itself any particular intelligible form or determinate essence prior to thinking. The object of thought has *in itself* the cause of its being thinkable, while the mind is thinkable by virtue of this object existing within it, in the sense of first actuality of mind which is identical with the objects it understands.

The transparent is not always actively able to fulfill the role of medium in sensation. The transparent is sometimes only potentially transparent, that is, the intervening medium is sometimes dark. It is only when the transparent is actively transparent, that is, when it is light, that color as the object of vision can be seen.

Aristotle writes:

> Light is the activity of the transparent *qua* transparent. Potentially, that in which there is this [i.e., light], there is darkness. (II.7.418b9–11)
>
> It seems that light is the contrary of darkness, but darkness is the privation [στέρησις] of such a state [ἕξις] from the transparent, with the result that it is clear that light is the presence of this [state, ἕξις]. (II.7.418b18–20)

There is thus one underlying being, the transparent, which when in a potential, privative state, is darkness through which no vision can take place, even if the objects are present in this potentially transparent air or water. In contrast, when actively being that through which objects of vision can appear, it is light, the cause of their being actively seen.

It is this activity of the underlying transparent to which the mind, or aspect of mind, treated in III.5 is compared. Where light makes the objects of vision, potential colors, actually colors (which I take to mean "actually seen"),[66] active mind makes the potentially thought objects of the understanding, actually thought. Or, more precisely, νοῦς ποιητικός (active mind) is the very activity of thinking which makes the objects of knowledge (ἐπιστήμη) actively contemplated. It is the active consciousness of that which is implicitly understood in knowing (ἐπιστήμη), when the mind's attention is directed towards the content of what it understands. This is a dis-analogous aspect between light and νοῦς ποιητικός (active mind): whereas light is the activity of a third thing—the transparent—beyond object and perceiver, an external element which causes their active identification, thinking has no external medium: it is the mind itself which is the transparency through which objects actively appear to it. So just as transparency is equivalent to the mind itself, light as the activity of the transparent corresponds in the analogy to the activity of the mind itself, that is, active contemplation (θεωρεῖν).

But if ancient and medieval interpreters were generally wrong to understand the analogy of light as pointing towards the existence of something beyond thinker and object thought which is the cause of them both, they are absolutely right that such a transcendent cause beyond the division of subject and object exists for Aristotle, and is implicit in the analogy if one presses the correspondence between his analysis of thinking and his explanation of the role of light in vision. Recall that light, on this analysis, is not self-caused:

> Light is in a sense the color of the transparent, whenever it is in actuality transparent, *by the agency of fire or some other such body above*. (II.7.418b11–13)

> [Light] is the presence of fire or some other such thing in the transparent. (II.7.418b16–17)

Beyond the activity of the transparent there is the source of illumination, either fire or one of the bright heavenly bodies. The question then is whether our text in III.5 identifies some element in thinking analogous to the source of light in the transparent.

◆ ◆ ◆

One might ask, however, why does Aristotle employ the language of *two* intellects if these are inseparable aspects of one intellect, the passive, receptive aspect and the side of active conscious awareness? The structure of the Greek clearly indicates a much deeper distinction than, for example, the analogous distinction in perception, that is, the material affection of the organ by the sensible form and the formal awareness of this affection. This latter example is genuinely inseparable: as Kosman writes, "There is nothing *in addition* to the πάσχειν τι which *constitutes* the awareness of perception,"[67] and again, "The separation of sense and the faculty of apperceptive awareness neither can nor need be achieved."[68] One could never refer to the passive and active aspects of sensation as separate perceivers, as these are merely the material and formal aspects of one event. With the analogous distinction in mind, however, the Greek structure we are considering in III.5 clearly does suggest two distinct minds: "καὶ ἔστιν ὁ μὲν τοιοῦτος νοῦς τῷ πάντα γίνεσθαι, ὁ δὲ τῷ πάντα ποιεῖν [and there is on the one hand a mind of such a kind by becoming all things, and on the other hand (a mind of such a kind) by making all things]" (III.5.430a14–15). This must be accounted for, lest we be guilty of the sin identified by Caston:

> Why on earth should Aristotle have thought there were *two* intellects? On this question, commentators have often been as loyal as the Emperor's councilors, pretending there isn't a problem at all. They smooth over Aristotle's plain talk of two intellects by speaking of two functions or aspects of a single intellect instead.[69]

We must face head-on that while the analogous passage in the analysis of perception really does identify two aspects of one perceiving organism, Aristotle is clearly talking here about two minds in a much more distinct fashion.

But on the current interpretation the moments are already far more distinguishable than in perception. For these are two separate events, distinguishable in time, by two minds, which, though they can very well belong to the same human individual, are very different kinds of beings. In III.4, we are speaking of the ignorant, purely potential mind of the neonate who "belongs to the class of knowers and ones who possess knowledge [ὁ ἄνθρωπος τῶν ἐπιστημόνων καὶ ἐχόντων ἐπιστήμην]" (II.5.417a22–24),[70] prior to having developed any settled understanding or epistemic state of possession (ἕξις), and explaining how this mind makes the transition towards being an actual knower (if still potential because not actively thinking about its knowledge). Here in III.5 this mind, which is all its objects not at all in actuality, but only in potentiality, and in fact, is nothing prior to thinking, is referred to twice as the matter (ὕλη). This fits perfectly with how Aristotle distinguishes the two kinds of potential mind in II.5: "a genus of such a kind [i.e., the genus of human defined as a potential knower] and the matter [τὸ γένος τοιοῦτον καὶ ἡ ὕλη]" (II.5.417a27). Let us recall once again the passage at length, since it is crucial for an understanding of the distinction in II.5:

> There is someone knowing as we would call a man "knowing" because the man belongs to the class of knowers and those who possess knowledge. But we also call someone "knowing" as already having the knowledge of grammar. Each of these is not potential in the same way, but the one because he is the genus of this kind and the matter [ὁ μὲν ὅτι τὸ γένος τοιοῦτον καὶ ἡ ὕλη], the other because he is able to contemplate when he wishes [ὁ δ' ὅτι βουληθεὶς δυνατός θεωρεῖν], as long as nothing from outside should prevent him. But the already actively contemplating is knowing this A in the strictest [κυρίως] sense. (II.5.417a22–30)

Notice the very same structure indicating two distinct kinds exists here as we find in our distinction of two intellects in III.5, this time referring to two distinct kinds of potentiality, one belonging to an infant, the other belonging to a learned adult. These are the two senses of "being a potential general" that Aristotle later identifies: the way a boy is a potential general when he does not yet know anything about strategy or warfare but belongs to the genus which is able to learn this; and the way an adult is a potential general once he has learned all the necessary skills for the job and needs only to actively put them into use.[71] It would not seem out of place to speak of these two cases of mind as two distinct minds.

The kind of transition under discussion in III.5, effected by νοῦς ποιητικός (active mind), has also been previously analyzed in chapter II.5:

> The one possessing understanding [ἐπιστήμη] becomes someone actively thinking, which either is not alteration, for it is the development into itself and to activity [ἐντελέχειαν], or another kind of alteration. There it is not right to say that the thinker, whenever he thinks, is altered, just like the builder when he builds. (II.5.417b5–9)

Here there is absolutely no transition besides the transition from potential to actual. With the nothingness of the merely potential infant mind, ignorance is destroyed through learning. This initial state is not preserved in the transition. There is thus a change (κίνησις), even if this mind is in an important sense still impassible (ἀπαθές), because through this change the child is simply becoming or realizing its own nature, and because there was no positive characteristic destroyed in the transition. But with the transition from knower to active thinker, absolutely nothing is lost: this is a transition free of all change (κίνησις), and this is why Aristotle calls it "σωτηρία" (II.5.417b3), a complete preservation in which absolutely nothing is lost; what is implicitly known is not altered except for the fact that it is actively contemplated.[72] Further, there is no distinction between the activity and the cause of the transition to this activity; for it is the very activity itself (the active thinking awareness directed at the unthought knowledge) which is the cause of the transition from potentiality to actuality.[73]

So while Aristotle in III.4 was able to consider potential mind and its transition towards the mind possessing knowledge as unaffected (ἀπαθές) in the qualified sense that it was, after all, not ultimately becoming other than itself when its ignorance was destroyed, but it was becoming itself more fully, there is also a sense in which this transition is not fully unaffected (ἀπαθές). Given that its previous quality is destroyed in the process, it does suffer change. He was able to refer to this potential mind as unmixed, since it could not have any formal determination if it is to be receptive of all formal determinations—this separated it from body, which is of necessity qualified in some determinate way. But the actualization of this potential mind is only unmixed in a qualified way, since it is through abstraction from the image, itself bodily and a product of an active sensation, that potential mind learns or receives forms. The actualization of this second mind has no such external involvement or dependence on an image (though the epistemic memory that it illuminates does), and it is thus unmixed in a more precise sense than first potentiality or first actuality. For this reason it is thus separate from body in a deeper sense also. For in perception, as we have seen, the active awareness which distinguishes sensitive from non-sensitive affection is in no way separate from the affection of the organ which receives the sensible form. In thinking, though, the receptive moment and the moment of awareness are separable (though they can presumably occur together in one event, since one must think something in order to learn it. As Kosman writes, "In general a ἕξις is established by those very activities for which it is a dispositional capacity").[74] Thinking awareness, as opposed to sensitive awareness, is genuinely separate (χωριστός); even by the standards laid out in I.1, it is not dependent upon *phantasia* at all. Thus Aristotle writes of the conscious awareness that makes the known objects actively contemplated: "And this mind [νοῦς] is separate [χωριστός] and unaffected [ἀπαθής] and unmixed [ἀμιγής], being in its essence [οὐσία] activity [ἐνέργεια]" (III.5.430a17–18).

That which makes the transition from knower to thinker is simply conscious awareness, the intellectual transparency through which what we understand appears to us. By this awareness the darkness of uncontemplated knowledge is illuminated and everything potential is made actual. All that is left for the mind that has the dispositional understanding of knowledge (ἐπιστήμη) is to turn on the light to illuminate the dark room of its uncontemplated content, its objects with which it has become identified through learning, and the mind does this by itself whenever it wishes. This light is the conscious attention of our mind. The essence of this added element is *energeia*, for activity is all that needs to be added to the understanding mind to make it thinking in the fullest sense and to make its objects thought in the fullest sense. The essence of νοῦς ποιητικός (active mind) is simply actuality or activity.

Once Aristotle says of νοῦς ποιητικός (active mind) that its essence is *energeia*, clearly there is some connection with that principle disclosed in *Metaphysics* book Lambda XII "whose very substance is *energeia*."[75] But it is important not to get ahead of ourselves with the passage at hand. At this point in the text we are speaking of that thinking conscious awareness responsible for actualizing the epistemic memory of settled understanding. It is through the agency of this consciousness, which the knowing human can turn on "whenever he wants," that the full actuality of human thinking is achieved. This is not yet God. But we will soon discover that in fact, this awareness, when separated from the mere potency of the unthinking knower, is the same in kind as the divine activity.

This most active and activating part of thinking, Aristotle next remarks, is the most noble feature of all living activities. For thinking is more honorable than the other living activities,[76] and this active aspect of mind is the most honorable feature of thinking, since "the agent is always more honorable [τιμιώτερον] than the patient, and the principle than the matter" (III.5.430a18–19). Thus in disclosing the active consciousness of mind, its second actuality, we have discovered the highest and noblest living activity, an activity both independent of body and independent of *phantasia*. The implicit conclusion of this discovery, which Aristotle makes explicit in what follows, is that as the highest activity, this must be what God is doing. This is precisely the argument one finds in *Metaphysics* XII.7, where Aristotle writes: "That which is capable of receiving what is thought of, that is, substance, is thought; it is *active* when it grasps it, so that it is the latter rather than the former that is the divine which thought seems to involve, and active thinking [θεωρία] is most pleasant and best."[77] This active thinking is the highest living activity in which we can engage, and it is the one activity which is fully divine: in actively contemplating, we are doing precisely what God always does.

Having thus discovered the living activity independent of body, one of the most fundamental tasks of the *De Anima* has been achieved. Soul has been discovered in its own nature apart from body—and this soul is simply *energeia*, the active thinking consciousness responsible for all thinking. Consequently, because we have discovered one of soul's living activities to be independent of body and imagination, we have been able to conclude that this activity *can* in fact exist apart from the other activities. There is a being whose only living activity is active thought, and this being, since its life is the best there could be, is God.

Aristotle notes,[78] once again, actual understanding (ἡ κατ' ἐνέργειαν ἐπιστήμη)—that is, first-actuality knowing—is the same as the thing (τῷ πράγματι; III.5.430a19–20).[79] And while it appears in a way that this knowing (ἐπιστήμη), which is potential thinking, comes prior to thinking, since objects must be learned as known (ἐπιστήμη) before they can be thought, on the whole this is not true—active consciousness is first. Even the neonate has νοῦς ποιητικός (active mind), despite the fact that it has no learned objects or knowledge (ἐπιστήμη) to illuminate, since this receptive side of its thinking is empty. But νοῦς ποιητικός (active mind) must always be present, or else the learning that would fill the potentiality of its mind with actually understood objects would be impossible, since one only learns and discovers truth through active, conscious thinking. Thus νοῦς ποιητικός (active mind) plays an important role and is present from birth, though it has nothing of which to be conscious until it finally acquires some kind of knowledge (ἐπιστήμη).[80]

Aristotle then writes of this highest activity: "But it does not sometimes think and sometimes not think [ἀλλ' οὐχ ὁτὲ μὲν νοεῖ ὁτὲ δ' οὐ νοεῖ]" (III.5.430a22). Compare this with what he says of the transparent in II.7: "For the same nature is sometimes dark and sometimes light [ἡ γὰρ αὐτὴ φύσις ὁτε μὲν σκότος ὁτὲ δὲ φῶς ἐστίν]" (II.7.418b31–419a1). If the parallel between the transparent and the human mind holds, it seems that Aristotle is here contrasting human intellect with divine intellect. Human intellect sometimes exercises its knowledge by actively thinking it, and sometimes does not actively exercise this knowledge, leaving it in potency, or darkness. In contrast, the divine intellect, which is separate from any other activity and which has no potentiality, is always thinking.

Aristotle closes his analysis of the role of light in vision in II.7, however, by noting that the cause of the activity of the transparent, or light, itself is always active, whether or not the transparent is light or dark, actively transparent or merely potentially so: "And fire is seen in both, that is in the dark and in the light, and this from necessity. For the transparent becomes transparent by virtue of this" (II.7.419a23–25). The cause of light or the activity of the transparent, that is, fire or one of the upper bodies, is lit independently of whether transparency is actively transparent. It is the cause of its own light, and therefore is lit and visible even when the transparent is inactive and dark.

Thus both the active transparent and the cause of light in the transparent are light. The difference between them is that the former is an intermittent active state of an underlying object which is also intermittently inactive and is caused by the presence of something other than itself, whereas the latter is eternally active with no potentiality and is wholly the cause of its own activity.

The same relation holds between human mind and divine mind. Human mind is not necessarily active, since one's knowledge need not always be actively contemplated. But the full active awareness of our thinking apart from the receptive aspect of human mind is identical to the divine thinking activity, with the difference that active human thinking is the activity of some independently underlying potential for that activity, while divine thinking is pure activity completely devoid of any potentiality and without anything underlying it. It is clearly this kind of intellect to which Aristotle refers in the concluding section of the chapter: "When it is separated [χωρισθείς],[81] it alone is that which it is, and this alone is immortal and eternal" (III.5.430a22–23).

As we have seen, because this formal case of thinking is independent of body or any bodily process, it can exist in separation. When we consider νοῦς ποιητικός (active mind) not as that part of us which illuminates our potentially contemplating mind and its potentially contemplated objects, but in itself separate from everything else, we have arrived at the nature of the divine activity. νοῦς ποιητικός (active mind), when it occurs separately, alone of all things is just that which it is—a formulation indicating that in essence it has no potentiality—it is fully active, actual being, with no underlying potentiality to be otherwise. Alone of all things it is eternal and immortal. Aristotle here is talking about that being in which active thinking occurs separately, with no other psychic powers—this is clearly God and only God, since in humans νοῦς ποιητικός (active mind) does not occur independently of mind's receptive side. And the adverb μόνον ("alone") makes clear that we are speaking only of God, νοῦς ποιητικός (active mind), as separate, a principle of pure transparent consciousness: this eternity and immortality could not be predicated of human mind—even its most honorable part.

The last lines of the chapter thus remind us of the difference between human mind and divine mind. "But we do not remember, because[82] this mind is unaffected [ἀπαθές] but the mind which is able to be affected is destructible [οὐ μνημονεύομεν δέ, ὅτι τοῦτο μὲν ἀπαθές, ὁ δὲ παθητικὸς νοῦς φθαρτός]" (III.5.430a23–25). Here Aristotle is anticipating a possible objection which might be made to his analysis of νοῦς ποιητικός (active mind): how, Aristotle, could you imply that mind in us is unaffected (ἀπαθές), given that our minds *do* decay? The mind which was, at the height of its scientific understanding, able to contemplate its knowledge at will, suddenly becomes no longer able to do so. The mind returns, in effect, to the ignorance of the child prior to learning. Recall the passage we cited from I.4,[83] where Aristotle poses the question of how to reconcile on the one hand what appears to be mind's impassivity, and on the other hand that it seems to be affected, especially in old age. But Aristotle there argues that in perception, when the aged lose their vision, this is not due to a difference in their form or soul, but rather the bodily instrument by which the soul sees. Replace the faulty eye, Aristotle says, and the old man would see like a young man, which leads us to the conclusion that "old age is not an affection of the soul, but that in which the soul exists [i.e., the body], just like drunkenness and disease" (I.4.408b22–24). Any activity of the individual which is dependent on body can be worn out—this includes discursive thinking (διανοεῖσθαι) which depends on images, and emotions like loving and hating. In the sentence most relevant to our statement in III.5 about not remembering, Aristotle explains the failure of memory in exactly this way:

> On account of this [i.e., the compound individual who possesses mind] being destroyed, one neither remembers nor loves. For they were not part of this [i.e., the mind] but of the community [of mind and body], which has perished. But perhaps mind is something more divine and unaffected [ἀπαθές]. (I.4.408b27–29)

It is the inevitable decline of the body of the aging that explains mind's losing its ability to activate itself at will. Since, as Aristotle has argued, the active consciousness of mind is impassible, it cannot be this that fails when mind is no longer able to perform its previous activities. It is thus here ascribed to not being able to remember the content which consciousness actively grasped. This "something other within" which is worn out (καὶ τὸ νοεῖν δὴ καὶ τὸ θεωρεῖν μαραίνεται ἄλλου τινὸς ἔσω φθειρομένου; I.4.408b24–5) is the seat of the images necessary both for learning and for preserving the knowledge learned, without which no active contemplation (θεωρεῖν) is possible. The activating condition is not destroyed, but its necessary conditions are no longer present. Aristotle clearly states in III.8 that "whenever one actively thinks [θεωρῇ], it is necessary simultaneously to think a certain appearance or image [φάντασμα]" (III.8.432a8–9). Once the basis for images is destroyed, one loses both the ability to learn and the ability to remember what has been learnt, returning in a sense to one's childlike ignorant state, lacking the content for active consciousness to illuminate.[84] This decay occurs because of the wearying involvement of the body with contrariety, which erodes the necessary conditions of receptivity for human thinking—his point in III.5 being that active consciousness in us does not decay and is not responsible for this inability to think.

The human mind, referred to here as νοῦς παθητικός (mind which has the capacity to be affected), is thus qualified as such, because thinking is what it is in the human only insofar as it grasps an object initially other than itself. As we have seen, this is accomplished initially through the affections of sensation, and subsequently the affection of the objects of thought learned through images. Our knowing, though manifesting divine, purely active consciousness, is essentially determined by its relation to being affected by its objects. As he writes in the *Eudemian Ethics*, "With us welfare involves a something beyond us, but the deity is his own well-being."[85] Our thinking, though always a self-thinking and separate in its active exercise, cannot be understood apart from this passivity and relation to objects other than itself—the mind has become its objects, but these objects are ultimately distinct from mind, in the sense that thoughts are always *about* something. As Aristotle writes in *Metaphysics*: "Evidently knowledge and perception and opinion and understanding have always something else as their object, and themselves only by the way."[86] In perception, the perceiver sees that it sees and hears that it hears, but only insofar as it has been affected by its object, as the senses do not perceive themselves directly. As we have seen, this is true of thought in a more complex way. Thought is not activated by an external object, but it is affected by the intelligible form in the underlying images, and these images are ultimately images of perceptions which in turn are of objects. So the mind always thinks itself, but *only* as determined by its object by having learned them—mind cannot think itself as the nothingness prior to any determination. In a passage explaining that thinking and perception are desirable in that one desires to become determinate like one's objects, Aristotle explains that

> we are not in ourselves possessed of each of such characters, but only by participation in these qualities in perceiving and knowing—for the perceiver becomes perceived in that way and in that respect in which he first perceives, and according to the way in which and the object which he perceives; and the knower becomes known in the same way.[87]

In contrast to this, the divine active exercise, conceived of as separate from all the passivity which characterizes human thinking, receives nothing from without. Human thinking requires an object in order to become determinate; divine thinking is determinate in itself.

It is to this essentially relational aspect of human cognition—its thinking and the perception required for thinking—which Aristotle refers in his formulation νοῦς παθητικός (mind in its capacity to be affected). Besides the various affections of the living being required for survival and perception of the external world, thought is affected in both of the qualified senses of being affected (πάσχειν) identified by Aristotle in II.5:

1. In the transition from purely potential mind to mind possessing knowledge (ἐπιστήμη)—where its initial emptiness and ignorance is destroyed by the objects of its acquired knowledge, but which is affected only qualifiedly in the sense that this transition does not simply make mind other than itself, but develops into a state of possession (ἕξις) and its inner nature.
2. In the transition from this acquired knowledge (ἐπιστήμη) to the active contemplation of this knowledge; there is affection only in the sense of the transition from potentiality to actuality, in which what existed potentially is in no way destroyed, but rather fully preserved, in the transition.

For these reasons Aristotle refers to human mind as παθητικὸς νοῦς (affected mind). Neither of these can be said of the divine mind, which in comparison is unconditionally unaffected (ἀπαθές). The former is thus destructible, while the latter is eternal and immortal. But νοῦς ποιητικός (active mind) understood as active consciousness, whether one takes it as an aspect of human mind or as separate and on its own in the divine activity—is the cause of all thinking: "Without this nothing thinks" (III.5.430a25). Hence through identifying νοῦς ποιητικός (active mind) as the conscious awareness of active thinking—the principle (ἀρχή) or formal principle of mind (νοῦς)—Aristotle has explained both the condition that, when present, distinguishes a thinking being which is determined by an intelligible form from a non-thinking being determined by its form, as well as explaining why the epistemic mind that has become its objects is not always thinking. In the same way that he closed III.2.427a14–16 on the awareness accompanying all perception, Aristotle could just as well have closed this chapter on active mind with the words: "concerning the principle [ἀρχή] by virtue of which we call a living being intellective, let this account suffice."

De Anima III.6—The Relation of Mind and Its Object to the Lower Activities and Their Objects

In *De Anima* III.6, the last chapter of that treatise devoted entirely to his treatment of theoretical intellect, Aristotle deepens his analysis of the activity of mind and its identity with its object explained in III.5. Though III.5 is surely the most debated passage in the treatise, III.6 is perhaps the most difficult chapter in the whole work and, probably due to its obscurity, has elicited surprisingly little commentary from modern interpreters.[88] It is not immediately clear what is even the subject matter of the chapter; he is analyzing the thinking of indivisibles (τῶν ἀδιαιρέτων νόησις), yet what these indivisibles are is a matter of some dispute. Most agree that by indivisibles he means the essence (τὸ τί ἦν εἶναι) of an object. But even for those who can agree on what the basic subject matter of the chapter is, exactly what he is saying about these indivisibles and their relation to our thinking is not obvious.

In III.3, Aristotle argued that identification of sense and intellect made understanding error impossible.[89] Having now differentiated thinking from sensation and offered his account of thinking, Aristotle returns to the question of error, comparing the infallibility of proper sensation to the infallibility of the thinking of essence. By the opening of III.6, a reader of the *De Anima* might be inclined to think at this point in the argument that even if the thinking of essence were infallible, that all the rest of thought's operations which are based on this essential grasp would be fallible and accidental. For though the building block of all sensation, the proper object, is grasped infallibly, once anything is combined with this perception, error can occur.[90] I argue that the purpose of III.6 is to show how the mind in fact remains wholly self-related in the thinking activity of demonstrations and definitions derived from the underlying synthesizing and dividing of the infallibly grasped essence.

Aristotle claims that, like proper perception, both active contemplation (θεωρεῖν) and uncontemplated knowledge (ἐπιστήμη), the potentiality of this activity, are infallible. This, he explains, is because the objects of thought are undivided (ἀδιαίρετον), while falsity always has to do with a synthesis of terms.[91] This was already implicit in his account of falsity in sense objects: the proper objects of sense admit of no falsity, since they are the undivided building blocks for any non-proper object of perception, while both the common and incidental sense objects admit of falsity because they are syntheses of a proper object of sense with some other perceptual object. One cannot perceive motion or size or the son of Cleon without there being some underlying proper object of sense accompanying that object in a non-inferential compound sense-object (αἰσθητόν). Yet with the case of proper objects of sense—white or hot—each is undivided in the sense that one cannot resolve the awareness of these most primitive objects of sense into further component parts.

Akin to the fallibility of accidental perceptual predication is the synthesis of two thoughts—σύνθεσις νοημάτων—which can admit of falsity. What is this νόημα (*noema*) and how does it differ from the direct object of thought—the νοητόν (*noeton*)? The word is mentioned only once before in *De Anima* I.3 in a passage we will attend to in a moment. It occurs once in III.7,[92] and twice in III.8.[93] Just like the αἰσθήματα (*aisthemata*) examined in the last chapter, which should be understood as the affections at the periphery of the sensitive animal as distinct from the fully active sensation which has reached the origin and principle (ἀρχή) of perception, these νοήματα (*noemata*) are thoughts on the way to the active thinking of an essence, but are not yet themselves the objects of thought (νοητά). They are spoken of in each instance as the elements of a synthesis, in contrast with the objects (νοητά) which are thought on their own.[94] Following the example given by Aristotle at III.6.430b6, when I am making a noetic judgment that "Cleon is white," "Cleon" and "white" are the νοήματα (*noemata*) of the thinking synthesis[95] my mind produces.[96] Besides the excerpt from Empedocles on love as the unifying force responsible for "synthesizing separate terms," Aristotle also cites the synthesis "incommensurable" and "diagonal" in the thought "the diagonal is incommensurable" (III.6.430b28–31).

This kind of noetic predication involves the synthesis of the νοήματα (*noemata*), Aristotle argues. These terms are also implicitly combined with a certain instant of time: "But it is not only false or true that Cleon is white, but also that he was or will be" (III.6.430b4–5). A synthesis that makes the claim not only that Cleon is white right here at this moment, but that he was white and will be white, synthesizes all the moments of Cleon's existence into the judgment. Aristotle writes that if thinking is "of things that were or things that will be, then we think the time in connection [to the νοήματα (*noemata*)] and synthesize it" (III.6.430a31–430b1). This adds further possibility of error, since a synthesis which is true of Cleon in the winter months may become false at some future moment or may have been false in a past moment if his color does not always remain white.

All these syntheses admit of falsity, that is, the predication of "y" to something that is "not-y." This kind of synthesis is the only condition under which something can be false. What is essential to synthetic thought, Aristotle concludes, is that the terms are in themselves separate and unconnected, and it is the mind which produces unity out of them: "The producer of unity [τὸ ποιοῦν] is in each case the intellect" (III.6.430b5–6). Thus the unity is not in the object itself, but in the unifying activity of the thinking mind.[97]

Aristotle may have in mind here the way Plato argues that essence is grasped through dialectic, as a process of collection and division, that is, collecting and separating the right subjects and predicates. In later dialogues like *Sophist*, *Statesman*, and *Philebus* but also clearly present in *Phaedrus*, thinking the essence of something is accomplished through this very activity of collection and division, and all objects are constituted out of a primary contrariety of limit and unlimited or sameness and otherness. For Aristotle, in contrast, objects are not constituted out of contraries, but are unified substances (οὐσίαι) within which contrariety is comprehended, and thinking the essence is thus a grasp of that unity prior to the synthesis of contraries. With the Platonic view, in Aristotle's account, the unifying form is not in the things but in the knower.[98] This is one of Aristotle's most basic criticisms of all his predecessors, that "nearly all thinkers agree that being and substance [οὐσία] are composed of contraries."[99] In substance Aristotle takes himself to have discovered the unity in objects prior to division and comprehensive of it.[100] Corresponding to this object he is showing in *De Anima* how he has discovered a thinking activity beyond Platonic dialectic, which he states is "merely critical," having to do only with the truth and falsity of synthesis and division (διαίρεσις).[101] Beyond criticism, Aristotle says that "philosophy claims to know," and philosophy "differs from dialectic in the nature of the faculty required."[102] *De Anima* III.6 is in a sense an explication of this faculty beyond the merely critical stance of dialectic.

Aristotle wants to show that thinking in its essence lies beyond these activities of synthesis and division. Of course synthesis and division are crucial aspects of what thinking does, but when the essence of something is grasped, what is grasped and what does the grasping are unities prior to any division. In the conclusion of the chapter, Aristotle will seek to show that certain forms of synthetic and dividing mental operations, namely demonstration and definition, do not actually involve the accidental and external connections imposed by mind, but are rather to be included in the thinking (νόησις) of indivisibles and regarded as infallible. These activities, which do involve synthesizing further terms with the essence, depend upon this prior and more fundamental grasp of an essence comprehensive of all the object's division and multiplicity within itself.

◆ ◆ ◆

Let us step outside the chapter for a moment to look back at the passage from I.3 where the concept of νοήματα (*noemata*) and their synthesis is first introduced, for Aristotle there introduces certain problems which must be recognized in order to understand what he is arguing in III.6.

In I.3 Aristotle offers a series of refutations of the idea that the soul is self-moving, arguing that change (κίνησις) (whether self-caused or caused by another) cannot belong to the soul at all, at least in the sense of *directly* being in motion.[103] Aristotle opens the chapter through a series of puzzles (ἀπορίαι) involved in this notion of soul moving the body through being itself self-moved. One especially important criticism of this idea is the following:

> But if the soul moves itself, it is also itself moved, with the result that, if ever change [κίνησις] is a displacement [ἔκστασις] of that which is moved *qua* that it is moved, then the soul must depart from its essence [οὐσία], if it does not move itself incidentally, but the change [κίνησις] is in itself part of its own essence. (I.3.406b11–15)

The soul in moving itself would thus become separated from its own nature. The soul prior to moving itself could not preserve itself in the soul at the end of the motion. Plato attempts to solve this and other problems inherent in the idea of self-motion by considering the motion of the soul to be the most perfect kind of motion, that is, the circular motion of the heavenly bodies, forever returning upon itself. The soul in moving itself would thus not lose itself, since the end of its motion would be the same as the beginning; the soul therefore would not lose its essence (οὐσία). Thus circular motion would solve certain problems which arise if one considers the soul's self-motion in terms of linear motion, where beginning and end of the motion exclude each other. To see whether this solution to the problem of self-motion withstands rational scrutiny. Aristotle focuses his criticism in the second half of the chapter (I.3.406b26ff.) on Plato's *Timaeus*.

As Aristotle notes, in identifying the soul as circular motion, Plato was clearly trying to express something about thinking in contrast with the lower activities of soul like sensation and desire, which would be characterized as linear motion.[104] As we have seen, this is an idea Aristotle himself affirms: that in sensation, change (κίνησις) is involved, whereas in thinking there is none.[105] But is circular motion an adequate way of describing this unchanging activity beyond any alteration? We need not go through all of Aristotle's criticisms of the *Timaeus* conception, but two criticisms in particular are important for understanding III.6. Aristotle first introduces the νόημα (*noema*) when he argues that "mind is one and continuous, just as thinking is. And thinking is the thoughts [νοήματα] it thinks" (I.3.407a6–8). Mind will thus be ultimately unified in just the sense that the connections between its thoughts are unified. But thoughts do not follow each other like one point follows another on the same line, with one point simply alongside the next—thinking should not be considered on the model of spatial movement. Rather, thoughts in a chain of reasoning are connected as an ordered series (like numbers).[106] So it is important to understand exactly how thoughts are connected in order to understand the nature of the activity of mind. The continuity of mind will correspond to the continuity of the concepts it connects.

After identifying certain problems with thinking about practical mind as circular motion endlessly revolving, at I.3.407a24 Aristotle then raises a set of similar problems involved in thinking of theoretical mind as circular: "And instances of theoretical thinking are similarly limited. For every reasoning [λόγος] is a definition [ὁρισμός] or a causal explanation [ἀπόδειξις]" (I.3.407a24–26).[107] There are two kinds of reasoning—definitions and causal explanations—which simply do not fit this description of the activity of thinking as circular motion starting from a beginning which the reasoning returns to in the end.

> But causal explanations both start from an origin [ἀρχή], and have in a way an end [τέλος], the reasoning [συλλογισμόν] or conclusion. But if they do not come to a conclusion, they do not however return again to the beginning [ἀρχή], but advance in a straight line always adding middle or extreme terms. But circular motion is always returning to its beginning [ἀρχή]. (I.3.407a26–30)

If causal explanations (ἀποδείξεις) were truly circular, they would not be explanatory, simply restating the beginning point or premises as their conclusion. But because there is a difference between the beginning and end of a causal explanation, it is genuinely informative. Yet in order to be informative, the movement must be linear rather than circular and limited rather than endless. Aristotle then concludes his criticism by noting that the same thing is true of definitions: "And definitions are all limited" (I.3.407a30–31). A definition might also be considered circular, in that what one predicates of the subject is not different from the subject itself. But there has to be some difference between the terms, or else the definition would be purely tautological. A circular definition of man would be: man is man. A genuinely informative definition of man—rational animal or two-footed animal—will not be simply endlessly returning to the beginning, but will also have this character of limited linearity.

If this is the case, however, and the changeless motion of the circle endlessly returning upon itself does not characterize thought, how to explain what happens when one moves from a premise to a conclusion or a subject to its defining predicate? If the thinking of the beginning point or the subject simply loses its nature or essence (οὐσία) in the transition to its predicate or conclusion, then all thinking beyond the grasp of undivided essence will be simply accidental, and no connection in thought will involve any necessity whatsoever. All noetic syntheses would be just as fallible as perceptive syntheses of proper and common objects or proper and incidental objects. Aristotle gives a hint as to what his own solution will be to this problem when he argues further against the mind as circular self-motion doctrine that "thinking [νόησις] seems more like a certain kind of rest and stopping than like movement" (I.3.407a32–33). I argue that this solution is to be found in III.6.

◆ ◆ ◆

To illustrate his point about how the divisions and multiplicity present in the object of thought are grasped, Aristotle uses the quantitative examples of cognizing a line and cognizing a point. For there are, he argues, two meanings of being undivided (III.6.430b6). The first sense corresponds to the example of a certain length which is undivided (undivided in actuality), but divisible into smaller constituent parts (divided in potentiality). One could grasp this length as an undivided whole. Though it could be separated into constituent parts, one's grasp of the line is not a synthesis of these potentially existing parts, but an undivided grasp of the whole comprehensive of and prior to these potential divisions.

Were one to grasp the object in this synthetic sense, grasping one actually divided segment of the line and then another, this process would take up time: "Thinking each of the halves separately, it also divides the time just like the lengths" (III.6.430b11–13). In other words, if mind thinks the line as two halves, it will think one and then the other in distinct periods of time as distinct as the lengths themselves. Further, if one thinks the line as a unity which synthesizes these two distinct halves, this unity will take up the same time it would take to think one and then the other in succession. The time taken to think the compound is itself a compound of the time taken to think each half separately.[108] But in grasping the object as a whole comprehensive of these implicit distinctions within it, one grasps the object completely as an undivided whole in every single moment, existing in this sense outside of time (which is the measure of change or κίνησις). So if one grasps the object as an undivided whole prior to division, one thinks the object in undivided time prior to the division into distinct temporal moments, whereas if one grasps the object as divided into parts, the thinking itself will occur through divided time. Beyond change or process (κίνησις) and consequently lying outside of time, this thinking of the indivisible in this sense passes the criterion for being considered an *energeia*.[109]

Aristotle then translates the conclusion of his geometrical analogy into the actual object under investigation in this chapter: how the object of thought, the form or essence of the object, is grasped, and what the relation is between the undivided grasp of the form and the multiple distinctions and oppositions that lie within it in potency. He writes: "But one thinks the undivided—not the quantitatively undivided but undivided in form—in an undivided time and by an undivided [activity] of the soul" (III.6.430b14–15). When one thinks the intelligible form of the thing, its essence or οὐσία, all conceptual distinctions in the object and all distinctions of its temporal development are comprehended within it. The moments of time relative to the object are comprehended by the essence, precisely because a being never escapes its essence while remaining itself; no matter what changes it undergoes through time, the essence will remain the same so long as it exists. Thus the essence of something, that which exists in each thing as undivided (and inseparable from it),[110] makes all the potentially divisible conceptual and temporal moments of the thing into one. This immanent unifying principle is to be contrasted with the external unification by mind of the divisions in an object evoked by Aristotle earlier in the chapter (III.6.430b5–6). In this way, the divisions in an object, either conceptual or temporal, are grasped in and through the understanding of the undivided substance underlying and comprehending them. And in the thinking of this comprehensive essence, given that the mind is identical with its object in the activity of thinking, the mind is also undivided and outside of time.

Aristotle then contrasts this undivided unity comprehensive of distinction within itself with another geometrical analogy. The second sense of the undivided (ἀδιαίρετον), opposed to the line which was actually undivided but divisible, is the point (στιγμή), conceived as a division within this larger whole (the line). This point is itself a division (ἡ δὲ στιγμὴ καὶ πᾶσα διαίρεσις [III.6.430b20]), but cannot be further divided. It is therefore actually divided but potentially undivided.

What then is the relation between the undivided grasp of the whole, and the distinctions or divisions within this whole? Aristotle further explains this relation between grasping the object as undivided through its essence and as divided through its various attributes by comparing it to the way one grasps the privation of something through its positive form (III.6.430b20–21). One knows the privation through knowing the positive form, although one knows neither the positive characteristic nor its privation by merely knowing the privation. Analogously, because the essence contains its necessary attributes within it, then in a causal explanation (ἀπόδειξις), both the middle and the conclusions are potentially contained within it, and are simply unfolded or made explicit through syllogistic reasoning. Thus once one is thinking the essence and has made one's mind identical to it, one's mind has then become comprehensive of these implicit divisions and distinctions within the object. Aristotle writes: "It is necessary for the knower to be [the contrary] and to contain it in itself" (III.6.430b23–24). Thus mind does not lose its grasp of essence in doing science, that is, in demonstrating further conclusions of its beginning (ἀρχή). The subsequent terms or propositions of the syllogism are contained within the premises, simply exhibiting the nature of the effects of which it is the cause. In this way the activity of causal explanation (ἀπόδειξις) is contained within the thinking of essence, and the conclusions, far from being merely accidentally predicated of the origin (ἀρχή), are comprehended and exhibited by unfolding what is already there within it.

This leads us to reaffirm what we concluded about the nature of mind in III.4–5, this time from the perspective of the nature of the object with which the knowing mind has become identical: "If there is no contrary to a certain one among the causes, the knower [i.e., the knower that knows this cause] knows itself and it is *energeia* and separate" (III.6.430b24–26). When mind knows the essence or οὐσία of a thing comprehensive of its potential divisions—for it is characteristic of an οὐσία (substance) that there is nothing contrary to it[111]—this mind is not thinking something external to itself or the object when it thinks the divided moments of its object. In this case it is not as if one had to import distinctions from without and then subsequently synthesize them with the underlying essence. Rather, the mind is here thinking itself as identified with the essence it thinks. In this way the mind is separate from all externality—a complete self-relation, even when engaged in syllogistic proofs that certain attributes belong to an underlying essence. This is further identified as *energeia* for reasons already cited: it is an activity beyond all process or change, lying consequently outside of time. This is the sense of Aristotle's comment in I.3 that "thinking [νόησις] seems more like a certain kind of rest and stopping than like movement" (I.3.407a32–33). For though thinking is not simply static and inert, in its activity it remains itself completely.

This is not only true of mind's apodictic activity, but also when the mind predicates the essential definition of the essence. Aristotle goes on to argue:

> Assertion [φάσις] predicates something of something, like affirmation [κατάφασις], and all these are either true or false. But this is not always the case with mind; it predicates the definition [τί ἐστι] of the essence [τὸ τί ἦν εἶναι], and this is not an instance of predication. (III.6.430b26–29)

When one unites the essence of something with its essential definition, though it is not simply a tautology, it is not a synthesis of extrinsically related terms, but again, a simple unfolding of distinctions inherent in the thinking (νόησις) of the indivisible essence.[112] Once again, the activity of defining an essence is comprehended with the thinking (νόησις) of the indivisible essence. There is no synthesis, and hence no possibility of falsity. The relation is wholly intrinsic to the mind and the essence it knows, and occurs within the prior unity of this noetic identity.

Chapter III.6 then ends where it began, by comparing the infallibility of active sensation's identity with its proper object with mind's active thinking of indivisible essence. Just as the proper object of sensation is the fundamental undivided building block for all the subsequently more complex and synthetic perceptive predications, the essence is the proper object of thinking, serving as the building block for the synthetic operations of mind in causal explanation (ἀπόδειξις) and definition. But now we can recognize the deep difference between sensation and thinking. All the connections made in perception are accidental. Recall that the common sensible object is only incidentally related to the proper sensible object,[113] as is of course the incidental sense object. There is no necessary connection of the proper sensible white to either a common sensible like shape or an incidental object like the son of Diares. Thus both kinds of sense object which depend upon the grasp of the proper object are completely fallible. This grasp of the proper sensible is not comprehensive of any predicates, whether of the common (III.1.425a15; III.3.428b22–24) or incidental sense objects, both of which are merely incidentally related to the proper sense quality. Further, the proper object is not comprehensive of time. The total particularity of the proper sensation is true only in the moment it is being actually perceived: as Aristotle states elsewhere, "Nor is there memory of what is present, but only sense-perception. For by the latter [i.e., sense-perception] we do not know what is future or past, but what is present only."[114] This punctual indivisibility of the proper sense object, which is indivisible in the sense of the point rather than the line in Aristotle's mathematical analogy, is to be contrasted with the indivisibility which characterizes the comprehensive universality of the thinking of an object's substance, having absorbed all the object's potential distinctions and changes over time into itself.

Let us close our reflections on III.6 by considering once again Aristotle's methodological reflections on the relation between knowing something's essence and its attributes:

> It would seem that knowing the essence [τὸ τί ἐστι] is useful in relation to knowing the causes of the attributes of the οὐσίαι, just as in mathematics, to know what is "straight," "curved," "line," "surface," contributes to behold the number of right-angles to which the angles of a triangle are equal. But also conversely the attributes contribute a great part towards knowing the essence [τὸ τί ἐστιν]. For whenever we are disposed to show all the attributes according to *phantasia*, either all of them or most of them, then we are best disposed to speak of the οὐσία. For the beginning [ἀρχή] of all causal explanation [ἀπόδειξις] is the essence [τὸ τί ἐστιν], with the result that definitions which do not contribute to knowing the attributes, and not even to easily guess concerning these things, are clearly spoken dialectically and are all empty. (I.1.402b16–403a2)

Through induction (ἐπαγωγή), the attributes which are grasped according to images, originating necessarily from attributes grasped in perception, can lead eventually towards the grasp of the essence. At that point, these attributes grasped in perception and communicated to mind through images which were grasped fallibly and without any necessary connections between them can be subsequently understood in their necessary connection to the thinking of essence. In this way, everything that was grasped of an object in sensation—its color, odor, shape, size, and so on—all this is comprehended within the grasp of the object as substance (οὐσία) as the potential divisions within this essence, attributes which can be manifested by the mind in proofs and definitions. Consequently, even those activities by which these attributes are grasped—the five proper senses (and even the generation of their organs through the nutritive activity), common sense, incidental perception, imagination, the various modes of discursive thinking employed in induction (ἐπαγωγή)—all these are similarly contained within mind in active contemplation as the potentiality of which it is the full actuality.

In the terms of Aristotle's geometrical analogy employed in II.3, "the prior term in the series is always contained in potency (by the subsequent term), both for figures and for ensouled beings, for example the triangle in the quadrilateral and the nutritive in the sensitive" (II.3.414b28–32). One reaches the thinking of the essence through the various distinctions grasped in sense and imagination. But when one returns to them in light of its thinking of essence, this is not a departure from thinking (νόησις) back to sense and imagination, but this occurs within the activity of thinking, which thus remains distinct (χωριστός) from them, meaning that it does not need to go back into sense or images in order to find attributes which are then subsequently extrinsically related by an act of mind. The object of thought contains within itself in potency its various divisions and distinctions—these are not simply externally related in the various distinctions grasped in sensation—and consequently thought contains within itself the various powers of soul by which these distinctions and divisions are grasped. In this way, Kurt Pritzl is right to argue that "*De Anima* 3.6 is an integral part of the main argument of *De Anima* 3.4–8."[115] For it is in III.6 that the acquisition and contemplation of essence treated in III.4–5 is connected to the thinking movement of definition and causal explanation.

Conclusion

In the opening of *De Anima*, Aristotle defines the principal object of his investigation to be the nature (φύσις) and substance (οὐσία) of the soul. We seek to know the nature of the soul in terms of what it is in itself, not in terms of what belongs by virtue of its association with the body. This can be revealed most clearly if we can observe the affections of the soul proper to it (ἴδια πάθη), apart from its relation to the body. It is in studying the mind that we see most explicitly what the nature of soul is. In doing so, we have discovered that the nature of soul apart from body is *energeia*—a completely self-fulfilling, self-preserving and self-related activity through which the living being remains identical with itself. This principle is present as the impassibility (ἀπάθεια) we have detected in all living beings. Their unaffectedness (ἀπάθεια) is manifested in how the plant is able to maintain itself in the assimilation and destruction of its environment, as well as how the animal is able to be determined by the objects in its environment in their own nature without either destroying them or losing itself in the process. In both these cases the living being preserves itself through its being affected by external objects beyond the destructive affections that characterize inanimate nature. As its living activities become progressively more comprehensive and receptive of what is different from and opposed to them, the living being becomes more able to preserve itself in its identification with its corresponding object. This unaffected aspect of living activities is thus exhibited both in the self-maintaining activity of nutritive soul and the general sensitive awareness of sensitive soul. Yet only in thinking and rational awareness do we see a living activity that involves absolutely no such process or change (κίνησις), whether growth, alteration, or locomotion, precisely because it is not a bodily activity, and is not a relation to an object outside the soul. By virtue of the fact that we can investigate the activity of soul independently of body by investigating mind, we are better able to understand what its nature is even in the exercise of life's lower activities though more obscurely.

By discovering these affections (πάθη) of soul which are not bodily, Aristotle also discovers that there can be a being that thinks independently of the embodied activities to which human thinking is necessarily bound. It is towards the life exhibited in this principle that all lower forms of life tend, including human life. It is surely in this way that Aristotle's idea that God moves the world by being loved[116] is to be understood: the divine activity of thinking exhibits the kind of life that all living beings desire to attain in their desire for self-actualization to progressively successful degrees.

One grasps the nature of something not by looking at its most primitive appearance or some other stage in its development, but at the nature the being in question exhibits at the summit of its development. Similarly, one must look at the fullest actualization of soul in order to understand its nature, and the serial logic of the hierarchy of living activities implies that the lower activity is always taken into the higher as its potentiality. For nutritive soul, which must be perpetually active in order for the living being to survive, is at the level of sensation distinguished into potential and actual exercise. The activity of nutritive soul is the potentiality for sensitive soul: the animal is maintaining itself in nourishing itself even when the sensitive activity which defines it is merely latent in sleep. The same kind of further differentiation then occurs in the transition from sensation to thinking. Here thinking becomes further differentiated into potentiality, first actuality, and second actuality, and the sensitive apprehension of the world is a potency for the sake of the actualization of our thinking relation to the world. Just as nutrition exists for the sake of sensation, sensation exists for the sake of thinking, and, as Aristotle shows in III.6, it is contained within our thinking relation to the world. While these activities exist for the sake of thinking, thinking exists for the sake of nothing further: "This activity alone would seem to be loved for its own sake; for nothing arises from it apart from contemplating."[117] This relation of instrumentality that holds between the lower and the higher is most obvious in the human, who contains all these activities in one soul rather than as distinct activities characterizing taxonomically distinct kinds of living beings (i.e., plants and animals and the various species of each). But plants and animals are not striving directly towards the mode of being exhibited by humans, but rather towards the divine thinking activity disclosed in III.5, which is the point towards which even the human mind tends.

Soul, in its own nature apart from body in thinking, has been defined as *energeia*. The conclusion of Aristotle's argument, left merely implicit in *De Anima*, is explicitly stated in *Metaphysics* XII.7 in the most striking terms:

> And life also belongs to God; for the actuality of thought is life, and God is that actuality. And God's essential actuality is life most good and eternal. We say therefore that God is a living being. Eternal, most good, so that life and duration continuous and eternal belong to God; for this *is* God.[118]

Life is unqualifiedly defined as the perfectly self-preserving, self-related activity of thinking. Active thinking is *energeia* beyond any change (κίνησις) or potentiality, the actuality for which all other living activities are potentialities; it is in this sense that the argument of *De Anima* is the progressive unfolding of one substance from its most primitive appearance into its most developed actuality. And unlike humans, God is nothing but this active thinking, pure *energeia*. Though God is not soul, since soul is the principle of life in embodied living beings, the living activities of these embodied beings are fully grasped only in relation to the principle in them which is apprehended in its separation and purity in the divine life, which exhibits all those characteristics mortal living beings seek to manifest to varying degrees of success.

Though this pure life of God can be achieved by the human in contemplation,[119] Aristotle is clear that if the plant is most properly defined by the nutritive activity of soul, and the animal is most properly defined by the sensitive activity of soul, it is God and not the human who is most properly defined by the *energeia* of active contemplation:

> But such a life would be too high for man; for it is not in him in so far as he is man, but in so far as he has something divine present in him; and by so much as this is superior to our composite nature is its activity superior to that which is the exercise of the other kind of excellence. If intellect is divine, then, in comparison with man, the life according to it is divine in comparison with human life. But we must not follow those who advise us, being men, to think of human things, and being mortal, of mortal things, but must, so far as we can, make ourselves immortal, and strain every nerve to live in

> accordance with the best thing in us; for even if it be small in bulk, much more does it in power and worth surpass everything.[120]

The human is not defined as the theoretical living being, but as practical mind (νοῦς). Taxonomically this distinguishes human life from animal life on the one hand and God's life on the other: thus the human is precisely classified as being a political animal, using intellect to rule his practical affairs. Investigating this properly human side of mind would lead us beyond the scope of the present chapter into the last sections of the *De Anima* on soul as the cause of animal motion and practical mind as the cause of human practical activity. But the difference between humans and other animals, as we have seen, is that the highest living activity characteristic of God, though it is sought by every other kind of living being, is actually attainable for the human intermittently. It is therefore contradictory and unnatural for humans, alone of mortal living beings able to attain what is universally desired, to ignore this divine element in us, just as contradictory and unnatural as it would be for a plant to stop nourishing itself or an animal to stop perceiving and moving.

Aristotle closes his reflections on divine being in *Metaphysics* XII by investigating what is the relation of this principle to the world it rules. He asks

> in which of two ways the nature of the universe contains the good or the highest good, whether as something separate and by itself, or in the order of the parts. Probably in both ways, as an army does. For the good is found both in the order and in the leader, and more in the latter; for he does not depend on the order but it depends on him. And all things are ordered together somehow, but not all alike—both fishes and fowls and plants; and the world is not such that one thing has nothing to do with another, but they are connected. For all are ordered to one end.[121]

Following the military metaphor, God is both separate from the world and also present in the parts as the end towards which all subordinate members are ordered. They all ultimately seek the end dictated by the ruling leader. I hope to have shown in the course of this argument that according to the analysis of soul and life in *De Anima*, one could just as well substitute the divine predicate "life" for "good" and this relation would equally hold. God is the one life independent of all other living activities, but all life involves one common structure that is realized in progressively more successful forms as one moves through nutrition and sensation to thinking. All living beings seek the full actuality of thinking and everything that our analysis of thinking has shown this actuality to involve: self-sufficiency, independence from externality, complete identity of thinker and object, uninterrupted eternal self-preservation, and independence from body, matter, and potentiality. Aristotle elsewhere[122] says that through having perception animals possess mind, but obscurely; perception is thus the same basic activity as thinking, yet not so fully realized. The same, I contend, could even be said of plants, although they lack all cognition. Humans, like plants and animals in their various ways of assimilating their environments to themselves, strive to achieve this divine mode of living. What distinguishes the human is that, while animals and plants necessarily fall short of divine actuality in their respective self-actualizations, the human in its own full self-actualization through contemplation attains what other modes of life were unsuccessfully seeking.

CHAPTER 5

The Soul That Moves the Body: Mortal Self-Motion and the Circular Motion of the Outermost Sphere

Living, ensouled beings can be marked off from unensouled beings by the fact that they are cognitively aware of their world, and that they move themselves through space. Thus soul is above all else the cause of the living being's cognition and self-movement.[1] Although this characterization has to be qualified[2] by Aristotle's discovery of the essential connection between soul, life, and the nutritive activities of self-nourishment, growth and reproduction, activities which involve neither awareness nor locomotion in II.4, the work as a whole remains governed by this dichotomy. In II.5–III.6, Aristotle has treated the various modes of theoretical awareness: the five senses, imagination,[3] and thinking. At the opening of III.9, Aristotle recapitulates the distinction between cognition and motion, and moves from the first division on cognition[4] (which he calls κριτική) to the second division on the soul's role as mover of the body through space. The three chapters that follow (III.9–11) focus on the kinetic function of soul.[5]

Given the centrality of this cognitive (κριτική) / locomotive (κινητική) distinction to both the structure and argument of the *De Anima*, it is surprising just how short and elliptic Aristotle's treatment of the soul's involvement in animal locomotion is.[6] The basic point I would like to argue about Aristotle's chapters on the soul's causal role in animal locomotion is that they should be understood as mirroring the argument of Aristotle's treatment of cognition in the first division. While the "critical" side of soul's activity comprehends both sensation and thinking, the argument of III.9–11 tries to establish that the primary distinction on the desiring or moving side of soul's activity is between ἐπιθυμία—appetitive desire—and βούλησις—rational desire. Two points that Aristotle has made about theoretical cognition are being made analogously in this section devoted to practical, locomotive cognition:[7] that sensation and thinking are not really independent or opposed powers,[8] but rather degrees of realization of one activity; and that the analysis of the highest activity of cognition offers a glimpse into the nature of God's activity.[9]

I argue that Aristotle's treatment of how soul moves the body accomplishes three distinct but related objectives.

First, the analogy between sensation and thinking on the one hand, and appetitive desire (ἐπιθυμία) and rational desire (βούλησις) on the other, undermines the notion that the nutritive, sensitive, intellective and desiderative activities are activities of distinct *parts* of the soul. Rather, Aristotle's argument shows that ultimately all these activities are contained on both sides of the primary division between soul's cognitive (theoretical) and locomotive (practical) powers.

Second, just as he sought to show that sensation is not opposed to thinking but rather that the actuality of sensation is a potency for the actualization of thinking, Aristotle wants to show that appetitive desire is not opposed to rational desire, but rather that appetitive desires are the origin and basis of rational desires, and that they are necessary for rational desires to motivate the human to move or act.[10]

Third, Aristotle wants to show, against Plato, that our practical activity is not simply a loss of the self-sufficient independence exhibited in our theoretical activity. Like theoretical activity, practical activity exhibits the same character as *energeia* beyond process (κίνησις), in which the beginning and end of practical activity coincide. Putting the argument in a cosmological context, Aristotle shows how the harmony of rational and appetitive desire in virtuous practical activity mirrors the most perfect, self-sufficient motion in the universe—the circular motion of the outermost sphere.[11]

The Separability of Locomotive Soul

At the conclusion of III.7, after his introductory comments about desire, Aristotle asks the following question which has often perplexed interpreters:[12] "Whether or not it is possible for mind to think something separate, since it is not itself separate from extension, must be examined later [ἆρα δ' ἐνδέχεται τῶν κεχωρισμένων τι νοεῖν ὄντα αὐτὸν μὴ κεχωρισμένον μεγέθους, ἢ οὔ, σκεπτέον ὕστερον]" (III.7.431b17–19). Is it possible for mind to think something separate from the extended, sensible world when it does not itself operate independently of this world? The question can appear strange given the points about theoretical mind discussed in III.5: mind in its active contemplation of its own knowledge is separate, unaffected, and unmixed. It operates beyond change, insofar as it is already identical with the content of its contemplation, so that nothing is either added or subtracted from itself prior to the activity of its thinking. The theoretical mind contemplating its knowledge of intelligible form operates independently of sensation and the sensible—mind thinks its own content independently of any dependence on anything outside itself. This is the grounds for its ability to think whenever it wants, since it contains everything necessary for its activity wholly within itself. Why then is Aristotle here raising doubts as to whether mind can think something separate from sensible extension, since it is not itself separate?

Given the fact that III.7 has been dedicated to mind in its practical, desiring mode, and that the remark seems incompatible with what has just been concluded about theoretical mind, I take this to be a question about the operation of practical mind[13]—in fact, it is *the* question of Aristotle's treatment of how the soul moves the body. The problem is this: in all practical activity, there is a necessary, absolutely ineradicable engagement of our senses with the sense objects immediately present in the always changing external environment. Given this unavoidable need in animal movement to sense the circumstances of one's immediate surroundings, the practical mind cannot operate independently of the sensible world. In light of this constraint, can it "think something separate" from the sensible world? In other words, can it attain to any general truth about the practical world that isn't simply determined and dragged around by the effect of an immediately present sensible object on the organism? Is there an inner freedom to practical activity which maintains an independence of the causal effects of the environment on the self-moving animal?[14] Can it operate according to itself and its own practical thoughts independently of the appetitive impulses generated from without by the objects currently presented to it?[15] Can it even have such a thought? If it can, then there is a way that practical mind might not simply just lose itself in sensible change and externality, and in its own qualified way, distinct from the independence which characterizes the theoretical mind, it might be able to operate in independence of the external.[16] If the practical mind cannot think the separate, then the accomplishment of chapter III.3 on imagination—the separation of a thinking activity distinct from sensation through the intermediate term of *phantasia*—is negated in practical thinking, and the ancient identification of thinking and sensation, where thinking is always relative to a present object, dependent on changes in the body and the changing environment, would hold true for our practical thinking.[17] As Aristotle says, this question of practical mind's "thinking the separate" must be examined later—and I propose it is principally the answer to this question that Aristotle seeks in his treatment of how the soul moves the body in III.9–11.[18]

Importantly connected to the question of whether and in what way the practical mind can move the body in pursuit of an end originating from within itself independently of sensible externality is the question of where to locate the soul's causation of animal and human self-movement relative to one of Aristotle's most important conceptual distinctions: the difference between motion (κίνησις) and *energeia*. A motion (κίνησις) is an activity that is fundamentally incomplete, in the sense that it does not contain its end within itself, but rather is directed towards an end that remains distinct from itself throughout its activity. In motion (κίνησις) the beginning point of the change, as well as every intermediate stage on the way to the result, excludes the end, and conversely, the end excludes the process, such that a motion (κίνησις) ceases once its end is attained. In contrast to motion (κίνησις), an *energeia*, that is, *energeia* in the strictest sense, is fundamentally complete. The end is wholly present and in the possession of the agent at every moment of its activity. The beginning and end of the activity always coincide, which Aristotle illustrates by showing how in an activity the present (ongoing) and perfect (completed) tense are inseparable. It is significant to note Aristotle's examples to illustrate the character of *energeia*: the cognitive examples of seeing, understanding, and thinking (at every moment of active seeing, we are seeing and have seen, are thinking and have thought).[19]

At this point of the *De Anima*, where Aristotle turns from an analysis of perception and thinking to how the soul moves the body through space, it might seem that we are making a simple transition from the study of *energeia* to the study of motion (κίνησις). It seems initially implausible that animal and human self-movement through space could be anything but motion (κίνησις). When I walk from home to school, I am not at the end point until the activity ceases—beginning, end, and intermediate points all exclude each other. So in the turn from the analysis of cognition—especially from the culmination of that investigation in III.5 where active contemplation of the mind's knowledge is shown to be an *energeia* beyond the change (κίνησις) required for both nutrition and sensation to occur—do we simply move from completeness to incompleteness? But notice that in his discussion of motion (κίνησις) in *Metaphysics* IX, Aristotle focuses on the change that occurs on the side of the mover, and on the change that occurs on the side of the thing moved. But what about *self*-motion? Does the label motion (κίνησις), the *energeia* of the incomplete, exhaust the nature of self-moved motion, where mover and moved are united in the organism?

It is important to note that there *is* a form of movement through space which does not seem to exhibit characteristics of motion or change (κίνησις) understood as opposed to *energeia*—that is, of course, *circular motion*, which

Aristotle calls the *first* motion (πρώτη φορά).[20] Movement in a circle moves from the same point to the same point, while rectilinear motion moves from a point to its contrary (up to down, right to left), or at least to a point which is other than the beginning.[21] In circular motion beginning and end are united,[22] so that its activity is constantly returning upon itself.[23] This motion is complete in itself because it cannot be added to, whereas rectilinear motion can be extended indefinitely.[24] One cannot distinguish beginning, middle, and end as separate moments of a process, and thus in its motion it does not change, never losing what it is through the course of its activity.[25] It is thus motion beyond change (κίνησις)—the closest that something moving and extended in space can come to what Aristotle calls *energeia* beyond change, an activity which perpetually preserves its origin and does not lose itself in its result.[26]

Aristotle criticizes his predecessors for not having adequately distinguished the soul from the body it moves, "supposing something not itself in motion to be unable to move another, taking the soul to be one of the things in motion" (I.2.403b29–31). In other words, previous thinkers draw the soul into bodily extension, so that the soul loses itself in sensible externality and change. For Aristotle, Plato tries (unsuccessfully)[27] to avoid this, at least in terms of the mind's thinking activity, by conceiving of the soul's thinking activity as the circular motion of the heavenly bodies. In the *Timaeus* passage cited by Aristotle, Plato identifies the motions of the heavens with the motions of the soul, distinguishing the activity of *mind* from the soul's embodied activities just as circular motion is distinguished from rectilinear motion. So while mind's circular motion returns upon itself, perpetually preserving its unmoved center through the course of its activity, both sensation and appetite are rectilinear, losing themselves in their ends or objects. In the Platonic view, the soul's practical engagements with the world, which always involve sensation and appetite, in no way contain their ends in themselves. In contrast, we know from the *Nicomachean Ethics* that Aristotle distinguishes *praxis* from *poiesis* by the fact that practical activity contains its end within itself.[28] In my view, this section of *De Anima* helps to clarify why Aristotle holds this view of *praxis*.

Aristotle has several criticisms of this identification of heavenly motions with the soul's theoretical activity, most of which stem from the problem that, in trying to distinguish thinking mind and its circular motion from the soul's embodied activities, Plato actually fails to distinguish soul from body, since only a body can move through space. I want to show that Aristotle rejects this too literal "physiology" of the soul, while ultimately accepting it in a qualified way. He seeks to show how the soul's movement of the body is in a nonliteral sense circular, and also that this applies not only to the soul's thinking, but rather that all self-movement manifests some degree of this self-returning circular activity.

Practically Interested Awareness—Locomotive Desire as a Mode of Cognition

Although Aristotle's treatment of the question of what in the soul moves the body begins most explicitly in *De Anima* III.9, he actually makes the turn to the soul's practical activity two chapters earlier in III.7, when he turns from our theoretical sensations to what could be called desiderative perceptions, that is, the sensation of objects as pleasant and painful. The movement to a consideration of desire is a transition to the question of how the soul moves the body, since he will show how desire is the cause of locomotion. What emerges from the argument is that desire is not really a distinct activity from perception, but that it is itself a mode of perception.[29] Aristotle is seeking to establish that desire and awareness, the two major divisions of the soul, are fundamentally unified—that desire is ultimately a form of what I would call "interested" awareness, to be distinguished from the disinterested awareness of the theoretical side of the various modes of cognition.[30] The result is that the distinction between movement and awareness, which the pre-Aristotelian tradition took to be the significant characteristics of ensouled life, is not only the chief structural division of the treatise, but the most significant and comprehensive division in Aristotle's conception of the soul.

What distinguishes our desiderative sensations and thoughts from our theoretical sensations and thoughts is the fact that the object is not just perceived as it is in itself, but as it stands relative to the good of the organism. In other words, it is a perception of an object as pleasant or painful, good or bad. In this way desiderative perception has an implicitly predicative structure: to desire something is just to perceive that the object is pleasant or good *for me*.[31] By perceiving it as pleasant or good, the perceived object exerts a pull on the organism; by perceiving it as painful or bad, the perceived object exerts a push on it. In other words, our desiderative perceptions are always *incidental* perceptions, perceptual syntheses of a proper sense object and an associated valuation, whether pleasant, good, painful, or bad.

To help illustrate this distinction, Aristotle offers the example of the beacon perceived as indicating an enemy (III.7.431b5–6).[32] He articulates various moments of the recognition that a beacon signifies an enemy, stages which should not be thought of as distinct steps in a reasoning process, but rather a breakdown of the moments in what may very well be an instantaneous perceptual recognition of the enemy. In the example, one *perceives* a fire.[33] This is a theoretical sensation—perceiving the object in itself. One *sees*, through the common sense,[34] the movement of the fire. When this movement of the beacon has been associated with the presence of an enemy, one recognizes this as belonging to an enemy. Indicating an enemy is not what the object is in itself—it is a property of the object as it relates to my own good, as presenting a danger or threat to me which demands some kind of practical response, a movement or an action. We can see here the intimate relation of theoretical and practical cognition. What in one situation might be a disinterested observation of a fire's motion, in a situation like the one given, the cognitive experience is a practical, action initiating one.

It is to this predicative structure, perceiving that something is pleasant or painful, that Aristotle refers as he moves for the first time in *De Anima* to this practical, desiderative relation to objects in III.7, and compares sensation to affirmation and negation: "And so perceiving is like mere speaking and thinking. But whenever something is pleasant or painful, just as if affirming or denying, it pursues or flees" (III.7.431a8–10). Practical perceptions are like affirmations, because just as one affirms "x is y" in a theoretical statement, the sensation that moves us has the implicitly predicative structure "x is pleasant."[35] To desire something is simply to perceive it as pleasant or good for me. Aristotle thus explicitly identifies the pull and push of desire and repulsion with this mode of sensitive awareness: "Both actual flight [φυγὴ] and desire [ὄρεξις] are the same, and the desiring capacity and the capacity for flight are not different, neither from one another nor from the capacity of sensation. But their being is different" (III.7.431a12–14).[36] This unity of sensation and desire is further deepened by locating our sensations of pleasure and pain at the center of our sensitive awareness. Feeling pleasure or pain is simply the active exercise of the seat of our sensitive awareness located at the center of the organism, not in terms of the proper or common sense objects, but in terms of the categories of goodness and badness: "And feeling pleasure and pain is being active with respect to the sensible mean[37] in relation to the good or bad as such" (III.7.431a9–11). What distinguishes the theoretical activity of the center of awareness from its practical, desiderative perceptions is the perception of them as "good" or "bad" for me (sensually speaking, pleasant or painful), as opposed to the proper perception of them as "white" or "sweet." But the activity of these desiderative perceptions is located in the very same part as all sensation, further establishing desire as a mode of cognition or awareness. The passage directly following this one on the common power which unifies the five senses (431a20–431b1) can seem out of place in the discussion of desire, unless one recognizes the purpose of recalling the doctrine of the common sense at this point in the argument. Aristotle is using the unity of the five senses through the sensible awareness common to the five senses and located in the heart to explain the unity of the sensitive and desiderative powers: "For there is a certain unity, in this way just like a limit. And these, being one by analogy and in number, are related to one another just as those [its objects] are related to one another" (III.7.431a21–24). Just as this power unites contraries within a genus of qualities (white and black in the genus of colors), as well as qualities belonging to distinct senses (white and sweet), so does it unite the proper sensible qualities of an object with its perception of the goodness or badness for the perceiving subject, the awareness of which constitutes desire.[38] As we will see, this reference to the unifying center of sensual awareness, whether of a theoretical or practical character, will come up again in III.10 in reference to the heart as the central material instrument by which the soul moves the body.

That desire is simply a different mode of awareness is even more explicitly articulated in III.10,[39] when Aristotle's positive answer to the question of what in the soul moves the body emerges: a synthesis of mind (νοῦς), broadly conceived as cognition, and desire (ὄρεξις).[40] But these are not to be conceived of as two separate powers which are synthesized.[41] What moves the body is desire, which simply *is* a mode of awareness of an object as pleasant or good, painful or bad. Desiring some goal and perceiving it as pleasant or good for myself are two ways of expressing the same activity. This kind of awareness exerts a pull or push on the organism.[42] Aristotle is here pointing out this unity[43] by showing that practical cognition and desire share the same fundamental characteristic: they are both directed towards an end or goal, that is, they are "for the sake of something [ἕνεκά του]": "But the mind currently under discussion is the one reasoning for the sake of an end, that is, practical mind [νοῦς]. It differs from the theoretical mind by its end. And all desire is for the sake of an end" (III.10.433a13–16). This end-directedness is what distinguishes desiderative cognition from theoretical cognition. It is to this that Aristotle refers a few lines down when he explicitly reduces cognition and desire to their common form.[44] Another way of stressing this cognitive-desiderative unity is the move to locate the cause of local motion in the *object* of desire in which cognition and desire are unified. Of course, an object of desire only moves me insofar as it is cognized,[45] but cognized as good in some way for me.

Perhaps the best image to understand Aristotle's point about the unity of cognition and desire which is always the cause of the animal's self-movement is the hinge (γιγγλυμός) which he uses to illustrate the physical cause of locomotion. In identifying the moving cause, Aristotle argues that its nature is double: "But the mover is double: on the one hand it is unmoved, on the other it is both moving and moved. And the unmoved aspect is the practical good, while the moving and moved aspect is the desiring capacity" (III.10.433b14–17). When Aristotle turns to the physical instantiation of the moving cause—the heart—he compares it to a hinge, made up of a convex unmoved socket and a concave moving ball. Extending this image used to explain the *physical* cause of motion (i.e., the heart) to the unmoved and moving movers in the *soul*, the cognition can be understood as the unmoved, fixed point, while the desire which follows necessarily from this cognition is the mover which is itself in motion. The socket here would be the cognition of the object, which acts as an unmoved anchor.[46] Insofar as the object is cognized as pleasant or good (or its opposites), the object exerts a pull or push on the organism, like the ball rotating in the hinge and directly swinging the door. These are simply two inseparable sides of one and the same event—the practical good is cognized as attractive and attracts as cognized.

Appetitive versus Rational Desires

Yet although the cause of animal self-motion is the desiring cognition, there is more than one kind of desired object: "The movers are many in number" (III.10.433b12). The other crucial distinction in *De Anima*'s account of human locomotion is the distinction between two primary forms of desire—appetitive and rational.[47] Establishing this distinction and determining how the two kinds of desire are related is another important goal of the argument in *De Anima* III.9–11. In III.7 when Aristotle first introduces the practical cognitions which move us, he treats the sensible perception of immediately present (τὰ παρόντα; III.7.431b8) sense objects as being pleasant or painful.[48] Beyond these sensations, there is also the sense awareness of sensible images originating in past active sensations of particulars. Thus the soul can turn its awareness to the image of a sense object currently absent, and this image can be cognized as pleasant or painful, hence carrying with it motivational force. This awareness of the image apart from the sensation of an external object allows for deliberation concerning future goals, since the organism is not bound to desire only what is immediately before it.

The fact that the soul is not bound in its desiring of images to sensations of external stimuli allows it to consider its good beyond the present moment and to consider what is good not at some particular moment but also in the future—and this in turn opens the possibility of thinking what is good for the human not in this or that particular moment, but in general. In this sense, beyond the awareness of these desiderative images, the practical soul can also "think the forms in the images," just as theoretical soul can think the essence of an object through reflection on images of it.[49] Like the difference between sensible and intelligible form on the theoretical side, the object of appetitive desire is a particular, while the object of a rational desire is a universal—a καθόλου ὑπόληψις καὶ λόγος (a judgment and thought of the universal) (III.11.434a17). This practical thought, distinct from the images out of which it emerges, also carries with it an attractive or repulsive force in the cognition of its object as good or bad, that is, this practical thought is also an object of desire (III.7.431b2–5).[50]

Aristotle characterizes these two potentially conflicting kinds of desires as βούλησις, or rational desire, and ἐπιθυμία, or appetitive desire. Mind, he explains, only moves as rational desire (βούλησις): "But as it stands mind [νοῦς] does not appear as moving without desire—for rational wish [βούλησις] is a desire. Whenever one is moved according to reasoning, one is moved according to rational desire [βούλησις]" (III.10.433a22–25).[51] As Moss states, "To be moved by wish is to be moved by intellect: one has a wish for something *because* intellect thinks that thing good."[52] The object of rational desire (βούλησις) is simply the object of the practical, desiring intellect.

But there is also a form of desire so independent of rational desire (βούλησις) that it moves the human against its reason in cases of incontinence: "But desire [ὄρεξις] moves contrary to reasoning; for appetite [ἐπιθυμία] is a certain desire [ὄρεξις]" (III.10.433a25–6). Appetite (ἐπιθυμία) is a desire for what appears immediately pleasant to the senses in the now, but in rational creatures who have an awareness of time beyond the present moment, opinions can be formed about what is good for the human being in general. The object of practical mind is a kind of object of desire (ὀρεκτόν), and should not be confused with the other practical powers ascribed to mind—especially the practical thinking (διάνοια πρακτική) which discovers the means to the end or desired object.[53]

Another way Aristotle speaks of this contrast between rational and appetitive desire on the side of the one desiring is the difference between imagining and thinking the object of desire, between a practical image and a practical thought. In the absence of a present sense object, the soul can cognize, just as if it were seeing, either appearances (φαντάσματα) or thought objects (νοήματα, *noemata*) (III.7.431b6–8); the object of desire moves either by being thought or by being imagined (III.10.433b11–12). Animals are moved *only* by desiderative, appetitive images, while humans *can* be moved solely by these (III.10.433a9–12)—for animals and for incontinent humans, the immediately pleasant is taken to be pleasant and good in an unqualified way (III.10.433b8–10).[54] This division between the sensually desired image and the rationally desired thought maps onto the two kinds of objects of desire: the apparent good (τὸ φαινόμενον ἀγαθόν) vs. the (actual) good (τὸ ἀγαθόν). For the animal, since the only kind of moving desire can be the desired image, no distinction between the apparent good sensually desired and the real good intellectually desired can emerge. For the human, both of these come into play, either in harmony with each other (where what appears good *is* good) or in conflict (where what appears good is not the real good).

As I brought out in the chapter on perception and imagination, the image is intimately tied to sensation as its result, but it is merely the potential beginning, the *matter* for thought (III.7.431a14–15).[55] Out of many internal sensual images, a practical opinion or thought can be formed. So the image plays an indispensable role in motivating movement or action (as we will see in the conclusion of this chapter, this remains true even after the practical thought emerges out of practical images). Even when the object of desire is a presently sensed object immediately present in the surrounding environment, it is the image and not the proper sensation alone which attracts or repels, because practical, desiderative perceptions are necessarily *incidental* perceptions. One perceives the sweet thing as pleasant—hence such desired images are essentially predicative. As Cashdollar has argued, "The second term of the percept has to have been a stored image which is spontaneously associated with the properly perceived first term,"[56] with the image of pleasure or pain associated to the perceived object acting as a kind of perceptual lens such that one perceives the object as sensually desirable or repellent.

Thus the key cognitive ingredient to any desire is *phantasia*, as something must *appear* as good or pleasant to us in order to exert a desiderative pull on us. The distinction between appetitive and rational desire (ἐπιθυμία and βούλησις) is reflected in the twofold nature of *phantasia*: sensible (αἰσθητική) and rational (λογιστική/βουλευτική).[57] The image involved in appetite (ἐπιθυμία) is through αἰσθητικὴ *phantasia*, a sensual appearance of an object which is experienced as pleasurable by one of the five senses. Here such an image is presumably produced by an actual sense experience of such an object, so that other instances of that object are perceived as potential sources of bodily pleasure. Appetitive desires and images belong to all animals. A rational desire or βούλησις is also an image[58] which associates a certain non-sensual object with being good for us—such an image is a rational (λογιστική or βουλευτικὴ) *phantasia*. The origin of such rationally desired images seems to be our reflection upon multiple sensually desired images or appearances:

> For whether one will do this or that, already this is the act of reasoning. And it is necessary to measure by one thing [ἑνὶ μετρεῖν]. For one pursues the better. Therefore one is able to produce a unity out of many images [ὥστε δύναται ἓν ἐκ πλειόνων φαντασμάτων ποιεῖν]. (III.11.434a7–10)

When there are conflicting goods, deliberative reasoning chooses between them. To measure between conflicting goods, some principle by which to determine which is better must exist for the deliberator. This measure is a unity produced out of many images. It is not simply given, but a rationally considered image of the good serves as the standard for ethical deliberation in cases of conflicting goods. This measure is an opinion about what is the practical good for a human being. Both the rational and non-rational animal have the sensual images which serve as the objects of non-deliberative desire for them, while for the rational animal, these images can serve as the material out of which the rationally synthesized image is produced (III.11.434a10–11).[59] The sensual image of appetite (ἐπιθυμία) is more widely shared across different kinds of animals, and serves as the necessary precondition for there being the rational images of rational desire (βούλησις). So there is a kind of desire (ὄρεξις) common to animals and to humans, namely, appetite (ἐπιθυμία), and in addition there is a desire (ὄρεξις) possessed only by thinking animals, βούλησις (rational desire).

Aristotle sometimes speaks as if thought (as distinct from desire) can oppose itself to desire as an alternative source of practical motivation—he speaks of the opposition between reason (λόγος) and appetite (ἐπιθυμία), with mind advising one action, and appetite another (III.10.433b5–10).[60] But in order for thought to motivate, it must be a desiderative thought, the thought of some object or goal as good for me.[61] A thought which is not a desiring thought carries no motivational force and thus cannot lead to action—thought as theoretical offers nothing about the object in terms of its desirability. When practical mind considers objects in terms of whether they are pleasant or good, painful or evil, if the object does not appear to it as such, no desire is produced (III.9.432b26–32). While Aristotle speaks of struggles between thought and desire, this can only make sense if one substitutes for thought "thinking desire."[62] Conflicts in practical motivations are always conflicts between desires.[63] Thus Aristotle opens his section on the struggle between appetite (ἐπιθυμία) and reason (λόγος) by considering what happens "when *desires* become opposed to one another" (III.10.433b10).[64]

Despite this opposition between rational and sensual desire (βούλησις and ἐπιθυμία), both share in common that they can cause the animal to move itself. As such they make up the capacity of the soul responsible for the animal's movement: τὸ ὀρεκτικόν, ᾗ ὀρεκτικόν (the desiring capacity, as desiring)—desire as comprehensive of the distinction of rational and appetitive. These are simply different species of the same genus of soul's power. The various modes of desiderative, interested cognition—chiefly appetite (ἐπιθυμία) and rational desire (βούλησις)—belong to the power of the soul Aristotle calls the desiring capacity (ὀρεκτικὸν). The various modes of theoretical, disinterested cognition—chiefly sensation and mind (αἴσθησις and νοῦς)—belong to the power of soul Aristotle calls cognitive (κριτική). Thus the difference between cognitive (κριτική) and desiring (ὀρεκτική) soul should not be thought of as a difference between cognition and desire, but rather two different forms of cognition or awareness, which I would qualify as theoretical and practical cognition.[65] Aristotle specifies three distinct but closely related differences between theoretical and practical cognition.

1. Practical cognition is intentional or end-directed—the organism is *aware* of something as a goal it seeks to achieve.[66] In theoretical cognition, by contrast, there is no end beyond the cognition of the object, that is, beyond being determined by the object as it is in itself.
2. Practical cognition does not just apprehend the object as it is in itself, but as the relation of the object to the perceiving organism. Aristotle makes the distinction between perceiving the object absolutely (ἁπλῶς) and in relation to something (τινί).[67]
3. The object of practical cognition is able to be otherwise (III.10.433a29–30), whereas the object of theoretical cognition is necessary and so not open to determination by the perceiving organism.

Beyond the Parts of the Soul

What are the implications of this view on how we should conceive the "parts" of the soul, a question that preoccupies Aristotle throughout his treatment of the soul's moving the body in *De Anima*? Having established all this about desire in III.7, Aristotle moves directly to the question of the soul's parts in III.9 (taking up again the *aporiai* with which he closed his historical account in book I; I.5.411a26ff.), in order to problematize any view that thinks of the soul having parts which exist independently of one another. The questions about the soul's parts are Aristotle's very first questions in his treatment of how the soul moves the body. On the one hand, is the power that moves the soul a part separate from the parts responsible for the other powers? If so, is it one of the parts already treated in the argument of *De Anima* (nutritive soul, sensitive soul, intellective soul) or another part beyond these? Or, on the other hand, is the whole soul responsible for moving the body? I suggest Aristotle's answer to these two possibilities, as is usually the case with him, is that both and neither are right—in a sense the part responsible for movement is distinct from the powers already discussed, in a sense it simply *is* these powers, and in a sense it is not some one part but the whole soul, while in a sense it is one part of soul. How can all these be right? Because the moving cause in soul is the practical, locomotive side of the very same powers already treated in the analysis of theoretical cognition.

The first chapter devoted explicitly to animal self-movement indicates that one of Aristotle's chief concerns in these chapters is the question of the soul's parts. After he lays out the various *aporiai* concerning the soul's parts, and which of the soul's parts is responsible for moving the body, in III.10 we get the outlines of Aristotle's own positive view of the principal divisions of the soul's powers:

> To those who distinguish parts of the soul, if they divide and separate according to the capacities, very many parts emerge: the nutritive [θρεπτικόν], sensitive [αἰσθητικόν], intellective [νοητικόν], deliberative [βουλευτικόν], and further the desiderative [ὀρεκτικόν]. For these differ more from one another than the appetitive [ἐπιθυμητικὸν] and spirited [θυμικόν]. (III.10.433b1–4)

Aristotle clearly does not fully embrace the language of parts here, as if he were listing the five parts of the soul. He takes a somewhat ironic distance from "those who distinguish parts of the soul." But at the same time he proposes these five powers as more convincing than the Platonic tripartition. The sense and thinking capacities (αἰσθητικόν and νοητικόν) belong to the theoretical (κριτική) power of the soul, representing its appetitive and rational modes. The capacities called βουλευτικόν[68] and ὀρεκτικόν I take to refer to the parallel distinction between the appetitive and rational modes of desire, matching up with the ἐπιθυμία/ βούλησις distinction evoked right before the current passage, with ὀρεκτικόν (desiring) here employed rather loosely[69] in reference to non-rational desires more generally, comprehending within it the Platonic distinction of appetitive and spirited capacities (ἐπιθυμητικὸν and θυμικόν).[70] This parallel structure points to why Aristotle cannot accept any straightforward partition of the soul into separate parts. The sensual modes of the soul's theoretical and practical cognitions—αἰσθητικόν and ὀρεκτικόν, are essentially united,[71] as are their rational modes—νοητικόν and βουλευτικόν (which I argue includes within it rational desire or βούλησις). So appetite (ἐπιθυμία) and sensation (αἴσθησις) are united, because appetite (ἐπιθυμία) is simply a desiring or practical form of sensation (αἴσθησις). Thinking (νόησις) and rational desire (βούλησις) are united, because rational desire (βούλησις) is a desiring or practical form of thinking (νόησις). Prior to the distinction between awareness and local motion, there is the nutritive power analyzed in II.4, the first of the five divisions. The division of the soul's powers thus looks something like the depiction in the figure below (why these powers can't really be conceived of as parts will be elaborated below).

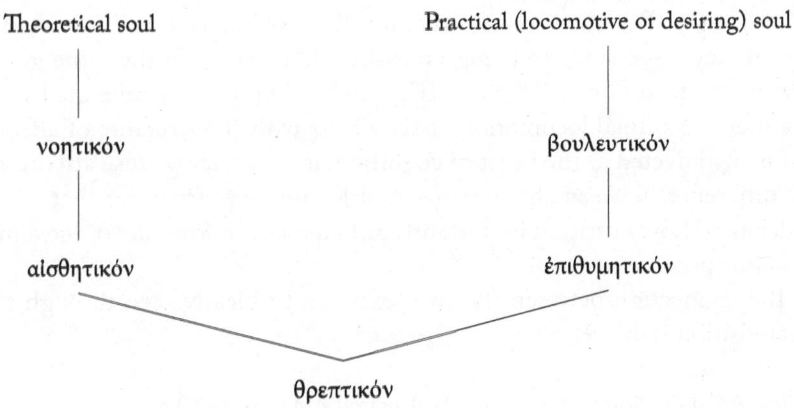

What, precisely, then, is the relation of this nutritive power to what is clearly the primary division of Aristotle's psychology—theoretical cognition and desire?

In II.4, Aristotle closes the chapter by discussing two structures which show that although nutrition involves no awareness or self-motion, its activity anticipates the emergence of both consciousness and self-movement in animals. As I argued in chapter 2, he first discusses the structure of nutrition, one which is already present in the general treatment of affecting and being affected in *On Generation and Corruption* I.7, which becomes central to his treatment of the various modes of awareness, namely the stages by which two initially distinct terms become identified through a process of alteration in either the agent or the patient.[72] The reader of the argument must be attentive to the differences in the common structure of affecting and being affected to discern the development from nutrition to sensation to thinking.

In this way, self-nourishing activity, when it takes an object distinct from itself, breaks it down through digestion so that it becomes identical to itself, and assimilates it to its own body, should be regarded as proto-cognitive. As one then moves from nutrition through sensation to thinking, one gradually preserves the identity of the object in itself, without losing its own identity, more and more fully through the various modes of the identification of organism and object.

In the same way that the discussion of this common structure reveals the pre-cognitive activity of nutrition to be proto-cognitive, Aristotle also shows the pre-kinetic activity of nutrition to be proto-kinetic. Nutritive soul does govern one form of the organism's change (κίνησις), quantitative change (κίνησις) or growth,[73] but that nutritive soul plays no causal role in change of place or locomotion is clear from the stationary character of plants (III.9.17–19). But the second structure discussed at II.4.416b21, identifying the key ingredients in being nourished, is taken from the more general treatment of motion in *Physics* VIII,[74] and is importantly reiterated in the treatment of animal locomotion at III.10. As with the structure of affecting and being affected at the heart of cognition, it is by paying close attention to the difference between the nutritive and locomotive structures that we can understand how nutrition importantly anticipates the structure of movement through space.

The connection between the two texts can be clearly seen through their juxtaposition (table 9).

TABLE 9. Nutrition and Motion: *De Anima* II.4.416b21–30 and III.10 433b13–21 Compared

De Anima II.4 416B21–30	*De Anima* III.10 433B13–21
ἐπεὶ δ' ἔστι τρία, τὸ τρεφόμενον καὶ **ᾧ τρέφεται** καὶ **τὸ τρέφον**, τὸ μὲν τρέφον ἐστὶν ἡ πρώτη ψυχή, τὸ δὲ τρεφόμενον τὸ ἔχον ταύτην σῶμα, ᾧ δὲ τρέφεται, ἡ τροφή. ἐπεὶ δὲ ἀπὸ τοῦ τέλους ἅπαντα προσαγορεύειν δίκαιον, τέλος δὲ τὸ γεννῆσαι οἷον αὐτό, εἴη ἂν ἡ πρώτη ψυχὴ γεννητικὴ οἷον αὐτό. **ἔστι δὲ ᾧ τρέφει** διττόν, ὥσπερ καὶ ᾧ κυβερνᾷ καὶ ἡ χεὶρ καὶ τὸ πηδάλιον, **τὸ μὲν κινοῦν καὶ κινούμενον**, τὸ δὲ κινοῦν μόνον. πᾶσαν δ' ἀναγκαῖον τροφὴν δύνασθαι πέττεσθαι, ἐργάζεται δὲ τὴν πέψιν τὸ θερμόν διὸ πᾶν ἔμψυχον ἔχει θερμότητα. τύπῳ μὲν οὖν ἡ τροφὴ τί ἐστιν εἴρηται.	**ἐπεὶ δ' ἔστι τρία**, ἓν μὲν **τὸ κινοῦν**, δεύτερον δ' **ᾧ κινεῖ**, ἔτι τρίτον **τὸ κινούμενον, τὸ δὲ κινοῦν διττόν**, τὸ μὲν κίνητον, **τὸ δὲ κινοῦν καὶ κινούμενον**, ἔστι δὴ τὸ μὲν κίνητον τὸ πρακτὸν ἀγαθόν **τὸ δὲ κινοῦν καὶ κινούμενον** τὸ ὀρεκτικόν (κινεῖται γὰρ τὸ κινούμενον ᾗ ὀρέγεται, καὶ ἡ ὄρεξις κίνησίς τίς ἐστιν, ἡ ἐνεργείᾳ), τὸ δὲ κινούμενον τὸ ζῷον ᾧ δὲ κινεῖ ὀργάνῳ ἡ ὄρεξις, ἤδη τοῦτο σωματικόν ἐστιν- διὸ ἐν τοῖς κοινοῖς σώματος καὶ ψυχῆς ἔργοις θεωρητέον περὶ αὐτοῦ.

De Anima II.4 416B21–30	*De Anima* III.10 433B13–21
Since there are three things (**ἐπεὶ δ' ἔστι τρία**), that which is fed (**τὸ τρεφόμενον**) and that by which it is fed (**ᾧ τρέφεται**) and that which feeds (**τὸ τρέφον**), that which feeds is the first soul, that which is fed is the body which has this [i.e. the soul], and that by which it is fed, the food. Since it is right for all things to be named from their end, and the end is to reproduce one like itself, the first soul would be the capacity to produce another like itself, and that by which it [i.e. the soul] feeds is double (**ἔστι δὲ ᾧ τρέφει διττόν**), just like that by which someone steers is both the hand and the rudder, the one moving and being moved (**τὸ μὲν κινοῦν καὶ κινούμενον**), the other only moving. So it is necessary for each thing to be able to digest food, and the heat works the digestion; therefore everything ensouled has heat. And so what food is has been said in outline.	Since there are three things (**ἐπεὶ δ' ἔστι τρία**), the one that which moves (**τὸ κινοῦν**), the second that by which it moves (**ᾧ κινεῖ**), and, further, the third that which is moved (**τὸ κινούμενον**), and that which moves is double (**τὸ δὲ κινοῦν διττόν**), the one unmoved, the other moving and being moved (**τὸ δὲ κινοῦν καὶ κινούμενον**), the unmoved is the practical good, the moving and being moved is the desiring power (for that which is moved is moved insofar as it desires, and desire is a certain kind of movement, one in activity), and that which is moved is the living being; and that instrument by which it is moved is desire, and this is already bodily—therefore one needs to consider this among those functions common to the body and the soul.

In nutrition, that which is passively fed (τὸ τρεφόμενον) is the ensouled body; in self-movement, that which is moved (τὸ κινούμενον) is the animal body. In terms of the cause responsible for the process, an important difference emerges between that which feeds (τὸ τρέφον) and that which moves (τὸ κινοῦν). The feeding agent is simply the first, "nutritive" soul—there is no distinction between an unmoved and moved aspect in this cause. In self-movement, by contrast, there is an unmoved mover—the practical good—and a moved mover—the desiring power. Further, an important difference exists also in the characterization of the third ingredient of the process, the bodily instrument by means of which the soul causes the change. In nutrition, there are two types of bodily instrument by which the organism is fed (ᾧ τρέφει)—on the side of the organism[75] there is the heat which remains unchanged in the process (the organism maintains a stable internal temperature through the change), while on the side of the external object there is the food, which moves the body by itself being moved or transformed. In local motion, this difference in the bodily instrument of the motion (ᾧ κινεῖ) is drawn into the organism. The heart as instrumental bodily mover is one organ (the heart) distinguished into two aspects indivisible from one another, like the convex socket and concave ball in a ball and socket joint.

What then is the significance of the differences between the common structure of an animal's self-movement and the organism's self-nourishment? Nutritive soul differs from kinetic soul in terms of its lack of internal differentiation, both in the soul and in the body. Because there is no difference in the nutritive soul between unmoving and moving aspects of the mover akin to the difference between the unmoving awareness of a practical good and the moving push or pull it exerts on us, the plant can have no awareness of itself as distinct from objects in its environment. Because there is no awareness of objects distinct from itself, there can be no desire—without the awareness or feeling of an object which one does not yet possess, there can be no desire for something which one does not yet possess. Thus desire requires that the object be simultaneously present and absent to the one desiring it, and without this inner differentiation of the soul, this co-presence would be contradictory. Desire requires an awareness of the distinction between self and environment, for one cannot feel pulled towards or pushed away from an object without the awareness of something distinct from oneself.

This same inner differentiation is reflected in the bodily instrument through which the soul affects the change in question (nutrition and self-motion). While the difference between unmoved mover and moved mover is in the nutritive process the difference between the heat of the organism on the one side and the nourishing object in the external environment on the other, this distinction for the self-mover is drawn into the organism itself. Heat in nutrition becomes the heart (after all, the hottest organ in the body) in sensation and awareness.[76] But the sensitive-desiring animal in contrast relates to its object as itself, that is, the animal relates to itself as determined by its object. As being aware of the object, there is an identity between object and organism. But insofar as the object is desired, it is represented to the animal as not yet possessed. It is a condition for the soul's movement of the body that the organism have changes that are, as Aristotle puts it, goal-directed, that is, "for the sake of something." This involves the synthesis of an image and a desire.[77] In terms of the bodily instrument, this duality is reflected in the homoeomerous (materially uniform) and anhomoeomerous (materially complex) parts of the heart, the former being required for the heart to be the center of sensation, the latter for it being the origin of bodily movement.[78]

As Aristotle does not go into detail on this point about the heart which he deems too physiological for the psychological investigations of *De Anima* (III.10.433b19–21), let us return to the question of the soul's parts in light of this kinetic structure common to nutrition and locomotion. The primary division between soul, as causing both awareness and motion, can be found in an inchoate way even in its nutritive activity prior to awareness and motion. When viewed as both proto-cognitive and proto-kinetic in this way, it is clear that Aristotle wants us to see the distinction between nutrition, sensation, and thinking as existing on both sides of this division—all three are both theoretical and practical.[79] This shows how both the cognitive and kinetic powers of the soul fit into the serial ordering of the kinds of soul, and how the analogy between the kinds of soul and the kinds of figure outlined in II.3 applies also to various kinds of desiring soul. It is thus also true for the proto-kinetic structure of nutrition, for appetitive desires and for rational desires that "the prior always exists in the posterior of the series in potency" (II.3.414b29–30).

While we can now understand why Aristotle rejects Plato's tripartition of appetite, spirit, and reason (since desire [ὄρεξις] contains all these distinctions in itself, while mind is present in both theoretical and practical modes), it might seem surprising that he also wants to reject his own bipartition of rational and irrational, a distinction which pervades his own ethical writings.[80] This is especially surprising if, as I am suggesting, one of his chief objects of investigation in these chapters is the division and relationship between desire in its rational and appetitive modes. On both the theoretical and desiderative sides of the soul, there are sensual powers—sensation (αἴσθησις) and appetite (ἐπιθυμία)—and rational powers—mind (νοῦς) and rational desire (βούλησις). Why can this not be characterized as a basic opposition between rational and non-rational powers?

The answer to the question is hinted at in the chapter on psychology in *Nicomachean Ethics*, where Aristotle makes precisely this division in the soul's powers. There he makes the following qualification of this division into one power which has reason, and another that is irrational:

> But whether these are distinct just as the parts of the body and the whole are divisible into parts, or whether they are two in thought but naturally inseparable just as the convex and concave on a circumference, this makes no difference in relation to the present investigation.[81]

While these questions might not matter for the practical philosophy of the *Ethics*, the theoretical reflections on the soul are precisely where one should expect precision on such matters. What exactly is implied about the unity of the rational in non-rational powers of the soul's desiderative cognitions (i.e., the relation between rational and appetitive desire [βούλησις and ἐπιθυμία]), in this image of inside and outside of the circumference of a circle as the relation of concave to convex? What would it mean that our rational and appetitive desires are related as the concave to the convex?

Rationally Virtuous Activity and the Circular Motion of the Outermost Sphere: The True Relation of Rational and Appetitive Desires

The final chapter on animal self-movement (III.11) turns to this question of the relation between appetitive desire and rational desire. An ἐπιθυμία, or a desired appetitive image, clearly has a certain separability or independence of βούλησις, a rationally desired thought, for in non-rational animals without thinking or reasoning, there are only sensual images, and on their own these are capable of moving the animal. When Aristotle turns to the question of whether the simplest, incomplete animals[82] have desire—those which are stationary and have the sense of touch but none of the distance senses—the purpose of the discussion is to establish the independence of the most primitive, simple appetites,[83] appetites which exist in complete independence in these most primitive animals, but which are also operative in more complex animals, including rational animals. This serves to identify the most common, shared manifestation of desire. Insofar as such animals have the sense of touch, they feel pain and pleasure, and consequently feel some kind of basic appetite (ἐπιθυμία), which presupposes some kind of sensual image. But Aristotle argues that "just as they are moved indeterminately [ἀορίστως], so also are these [ἐπιθυμία and φαντασία] in them" (III.11.434a4–5). What Aristotle means here by ἀορίστως or indeterminately,[84] can be discerned from a passage in book I about practical thinking: "For of practical thoughts there are limits, as they are all for the sake of another" (I.3.407a23–4). All practical thinking has a limit or an end point, namely, the goal it cognizes as distinct from itself yet good for it—in other words, the object of desire. πέρας (limit) and ὅρισμα (boundary) are interchangeable here—both represent the end point of the organism's desire. To have an indeterminate image of a desirable or repulsive object simply means that the image or desired object is not experienced as something distinct from the organism—the animal might experience contact with some object as painful and contract its body in response. Here there is no cognition or image of an object distinct from itself towards which it is pulled; the experience is of itself and the way it is affected by contact with its environment (i.e., it feels its pleasure or pain). Importantly, these "indeterminate" desires persist in more complex animals, even rational ones—think of a human being accidentally touching the hot element of a stove and unthinkingly pulling back. Why bring up this phenomenon in the course of the developing argument about desire and locomotion? Here we see the transition from merely nutritive activities, which, having no sense of an object distinct from itself, has neither awareness nor desire, to the activities of sensitive and desiring animals, who perceive a world of objects distinct from themselves and can respond to the push or pull which desire for or repulsion from these objects exerts upon us. The indeterminate appetites and images of these simple stationary animals serve as a bridge between plants and more complex animals. More importantly, such an appetite (ἐπιθυμία) completely devoid of any trace of rationality shows itself to be capable of separable existence from higher desires. There is thus a real distinction between our appetitive and rational desires. The ensuing argument treats the question of how we should conceive the relationship between these.

A hierarchy of desired images emerges in what follows. The most primitive, stationary animals have indeterminate images or desires. Non-rational self-moving animals have these indeterminate desired images, but also properly sensible (αἰσθητική) images—appearances of sensible objects which appear to the animal as pleasant for it, and as distinct or separate from it, such that they can instigate movement through space towards them. Rational animals have both these desired sensible images, along with the images Aristotle qualifies as rational (βουλευτική and λογιστική).[85] In his brief account of how the object of rational desire (βούλησις) comes about (III.11.434a7–10), Aristotle suggests that this universal object of practical knowledge emerges out of the synthesis of various practical images which results from deliberation; once this practical truth has been grasped by practical mind, this rational desire (βούλησις) can then serve as a measure of the goodness of sensible desires. In deliberating about whether to choose this or that appetitive good, a rational opinion (δόξα) about what is good is produced as a synthesis of these goods which then acts as a measure of which desired objects are better and which are worse. The rational desire—the βουλευτική / λογιστική appearance or βούλησις[86]—comes to be out of appetitive desire, and as such no organism can have rational desire without appetitive desires. But having emerged as a synthesis of appetitive desires, the rational desire then attains independence from the appetitive in that it can act as a measure for it.

The lower animals thus do not have such opinions or beliefs about what is good in general[87]—these involve deliberative or rational images which emerge from synthesizing many sensual images into a general belief. The conclusion of this argument is that there is a form of rational desire—a βούλησις—which cannot emerge without the appetitive desires that are more widely shared among animals, but which is distinct from this lower form of desire (ἐπιθυμία), and belongs only to humans.

Having clearly distinguished rational from appetitive desires, Aristotle discusses three ways in which the two can be related in human practical activity. The text is absurdly condensed, and every line could be interpreted in various ways; the following reading gets its support from how it is able to make sense of the passage in the context of Aristotle's overall argument in III.9–11:

> Therefore desire does not imply the rationally deliberating capacity. And sometimes the former defeats and moves the latter, but sometimes the latter does to the former, just as a sphere moves a sphere, so does one desire defeat and move another desire, whenever there is incontinence. But by nature the upper is always more ruling and moves the lower. So there are now three motions.
>
> διὸ τὸ βουλευτικὸν οὐκ ἔχει ἡ ὄρεξις· νικᾷ δ’ ἐνίοτε καὶ κινεῖ ὁτὲ μὲν αὕτη ἐκείνην, ὁτὲ δ’ ἐκείνη ταύτην, ὥσπερ σφαῖρα <σφαῖραν>, ἡ ὄρεξις τὴν ὄρεξιν, ὅταν ἀκρασία γένηται· φύσει δὲ ἀεὶ ἡ ἄνω ἀρχικωτέρα καὶ κινεῖ· ὥστε τρεῖς φορὰς ἤδη κινεῖσθαι (III.11.434a11–15)

Not every desire (ὄρεξις) is a rational one (βούλησις), for appetite (ἐπιθυμία) is a desire distinct from rational desire (βούλησις), and these two desires can conflict (notice again how this is not a conflict between reason and desire, but between two kinds of desire). Two kinds of action can emerge out of these conflicts, depending on which of the desires triumphs. When rational and appetitive desires clash and the appetitive desire emerges victorious, this constitutes a case of incontinence. When the rational desire overcomes the appetitive desire, this is a case of continence.[88] Neither constitutes genuinely virtuous action, which only emerges with the third kind of motion, in which the higher rules and moves the lower. Here the appetitive (lower) desire does not conflict with the rational (higher), because the former is so thoroughly governed and caused to be desirable by the latter such that it does not have the independent ground upon which it could oppose it. This is the soul that has developed the virtues of character which naturally desires what its practical knowledge knows to be good for humans in general.

None of this however speaks to Aristotle's famously obscure reference to how these three motions correspond to the spheres, what Hutchinson calls "the analogy of the sphere."[89] I want to argue, along with some ancient commentators,[90] that we have here a comparison between the different kinds of desires as causes of motion in the human being, and the heavenly spheres as causes of the movement of the heavenly bodies. As such, I want to provide a new answer to Andrea Falcon's question: "How much of what Aristotle says about soul is relevant to the study of celestial life?"[91] by suggesting that his study of celestial life has a determinative role in his study of soul, particularly in the study of the soul's causation of bodily movement. As mentioned above, in book I of the *De Anima* Aristotle explicitly criticizes such a correspondence between heavenly motions and the movements of the soul as found in Plato's *Timaeus*. There Aristotle reports how the *Timaeus* "physiologizes" about how the various activities of soul are caused by movements of the soul which correspond to the movement of the heavens. Thinking is there identified with motion in a circle, while sensitive and appetitive activities are characterized as rectilinear. For Hutchinson,

> The "spheres" to which Aristotle is referring in our *De Anima* passage are, then, Platonic soul-circles, which he uses as an illustration (I am not suggesting that Aristotle believes in soul-circles) because they are familiar to his students and because they indicate exactly the Platonic philosophy of motivation which Aristotle is recycling.[92]

Hutchinson dismisses the possibility that the reference could be to Aristotle's own views on the heavenly spheres, because "in Aristotle's universe the spheres are not part of any cause of disorder, only part of a system of order, and it is difficult to see, under this interpretation, what the point is of the remark that it follows from the natural superiority of the knowing part that there are three motions."[93] But is it the case that Aristotle's system of spheres is simply a system of order without tension or struggle? For each of the heavenly bodies, Aristotle adopts the model of spheres from Eudoxus and Callippus in which the complex motion of a planet is explained by a system of concentric spheres. One of Aristotle's innovations relative to the astronomy of his predecessors is his view that ultimately this multiplicity of planetary systems of spheres work together in one system comprehending all the planets and their movers.[94] But the other innovation he introduces, necessary in order to make this reduction to one harmonious system, is the idea of "counteracting spheres" (ἀνελιττούσας σφαίρας). What must be counteracted is the effect of the preceding spheres, so that the outermost sphere of each planetary system can impart the motion of the sphere of the fixed stars at the outermost periphery of the system as a whole. As a result, the counteracting spheres must move in the opposite direction of each sphere to cancel their influence.[95] Thus while it is true that an overarching harmony exists among the spheres, this harmony is the result of opposition within the multiplicity, such that from the perspective of any *part* of the system, lack of harmony is the result. Only with the perspective of the whole system can the overriding harmony, which is the harmony of each part with the outermost sphere of the fixed stars, be seen.

What is the point of comparing this system of spheres to the various kinds of conflict between appetitive and rational ends? The sources of human motion or action are many, and these can counteract and overcome one another. Within the system of spheres the outer imparts motion to the inner, but this is in turn counteracted by the unwinding spheres. These interactions between spheres correspond to the first two kinds of motions, where rational desire overcomes appetite and appetite overcomes rational desire. Yet beyond such conflicts, from the perspective of nature, the higher controls the lower ends, contains them all within itself, and overcomes their opposition, revealing their essential unity. As including all such ends within itself, the outermost sphere is beyond opposition to anything—in this way it is supremely self-sufficient and independent. In that there is no *other* outside of it which could move it, it is the paradigmatically self-moving mover, a self-mover whose wholly self-initiated motion is the paradigmatic local motion to which all other self-movers aspire to varying degrees of success. Aristotle wants to show how this perfect and complete self-motion is most closely approximated by the best kind of mortal self-motion, the self-motion of rationally virtuous human activity.

The conclusion of Aristotle's treatment of locomotion is his analysis of what is often called the practical syllogism. Although it has gone generally unnoticed, this formulation of the practical syllogism takes up and concludes Aristotle's reflection on the relation of rational and appetitive desire. In the context of the unfolding argument, this discussion is meant to be an illustration of the third kind of the aforementioned three movements: the practical activity of the practically wise and ethically virtuous agent whose appetitive and rational desires are harmonious. Three moments are distinguished in this agent's practical activity:

First, the practical knowledge of what is good for the human to do in general. Aristotle writes that it is a judgment (ὑπόληψις) and account (λόγος) of the universal (καθόλου), which says in general: it is necessary for such a person to do such a thing. The language of necessity here could be just as well expressed in terms of goodness—it is best for such a person to do such a thing. This is the element of practical knowledge (τὸ ἐπιστημονικὸν)[96] in rational practical activity.[97]

Second, the sensitive awareness of the particular situation and circumstance. Here, the action that is generally understood to be good in practical knowledge (the general opinion that it is good for such a person to do such a thing) is instantiated in the immediately present circumstance of the agent. In other words, the perception that all those conditions taken to be good in the rational agent's practical knowledge actually obtain here and now in this particular situation.

Third, the resulting action or movement of the body which realizes the general principle of practical knowledge.

In terms of the discussion of the relation between our rational and appetitive desires, the general practical knowledge is a rational desire, a βούλησις, that is, an image which presents a certain kind of action as being good for the human being and hence desirable. The sensitive perception of the particular circumstances in the agent's immediately present environment is an example of an appetitive desire, an ἐπιθυμία, where the sensual image of what is immediately present is determined as pleasurable or good for me. This is an example of the third kind of movement discussed above, where the higher rules the lower, not through a struggle which it wins (continence), but where what is sensually desired as an appetite is harmoniously determined by what is rationally desired. That this goal right now appears good to me in this moment is causally determined by the fact that I generally believe such a goal to be best.[98] The desirability of the present circumstance is transferred from the general rational desire of practical knowledge. Thus the rational desire (βούλησις) causes and thoroughly governs the appetitive desire (ἐπιθυμία), and it contains the whole motivational process as uniting the origin and end of the action. Appetitive desire does not oppose rational desire in the best kind of action because it is wholly contained within it as a particular instantiation of the more general desire.[99] Like the circular motion of the outermost sphere, there is nothing outside of this rational desire which could oppose it—and while the rational agent, as opposed to the outermost sphere, has a surrounding environment (περιέχον) distinct from it, its appetitive desires for this externality are so thoroughly governed by what it rationally believes to be good for the human being that there is in a real sense nothing distinct from this practical knowledge. In this way, although sensible desires are required to initiate locomotion, this movement remains thoroughly self-initiated and moved from within.[100]

To go back to the analogy of the sphere, we have here a completely harmonious relation between a containing sphere and that which it contains.

They are, according to the analogy of the sphere, like the inside and outside of the circumference. This, I suggest, is what Aristotle, at *Nicomachean Ethics* I.13, means by conceiving the rational and non-rational powers of the soul's practical side as inseparable, in the manner of the convex to the concave on a circumference. As Aristotle writes in a different context (the relation between the four elements), "For the higher is always in relation to what is under it just as form is to matter."[101] The appetitive desire is matter or potentiality to the rational desire as its form or actualization, just as on soul's theoretical side, thinking is the form or actualization of sensation. Here is another instance of the serial ordering outlined in II.3 which serves as the structural linchpin of the whole treatise. The earlier powers of the soul exist in the later ones in potency. Through grasping the ultimate term in the series, we see what the lower terms in their independence were ultimately seeking to varying degrees of success. Practical mind and its rational desire (βούλησις) are related to non-rational desire or ἐπιθυμία as potential to actual, or matter to form.[102] In this sense, the distinction between nutritive, sensitive, and intellective soul—viewed from *both* the theoretical and practical sides of soul's activity—is not adequately understood through a language of parts which lie outside one another. The three powers are degrees of potentiality of one actuality, which can exist separately only in the sense that a being with only the lower powers can exist apart from the higher. The movement from appetitive desires to rational desires can be thought of according to the same developmental logic which governs the development of a living being from seed to fully formed organism.

The main point in this passage devoted to the practical syllogism is that our rational desire (βούλησις) for what is good in general remains unmoved in moving us, while the appetite (ἐπιθυμία) for the immediately present sensual good moves us while also being moved. Here we have found the moment of independence or separation from the flux of our sensation of changing practical circumstances. Practical knowledge—the general belief about what is good for the human—is the unmoving socket of Aristotle's hinge. The virtuous agent's practical knowledge of what is best for the human being is not simply dragged around by impulses presented to us from the external environment. It remains fixed as a kind of anchor orienting all the practical engagements of the completely virtuous agent with the world. Before this particular circumstance presented itself, I believed such an action to be good, and after my action, I will continue to believe it—there is no change in my practical knowledge through the course of the action. As a result, this kind of action is the most self-initiated, and so least determined from without, since the desirability of the immediate environment is caused by the inner determination of what is good. But note of course that although this represents an unmoved moment in our motivation to action, this unmoved character is qualified by Aristotle—it remains *more* (μᾶλλον) at rest than any other desire.[103] After all, what we take to be generally good can be affected, even improved, through new particular experiences.

Our sensible cognition of the immediate particular circumstances as good is in motion precisely because the object of desiring perception is itself moving—when this particular circumstance presents itself, what previously did not appear desirable now presents itself as desirable. But without this moment of sensibility, the rational desire moves nothing.[104] The appetitive desire for the immediately present good is the ball of Aristotle's hinge. Though the unmoving rational desire (βούλησις) ultimately causes the object of appetite (ἐπιθυμία) to be desirable in the first place, this rational desire cannot cause action unless accompanied by an immediate desiring cognition for a present object. It is this appetitive desire for the particular goal that immediately moves the agent—and the rational desire which caused the appetitive object of desire to be desirable only moves in a mediated way.

Conclusion

The answer to the original question of Aristotle's treatment of practical self-motion has emerged: practical mind, although it cannot be completely separate from the extended, sensible world, can in fact "think the separate." Our rational, practical knowledge of what is best for humans in general is a separate, independent moment in the human motivation to move practically in the world. And in this way, as Aristotle has shown, rational human self-movement or practical activity most closely approximates the circular, self-sufficient motion of the outermost sphere of the universe. In the study of theoretical cognition, the highest activity of human thinking, that is, the active contemplation of intelligible form, manifests a startling approximation of the divine activity of thought thinking itself. Here, in the study of practical or desiderative cognition's movement of the body, the highest mode of human desiderative cognition, in its self-initiating activity comprehensive of all possibly contrary desires, points towards the perfectly comprehensive and self-initiating divine motion of the outermost sphere, which is the ultimate source of all other motions. With the emergence of divine separate intellect in III.5, very little is explained about the principle the argument has disclosed, because the divine mind exceeds the limits of psychology as the study of the formal principle of mortal beings.[105] Here, in a similar way, the culmination of the argument has discovered the divine principle of all motion through space, but only the barest mention is made, since the study of such a being exceeds the limits of *De Anima*'s investigation. But this principle makes explicit what all self-moving movement (κίνησις) is ultimately seeking and attaining to various degrees—its form or final cause. In this sense, the theological culmination is not extraneous to the argument: it is integral to the project of the *De Anima*. As Aristotle argues in *De Caelo*, the motion of the heaven—defined as the outer periphery of the world—is the measure of all other motions, because it alone is continuous, eternal, and immortal.[106] As Aristotle has already argued in *De Anima* II.4 in another context, it is this divine eternity that all beings seek (II.4.415a26–415b7).

Importantly, the structure of a fully rational, completely virtuous soul's practical activity, where the unmoved rational desire causes and comprehends within itself the moving appetitive desire, is also present in all the lower forms of desire, if only imperfectly. This distinction between unmoved and moved mover occurs within all self-movers, although in simpler animals such a distinction is not nearly so articulated. While in the practical syllogism, the unmoved and moved movers are two distinct desires (rational and appetitive),[107] in simple appetitive desire the distinction simply lies between the cognitive and appetitive aspects of the same desiring cognition. Recall that in III.10, in the general account of how the soul moves the body (III.10.433b13–27),[108] the moving cause of the body was twofold: the cognition of the practical good remains as an unmoved fixed point, while the desire for this good exerts a psychological push or pull on the agent—it is a moved mover. In the practical syllogism, both the rational and appetitive objects of desire are simultaneously cognized and desired, but the rational desire here plays the cognitive role, while the appetitive desire plays the attracting, desiderative role.

This division common to all self-movers between an unmoved cognition and a moving desire holds true even with the purely appetitive desires of animals who have only sensible images of particulars, and even of the "indeterminate" desires and images of primitive, stationary animals who react to the pain and pleasure from contact with their immediate environment. Further, although animal motion is rectilinear, Aristotle tries to show through this section that because animal movement is self-initiated to some degree, initiated by the image of the good pursued within its field of awareness, that the beginning and end of this self-motion coincide, giving it a certain figurative circularity—the object of desire (as cognized) initiates the motion; as attained, it completes the motion. The heart's role as bodily instrument, as the seat of both awareness and desire at the center of the animal, is in this way also the identity of beginning and end. In fact, the whole animal is compared to a circle (ὥσπερ ἐν κύκλῳ) (III.10.433b26), with the heart at the unmoved center as the principle of the motion at the periphery. The same is true for the structure of practical deliberation. The object of desire is the beginning of the deliberation, which moves backward from the end or goal through various steps until one reaches an action or goal immediately executable. Then the actions lead back through these steps towards the beginning, that is, the ultimate goal originally represented to the agent. All this language of circles, of beginnings and endings of movements being identical, is not accidental. This helps show how at every level of desiring activity, there is present something of the perfect, self-complete circular motion of the outermost sphere of the fixed stars, the periphery of the world outside of which neither time nor motion nor matter exists.[109] But only God is unqualifiedly self-moving.

The primary division of the soul is between theoretical cognition which seeks to know its object by becoming identified with its object as it exists in itself, and practical cognition, which, perceiving the world not in itself but in relation to its own pleasure or good, seeks rather to possess its object on the organism's terms, as a goal to attain or a change to effect in the realm of what can be otherwise than it is. The account of each division appeals to one side of divine activity: the paradigm of the soul's theoretical activity is the immaterial separate divine thinking of III.5; the paradigm of the soul's *kinetic* or practical activity is the circular motion of the outermost sphere of the fixed stars, comprehending all other motions in itself as their cause.[110] While the former principle is characterized as separate, unaffected, unmixed, immortal, and eternal, a pure *energeia* beyond all change (κίνησις), the outermost sphere (i.e., "the essence [οὐσία] of the last periphery of the universe, the natural body which is on the ultimate circumference of the universe")[111] is called divine (τὸ θεῖον), one, unique, perfect or complete, immortal, eternal, unaffected by mortal difficulties, active without any effort because beyond any necessary compulsion.[112] Like the immaterial thinking activity discussed already in *De Anima*, Aristotle speaks of the outermost sphere as existing "beyond" all other bodies, "prior" to them, and that it is "more divine" than them.[113] As Aristotle says, his view of the divine nature as including not only the immaterial unmoved principle beyond the world, but also this outermost limit of the world and its circular motion, confirms the ancient belief that "there is something immortal and divine among those beings having motion, and of those having motion such that their motion has no limit, but rather is the limit of the other motions."[114]

Aryeh Kosman, in an article devoted to "Aristotle's Prime Mover," has suggested that the self-moving outermost sphere of the fixed stars and unmoved divine self-thinking form are "the soul and body of a single divine entity";[115] the implications of this thought resonate deeply for our overall interpretation of Aristotle's philosophy. Kosman writes:

> For the unchanging mover of the *Physics* is the principle of the outermost heaven's motion, analogous in ways that I shall suggest to its soul, and the prime motion that is the principle and source of natural change is thus the self-movement of that outermost heaven, the motion whose proximate cause is that principle or soul-analogue[116] . . . The notion of a divine first mover is thus no simple concept in Aristotle. At one level, the Prime Mover is the ceaseless encircling motion of the outermost heavenly sphere. We may want to distinguish between this self-moving sphere itself and the principle of its motion, as between the outermost heavenly body and its soul. But given that it is *self*-moving, and given Aristotle's understanding of soul as nothing other than the active principle and formal being of the living body, it is not surprising that in the *De Caelo* the first mover is indifferently thought of as the outermost moving sphere of the heavens itself and as the divine unchanging being that informs that sphere, indifferently thought of, we might almost say, in the two sense of *primum movens*.[117]

This double character of divinity for Aristotle is thus intimately related to his psychology, both in the sense that the two sides are analogous to the relation between body and soul in mortal living beings, and also in the sense that in this being what is only vaguely achieved at lower levels of living being is very closely approximated by the theoretical and practical sides of human rational activity, and then fully realized in the complete actuality of divinity.[118] And when one considers that this distinction in Aristotle's psychology between its cognitive (κριτική) and locomotive (κινητική) power provides the biological basis for the primary distinction of the *Nicomachean Ethics* between theoretical and practical reason,[119] one begins to glimpse the underlying structural unity of Aristotle's first philosophy, physics and practical philosophy.[120]

Appendix: A Qualification about the Desire of Theoretical Mind

In this chapter I have distinguished soul as the cause of theoretical cognition from soul as cause of locomotion, that is, soul as practical and desiring, what I have called practically interested cognition. But just as we have shown cognition to play an integral role in animal self-motion (since desire *is* a particular mode of cognitive awareness), desire plays an important role in the soul's theoretical impulse to know the world as it really is in itself. All humans, as Aristotle says, *desire* by nature to know, a desire which is at work in all its modes of cognition, from the simplest sensation of the external world through its memory, experience, and craft knowledge to its theoretical knowledge of necessary truth and the wisdom which grasps the highest causes. This is a desire which Aristotle in the *Eudemian Ethics* characterizes as lying at the heart of why we desire to live—because we have a fundamental desire to become determinate through becoming the object known and being aware of this determinacy.[121] In the *De Anima* itself, once an external object has been internalized as an image, activating our awareness of it is "up to us, whenever we want" (III.3.427b18–20)—since the content is in the soul, the only thing which can explain the passage from the potency of possession to the active awareness of the image is our desire to attend to it. Similarly, the person who has acquired possession of theoretical truth, which is the capacity for active contemplation of the truths we know, actively contemplates her knowledge when she wants, providing that nothing external prevents this activation (II.5.417a27). In the passivity of sensation, one perceives independently of desire, since the active cause of sensitive awareness is the external sense object. But once soul has become its objects through memory and knowledge, it is only by *desiring* to actively contemplate its possessed knowledge that it is actualized.

In other words, the transition from *De Anima* III.4 (which treats the process of learning or acquiring intelligible form and thus becoming a knower) to III.5 (which treats the transition from actually knowing to actively contemplating what one knows) is accomplished primarily through desire. It is our desire for active contemplation which explains this transition from potentiality to actuality.[122]

This coincidence of the theoretical and the practical, of the disinterested and interested cognition which we find in the active exercise of our highest theoretical power is significant. At lower levels of the soul's activity, not only is desire not the cause of the soul's theoretical modes of cognition, but the theoretical and practical are in tension with one another. Our theoretical relation to the external object of sense grasps the object as it is in itself, while our practical, desiderative awareness of objects as ends or goals for us grasps the world only in terms of what is pleasant or good for me.[123] These two modes of awareness are distinct and potentially opposed. But once the soul has learned and internalized the intelligible form of its objects, there is a practical desire to possess this content as fully and actively as possible through contemplation. This desire is completely harmonious with the theoretical act. Here the overcoming of the opposition between theoretical cognition and desiderative cognition in our highest theoretical activity itself anticipates and approximates the unity beyond opposition of the two sides of divinity I have identified—the eternal actuality of divine thought thinking itself, and its first external expression in the perfect circular activity of the outermost sphere, a relation which Aristotle constantly reminds involves no constraint or opposition whatsoever.

ABBREVIATIONS

The following abbreviations are used throughout the notes:

APo.	*Posterior Analytics*
DA	*De Anima*
DC	*De Caelo*
DM	*De Motu Animalium*
DP	*On Plants*
DS	*De Sensu*
Eth. Eud.	*Eudemian Ethics*
Eth. Nic.	*Nicomachean Ethics*
GA	*On the Generation of Animals*
GC	*On Generation and Corruption*
HA	*History of Animals*
Insomn.	*On Dreams*
Juv.	*On Youth and Old Age*
Long. Vit.	*On Length and Shortness of Life*
Mem.	*On Memory*
Metaph.	*Metaphysics*
Meteor.	*Meteorology*
MM	*Magna Moralia*
PA	*On the Parts of Animals*
Phys.	*Physics*
Pol.	*Politics*
Prot.	*Protrepticus*
Resp.	*On Respiration*
Top.	*Topics*

NOTES

Preface

The epigraph is from *Metaph.* XII.7.1072b26–30.

1. Gadamer 1980, 200.

2. *Metaph.* VII.7.1032a18–19.

3. See *Metaph.* XII.10.1075a15–25, where the order of nature is compared to the order of a household. The ordering principle is free, inwardly determined, governed by a purely inner necessity, while the lowest members are open to the indeterminacy of chance and determined almost completely from without.

4. *DM* I.

5. See *PA* I.5.645a17–23: "Every realm of nature is marvelous: and as Heraclitus, when the strangers who came to visit him found him warming himself at the furnace in the kitchen and hesitated to go in, is reported to have bidden them not to be afraid to enter as even in that kitchen divinities were present, so we should venture on the study of every kind of living being without distaste; for each and all will reveal to us something natural and something beautiful."

6. Jonas 2001, 2.

7. Jonas 2001, 2.

8. Jonas 2001, 83.

Introduction

1. All translations of *De Anima* are my own. Translations of other Aristotelian treatises are taken from the Oxford translation, with occasional revisions. Hereafter in-text citations are of the *De Anima*. In terms of modern scholarship, in cases when there are no existing published translations of French and German scholarship, I have provided my own English translations.

2. The division is made with reference to Aristotle's philosophical predecessors at I.2 403b25–28, where Aristotle says that we have "nearly [σχεδὸν]" adopted this distinction from them; at I.5 409b19–27, where the soul's being barely corporeal is added as a third distinguishing characteristic; and at I.5 410b16–19, where the ancient thinkers' distinction is criticized for not covering all soul (non-locomotive sensitive soul and nutritive soul). At I.5 Aristotle implicitly adopts the division, with understanding (γιγνώσκειν), perceiving (αἰσθάνεσθαι), and opining (δοξάζειν) on one side, and appetitively desiring (ἐπιθυμεῖν) and rationally desiring or willing (βούλεσθαι) as forms of desire (ὀρέξις) on the other, alongside locomotion (which is included, surprisingly, as distinct from desire), and the nutritive activities of growth and decline. The division is laid down, seemingly as Aristotle's own view, at the opening of III.3 and III.9.

3. The key passages on core-dependent (πρὸς ἕν) relations are *Metaphysics* IV.2 1003a33–34 and VII.4 1030a34–1030b1.

4. As Falcon (2005) points out, mind (νοῦς) is only attributed to humans in a qualified way—Aristotle seems to reserve mind (νοῦς) in the strictest sense for divine disembodied

intellect. As Falcon (2005, 96, fn. 18) writes, "Evidently, *nous* refers primarily to divine being and the reference to human thinking is derived from this primary meaning. Needless to say, this fact is relevant for the project of finding a unitary account of thinking: that is, an account that unifies divine, celestial and human thinking." But for Falcon, this kind of account exceeds the scope of *De Anima*, in which Aristotle "restricts his investigation to a study of perishable life, to the exclusion of imperishable life" (2005, 92). Falcon there cites two references to perishable living beings at 413a31–32 at 415a8–9. But just because Aristotle there restricts his observation about the dependence of higher activities on lower activities to perishable beings, does not mean that this defines the scope of his investigation in *De Anima*. While I agree with Falcon that neither celestial motion nor divine thinking can be "reduced" to sublunary natures and mortal living beings, and that there is a radical break or discontinuity between sublunary and supralunary being, my interpretation of the *De Anima* aims to undermine his claims that "celestial souls go beyond the scope of the investigation offered in the *DA*," and that "*no serial relationship* exists between the perishable and celestial souls" (2005, 92).

5. Against Richardson-Lear (2004), I argue mind *can* be the form of all these other cognitive and proto-cognitive activities, precisely because of their analogical unity. See Whiting (2002, 199), for the claim that practical mind is the form of the desiring part of the soul.

6. This is the self-motion of a human agent whose rational desires thoroughly control and contain its appetitive desires beyond all psychic struggle or disharmony.

7. This question has recently been raised by Falcon (2009), which is largely based on the larger investigation in Falcon (2005).

8. See Falcon (2009) 176–77: "The decision to restrict the investigation of the soul to perishable souls, to the exclusion of imperishable souls, is already taken at the outset of the positive account of the soul offered in the second book of the *De anima*."

9. At the outset of the investigation, the least specific possible reading of ζῴων is necessary: not animals, but rather "living beings." Whether and how plants and gods fit into this picture needs to be answered through the course of the argument.

10. Falcon (2009) writes helpfully about this line: "Even though the investigation of the soul contributes directly and most obviously to the study of nature, its importance goes emphatically beyond the boundaries of a science of nature" (167, fn. 1).

11. One significant difference between *De Anima* and *Protrepticus* is that Aristotle does not bring his analysis of the various kinds of life into the immersion in nature to the same extent, that is, he does not consider the nutritive activity of plants. Living is rather defined, as it is for Plato, by the presence of perception. See Aristotle 2002, *Protrepticus*, trans. D. S. Hutchinson and Monte Johnson (http://www.chass.utoronto.ca/~phl102y/Protrepticus.pdf), 74.

12. Hutchinson and Johnson date the work in the late 350s. For their reconstruction of the work, see Hutchinson and Johnson (2005).

13. *Prot.*, 86.

14. Ibid., 87.

15. Ibid., 87. Aristotle transfers this conclusion from living to being (thus extending its scope to non-living beings), since, as he notes in *De Anima*, "for living beings life [τὸ ζῆν] is existence [τὸ εἶναι]" (II.4.415b13). In *Protrepticus* Aristotle writes: "Now if for any living being to be alive is the same as to be in existence, it is clear that the wise person would surely exist to the highest degree and in the most proper sense, and most of all at that time

when he is exercising his faculty and actually contemplating what is most knowable of the things that exist" (*Prot.*, 88).

16. *Prot.* 88.

17. Ibid., 81.

18. "Therefore everything that is done skillfully comes into being for the sake of something, and this purpose of it is the best thing. . . . And yet that which comes into being according to nature does so for the sake of something and is always constituted for the sake of something better than the product of skill" (ibid., 79–80).

19. Ibid., 68–69.

20. Ibid., 74.

21. Ibid., 67.

22. Ibid., 72.

23. Ibid., 82.

24. *De Caelo* I.10.279a21.

25. Ibid., I.9.279a28–30.

26. *History of Animals* VIII.1.588b4ff.

27. *DC* II.12.292b1–19.

28. A similar thought is expressed in *Eudemian Ethics* I.7: "Now this (happiness) is admitted to be the greatest and best of human goods—we say human, for there might perhaps be a happiness peculiar to some superior being, e.g., a god; for of the other animals, which are inferior in their nature to men, none have a right to the epithet 'happy'; for no horse, bird, or fish is happy, nor anything the name of which does not imply some share of a divine element in its nature; but in virtue of some other sort of participation in good things some have a better existence, some a worse" (I.6.1217a20–29).

29. *On Generation and Corruption* II.11.336b27–31.

30. *Eth. Eud.* VII.12.1244b22.

31. Here I follow Kosman's analysis of how one should read the problematic Greek text at this point as τὸ αὑτὸν αἰσθάνεσθαι and τὸ αὑτὸν γνωρίζειν, meaning one's own perception and one's own knowing. These, Aristotle points out, are more desirable to us than knowing in general, as we see by the fact that our own knowing is more desirable to us than someone else's knowing. See Kosman (2004, 136–39).

32. *Eth. Eud.* VII.12.1244b35ff.

33. Ibid., VII.12.1245b17–19.

34. This desire for the indeterminate to become determinate is part of a more general ontological principle in the universe, that is, the desire of matter for form: "For admitting that there is something divine, good, and desirable [i.e., form], we hold that there are two other principles, the one contrary to it [i.e., privation (στέρησις)], the other such as of its own nature to desire and yearn for it [i.e., matter (ὕλη)] . . . what desires the form is matter" (*Physics* I.9.192a16–22).

35. Kosman puts the matter well in his discussion of this same passage in the *Eudemian Ethics*: "Consciousness is thus a power of *receptivity*. It is a power of openness to determination by the other, a power that is given at once active being and determinacy only in so far as it receives that determination from its object. . . . We are, as it were, beings of indeterminate determinacy, our essential nature involving the openness to a determination received only through participation in the objective other" (2004, 135).

36. Blumenthal explains how Iamblichus either devised or canonized this interpretative rule (1979, 315).

37. Blumenthal, citing Simplicius's commentary on the *Categories* (VIII.13–15), explains why the question of aim (σκοπός) is important: "If one identifies the aim of the treatise correctly that will guide our thinking (διάνοιαν) is that we are not carried hither and thither in vain, but rather refer everything to it" (1996, 29).

38. Blumenthal 1996, 30–31.

39. As Blumenthal notes, Alexander "is the only major commentator whose work survives in any considerable quantity who wrote before Neoplatonism. Shortly after Alexander the kind of thought that is conveniently described by this label came to dominate Greek philosophy, and nearly all pagan philosophy and philosophical scholarship was pursued under its influence, if not by its active adherents" (1976, 305).

40. *Metaphysics* VII.7.1072b17–18.

41. Quoted in Kosman (1988, 183).

42. Blumenthal writes, "Neoplatonists saw the individual soul as a descending succession of forms or as a series of reflections from, or images of, the highest part. Thus for instance the sensitive soul was a reflection of the rational soul, the vegetative of the sensitive and sometimes a further sub-sensitive phase was distinguished whose function was to inform matter" (1976, 309).

43. Themistius is closer to Aristotle's argument in his interpretation than more Neoplatonic commentators, who seek to show how the higher levels of soul produce the lower. As Blumenthal notes, "Themistius follows Aristotle in regarding the human soul as a continuum, built upwards from the lower faculties rather than extending down from on high as did the Neoplatonists" (1996, 23).

44. See, for example, Johansen (1998, 20–21, fn. 5).

45. See, for example, Charles Kahn (1966, 17–18); Joseph Owens (1951, 30ff.); Myles Burnyeat (2002, 52).

46. Burnyeat 2002, 52. On II.5 he notes that "the essential incompleteness of II 5 has not been appreciated."

47. Blumenthal 1996, 28.

48. Blumenthal 1976, 309. See also his treatment of Neoplatonic commentary on the sub-sensitive soul in Blumenthal (1996, 111–120).

49. See *Phys.* I.1 for an account of how the whole is present unclearly in the beginning, and moving to the cause is simply a matter of making clear what is initially present.

50. Namely, measuring what is sought by the soul in reproduction against the satisfaction of this desire in the divine eternity in II.4. We will discuss this passage in our chapter on nutritive soul.

51. Blumenthal notes that the Neoplatonic commentators shared "the aim of making Aristotle self-consistent through a knowledge of his whole philosophy" (1976, 311). He cites a passage from Elias's commentary on the *Categories* which makes this aim explicit.

52. In his introduction to Aquinas's commentary on Aristotle's *De Anima*, Ivo Thomas writes: "In the first place the run of Aristotle's text, jerky, pithy, even haphazard in appearance, is expounded as a minutely linked sequence of thought. Each *lectio* begins by showing the place within the whole work of the passage immediately under consideration; this passage is then logically divided and subdivided down to its atomic phrases. Only after this formal analysis of the text has been made does the commentator go on to explain the material embodied in it" (Thomas 1951, 13).

53. Ivo Thomas writes of this view of the treatises as demonstrative science that "the medievals found a fully planned and largely developed scientific system, based on copi-

ous experimental data, harmonizing these under indemonstrable self-evident principles of reason by means of achieved definitions and deductive chains of argument" (1951, 14). As W. J. Hankey writes on Aquinas's interpretative approach: "In his Aristotelian and other commentaries, he not only looks at the content through Neoplatonic spectacles, but, indifferent to its own form, he divides and restructures it into a systematic chain of arguments" (1987, 8).

54. Aquinas, XIII, Fifth Article.

55. Ibid., XIII, Second Article.

56. Ibid., XVIII, Third Article.

57. See, among others, Lawson-Tancred (1986, 49).

58. See Hett's comments in his introduction to *De Anima* (1936).

59. Hicks 1907, xlii.

60. Rorty 1992, 12.

61. Nussbaum 1992, 4–5.

62. On this trend, see Lawson-Tancred (1986).

63. See Walter Brogan (2005, 17): "Hermeneutic philosophy is inauthentic when it imposes structures from outside on what is being investigated, rather than following the movement from out of itself, and making this movement of facticity explicit in its origin."

64. Heidegger does recognize that the grounds for a systematic reading of Aristotle are present in Aristotle's writing, for instance in the way that Aristotle measures the reproductive activities of nutritive soul against divine eternity in II.4. Yet he argues, I think rightly, that this is not generally the way Aristotle proceeds. Brogan writes: "He [Heidegger] attempts to show that σοφία has to do with divine movement, not the movement of living being. The mistake that has pervaded the tradition, namely, interpreting all being on the basis of what is revealed in σοφία has its roots in a certain theological bias, as Heidegger laid out in an earlier part of his text. But it can also be traced to a certain ambiguity on the part of Aristotle. To a certain extent, Aristotle's concern about the eternal and necessary movement of divine being causes him to define living being in terms of what it is not, that is, in terms of its not being necessary and eternal. This covers over, to some extent, the more original and positive access to the peculiar kind of movement and being that is involved in the case of living beings" (2005, 17).

65. "Heidegger's pervasive claim in this essay is that philosophy *is* life, that is, the self-articulation from out of itself of life. This is why Heidegger says that genuine philosophy is fundamentally atheistic. To the extent that theology takes its cue from outside factical life, it can never do philosophy. All philosophical research, and Aristotle is seen as paradigmatic, remains attuned to the life situation out of which and for the sake of which it is inquiring" (Brogan 2005, 12).

66. Kahn 1966, 5 [48].

67. Kosman 1975; 1987; 1988; 1992; 2000; 2004.

68. Ibid., 1992, 356.

69. Ibid., 357.

70. Ibid., 1988, 185.

71. Polansky 2000, 57.

72. Ibid., 58–59.

73. Russon 1996, 784.

74. Ibid., 786.

75. Shields 1999.

76. Ibid., 188.
77. Ibid., 189–91.
78. Bodéüs 1993, 50–51.
79. As a preliminary response, one need only look at *Posterior Analytics* II.19.99b34–100b19 for an account of sense perception in animals as a prefiguration of mind (νοῦς) which undermines Bodéüs's dismissal.
80. Hegel 1971, 3.
81. In order to fill out the details of this reading, one must turn to Hegel's own treatment of the soul in the *Encyclopaedia*, especially the section on the Idea as life in the *Logic* §§ 213–44, the section on organic life in the *Philosophy of Nature* §§ 337–76, and the section on subjective spirit in the *Philosophy of Spirit* §§ 377–482.
82. For Hegel, this lack of a systematic approach has its interpretative advantages for readers of Aristotle. Although the moments are not explicitly connected and related to the concept by Aristotle himself, Hegel writes that "on the one hand, this mode presents a complete series of the moments, and on the other, it arouses personal investigation for the discovery of necessity" (1995, 132).
83. Hegel 1995, 132.
84. See, for example, *Encyclopaedia* 380: "The species and grades of mental evolution, on the contrary, lose their separate existence and become factors, states and features in the higher grades of development. As a consequence of this, a lower and more abstract aspect of mind betrays the presence in it, even to experience, of a higher grade. Under the guise of sensation, for example, we may find the very highest mental life as its modification or its embodiment" (Hegel 1971).
85. For this reason, in order to clarify Aristotle's argument one must do what he in fact does not do, that is, refer forward in the progression of souls in order to clarify what is going on at a lower stage. See Hegel (1971, 380).
86. Hegel 1995, 137.
87. Ibid., 249.
88. Ibid., 251.
89. Although I only refer to book I sparingly in what follows, I do not leave it aside in agreement with Hamlyn's assumption that there are only a handful of "passages from Book I relevant to the argument in Books II and III." See his abridged selection of passages in Hamlyn (1968, 1–7). I am in full agreement with Bodéüs when he writes: "It is a mistake that certain interpreters relegate to historians of pre-Aristotelian thought the job of considering in itself the first section of the text in which the philosopher turns to a criticism of his predecessors" (1993, 26). I hope to return to this dialectical treatment of previous views on soul in a future study, but for now I can thankfully refer the reader to two excellent recent studies on book I which give an account of Aristotle's argument and its relation to what follows, both of which implicitly support the view of *De Anima* I am arguing for. See Viano 1996; Menn 2002. Viano's conclusion about the overall argument of book I in particular supports my thesis about the book as a whole: "In relation to the definition of the soul, this doxography was constructed by Aristotle especially according to the determination of the soul in its highest sense as mind [νοῦς] (see II.3). In fact, the mind [νοῦς], which comes after the other faculties and represents the final form or act of the human, the true soul which includes in itself the others, is the surpassing of the problem of reuniting the psychical and the pure noetic model into a unity" (Viano 1996, 79).

Chapter 1

1. Beyond the ancient and medieval interpretations of these chapters (esp. Alexander of Aphrodisias, Simplicius, John Philiponus, Albert the Great, and Aquinas), and the modern interpretations offered in more general commentaries (esp. Hicks, Rodier, Ross, Bodéüs, Hamlyn), there are several articles that have been devoted exclusively to these chapters on definition and method: J. L. Ackrill (1972–1973, 1979); R. Bolton (1978); W. Charlton (1980); M. de Corte (1939); S. Mansion (1973); Stephen Menn (2002); J. Owens (1971); Rosamond Kent Sprague (1996); and Johannes Hübner (1999).

2. In his recently published book devoted to these three chapters of *De Anima*, Martin Achard has very usefully classified the main positions taken on the argument, and I am much indebted to his analysis (2005, esp. 15–17).

3. Held by Aquinas and R. D. Hicks.

4. Albert the Great, G. Rodier, M. De Corte, R. Bolton.

5. Alexander of Aphrodisias, G. Rodier, R. Bodéüs.

6. Aquinas, J. Barnes, H. Lawson-Tancred, R. Polansky.

7. Martin Achard shows that what unites most of the diverse interpretations of *De Anima* II.1–3 is that the problems of the three chapters, though obviously internally related and interdependent, "have almost always been approached in an independent way in the literature" (2005, 18). Unlike Achard, I do not think that one needs the *Posterior Analytics* to make sense of *De Anima* II.1–3. Achard describes the goal of his study as follows: "We will attempt simply to show that certain chapters of the second book of the *Posterior Analytics* hold the key to untying the most fundamental *aporiai* of the text of chapters II.1–3 of *De Anima*" (2005, 28).

8. I.5.410b6–23. Aristotle in this passage is first concerned that no soul be excluded from the definition, and then that no being without a soul be falsely included.

9. I.5.410b24ff.

10. Achard (2005) shows convincingly, in my view, that the most common definition (κοινότατος λόγος) yields the genus of soul.

11. *Pol.* I.1.1252b32–33.

12. The view is so prevalent that one could cite virtually all modern interpreters of Aristotle. For particularly clear expressions of it, see Bodéüs (1993, 50–51), or Fraser (2003, 136, 139, fn. 8).

13. See *Metaph.* XII.7.1072b13–30.

14. See Fraser (2002, 45): "The categorical structure of being *qua* being is understood in terms of the demonstrative explication of a single genus and nature: οὐσία. And the science of οὐσία, upon a still deeper reflection, turns out to be identical to the science of super-celestial οὐσία, viz. theology, since the principles of divine substance are, for Aristotle, the principles of the substantiality of all else."

15. An important difference between the serial logic of the categories and the serial logic of the hierarchy of soul is that the non-substantial categories of being are realized in their focal sense of substance-being, while we have substances already from the lowest level of living. Having discovered substance-being, the argument of the *De Anima* can be seen to extend the argument by looking at the various levels of substance until the structure of substance appears in its clearest form: thought thinking itself. This difference has important consequences: while none of the non-substantial categories of being can exist without their focal meaning substance, which alone has independent and intrinsic (καθ' αὑτό) existence, all the kinds of living can exist separately. The different degrees of

existence in itself (καθ' αὑτό) are distinguished according to the extent each kind of soul can exist separately from its environment, from a being other than itself. One could say that while substance is the focal sense of being, living activity is the paradigmatic sense of substance, and God's thinking is the focal sense of all life (and thus of all substance).

16. My disagreement with Fraser hinges on what constitutes independence and separation in *De Anima*. While Fraser looks to which level of soul can exist apart from the others, I shall argue that the more relevant sense of independence lies in the degree of dependence of the soul on another being external to it, its environment. Only with active thinking is the object of the activity wholly internal, without any reference to the external, and thus wholly independent.

17. 402b16–25: "It would seem not only that knowing the 'what it is' is useful for knowing the causes of the attributes of the substances (just as in mathematics knowing what straight, curved, line, and surface are is useful for recognizing how many right angles equal the angles of a triangle). But conversely the attributes contribute a great part for knowing the 'what it is.' For whenever we are able able to explain the attributes according to appearances, either all of them or most of them, then we will be able to speak most finely about the *ousia*."

18. I am indebted to two of my students, Evan King and Benjamin Max Manson, for pressing the point to me that the most common definition (κοινότατος λόγος) can in fact yield some grasp of the essence, even if the soul's nature and essence is not fully understood until it is grasped through its fullest actuality.

19. See Johannes Hübner (1999). The principal differences between Hübner's interpretation and my own are (1) he seems to take the most common definition (κοινότατος λόγος) as Aristotle's satisfactory definition of what soul is most fundamentally, whereas I argue in what follows that it is a necessary but transitory moment in the argument; (2) he wants to argue that the first activity that is soul is actually the activity one finds in the embryo, whereas I understand the embryo prior to its distinct, separate existence to be the matter that is life potentially; (3) he sees his position on soul as activity as being incompatible with the traditional interpretation of soul in II.1 as a collection of latent or unexercised capacities, whereas I see the two views to be ultimately compatible. None of these differences affect my dependence upon and agreement with Hübner's argument in this section.

20. *Pol.* I.1.1252a17–18 (translation mine).

21. Bodéüs asserts that the most common soul, though it used the nutritive soul as its first reference, was not a proper definition of nutritive soul (1993, 151 fn. 2).

22. Polansky 2007, 146, fn.1.

23. Although Martin Achard (2005, 159–62) has recently maintained that scholars have been misled to believe that Aristotle's quest for the most common account of soul is fundamentally Platonic, I am in agreement with De Corte, who writes that "adopting a unitary method of a demonstrative kind for the discovery of the essence of the soul comes down to making the soul into an idea" (1939, 461).

24. Plato, *Phaedrus* 237b-c.

25. Ibid., 263a.

26. Ibid., 265d–266b.

27. As Martin Achard (following Aquinas) has noted, on the way to his first attempt at formulating the most common definition of soul Aristotle proceeds through a series of two divisions, which lay out all the distinctions that are incorporated into the subsequent

definitions. See the helpful diagram and explanation of these divisions in Achard (2005, 36–39). I do not think, however, that identifying Aristotle's procedure as division in this section has as much explanatory power as Achard ascribes to it.

28. This helps avoid the error committed by Thales, who saw soul as existing in all natural being, including the elements. See *DA* I.5.411a7–16.

29. Categorizing the living being as compounds (συνθέτη) at this point introduces the problem of the nature of the unity of the living being, which will recur throughout the chapter. This point in the argument is very similar to the point which Aristotle reaches by VII.17.1041b11ff. of the *Metaphysics*, where one has recognized that substance is matter and form together, but not merely as the mixture or coordination of two independent elements.

30. Hübner argues that Aristotle's distinction between knowledge (ἐπιστήμη) and active contemplation (θεωρεῖν) is not referring to the later three-level theory of potentiality and actuality which is articulated in the section on sensation, and that Aristotle is using this distinction in another context at this point. I do not think, however, that Hübner's important emphasis on the activity of soul in this definition is incompatible with associating the definition of soul with first-actuality/second potentiality, since the capacity for further activity is itself inextricably active.

31. The active exercise of the knowledge exists as prior in the soul of the teacher.

32. See King (2001, 3): "This definition is then given concrete form in the functions or parts of the soul, but it is closely associated from the outset with the nutritive soul, that is, the soul responsible for nutrition, since all living things, in all their parts, must achieve this actuality or activity."

33. "Concerning the soul by virtue of which an animal is so called (and this is in virtue of the sensitive part of the soul) – does this exist originally in the semen and in the embryo or not, and if it does whence does it come? For nobody would put down the embryo as soulless or in every sense bereft of life (since both the semen and the embryo of an animal have every bit as much life as a plant), and it is productive up to a certain point. That then they possess the nutritive soul is plain (and it is plain from the discussion elsewhere about soul why this must be acquired first) [Note: it seems possible that this may even be a reference to the passage of *De Anima* now under consideration]. As they develop they also acquire the sensitive soul in virtue of which an animal is an animal" (*On the Generation of Animals* II.3.736a29–736b1).

34. The first part of the chapter, seeking the most common definition, seeks to identify the limit between what counts as life and what does not through defining the emergence of life in birth. The second part of the chapter (the comparison of the soul with the axe and the eye) concerns itself with the end limit, looking at various ways in which form and matter are separated, to draw the limit between the living and non-living through the death of the organism.

35. It is based on these passages that I have minor disagreements with Hübner's account. This seems to show (1) that the idea of soul's common definition as activity is not in fact at odds with the three-level doctrine of potentiality and actuality, since the second potentiality is an activity anyways, and the first potentiality is, in accordance with the doctrine just outlined, non-active body potentially possessing life; (2) it is not wholly right to identify the embryo and this first activity, since the embryo is not actively living until it is separate and able to engage in nutritive activities.

36. *GA* II.3.736b8–13.

37. "We assume that one who is exercising sense-perception is awake, and that every one who is awake perceives either some external movement or else some movement within himself" (*On Sleep and Waking* I.454a2–4).

38. See, for example, *Eth. Eud.* II.1.1219b22–24: "For in sleep the vegetative part is more active, while the perceptive and the appetitive are incomplete in sleep."

39. Aristotle makes explicit that this cannot be the case in *Generation of Animals* V.1: "For life most of all appertains to wakefulness, on account of sensation" (V.1.778b31–32).

40. I agree completely with Stephen Menn's assessment of the role of book I in the argument: "Aristotle is proposing to his readers a criterion for judging his own account of what the soul is, namely that it should resolve the ἀπορίαι raised in *De Anima* I, or, perhaps more precisely, that it should satisfy the different expectations about soul that Aristotle's predecessors had been trying (explicitly or implicitly) to satisfy, but that he has shown they have failed to satisfy" (Menn 2002, 103).

41. At this point, it remains unclear whether this opening sentence is a criticism of the abstraction of the definition in II.1, or merely the statement of the new beginning which takes up the most common definition (κοινότατος λόγος) as its most unclear and manifest starting point, moving to the principle. Taken in isolation, the sentence can plausibly be taken in both senses, but I hope through the interpretation that follows to convince of the truth of the first reading.

42. πάλιν can mean simply "anew," or "beginning again," both of which also make perfect sense in this context, but it seems that in this particular case Aristotle is talking about a new beginning from the particulars to the universals, rather than from universals to particulars.

43. Aristotle makes this clear in the *Parts of Animals*, when discussing the difference between investigating eternal and mortal substances. He writes that "the former are excellent and divine, but less accessible to knowledge. The evidence that might throw light on them, and on the problems which we long to solve respecting them, is furnished but scantily by sensation; whereas respecting perishable plants and animals we have abundant information, living as we do in their midst, and ample data may be collected concerning all their various kinds, if only we are willing to take sufficient pains. Both departments, however, have their special charm. The scanty conceptions to which we can attain of celestial things give us, from their excellence, more pleasure than all our knowledge of the world in which we live . . . On the other hand, in certitude and in completeness our knowledge of terrestrial things has the advantage. Moreover, their greater nearness and affinity to us balances somewhat the loftier interest of the heavenly things that are the objects of the higher philosophy" (*PA* I.5.644b25–645a4).

44. See *Meteorologica* IV.12.390a14. Here we see that the lower on the hierarchy are less clear than the higher. Plants less than animals, flesh and touch less than tongue and taste, because their formal articulation (λόγος) and function are less clear.

45. *DP* I.1.815a10–12. If the author of this treatise is not Aristotle, which seems to be the scholarly consensus, it is clear that the student on this point has grasped his teacher's thinking.

46. This νῦν (now) can equally refer to either "definitions nowadays," that is, the prevailing Platonic approaches which have a hold on Aristotle's contemporaries, or more specifically to the immediate context of the most common definition (κοινότατος λόγος) of the previous chapter. As we have seen that Aristotle's method in II.1 is fundamentally Platonic in inspiration, there is no opposition between the two options.

47. See especially Rosamond Kent Sprague (1996). It is further assumed by Sprague that the fault which plagued the II.1 definition is remedied by a proper syllogism somewhere present in II.2, starting with the premise "soul is that by which we live, perceive, think," and ending with the formula at the end of the chapter: "soul is a certain actuality and λόγος of a certain thing having a potentiality."

48. Although Sprague admits that she has "had little success in attempting to construct syllogisms of which the definitions of II.1 are the conclusions" (1996, 108 fn. 6), this is not, as she suggests, the fault of the definition in II.1, but is because neither book II.1 nor book II.2 should be read as offering syllogistic demonstrations of essence.

49. As Aristotle makes clear in *APo.*II.8, definitions can only result from demonstrations when the cause is other than the object (for example, with eclipses). This is not the case with soul. And even in these cases, conclusions of demonstrations never predicate the definition or essence of the object being defined. I thank David Bronstein for pointing this out to me.

50. See Hicks (1907, 322–23) and Heath (1949, 191–92). Hicks describes the latter example in the following terms: "The problem in VI.13 is to find a mean proportional between the two straight lines; and we find that by placing the two lines in one straight line AC, describing a semicircle on the whole line as a diameter, and from the point *B* where the two lines meet drawing a line at right angles to *D* a point on the circumference, a mean proportional, i.e. a line which stands to the one line in the same ratio as it itself stands to the other, is obtained; so that AB:BD::BD:BC . . . It will be observed that BD, which is the mean proportional between AB and BC, is also the side of the square equal to the rectangle AB.BC."

51. Life falls immediately into these senses of living, just as being falls immediately into the various senses of being in the categories. Notice that having only local motion allows heavenly bodies to be considered living. See Bolton (1978, 261). Though there is nothing that exists with sensation alone, thinking alone allows God to be included in this account, while local movement alone allows the heavenly bodies to be included.

52. Another recent interpretation of Aristotle's definition of life in *De Anima*, one which does not fit into the main divisions I outlined above, has been offered by Gareth B. Matthews in his "*De Anima* 2.2–4 and the Meaning of Life." There Matthews argues, based upon the passage currently under consideration, that Aristotle defines life by listing a certain number of properties of living things, at least one of which must be possessed by a being for it to be considered alive. More specifically, he says that a certain being is alive, if it is able to exercise one of the self-perpetuating powers belonging to its species (1992, 192). Within the context of the argument of the whole, this is not tenable as an interpretation of an acceptable Aristotelian definition, but Matthews does bring up one point which is crucial in order to understand how he views a core-dependent (πρὸς ἕν) definition as necessary for determining the nature of "life." He takes seriously the consequences of the fact that Aristotle considers God to be alive, though he does not participate in any of the dynamic activities besides thought. Thus life cannot be defined by nutritive activity, as many think, if the definition is to be properly universal and thus inclusive of all instances of living. See Shields (1999) for the importance of this point for grasping the core-dependent (πρὸς ἕν) definitional structure of life.

53. Aristotle does not begin with a determinate species of living being, such as the most primitive species of life, plants, but with τὰ φυόμενα, things growing. We are here considering all life from its beginning, which, in the *Politics*, Aristotle makes clear is the objective

beginning point in every investigation of a series: "He who thus considers things in their first growth and origin [ἐξ ἀρχῆς τὰ πράγματα φυόμενα], whether a state or anything else, will obtain the clearest view of them" (*Pol.* I.2.1252a24–25). I will say more about the parallel between method in *Politics* and the *De Anima* in the conclusion of this chapter. The fact that Aristotle refers to growing things and not to plants is passed over by most translators besides Bodéüs and Barnes. Yet even Bodéüs explains the use of φυόμενα (things growing) somewhat extrinsically to the argument: Aristotle likely chose this term because he wanted to include primitive marine life within his consideration (Bodéüs 1993, 141n4).

54. Recall these activities as they are introduced into the account at II.1.412a14.

55. The brief remark on the specific nature of living growth as distinguished from the increase of the inanimate elements occurs here because in discussing the proper characteristic of each soul, one must identify those powers which are present at that level of soul but lacking in the level below. Because the nutritive soul is the very first appearance of life from out of the non-living, it must be distinguished not from a lower form of soul, but from the inanimate. He must clearly distinguish this most primitive, initial activity from non-living being. All living things manifest this principle that separates them from non-living natural beings by the fact that they grow in all directions, and do not merely move or accumulate themselves relative to their natural place, which, as opposed to the center of growth internal to living beings, lies outside of themselves (perhaps the most primitive indication of the *entelecheia* of life, having one's principle within itself).

56. It is significant that the word for taking in food is also the word one uses for apprehending by the senses *and* the word used for grasping with the mind. This is a linguistic indication of the structural analogy at all levels of the soul.

57. Although it is not mentioned at this point of the argument, there exist within nutritive soul higher functions, such as reproduction (see II.4), but taking away a plant's ability to reproduce does not prevent it from being a plant. The same thing will be observed of animals. There are thus affections (πάθη) of each level of soul which are inseparable for its being what it is, and affections (πάθη) which, though necessary for defining the particular kind of plant or animal that it is, are superfluous to finding under which of the kinds of soul it falls.

58. Here I believe Aristotle is referring to desire and locomotion.

59. "The soul is the principle of these aforementioned activities and is defined by these, that is by the nutritive, sensitive, intellective [διανοητικῷ] and by movement" (II.2.413b11–13).

60. "On account of what cause each of these happens [συμβέβηκεν], we will explain later" (II.2.413b9–10). My interpretation of this line is admittedly contentious, and runs contrary to the traditional (and perhaps more natural) reading of the sentence as referring simply to the fact that touch can exist separately from the other senses in lower animals just as the nutritive soul can exist independently from the sensitive in plants. On this traditional reading Aristotle simply postpones giving the reason for this fact until *De Anima* III.12 and III.13, where he explains that an animal with locomotion but no sense of touch could not preserve itself through fleeing and pursuing the appropriate objects, since it would have no awareness of its potentially destructive direct contact with other bodies. My own tentative interpretation understands the referent of ἑκάτερον τούτων (each of these) to be activities of nutrition and sensation just mentioned, rather than merely the separate existence of touch. Two points should be noted about this sentence. First of all, the verb συμβαίνειν (to stand with, coincide, to happen) used here recalls I.1.402a7–11,

when Aristotle states that his goal is to know first the nature and substance of soul, and then the attributes of this nature (ὅσα συμβέβηκε περὶ αὐτήν). The συμβεβηκός (attribute) is then identified with the affections (πάθη), and divided into two kinds—one which belong properly to the soul in itself, and ones which belong to the living body, the compound of soul and body. In this passage of II.2, it seems possible that Aristotle, referring to the nutritive and sensitive powers, is referring to those attributes (συμβεβηκά/πάθη) which follow from the body-soul compound, while thinking refers to the attributes (συμβεβηκά/πάθη) proper to the soul in its inner identity. The second point is that most interpreters do not make the connection between this comment about the cause, and the context of the discussion of II.2 more generally as seeking not just the fact but the cause. For this reason, they look for the answer to this question in the last chapter of *De Anima*. Yet if the current interpretation is correct, the reason is that which is disclosed by discovering the ultimate term of the series as that for the sake of which each exists. The fact that the cause is not yet disclosed is reiterated in the context of the next section at II.2.414a1–2, which can also be perhaps more plausibly read along the lines of the aforementioned traditional interpretation.

61. See, for example, *Timaeus* 69e ff.

62. This is perhaps one sense in which starting from the simple vital activity of plants with their limited number of activities, certain features of the soul are more manifest to us.

63. As I point out elsewhere, one of the characteristics progressively manifested as one moves up the hierarchy of life is *indivisibility*. Thus the lowest form of life is most divisible, while the highest (God's thinking) is most indivisible.

64. Bodéüs notes that "Aristotle is not troubled by the fact that, in his own comparison, the soul is considered, on the one hand, as the material principle (of the knower), and, on the other, as the formal principle (of the living being)" (1993,145n2).

65. One cannot make sense of this passage or many others in Aristotle's corpus unless one heeds Kosman's warning concerning Aristotle's uses of the terms "form" and "matter": "We must remember that *form* is for Aristotle always specific to *being under a certain description*" (1987, 372). The distinction of form and matter is not firmly fixed: something which is form can become matter under a different description. In relation to our consideration of *De Anima*, the activity of sensitive soul is the form of an animal, but becomes matter or body in the context of the human, in that its full activity is the potential existence necessary for the exercise of the higher activity.

66. See Aristotle's various formulations for matter in *Metaphysics*: "By matter I mean that which is not a 'this-such' in actuality, but that which is a 'this-such' in potency" (VIII.1.1042a27–28).

67. As far as I can see, this is the unanimous consensus among interpreters, even Hübner (1999, 13), with whom I am otherwise in almost complete agreement.

68. *Top.* VI.10.148a25–31.

69. *Metaph.* VII.8.1034a7–8. The species is said synonymously of each member: Socrates and Callias are "different by virtue of their matter (for that is different), but the same in [species] form; for the form is undivided."

70. It is for this reason that ultimately the three principal kinds of soul are reduced to nutritive, sensitive, and intellective. Moving in space and desiring are necessarily related to various aspects of sensation, and thus do not ultimately constitute a different kind of soul (seeing that their division does not constitute a different kind of living being, that is, other than plant, animal, human).

71. Smell is a special case, since it is an intermediary between the cognitive and nutritive senses, sharing characteristics of both.

72. The context of their higher formal activity changes the nature of nutrition in animals in comparison with plants in several ways: the plant takes in food already processed by the earth's heat and is thus far more passive than the animal which takes the food and processes it within itself; being stationary, what it takes in is wholly determined by its location and natural environment; its reproduction occurs differently since the plant exists prior to the differentiation between male and female, containing in a sense both within itself prior to their distinction. All these differences are explained by the fact that in plants the nutritive soul is that for the sake of which the nutritive activity exists, whereas in most animals nutrition exists for the sake of perceptive/locomotive soul. On some of the differences between nutritive activities in plants, lower animals, and higher animals, see *HA* VII.1.588b30ff.

73. Plato, *Timaeus* 77.

74. οἰκεῖον here means a *particular* form, and also the most proper or precise expression of the series. It might also retain the sense of οἰκεῖον as manifesting a family resemblance—it has a look of its own but which is related to and derived from the traits of the other individuals in the family.

75. Interpreting this difficult passage would be much easier had Aristotle explained somewhere exactly how he understands figure to be ordered serially. He associates the triangle with the nutritive soul, the simplest manifestation of each term, and associates the quadrilateral with the sensitive soul, as the first stage beyond the most primitive manifestation. Most interpreters and translators assume that the series of figures corresponding to the series of souls would be triangle, quadrilateral, pentagon, hexagon, and so on. This seems to be unlikely, for two reasons. First, this account of the series of figures would be infinitely long, since one can simply keep adding sides to the figure. The hierarchy of souls, in contrast, culminates in intellect beyond which nothing is more comprehensive. Second, while the square contains triangles potentially within it in that one could divide it up in many ways and obtain triangles in actuality, the same cannot be said about squares existing potentially within pentagons. Since figure is defined, by Plato for example, as "the limit of a solid" (*Meno* 76a) or by Euclid as "that which is surrounded by some limit or certain limits" (*Elements* I.14), the key to the series parallel with the series of souls is that each subsequent term comprehends the lower terms within its limits. It seems to me likely that Aristotle took the circle to be the paradigmatic, most comprehensive figure containing all other figures within it (much as circular motion acts as the ultimate limit comprehensive of all rectilinear motion), in the same way that he takes thought to be the complete nature of soul, comprehending the lower activities within it. On the circle as prior to all other figures, see *DC* II.4.286b18ff. There Aristotle argues that, while triangle as the simplest rectilinear figure might be thought to be the primary figure, ultimately it is the circle and not the triangle which has priority among figures.

76. See Kyle Fraser's instructive comments on the causal explanation: "This transition from fact to reasoned fact does not generally come in one step, but involves a series of analyses, in which the scientist probes deeper and deeper into the essential nature of the genus in question, until he arrives at an unmediated aspect" (Fraser 2003, 133). On the reading I am offering, the two postponements until later of the question of the cause of the lower souls being the way the are (*De Anima* II.2.413b10–11; II.2.414a1–2) are not, as virtually all commentators think, a reference to the last two chapters of the treatise, but rather to the moment when mind (νοῦς) is discovered as the fulfillment and nature of the series.

77. Kyle Fraser explains how serial and the core-dependent (πρὸς ἕν) structures are not different: "Every serial structure can be regarded as a species of πρὸς ἕν connection" (2003, 139 n.8).

78. Kosman writes, in the different context of the core-dependent homonymy (πρὸς ἕν λεγόμενα) structure of the *Categories* but which applies just as much to the various kinds of living: "Two entities are πρὸς ἕν λεγόμενα if they are homonymous in this sense [i.e., what it means to live for each is different], but if in addition there is some third entity that is F, and what it is to be F for this entity is such that what it is to be F for the original entities may be understood in the light of it" (1984, 145).

79. *Posterior Analytics* II.1.90a15. See also Kosman 1973, 376.

80. Kosman 1994, 145.

81. As James Doull writes in reference to II.3 of *De Anima*, "The powers of the soul which appear in the development are not faculties of a substance but the unfolding of the substance itself" (2003, 47).

82. As a result, this method in accordance with the serial ordering of souls provides an answer to the initial *aporia* of I.1 (402a11–22): Is there a universal method always applicable to the search for the essence or nature of an object? Or does a distinct method need to be found for each distinct object of inquiry? The answer here is that a particular method applies in the case of soul by virtue of the fact that the different kinds of soul fall into a series of prior and posterior, where the earlier are taken up into the later. This method will apply to all such serially ordered members of a genus.

83. Menn writes that "because the *De Anima* 2.1 definition of soul is deliberately set up to demand clarification both by specifying the soul's powers and by specifying their acts and objects, the investigation of sensation (and so on) should be seen as filling in the account of what the soul is—even though Aristotle never again after *De anima* 2.4 explicitly calls the soul a form or an ἐντελέχεια" (2002, 107).

84. *Pol.* I.1.1252a4–7.

85. Ibid., I.1.1252b28–29.

86. Similarly, just as nutrition might be seen as the fundamental nature of life because it alone can exist apart from the other activities, the family can be seen as the true nature of association (κοινωνία) because it emerges first independently of the city, although the city cannot exist independently of the families it comprises. But this view of association (κοινωνία) would be as wrong as the view of soul we are criticizing that sees in plants the paradigm of life. See *Pol.* II.1.1261b11–13: "For a family is more self-sufficing than an individual, and a city than a family, and a city only comes into being when the community is large enough to be self-sufficing." The kind of independence is not the independence of existing in order of time or in frequency (being most common), but rather, the ability for the kind of soul or association (κοινωνία) to exist in independence from what lies outside it and to maintain itself continuously in existence.

87. Aristotle argues that the result of Plato's interpreting assoication or community (κοινωνία) synonymously is that the unity characteristic of the family applies identically to the state as a whole (see *Pol.* II.1).

88. *Pol.* I.1.1252a17–18.

89. *Pol.* I.2.1252a24. Recall Aristotle's statement at *DA* II.1.412a26–27: "And knowledge [ἐπιστήμη] [i.e., the mere possession as opposed to the active exercise] is prior in genesis with regard to the same being." It is striking, in terms of the analogy between *De Anima* and the *Politics*, that Aristotle begins in that later treatise with the form of com-

munity that is most natural, most governed by necessity, whose most perfect form results in reproduction. In all these ways the beginning point echoes the psychological beginning point with plants.

90. *GA* II.4.740a27–35.

91. *GA* II.3.736b11–13. See also *Pol.* VII.16.1335b18–19: "For the offspring derive their natures from their mothers as plants do from the earth."

92. "Hence it is that only one part comes into being first and not all of them together. But that must first come into being which has a principle of increase (for this nutritive power exists in all alike, whether animals or plants, and this is the same as the power that enables an animal or plant to generate another like itself, that being the function of them all if naturally perfect). And this is necessary for the reason that whenever a living thing is produced it must grow" (*GA* II.1.735a14ff.).

93. *GA* II.4.740a7–8.

94. *GA* II.4.740a24–27. This is true both for viviparous animals as well as animals born from eggs, whose yolk nourishes like the uterus.

95. "[The embryo] lives the life of a plant, for it receives its first growth and nourishment by being attached to something else" (*GA* III.2.753b27–29).

96. *GA* III.2.753b25–27.

97. *GA* V.1.778b20–24. Aristotle does mention that animals do occasionally awaken in the uterus (V.1.779a8–11).

98. "It is necessary then for the animal to sleep most of the time because the growth and the weight lie on the upper part of the body" (*GA* V.1.779a5–7).

99. *GA* V.1.778b25–6.

100. *HA* VIII.1.588a31–588b2.

101. *PA* IV.10.686b28–29. This physical manifestation of soul, heat, also determines the hierarchy of animals based on the predominance of soul over body: if "a further decrease occurs in the elevating heat, and a further increase in the earthly matter," we move from biped to four-footed to the no-footed and finally to plants, which have no sensation or movement whatsoever (see IV.10.686b28–687a2).

102. *PA* II.1.646a25–28; II.1.646a35–646b2. The context of this passage is to show how simple, uniform substances are prior in formation but posterior in essence (οὐσία) to the non-uniform parts as merely instrumental to these. Yet this principle applies equally to all levels on the hierarchy of natural being, from the elements to human soul.

103. See also *Phys.* VIII.7.261a13–14: "In general, that which is becoming appears as something imperfect and proceeding to a principle; and so what is posterior in the order of becoming is prior in the order of nature." Peculiarly, in this passage Aristotle writes that "all things that go through the process of becoming acquire locomotion last" (VIII.7.261a14–15). It is odd that thinking is not the last, if he is including humans among generated beings.

104. *GA* V.1.778b31–32.

105. See *PA* II.1.646a ff. for the parallel with house-building. The parallel is further explained in *Phys.* II.8.199a8ff.

106. *Pol.* I.1.1253a19–20.

107. Thus the answer to the question "what is the nature of soul" is "thinking." As it is for the individual thing, so it is for the series. That it is "the nature of the soul to know," in the same way that it is the impulse (ὁρμή) in all things towards such a community (*Pol.* I.2.1253a29–30), sheds new light on the opening lines of the *Metaphysics*.

108. *Pol.* I.1.1252b30–1253a1.

109. Ibid., I.1.1253a19–20.

110. See also *Metaph.* XIII.2.1077a1ff.

111. *DC* I.1.268a9. The fact that all these examples come in sets of three is significant, but I am not sure about the necessity of this pattern. Aristotle explicitly suggests that there is a kind of divine necessity to the series of three, which had been intuited by the Pythagoreans through the importance assigned to the number three in their religious ceremonies. They recognized that three was the number of the complete (τὸ τέλειον) and the whole (τὸν ἀριθμὸν τοῦ παντός).

112. *DC* I.1.268a30b5.

113. Ibid., I.1.268b5ff.

114. Ibid., II.4. Like the pure intellect relative to the human soul containing all lower souls within it, the circle is limited by only one surface, while the rectilinear figures contain several.

115. *Pol.* I.2.1252b29.

116. *Eth. Nic.* X.7.1177a27ff; X.8.1178a22ff.

Chapter 2

1. W. S. Hett in his introduction to the Loeb edition of *De Anima* dismisses the nutritive soul with one sentence: "Nutrition is not discussed at any length and needs no comment here" (1936, 4). In the most important collection of essays in English, *Essays on De Anima* (1992), no articles are devoted to the role of nutrition in the argument, and almost no passing references are made to the topic. Certain authors do show an awareness of the importance of nutrition for apprehending the structure of Aristotle's argument: Kosman, Lear, and Russon, in particular. The only articles I have found solely devoted to the questions of plant life and nutritive soul are S. Cantin (1946); Damian Murphy (2005); and Bernard Besnier (1997). Two recent and excellent books devoted to questions intimately related to nutritive soul are Gad Freudenthal's (1995) *Aristotle's Theory of Material Substance* and R. A. H. King's (2001) *Aristotle on Life and Death*.

2. Just as the acts (πράξεις) and activities (ἐνέργειαι) are prior to their capacity (δύναμις) according to reason (λόγος), the objects (ἀντικείμενα) are prior to the activities (ἐνέργειαι) for the same reason (διὰ τήν αὐτὴν αἰτίαν; see *DA* II.4.415a19–22).

3. "With us welfare involves something beyond us, but the deity is his own well-being" (*Eth. Eud.* VII.12.1245b18). We will have to return to this fundamental relational character of mortal psychic activity.

4. Plato seems to have made the same realization in his later psychological thinking. Whereas soul and the city were treated, in *Republic* and *Phaedo* for example, in isolation from what was external to them, in the *Timaeus* Socrates expresses the desire to understand them in relation to their interactions with otherness, in the following step beyond the politics and psychology of the *Republic*: "My feelings are like those of a man who gazes upon magnificent looking animals, whether they're animals in a painting or even actually alive but standing still, and who then finds himself longing to look at them in motion or engaged in some struggle or conflict that seems to show some of their distinctive physical qualities" (*Timaeus* 19b-c).

5. In his discussion of acting (ποιεῖν) and being acted upon (πάσχειν) in *On Generation and Corruption* I.7, dealing with exactly the same problems of "like by like" and "unlike by unlike" which he addresses in *De Anima* II.4, Aristotle diagnoses the problem with these

incomplete positions as follows: "The cause of the disagreement is that it is necessary to think the whole, but each of them happens to address a certain part" (*GC* I.7.323b17–18).

6. *Pol.* I.8.1256b15–22. It must be noted that if all things exist for the sake of man, it is for a specific reason: because man is that living being who is characterized by the ability to exercise thought. Thus all being exists ultimately, one could just as well say, for the sake of thinking.

7. Specifically, earth and water. See *GC* II.8.335a4ff.

8. As Kosman writes, "It is as though, in viewing the elements themselves as essentially instrumental for the higher forms of organic life, Aristotle sees the entire range of being as naturally constituted for the sake of the complex modes of animal activity" (1987, 389). Kosman uses the example of animal activity, but the same holds true for plant activity. He goes on to write that "motion, perception and mind itself are on this view the natural manifestations of modes of capacity and potentiality embedded in even the most elemental forms of nature" (1987, 389). While I am restricting the present study to the *De Anima* and the study of living being, it would be interesting to look to Aristotle's works on non-living nature to see the ways in which their being and activity also express the characteristics of divine being in even more unclear and distant ways than living being. See *GC* II.10 on this point.

9. To confirm that Aristotle does in fact see non-living nature as seamlessly integrated into the hierarchy of life described in *De Anima*, one need only look to the well-known passage from the *Meteorology* IV.12.389b27ff. There the elements are said to exist for the sake of homogeneous bodies, which in turn exist for the sake of the heterogeneous bodies like the parts of the body. At each level there is progressive dominance of form over matter.

10. Compare *GA* II.1.730b24–731a1.

11. See Bodéüs: "It seems to apply here, under the heading of 'intended goal,' to eternity (proper to imperishable beings), and, under the heading of 'subject served,' to the (perishable) being which has as its ends nutritive operations. It assumes a *distance*, proper to any natural being, between what it is and what it strives to be, whether this is within its reach or not, either totally or partially" (1993, 152n3).

12. Plants of course have no desire, since desire only emerges with perception with the emergence of animal life. This is why Aristotle adds that this is what is sought by all things when they "act in accordance with nature." This is the case for all things, even the movement of the elements prior to life. Thus they desire it only in the sense of being determined in their nature to have a tendency towards this. But to apprehend each particular unconscious activity as a manifestation of a desire for the divine activity, one must have before oneself the whole of nature and its development from level to level towards the divine before oneself. In isolation, the activities would not seem to have this character.

13. Jonathan Lear 1988, 101. Lear notes that the divinity of reproduction cannot lie merely in its eternality, since matter is also eternal for Aristotle but not divine.

14. Bodéüs interprets the object of the desire as persisting continuously through time by reproduction, and thus the various degrees of participation in this eternal divine activity are measured by the continuity of the being's lineage. See Bodéüs (1993, 152n3).

15. Of course, very striking in this passage is the use of the Platonic language of participation. Each lower instance of life seems to exist as *participating* in the divine, paradigmatic instance of life. In view of Aristotle's criticism of the Platonic doctrine of participation as "metaphorical," it is necessary to determine first of all, why Aristotle chooses this Platonic language, and secondly, how he sees the relationship expressed by this participation to be

not vulnerable in the same way to the accusation of metaphor he launches at Plato. This is a question we need to keep in mind throughout his account, as we get a clearer idea of what Aristotle means by participation of each instance in the divine.

16. *Eth. Eud.* VII.12.1244b24ff.

17. *Eth. Nic.* VII.13.1153b29–32.

18. Gonzalez 1991, 144.

19. *GC* II.10.336b17–337a7.

20. Ibid., II.11.338b8–13.

21. Evidently the possibility of extinction of species is not accounted for by this insight.

22. Aristotle speaks of soul as both cause (αἰτία) and principle (ἀρχή), yet in what follows focuses explicitly only on soul as *cause*. Yet this section is as much about soul as the principle, beginning, or source (ἀρχή) of the activities.

23. When he begins his investigation into nutritive soul, he writes that "first one must speak of food and reproduction" (II.4.415a22–23), omitting growth (three lines later, he writes, "to reproduce and to use [χρῆσθαι] food" [II.4.415a26]). Why does Aristotle here bring up these two activities at this point, for at least one other important activity characteristic of nutritive soul—growing—could have been mentioned? Later on, Aristotle seems to conceive of the three primary activities of the nutritive soul—self-nourishment, growth, and reproduction—as being ordered in a hierarchical relationship, much like the relationship between nutrition, sensation, and thought, since the higher cannot exist independently of the lower. The organism nourishes itself for the preservation and continued existence of its substance or essence (οὐσία); it must persevere in its existence for the sake of developing into its appropriate quantity or size through growing; and finally, having reached its full development with relation to itself, it can thus perform the ultimate function for which its exists, by producing another the same as itself, thus initiating the whole process again from the beginning.

24. "But what it is to be nourishment and what it is to be growth are different. For the ensouled being as a certain quantity is capable of growth, but as an individual thing and a substance, it is nourishment" (II.4.416b11–13).

25. In ascribing this power of holding together the body to nutritive soul, Aristotle answers the puzzles he raises at I.5.411b14–19 about which part of the soul, if any, is responsible for this preservation of the living body.

26. *GC* II.8.335a14–16.

27. *On Respiration* III.474a25; IV.469b17–20. See especially *PA* II.3.650a2–9: "Now since everything that grows must take nourishment, and nutriment in all cases consists of moist and dry substances, and since it is by force of heat that these are concocted and changed, it follows that all living things, animals and plants alike, must on this account, if on no other, have a natural source of heat; and this, like working of the food, must belong to many parts."

28. *On Youth and Old Age* V.469b25–27.

29. *PA* III.7.670a25.

30. *Resp.* XVII.478b33.

31. King captures the reflexive return upon itself of nutrition well: "But nutrition is not only *of* the body, it is *by* the body: the body not only benefits from nutrition, it also provides the tools to do so. Since these tools are the body, they are preserved by the process to which they are instrumental" (2001, 57).

32. This is what Aristotle means when he writes that "the food prepares it [the living being] to be active" (II.4.416b19). The process involved in nourishing itself is a preparation for the *energeia* which is its self-maintenance.

33. "What does come-to-be in growth is flesh or bone—or a hand or arm" (*GC* I.5.322a19–21).

34. "In so far as this acceding food is potentially the double-result—e.g., is potentially a quantity of flesh—it produces growth: for it is bound to become both *a quantity* and *flesh*. But in so far as it is potentially flesh only, it nourishes: for it is thus that nutrition and growth differ by their definition. That is why a body's nutrition continues so long as it is kept alive (even when it is diminishing), though not its growth; and why nutrition, though the same as growth, is yet different from it in actual being. For in so far as what accedes is potentially a quantity of flesh it tends to increase flesh: whereas, in so far as it is potentially flesh only, it is nourishment" (*GC* I.5.322a23–28).

35. "The sphere of growing and diminishing is believed to be magnitude [μέγεθος]" (*GC* I.5.320a28–29). Of course, the matter regarded as quantity is the same matter that underlies the substance, since quantity cannot exist except for in substance. See *GC* I.5.320b22ff: "Since there is also a matter out of which corporeal substance itself comes-to-be [corporeal substance, however, already characterized as such-and-such a determinate body, for there is no such thing as body in general], this same matter is also a matter of magnitude and quality—being separable from these matters in definition [λόγος], but not separable in place unless qualities are, in their turn, separable."

36. As we will see in the next chapter, this is to be compared with the structured qualitative change in perception. The organs are made up of a certain ratio or limit, and stretched beyond it they are destroyed.

37. *GC* I.5.321b22–28.

38. The sameness of nutrition and growth can be gleaned from several comments by Aristotle in the chapter. First of all, at the outset of the chapter when he refers to the functions of the first and most common soul, he says, "Reproduction and the use of food [τροφῇ χρῆσθαι]" (II.4.415a25). He neither refers to growth at all nor designates nutrition in his usual way (τροφή or τρέφεσθαι) because he is using a more general formulation which includes them both: using food. Second, throughout the chapter when considering what happens to the food in ingestion and digestion, he refers to nutrition and growth together (II.4.416a8–11).

39. See, for example, *GA* I.23.731a25: "To the essence of plants belongs no other function or act than the production of seed."

40. "Since the nutritive and reproductive powers of the soul are the same power, it is necessary to define nourishment. For it is distinguished from the other powers by this activity" (II.4.416a19–21).

41. See *GA* II.6.744b32–36: "For everywhere the nutriment may be divided into two kinds, the first and the second: the former is nutritious, being that which brings into being the whole and the parts; the latter is concerned with growth, being that which causes quantitative increase." See also IV.8.777a5–6.

42. See *GA* IV.1.766b7ff. for an account of the reproductive materials as the final stage of concoction of the nutriment.

43. Aristotle distinguishes food (blood) from useful residue (περίττωμα) and useless residue (σύντηγμα) (see *GA* I.18.724b25–26).

44. On blood, material for growth of parts, and reproductive matter as the stages of concocted nutriment, see Peck's useful remarks in his Loeb edition of *On the Generation of Animals* (1943, lxii–lxvii). An indication of this is Aristotle's passing observation that small animals reproduce more prolifically: "Just as with the other animals and plants whose nature is analogous to theirs [i.e., small] . . . the increase of size turns with them to seed" (*GA* I.8.718b13–15). See also his claim that fat animals are less fertile (*PA* II.5.651b14–17), because more of their matter is required to maintain their quantitative bulk, leaving less to be concocted into reproductive materials.

45. Aristotle identifies three essential factors in growth: that which grows is preserved and persists over and above the change in magnitude, each part of the magnitude grows, and the growth is effected through the addition of something to it (*GC* I.5.321a19–21; 321b11–15).

46. On the role of vital heat for informing matter in generation, see Freudenthal (1995, 24–29).

47. Russon writes that the soul is "the principle of identification with otherness," that its functions are "essentially actions whereby the self and the other are in some manner identified," and that the "form the identification takes differs with different kinds of soul" (1996, 784).

48. See, for example, Burnyeat (2002, 33 esp. fn. 12).

49. Burnyeat 2002, 33.

50. King notes the important connection between the II.4 discussion and *GC* I.7 (2001, 52).

51. See Kosman (1975, 514).

52. I have added some features, but nothing which runs against Kosman's schematization.

53. This discussion in II.5 occurs at 416b35ff. The parallel discussion of nutriment in terms of this philosophical conflict of identity and contrariety theorists is found in II.4 at 416a22ff. Both should clearly be read together along with the important analysis in *On Generation and Corruption* I.7 of this conflict in terms of the more general principles of acting (ποιεῖν) and being acted upon (πάσχειν).

54. This formulation is expressed in relation to perception, but is equally applicable to his account of nutrition.

55. Burnyeat, for example, writes in his excellent treatment of II.5 that "*De Generatione et Corruptione* I.7 323b1–15 is also the source of the opposite (Democritean) opinion that like is affected by like, *which makes its first appearance in the De Anima at the beginning of II.5* [italics mine]" (2002, 38). Yet Aristotle has already treated this view in relation to nutrition in the previous chapter, and the movement of the argument as a whole only becomes clear once this is recognized.

56. Burnyeat writes (very helpfully): "*De Generatione et Corruptione* is a work at the lowest level of Aristotle's world, where the elements change into each other (elemental generation and destruction), act on each other and on other things, and combine by mixture to form more complex stuffs like bronze and flesh" (2002, 38). This kind of change, he points out, is especially related to ordinary qualitative change, in which one quality replaces another by destroying it. As one moves from this inanimate activity up the hierarchy of living activity, this structure is transformed in significant ways.

57. *GC* I.7.324a4–9.

58. Ibid., II.8.335a10.

59. Russon is one of the only commentators who stresses the parallel between *GC* I.7 and Aristotle's dialectical treatment of nutrition, yet his formulation of how the two

passages are related differs somewhat from my own: "The sameness of genus in this change amounts to the participation of both subject and object in the nutritive relation, and the difference of species is precisely the difference of eating subject and eating object" (1996, 785). See also Johansen: "A single causal framework is applied to all the senses. Aristotle's first move in *De Anima* II.4 before he starts his discussion of perception in II.5 is to discuss nutrition. He picks up the key causal scheme from the *Physica* and *De Generatione et Corruptione* and applies it to nutrition . . . One could say here that sight is modeled on nutrition" (1998, 22).

60. *GC* I.7.324a10–14.

61. As the critics of the "like by like" theorists point out, interaction between identical terms implies that the terms remain unaffected (ἀπαθής). This theory thus cannot account for how the food is obviously changed in nutrition. Yet the reason these critics cannot see the truth in the "like by like" position is that they have not grasped the sense in which nutrition is an *energeia* that does not involve change between contraries, since the living being preserves what it is through the course of the activity – this state of impassibility (ἀπάθεια) and being unmoved is obviously not inertness, but is an activity in which the living being more fully realizes the end which already lies within itself. Hamlyn also does not grasp how nutrition is an *energeia* in this sense: "The suggestion that what is fed is not affected by the food seems odd" (1968, 98).

62. "But neither is it open to say that growth or diminution occurs in the way in which e.g. air is generated from water. For although the volume has then become greater, the change will not be growth, but a coming-to-be of the one—viz. of that into which the change is taking place—and a passing away of the contrasted body. It is not a *growth* of either" (*GC* I.5.321a10ff).

63. *GC* I.5.320b30ff.

64. Ibid., I.5.321a23–26.

65. It is what is the hottest in the organism which performs the digestion in nutrition, for of all the elements, "fire is the only one of them . . . which is fed" (*GC* II.8.335a16–18).

66. In the *Magna Moralia*, in an example using the elements of fire and water to illustrate how those in the friendship of utility are most contrary to or unlike one another, Aristotle writes: "If you like to set down fire and water as extreme opposites, these are useful to one another. For fire, they say, if it has not moisture, perishes, as this provides it with a kind of nutriment, but that to such an extent as it can get the better of; for if you make the moisture too great, it will obtain the mastery, and will cause the fire to go out, but if you supply it in moderation, it will be of service to it" (*MM* II.11.1210a15ff.).

67. "Living and possessing a soul exists with a certain heat. For there is no concoction, through which food turns into the animals, either without soul or without heat. For it is fire in all cases that does the work" (*Resp.* VIII.474a25–28).

68. Food is always a combination of the earthy (solid) and watery (liquid) (see *De Sensu* IV.441b25ff.; *PA* III.5.668b10). Consider here Aquinas's excellent comment: "Water may be generated by fire and *e converso*, but we do not say that water is fed by fire. Yet we can say that fire is fed by water, inasmuch as watery vapor nourishes fire. When water comes from fire there is no new coming-to-be of water; but fire can make use of and grow by means of watery vapours. Among the elements, therefore, only fire seems to be fed and only water seems to be food taking water to include all vapours and liquids" (II.4 section 335).

69. This is probably more appropriately referred to as its natural πνεῦμα (*pneuma*), which, as a kind of particularly hot air, lies somewhere between the elements air and fire.

70. The reason for the uni-directionality of the change is, at least in terms of the material description, well stated by Rodier: "The reason is that we only notice the one contrary which is ontologically superior to the other" (1900, 239).

71. *Meteor.* IV.2.379b32.

72. Ibid., II.3.358a12ff. See also *GA* I.18.724b26.

73. See *Meteor.* III.6.378–IV.3.381 for a good, relevant account of this phenomenon.

74. See *Somn.* III.456a30–456b7.

75. *PA* II.3 gives a concise account of nutritional concoction as a heating of food which separates the original food into nutritionally useful blood and a useless residue. This of course only applies to animals, since plants take in their food pre-concocted (see also *PA* IV.4). *DS* IV gives an account of what happens relative to the tasteable: in digestion it is the light that goes up and is transformed into blood in the vessels, while the salty and bitter heavy matter is left behind (IV.442a5).

76. Aryeh Kosman points out two of these moments, ingestion and digestion: "The nutritive capacity, for example my capacity to *eat*, is my capacity to take in nutriment (the power of ingestion) and to transform it into myself (the power of digestion)" (1992, 357).

77. *PA* III.14.674a13–14. See also *HA* I.2. It is difficult to decide which step of the nutritive process is analogous to the sense organ receptive of the form without the matter in sensation: the mouth which takes the object in from outside, or the stomach which acts as the receptacle of the ingested food. But Aristotle makes clear that the mouth is not actually involved in the digestion of the food; it simply prepares the food for digestion, by breaking it up and making it more easily concocted once in the stomach: "First of all there is the mouth and the parts inside the mouth, on which the first share in the duty clearly devolves, in such animals at least as live on food which requires disintegration. The mouth, however, does not actually concoct the food, but merely facilitates the action of heat upon it" (*PA* II.3.650a9ff.). In this respect the mouth is more analogous to the medium in sensation, transmitting the object to that which properly receives the object. Interestingly, the role Plato ascribes to heat in the *Timaeus* is more like the role of the mouth in Aristotle's view, since it is by the sharpness of the geometrical form of particles of fire that the food is broken down and turned into blood (Plato, *Timaeus* 80d).

78. The perfect form here is significant, since Aristotle's definition of an *energeia* or *praxis*, as opposed to a process (κίνησις), is an activity in which the perfect and the present form of the activity are always identical, meaning that the activity is complete in every moment. This is not the case in the transition of first potentiality to first actuality: it is only at the last moment of digestion that the undigested food becomes food "having been digested," at which point it is no longer what it was (undigested). The transition from first potentiality to second potentiality is a process (κίνησις) in which the contrary is destroyed by the contrary.

79. In fact, as can be gleaned from the sun's role in spontaneous generation, the sun can also be directly responsible for the production (γένεσις) of life. See, for example, *GA* II.3.736b30ff.; III.11.762b14; II.3.737a3; II.6.743a33.

80. "For since the revolving body is always setting something in motion, the movement of the things it moves must also be circular. Thus, since the upper movement is cyclical, the sun moves in this determinate manner: and since the sun moves *thus*, the seasons in consequence come-to-be in a cycle, i.e., return upon themselves; and since they come to be cyclically, so in their turn do the things whose coming-to-be the seasons initiate" (*GC* II.11.338b1ff.).

81. *Phys.* II.2.194b13. See also *Metaph.* XII.5.1071a11–17.

82. "Everything living has soul, and it, as we have said, cannot exist without the presence of natural heat. In plants the natural heat is sufficiently well kept alive by the aid which their nutriments and the surrounding air supply . . . If the surrounding air is excessively cold owing to the time of year, there being severe frost, the force of the heat dwindles; but when there are hot spells and the moisture drawn from the ground cannot produce its cooling effect, the heat comes to an end by exhaustion" (*Juv.* VI.470a19–31).

83. See *Meteor.* II.4.360a6. Freudenthal also points to some inconclusive evidence that Aristotle may have also thought the earth contained its own internal heat apart from the external heating of it by the sun (1995, 72).

84. Plato, *Republic* 509bff.

85. On the similarity between *Republic* and *De Anima* on this point, see Kosman (1992, 349ff.). I will be elaborating on the Platonic nature of Aristotle's analogy between thinking and vision in the chapters that follow.

86. The τὸ μὲν . . . τὸ δὲ structure of this sentence, in my view a chiastic one, parallels the typical use of οὗτος . . . ἐκεῖνος, to signify "the latter . . . the former," in which the latter element precedes the former one in the previous clause. Here the first τὸ refers not to the first item (the hand) but to the nearer item (the rudder), while the second refers to the first, more distant item (the hand). This reading is a possible one, since the antecedents of the respective τὸ's are not clear from the text itself.

87. Freudenthal 1995, 22ff. See also (29): "We can thus conclude that in Aristotle's theoretical framework *vital heat is heat charged with specific, formative movements*, which are precisely what makes it into *soul*-heat."

88. "The vital principle is in that which is hot [θερμόν]" (*GA* III.1.751b6); "The soul is incorporate in some substance of a fiery character" (*PA* II.7.652b10ff.); "Respiration takes place when the hot substance which is the seat of the nutritive principle increases" (*Resp.* XXVII(XXI).480a16).

89. Freudenthal writes: "It would seem that where both accounts are applicable, Aristotle holds an identity theory: Aristotle's physiological theory assigns to the vital heat the role of producing the forms of homoeomerous parts, a role which the psychological theory attributes to the workings of the nutritive soul. One and of a living body that it 'has vital heat' (using the theoretical vocabulary of biology) or that it 'has nutritive soul' (psychological idiom) are two ways to refer to a capacity to transform matter into substances having a characteristic λόγος" (1995, 30).

90. For a juxtaposition of the II.4 and III.10 passages which proves, I believe, that Aristotle is drawing attention to an important connection between nutrition and locomotion, see chapter 5 below, in the section "Beyond the Parts of the Soul."

91. Murphy 2005.

92. *Phys.* VII.2.245a1.

93. *PA* II.3.650a3.

94. Sorabji 1974, 74n28. Murphy glosses the literalist take on this as follows: "The literalist argues rather that the reception of form without matter means the eye becomes red (i.e., undergoes an ordinary alteration) without *receiving* any matter (e.g., particles of red paint) from the object of perception" (2005, 298).

95. Murphy 2005, 300.

96. Ibid., 2005, 301.

97. In II.4, when Aristotle speaks of growth, he refers to it as being essentially related to quantity, employing the word ποσός rather than μέγεθος. I take both to mean size or magnitude in each passage under consideration, but he uses ποσός in II.4 since he is speaking explicitly about the categories, whereas in II.12 he is discussing the quantitative bulk characteristic of bodies more generally. It is also important to note that Aristotle does refer to μέγεθος as lying at the heart of growth in II.4 at 416a17.

98. I am reading the ἐκείνου (with Bodéüs) as a reference to the first sense organ (not the μέγεθος).

99. The last part of this passage is frustratingly ambiguous, though the ambiguity has not been noticed by many interpreters. What does it mean that the plant has no principle to receive sensible forms, but is affected *with the matter*? Does Aristotle here mean the plant is affected along with the matter *of the object*, while an animal in perception is affected without the object being affected, or that plants are affected along with their matter, that is, their body, while animals when perceiving are not materially affected or altered? I will leave this question open until the discussion of perception.

100. It may be more appropriate to speak of the object of food as analogous to the organ of perception rather than the sense object, since in nutrition the object is assimilated to the organism, whereas in perception the organism is assimilated to the object. On this point, see Russon (1996, 786) and Burnyeat (2002, 45).

101. *GC* IV.6.313b8–10.

102. See *GC* IV.6.313b8–10.

103. In these as the objects of touch, see also *DA* II.11.423a27ff.

104. Recall the relevant passage of II.12: "Plants are affected in a certain way by the tangibles" (II.12.424a34).

105. Bodéüs 1993, 196 fn. 5 ("manque de régulation thermique interne constante").

106. See also *Long. Vit.* VI.467a18ff.; *Juv.* II.468a30; *PA* IV.6.682b30.

107. Aristotle states that the most basic kinds of animals generally have three parts: "For in all animals, at least in all perfect kinds, there are two parts more essential than the rest, namely the part which serves for ingestion of food and the part which serves for the discharge of residue. For without food, growth and even existence are impossible . . . And in all there is a third part, intermediate between the two, in which is situated the principle of life" (*PA* II.10.655b30–656a1). Though he goes on to explain in this passage how plants have no great variety of parts, they do generally have these three distinct functions, although to a less distinct degree: the roots are for ingestion of food, the top of the plant is the part out of which the residue is evacuated in the form of fruit and seed, and the middle, though not as distinct as the heart in animals (since no concoction is needed for its already concocted food), is generally that point from which the two ends grow out.

108. *PA* II.10.656a1ff. Following this passage Aristotle explains how the higher a living being is, the more differentiated their parts will be, presumably because they will be capable of a greater number of functions, and thus require more distinct instruments to carry these out.

109. *Long. Vit.* VI.467a28–30. Just above, Aristotle states that the reason why the plant can live when divided is that "every part of a plant contains potentially both root and stem" (VI.467a23–4).

110. *Resp.* XXIII(XVII).478b36.

111. *GA* II.23.731a21. The distinction of male and female and the role of each as the principles (ἀρχαί) in generation is the overarching theme of *Generation of Animals*. See

in particular I.18.724b10–12; I.24.731a1ff.; II.4.741a4ff.; IV.1.763b20, among countless other places in that treatise.

112. See *GA* III.10.759b30ff.

113. Freudenthal has a very useful analysis of the important of spatial orientation in the hierarchy of life (1995, 55–56).

114. "The nutritive part does its own work [ἔργον] better when the animal is asleep than when it is awake. Nutrition and growth are then especially promoted, a fact which implies that creatures do not need sense-perception to assist these processes" (*Somn.* I.455a1–4).

115. *Somn.* III.458b8.

116. Ibid., III.458a11.

117. Ibid., I.454b1; I.454b10–11; I.454b24–28.

118. God's life and thinking in general are consistently associated with leisure and pleasure by Aristotle.

119. *GC* I.5.321a34–35.

120. See Introduction, "Thinking as the Essence of Life in Other Aristotelian Treatises," as well as *Eth. Eud.* VII.12.1245a1ff.

121. *Eth. Nic.* VIII.3.1156a14–19.

122. While the friendship of utility corresponds to nutritive activity, the friendship of pleasure, characterized by feeling, erotic passion, and the pleasure of the moment, is better and corresponds to the subjective identification of perception. It is only with the virtuous friendship that one is identified with the object of love as its own being and nature (its *character*), just as it is in the thinking relation that one is identified with the object as it is in itself in its full nature.

123. This description of course characterizes not sensation per se, but the movement from second potentiality or first actuality to second actuality. Yet further down (II.5.417b16–18), Aristotle identifies the capacity for sense with this level of potentiality, since the transition from first to second potentiality occurs at birth of the sentient creature, which is already this second potentiality, needing only to be actualized to second actuality.

124. Of course animals and humans are able to refrain from eating and drinking when they want. But the point of the stomach-root analogy is that even when we stop eating, nutrition is still going on through the nutrients remaining in our body: the difference is that we are able to move around with the source of our food, since it lies within our own bodies, as opposed to plants. In both, however, nutrition is equally perpetually necessary for the continued existence of the organism.

125. See *Eth. Nic.* VI.12.1144a10–11.

126. The author of *On Plants* notices this tension: while higher living beings should be more self-sufficient (αὐτάρκης), the fact that the plant seems to contain within itself both male and female seems to make it more independent than animals and even humans. Yet he resolves this apparent problem by stressing that it would be wrong to consider these principles as actually distinguished and united in the plant, since they exist prior to this differentiation of reproductive principles: the real independence consists rather in independence from one's environment: "A plant, therefore, would have been discovered before the mingling had taken place, and it ought therefore to be at the same time an active and a passive agent. The two sexes cannot be found combined in any plant: if this were so, a plant would be more perfect than an animal, because it would not require anything outside itself in order to generate; whereas the plant does require the right season of year and sunshine and its natural temperature more than anything . . . But we must suppose

that the mingling of male and female in plants takes place in some other way, because the seed of a plant resembles the embryo in animals, being a mixture of the male and female elements" (*DP* II.817a15ff.).

127. This still implies the distinction between organism and its nutriment, however. Life within the egg should thus be viewed as analogous to the viviparous animal within the womb of the mother taking in nutriment through the umbilical cord, or the life of the plant rooted unmoving to its source of nutriment.

128. *HA* VIII.1.588b32.

129. *GA* V.3.783b22. For plants "the change from summer to winter is more important for them than the time of life," while in man "it is the seasons of life that correspond to summer and winter" (V.3.783b20–25; see also V.3.784a12–20 and V.6.786a30).

130. See Freudenthal's appendix on *The Vital Heat of Plants* (1995, 70–73).

131. *GA* III.11.762b13–15. See also *Parts of Animals* II.2.649a1–4: "In some of the bodies which are called hot the heat is derived from without, while in others it belongs to the bodies themselves, and it makes a most important difference whether the heat has the former or the latter origin." There must be some internal heat in the plant, however, since it is the absence of internal heat which for Aristotle distinguishes even plant life from inanimate nature: "That which external heat makes in external bodies, this happens by the nature of animals and plants" (*SS* IV.442a7–9). See also *PA* II.3.650a5–7: "Animals and plants alike . . . have a natural source of heat."

132. *Juv.* III.468b28.

133. Ibid., VI.470a20ff.

134. The sun is responsible for heating the surface of the earth (see *Meteor.* II.3.356b22ff.).

135. *PA* II.10.655b32.

136. "As for plants, though they are included by us among things which have life, yet are they without any part for the discharge of waste residue. For the food which they absorb from the ground is already concocted, and they give off instead their seeds and fruits" (*PA* II.10.655b33–36). See also *PA* II.4.650a21ff.: "For plants get their food from the earth by means of their roots; and this food is already elaborated when taken in, which is the reason why plants produce no excrement, the earth and its heat serving them in place of a stomach."

137. *PA* IV.4.678a13.

138. *PA* II.3.650a25 (italics mine). Interestingly, in this passage Aristotle associates this difference between animals and plants with the possession of locomotion. Because the plant is rooted in one place, that which performs this transformative activity in nutrition can exist outside of it in the element in which it is rooted. For the locomotive being, however, it must possess this capacity within itself so it will be present to it wherever it may roam, since nutritive activity must persist to maintain itself in existence.

139. *GA* IV.8.776b6–8 (italics mine).

Chapter 3

1. Following Rodier's (1900) emendation of αἰσθάνεσθαι to αἰσθητόν.

2. As we saw, this digestive activity is not universally part of self-nourishing organisms, since in plants it is the environment that is responsible for this digestive process.

3. Digestion is what has to happen on the side of the object to transform the object into the kind of matter that can nourish the animal, but it is not itself nourishing. This is seen clearly by the fact that a plant's food is digested before it is ever even assimi-

lated as nourishment. It cannot be, therefore, that the digestion is part of the activity of self-nourishment. The digestion is akin to the sounding of the bell in hearing. This is not part of the hearing, but by bringing the object from first potentiality to second potentiality, it constitutes a necessary condition for an actual instance of hearing to take place.

4. He refers to this affection of the five peripheral organs in *On Dreams* as "sensation in accordance with the part" (*Insomn.* III.461a4–5).

5. Aristotle does not mention the αἴσθημα (*aisthema*) in his treatment of perception in *De Anima*, but the idea is mentioned in III.8 in a remark about appearances (φαντάσματα): "appearances [φαντάσματα] are like αἰσθήματα [*aisthemata*], except without matter" (III.8.432a9–10). Because of the paucity of references to αἰσθήματα (*aisthemata*) in *De Anima*, I will leave this question aside in my treatment of perception, but it is helpful to my analysis of the structure of the argument that Aristotle elsewhere identifies the passive, receptive aspect in the sense organs as a distinct ingredient of perception. Most of the references to this phenomenon are in *On Dreams*, see II.460b3; III.460b29; III.461a19; III.462a31.

6. Burnyeat (2002) cites *DA* II.5.417a31–2; II.5.417b2–3; II.5.417b15; *Phys.* V.2.226b1–8; *GC* I.7.324a5–14.

7. One of the only commentators to notice that the distinctions at II.5.417b12–15 and II.5.417b1–7 refer to different transitions is Burnyeat: "These are not the same two types of being affected or altered as the two distinguished at 417b1–7. There ordinary alteration, due to contrariety, served as foil to preservation. Here it is foil to what I shall call *development*" (2002, 61).

8. Burnyeat is absolutely right in pointing out that Aristotle thinks that no standard alteration occurs in perception: "In the ordinary sense of these terms (being affected or altered) they signify the loss of a quality and its replacement by another (opposite or intermediate) quality from the same range . . . That is not what happens in perception, which is a different way of being affected and being altered" (Burnyeat 2002, 29). This is one of the contrasts between nutrition and perception, since the change of food is in fact a standard alteration of the food from its own being into the body of the living being which is nourished. Yet he takes the different or qualified way of being altered as being simple: it is change in the sense in which the initial quality is preserved without any destruction. Aristotle importantly distinguishes another way in which something is not a completely standard mode of alteration, yet which still involves a destruction of the original quality, that is, what I describe as nonstandard alteration #1.

9. Note here that Aristotle will first explain a qualified mode of quantitative change or *growth*, then a qualified mode of qualitative change or *alteration*, and finally a qualified mode of change of place or *locomotion*. This threefold distinction was introduced in *De Anima* I.3 at 406a12–13, and each mode of qualified animate change emerges gradually as one moves up the hierarchy of life.

10. I put aside the difficult and often debated question about whether the organ actually becomes red in seeing red, for example.

11. This is one of the chief differences between the receptive sides of sensation and thinking, as we will see. There is less of a destruction in thinking, since thinking has no independent qualitative determination which is affected in the reception of its object.

12. It is thus ambiguous precisely which of the terms of the relation should be characterized as acting (ποιεῖν) and which as being acted upon (πάσχειν).

13. This view of this section of Aristotle's treatment of sensation in *De Anima* is close to Kahn's (1966) outline (50), which understands II.5–12 to be treating the special senses, both the faculty and the organ.

14. I have argued that the five senses in *De Anima* II.7–11 are to be read hierarchically in a paper entitled "Aristotle on the Hierarchy of the Five Senses," presented at the Atlantic Region Philosophical Association on October 27, 2006. I hope to share the result of my study of the five senses in the near future.

15. This is not to deny that what is partly at work in these chapters is simply Aristotle's typical exhaustiveness in trying to think through the full details of the phenomena in question. Further, some details are included for other reasons unrelated to the hierarchy of the senses: the extremely detailed explanation of the role of light in vision in II.7 serves the purpose of filling out the analogy between light and νοῦς ποιητικός (active mind) in III.5, as I will argue in the next chapter.

16. Vision: *De Anima* II.7.419a9–21; hearing: II.8.419b8–10, II.8.419b33–35, II.8.420b14–16; smell: II.8.421b9, II.8.421b17–18; taste: II.10.422a34–422b10; touch: II.11.423b4–26. See also II.7.419a25–419b3.

17. *GC* I.6.322b22–23; I.6.322b29; I.6.323a22–25; I.7.323b29–324a9; I.7.324b8–9; *Phys.* III.2.202a6–7; VII.2.243a32–35; VIII.4.255a34–255b1; *Metaph.* IX.5.1048a5–7.

18. "That which is receptive of color is colorless [τὸ ἄχρουν], and that which is receptive of sound is soundless" (II.7.418b26–7). See also II.8.420a7–11, where the air is said to be both soundless and motionless (ἀκίνητος).

19. Relative to taste Aristotle mentions the example of someone who is ill to whom everything tastes bitter, "on account of perceiving with a tongue full of fluid" (II.10.422b8–10).

20. Because of this fragile and indeterminate quality of air, in hearing it is necessary that the object struck be smooth and continuous: this determinacy bestows itself upon the otherwise indeterminate medium, giving it the determination required to reach the inner air of the ear (see II.8.419b34–420a2). At II.8.420a8–10, Aristotle explains how by virtue of being easily dissipated (εὔθρυπτον), that it is without any sound of its own, and sound can only be produced if some surface can prevent its dissipation.

21. As shown in the last chapter on nutritive soul, plants are predominantly constituted out of earth, the lowest and most bodily of the material elements. As one moves through the senses, in touch the medium and organ contain all the elements, though earth predominates. In taste organ and medium are constituted of earth, but only when water is added through liquefaction. In the distance senses water and air constitute the media and organs. We can thus trace a progressive dematerialization of material activities as one moves through the hierarchy of living activities, as we ascend through the hierarchy of elements from most bodily to least bodily.

22. It seems peculiar here that Aristotle is speaking of the object as wet and not flavored, but to be flavored for Aristotle requires an underlying wetness. Hence once the tongue is too wet, it itself becomes tasteable and thus tastes itself rather than its object.

23. On the more determinate neutrality of touch, see *DA* II.11.423b30–424a10.

24. Unlike the medium and organ of the higher senses, which are constituted of air or water, the medium and organ of the tangible senses are constituted out of a mix of all the elements, with a predominance of earth (see II.11.423a13–15). For this reason it is susceptible to "blind spots" that the other more indeterminate senses are not: "That which makes something like itself in actuality, acts on something that is potentially such. Consequently we do not perceive the similarly hot and cold or hard and soft, but the ex-

tremes, as the sense is like a certain mean between the sensible extremes" (II.11.424a1–5). Perception requires both difference of species and similarity of kind, but if the organ and object are too close prior to their interaction, there is not sufficient difference to constitute an instance of perception.

25. Aristotle means here that we can also in a sense see a privation of color: one sees darkness in a sense (II.7.418b28–9).

26. For the two primary contraries of tangible objects, see II.11.423b27–29.

27. Taste: *De Anima* II.10.422b15–16; hearing: II.8.419b4–11.

28. Kosman 1987, 362. Kosman cites *Metaph.* VII.3.1029a19: "By matter I mean that which is per se neither this nor so much nor said in any of the other categories by which being is determined."

29. I take the terminology "remote" and "immediate" objects of perception from Kosman's discussion of this passage; see (2000, 320–321).

30. Victor Caston sheds important light on what Aristotle might have meant by focusing on what a signet ring communicates to wax: "It transmits information about the owner of the ring, by receiving his signet" (2005, 304).

31. Kosman 2000, 321.

32. Ibid.

33. The sense organ which is first affected is to be contrasted with τὸ ἔσχατον αἰσθητήριον—the last sense organ (III.2.426b16). In II.12 Aristotle is summarizing the passive, receptive, peripheral aspect of sensation which has been analyzed from II.7–11. In *Parva Naturalia*, however, Aristotle refers to the common seat of sensation (the heart) as the first sense capacity (τὸ πρῶτον αἰσθητικόν) (*On Memory* I.450a12; I.451a17) and the first sense organ (τὸ πρῶτον αἰσθητήριον) (*Somn.* III.458a28). In this context he means the preeminent or ruling part in the sense of "first principle." Here I am in agreement with Block (1988, 240).

34. The same problem appears in Plato's *Theaetetus* 184b ff., though Plato's solution is importantly different. For Plato the community of the senses, along with several of the other powers Aristotle ascribes to the common sense, implies thinking beyond perception. Aristotle clearly has this section of *Theaetetus* in mind as he writes III.1–2.

35. Several very good interpretations of the common sense exist, to which the analysis that follows is greatly indebted. Kahn's (1966) article is absolutely foundational in the literature, and the best work produced on the common sense since its publication builds on his excellent articulation. Kosman (1975) is the first analysis to make sense of the difficult argument of III.2, and my own study is greatly indebted to his findings. Finally, Jacques Brunschwig (1991) and (1996) gives a very helpful account of the argumentative structure of III.1–2. Gregoric (2007) is the most comprehensive study of this power to date.

36. Kahn 1966, 51.

37. Kahn 1966, 50. I reserve judgment for the moment on whether these two chapters "illustrate the same type of incomplete, partially incoherent, exposition which is found in a more extreme form in the following chapters on νοῦς."

38. Kosman explains this difficulty well: "The radical intentionality of perception, the fact that our perceptions are object saturated, insures the difficulty of specifying the awareness implicit in our perceptions, since the intentionality ensures that it will be the object of perception and not the awareness of that object which presents itself" (1975, 516–17).

39. I agree with Kahn that Aristotle is following a more general argumentative strategy present throughout his writings according to which "the aporetic technique aims at mak-

ing things difficult before they are simplified—at tying the knot before it is untied, so that the scope and importance of the solution may be seen" (Kahn 1966, 63).

40. Brunschwig 1991, 464 ("la communauté des sens, ou leur synergie").

41. Brunschwig (1991) brings out well the solution to the apparent contradiction between Aristotle's claim that the common objects are perceived intrinsically (καθ' αὑτά), and his later claim at III.1.425a15, that the common objects are perceived by each sense incidentally (κατὰ συμβεβηκός), an apparent contradiction solved through showing the need for the functioning together of the various senses. The commons are accidental to each proper sense, but are essential (καθ' αὑτά) to all the senses taken together. Modrak also argues that "the perception of common objects καθ' αὑτά is a case of the senses perceiving as one" (1981, 408).

42. Kahn mentions a further reason why a common sense is suggested though not stated in II.6 by the existence of common objects: "There is no suggestion, at this point of the exposition, that the several senses which perceive shape must therefore be related to some common faculty. Such an inference would probably be legitimate. For how could we recognize shape-as-seen and shape-as-touched as the *same* property if the sensation of sight and touch were wholly separate from one another? But Aristotle carefully refrains from drawing any such conclusion in *De Anima* II.5–12, because he is there concerned with the operation of the special senses as such, and does not wish to obscure their analysis by introducing complications from without" (1966, 52–53).

43. At III.1.425a21–22, it is unclear to me whether Aristotle means our simultaneous active perception of one object through both taste and vision, or the active exercise of one sense which grasps the proper object of another without the active exercise of that sense (e.g., perceiving the white object to be sweet without actively tasting it). I assume from his example that it is the latter, since one cannot (without great feats of the tongue and peripheral vision) simultaneously taste and see exactly the same object. This question is not determinative for the overall argument, however, since the second kind of perception relies on there having been an instance for the first kind at some point in the past. For example, for me to see the whiteness of sugar as sweet, this requires a prior simultaneous perceptive experience of both qualities in the same object by which we become "able to recognize [ἅμα γνωρίζομεν] them whenever they occur together" (III.1.425a23–4). Thus both possibilities ultimately depend on the integrated experience of distinct proper senses, which is the phenomenon under discussion in the passage in question.

44. It is difficult to tell whether or not the phrase ascribed to the common objects at III.1.425a15, "which we perceive incidentally by each sense," belongs to the hypothesis of a proper sense for the commons, a hypothesis which Aristotle rejects. Kahn (1966), following Theiler (1959), Rodier (1900), and the Greek commentators, argues that it does belong to this rejected hypothesis, so that Aristotle is here denying that common objects are perceived incidentally. But there is no contradiction between saying that the common objects are perceived intrinsically (καθ' αὑτά) by the common sense, but only incidentally (κατὰ συμβεβηκός) by each distinct sense.

45. "Saying that both are one is not for different senses" (III.1.425b2–3).

46. As Kahn rightly shows, the claim about the common power at this point of the argument is very minimal: "The common sense described in this passage is nothing but the coincidence of the special senses" (1966, 54).

47. Kosman 1975, 511.

48. Here Aristotle means the eyeball. It is in this sense that I am confident Aristotle intends the expression αἰσθητήριον πρῶτον at II.12.424a24, that is, the sense organ which is first affected. It is to be contrasted with the expression he uses later in the chapter, τὸ ἔσχατον αἰσθήσει (III.2.426b16). In II.12, Aristotle is summarizing the passive, receptive, peripheral aspect of sensation which has been analyzed from II.7–11, since it would be out of place to be mentioning the general awareness only disclosed in III.1–2 at that point in the argument (see note 33 above).

49. Kosman (1975) does not attend to this argument in his excellent treatment, though it simply contributes further proof in defense of his interpretation.

50. This unified aspect of sensation as responsible for the apperceptive element in sensitive awareness is expressed more explicitly than in the *De Anima* in a passage from *On Sleep and Waking* (II.455a13–23) addressing the very same problem he is addressing at the end of III.2: "Since every sense has something special and something common; special, as e.g., seeing is to the sense of sight, hearing to the auditory sense, and so on with the other senses severally; while all are accompanied by a common power, by virtue whereof a person perceives that he sees or hears (for, assuredly, it is not by *sight* that one sees that he sees; and it is not by taste, or sight, or both together that one discerns, and that sweet things are different from white things, but by a part common to all the organs of sense; *for there is one sensory function, and the controlling sensory organ is one, though differing as a faculty of perception in relation to each genus, e.g., sound or color*)" [italics mine]. An important aspect of this passage is that the unity of the perceptive parts throughout the organism is responsible both for apperceptive awareness and discriminating between objects of distinct senses.

51. Kosman 1975, 518.

52. Barker 1981. The problem, as Barker points out, is that commentators have wrongly assumed that what Aristotle is examining in this brief section coincides with the λόγος (*logos*) discussed in II.12, a discussion not of the actuality of sense as in III.2, but the *capacity* (first actuality) of each organ. The result is that they overgeneralized the conclusion of the III.2 passage to all sounds in general, making the argument confusing and even invalid, rather than recognizing how Aristotle is analyzing throughout a specific kind of heard object: the blended harmony.

53. Aristotle offers another detailed treatment in *De Sensu* VII of what happens when one perceives multiple objects within one proper sense at the same time, again comparing it with the phenomenon of perceiving a multiple of objects in distinct proper senses simultaneously.

54. The same expression is employed II.11.422b32–3, when searching for what the primary underlying object of touch is, equivalent to sounds, flavors, odors, and colors.

55. This question is not to be confused with the one raised at III.1, which had to do with perceiving the sweet by vision, perceiving the proper sense object of one sense by another.

56. Plato, *Theaetetus* 186e.

57. Kahn's image, borrowed from Alexander, is helpful: the proper senses are here viewed as "converging lines, joined at the center in a single, generalized faculty of sense" (1966, 56).

58. Both Kosman and Kahn (1966) state the matter well. Kosman writes, "The living body is a common, single sensitive organism, with, to be sure, a center in the heart, but a center which is not separate from but one with the various senses, which are at once special in their individual activities and common as modes of a single organic sensibility" (1975, 518).

59. That the center of sensation is understood as a mean of the various proper senses further explains the analogy Aristotle sees between different qualities within the range of one proper sense, and different qualities belonging to distinct common senses. The relation which the proper sense holds to the extremes of which it is a mean is like the relation the common sense as a mean holds to the objects of the various senses.

60. For this reason Bernard Hubert (1997) is correct in identifying the cause of an animal's unity with the common sense or the awareness spread throughout the whole sensitive organism: these represent the soul as formal principle of the animal.

61. As Kosman seems to suggest at the end of his account (1975, 519).

62. Aristotle makes several references to this principle (ἀρχή) of perception throughout his other writings on the soul. In *On Dreams* at III.461b3–5, he writes that "generally, the principle [ἀρχή] affirms the report of each sense, unless something more authoritative contradicts it." He argues that when the movements from the proper sense reach the principle (ἀρχή) that one seems to see and hear and perceive (III.461a30ff.) See other similar references at *Mem.* I.451a16; I.450a12; II.451a25. This principle (ἀρχή) Aristotle clearly locates in the heart as the controlling organ of all the animal's embodied functions: nutrition, sensation, and movement (see *Juv.* I.467b27–30; III.469a5–19).

63. The expression is Kahn's (1966, 63).

64. I hope that this analysis provides the beginning of a reply to the challenge posed by Irving Block to Kahn's argument: "If, however, Aristotle knew all along when he wrote the *De Anima* that there is only one sense located in the heart and the individual senses are simply factors or aspects of this one sense, why should he have employed such a fiction in the first place? What could have been the point of it?" (Block 1988, 238).

65. On imagination, Malcolm Schofield (1979) reopened interest in the topic, and most recently Michael Wedin (1988) has brought great clarity to the topic. There is a huge bibliography on the topic, and the most significant contributions can be found in the bibliography. I have found Victor Caston (1996) particularly helpful.

66. Caston puts the matter well against commentators who see no clear reason to address the question of *phantasia* at this point in the argument: "We cannot discount another possibility, namely, that phantasia is somehow necessary at this stage of Aristotle's exposition, prior to his accounts of thought, desire and action. Instead of interrupting the sequence, *De Anima* 3.3 might constitute an integral part of it" (1996, 23–4).

67. On these citations and their original contexts, see Hicks (1907, 454–55).

68. Caston 1996, 39.

69. Here and throughout the chapter Aristotle uses three strategies for distinguishing the various capacities discussed in the chapter. He tests for taxonomical separability, that is, whether there exists some being which necessarily has one of two certain capacities without the other; separability of the capacities or activities within a being possessing them both, or whether an animal with both capacities can exercise one without the other; and truth and falsity, that is, whether two capacities under investigation can be true and false, or can only be true.

70. This is the force of γάρ at III.3.427b14.

71. D. Frede 1992, 291.

72. This feature of imagination is also crucial for action (πρᾶξις), in that this critical distance opens up the possibility of deliberation over possibilities without being simply immediately motivated by impulses from one's environment (see for example III.7.431b4ff.).

73. Bodéüs's comments on this feature of imagination are excellent. He writes that, thanks to imagination, "mind therefore finds itself indirectly dependent upon sensible experience. And from the Aristotelian perspective, this undoubtedly signifies that, far from being in itself that which leads mind to err or to make a mistake, imagination, because it depends on sensible experience, is on the contrary that which guarantees mind that it will apprehend something which, ultimately, *always* corresponds to an objective reality . . . there is not, according to him, an imagined representation which does not derive, in some way, from a genuine sensation: There is nothing purely imagined" (1990, 25).

74. "[Imagination] establishes the connection between the intellect and its sensible objects" (D. Frede 1992, 288).

75. See also III.4.429b11–23, a passage we will treat in the following chapter.

76. As Aristotle writes, "αἴσθησις in act is of the particular, while ἐπιστήμη is of universals" (*De Anima* II.5.417b22–23). The image is not a universal concept, but it is more general than the complete particularity of an immediately perceived object, since its independence from this particular of sensation allows it to develop over time independently of that object. As D. Frede argues, "φαντάσματα are flexible and can be enriched by repeated observations, while immediate sense-perceptions cannot" (1992, 291).

77. Bodéüs 1990, 26. He writes further, "Not recognizing in the mind any other source but this, Aristotle could not take imagination (in its various forms) as the first cause of error, without at the same time looking to it as the first remedy of error" (27).

78. These are the concluding lines of the chapter on imagination, where Aristotle explains what he has accomplished by the argument in III.3.

79. The image is a potentially perceived alteration which at any time may or may not be perceived. Caston writes: "They are changes in the perceptual system that represent in virtue of their causal powers. But a phantasma will have those powers *whether or not* it actually exercises them (*Insomn.* III.461b11–19; *Mem.* I.450a27–b11; II.451b7–10). *The experience* a phantasma is capable of producing, therefore, *need not occur for the phantasma to have the content that it does*" (1996, 51–52).

80. In this section devoted to distinguishing *phantasia* from sensation (αἴσθησις), opinion (δόξα), knowledge (ἐπιστήμη), and thought (νοῦς), it seems significant that he treats sensation (αἴσθησις) as sensation of proper objects only, rather than including common and incidental sensation (hence its infallibility). Likewise in his treatment of thinking, he considers mind in its correspondingly infallible modes, first knowledge (ἐπιστήμη) and then νοῦς, which is the non-discursive grasp of essences beyond *phantasia*.

81. In order to understand Aristotle's conception of *phantasia*, it is useful to recall Caston's exceptionally apt comparison between *phantasia* and echo (see 1996, 47–48). Although Aristotle himself does not make any connection between his analysis of echo in II.8 and his analysis of *phantasia* in III.3 and almost surely intended no connection to be drawn, the fit between the two in Caston's analogy is remarkably illuminating.

82. Caston 1996, 49.

83. See Caston: "Sometimes this 'echo' is *modified* on its way to the central organ in a way that *alters* its causal powers . . . A phantasma can change and so deviate from the original stimulation" (1996, 49).

84. This suggests the important conclusion that the primary psychological distinction between soul as the cause of cognition and soul as the cause of motion is the difference between its powers for being acted upon (πάσχειν) and acting (ποιεῖν) respectively.

85. 427a17–21. For the same division reiterated at the outset of Aristotle's treatment of soul as the cause of the living being's actions and movements in space, see III.9.432a15–22.

86. Aristotle sets out to prove this at *De Anima* III.3.428b17–428b30.

87. That the common and incidental appearances (φαντάσματα) can be both false and true is more straightforward, for since their originative sensations can be either false or true, they can also be false even when the object is being actively perceived, that is, in the case that the sense object is itself false.

88. Caston argues that imagination is essential to incidental *and* common perception, and claims that it is insofar as these modes of perception involve *phantasia* that they are susceptible to error (1996, 42). The evidence that *phantasia* is necessarily involved in all perception of common sense objects is scant, however (Caston cites *Mem.* I.450a9–12; II.452b7–453a4). I would argue rather that it is by the fact that the object involves perceptual synthesis of terms that introduce the possibility of falsity into these two kinds of perception. In III.3 Aristotle is not discussing *phantasia*'s contribution to each of the three kinds of sense objects, but rather the distinct kinds of appearances (φαντάσματα) produced by each kind of object.

89. De Corte writes, "It is precisely because incidental sensibles do not, *qua* incidental, have any effect on the senses that they differ from the common sensibles" (1934, 92).

90. Cashdollar (1973, 165).

91. This would be almost like an automatic, unreflective, non-inferential version of the deliberate production of images (εἰδωλοποιοῦντες) involved in arranging a mnemonic system mentioned by Aristotle at III.3.427b18–20.

92. For the finest and most persuasive account of phenomenon, which Cashdollar calls "perceptive predication," see Cashdollar (1973, 161–67).

93. Cashdollar 1973, 163–67.

94. Cashdollar writes the following on the difference between perceptive and thinking predication: "The incidence within the inceived sensible is the reverse of predication of συμβεβηκότα as we usually understand it, for observation of the various examples suggests a reversal of the order of subject and predicate when compared with thought. The exemplary cases reveal that incidental perception is the true or false recognition of a particular substance which in the order of nature is prior to its attribute or incidental quality, but which quality is proper to one of the five senses . . . Since special perception then is of the category of quality, substance is for perception relegated to a secondary place along with usual secondary qualities . . . while thought would usually ask 'what is Cleon' or 'where is Cleon,' perception always asks 'what is the white,' 'where is the white,' or 'how big is the white.' When Aristotle speaks (III.2.426b8) of a 'subject' of perception (as we say 'object'), he means exactly that. Quality is no longer simply a κατηγορία (predicate) but a subject or substrate (ὑποκείμενον), the subject being from a proper perception, the predicate from another source" (1973, 162–63).

95. In his discussion of perception in *De Anima*, Kahn writes: "We are not here concerned with what James calls the perception of 'things,' something more complex and intellectual than mere sensation. This would involve Aristotle's doctrine of incidental sensation or sensation *per accidens*, which is not an act of the sense faculty as such and therefore lies outside the present study" (1996, 46). My view is in disagreement with Kahn in that I argue incidental sensation is indeed a form of sensation, not something more intellectual than sensation, and that there is consequently for him a perception of things prior to the emergence of thinking. For Aristotle, non-thinking animals are perfectly well

able to recognize objects, and this is because incidental perception is dependent not on thought but on *imagination*, which is integral to his account of perception.

96. Compare also the similar formulation at II.4.416b25, where first soul is defined as γεννητική οἷον αὐτό.

97. When this thinking is practical rather than theoretical, this imagination is called βουλευτική (III.11.434a7).

98. One further aspect of the parallel: just as reproduction is present in all beings with nutritive soul which are "complete and not maimed" (II.4.415a27)—in other words, living beings that are either not too rudimentary or individually defective (see Bodéus, 1993, 151n4)—imagination is present in all beings with sensitive soul, except perhaps those which are extremely rudimentary. In III.3 Aristotle mentions certain rudimentary animals which seem to be without *phantasia* (III.3.428a10–11), but in most other passages he takes imagination to be universally present in all sensitive beings, if only indeterminately in very rudimentary perceivers. For relevant passages on this question, see Caston (1996, 23n9).

99. Thus III.3 on imagination forms the conclusion of the section on sensation, and not III.2 on the principle (ἀρχή) or formal principle of sensation, as most suppose. *Phantasia* belongs to the sensitive soul just as much as reproduction does to the nutritive soul, which Aristotle makes explicit when he states that "the appearance [φάντασμα] is an affection [πάθος] of the common sense [κοινῆ αἴσθησις]" (*Mem.* I.450a10–11).

100. Kahn (1966) notes that 10 Bekker pages are devoted to sensation, with 3 devoted to intellect and 4 to all the other faculties combined. See Kahn (1996, 49).

101. In the argument that follows I remain neutral on the question of whether perception involves any material change which dominates recent Anglophone secondary literature. Though it is an interesting and important question, I do not think it is a question Aristotle had in mind in *De Anima*. The qualified senses of change (κίνησις) to which he refers in II.5 do not refer to the difference of material and immaterial changes, but rather to changes in which nature is lost vs. changes in which nature is preserved.

102. Kahn 1996, 62.

Chapter 4

1. Because the interpretative history of Aristotle's views on thought is so rich and complex, I avoid reference to other interpretations, except to acknowledge my sources and to clarify my own interpretation.

2. Eudemus was taken to be the author of the *Eudemian Ethics*, though beyond this source, Simplicius also makes reference to Eudemus's stance on the question.

3. Brentano 1992, 313.

4. The way I read book III of *De Anima*, chapters 7 and 8 open the discussion of practical mind. In contrast, almost all commentators see this transition as only occurring in chapter 9, with 7 and 8 constituting random compilations of reflections on the mind discussed up to that point in the work. Michel Fattal reads these chapters in the same way that I do: "It is within what could be communally called the noetic that one must situate chapter 6 of Book III of *De Anima*. After having treated his conception of theoretical intellect in chapters 4 and 5, Aristotle studies the acts and operations of νοῦς in chapter 6, and treats practical intellect in chapter 7" (1996, 421).

5. For this reason, though Caston is right in finding fault with certain medieval commentators who postulate an "agent sense" parallel to agent intellect (1996, 204), there is

a true insight in this. Perceiving that we perceive is indeed the apperceptive awareness equivalent to νοῦς ποιητικός (active mind), but in addition νοῦς ποιητικός is more than this. For unlike sense awareness where the objects and light are productive of the perception, in thinking νοῦς ποιητικός (active mind) internalizes both object and medium and is itself the apperceptive and the initiating moment of the activity of thinking.

6. Kosman rightly argues from the perspective of the rhetorical structure of III.4–5 that it would be surprising if III.5 were treating the transition from first potentiality to first actuality, the development of mind (νοῦς) as a state of possession (ἕξις)—as is argued by many commentators, when this aspect of thinking was covered explicitly in III.4: "We might, therefore, find it odd that Aristotle should have devoted a chapter at the heart of his discussion of νοῦς to spelling out a specific application of this general feature of acquired habits. If he had felt it necessary to give a specific account of νοῦς as first actuality, wouldn't the obvious point for him to do so have been in the heart of ch. 4 when first-actuality νοῦς is initially introduced?" (Kosman 1992, 352). But as I will argue later, Kosman obscures his point by denying, through a flawed analogy with perceptual identity of object and sense, the way that, in the state (ἕξις) of knowledge (ἐπιστήμη), the object and mind are identical (the identity does not hold just in the second actuality of active contemplation [θεωρεῖν]). This confusion obscures this clear division between the mental phenomena being analyzed in III.4 (mind as receptive) and III.5 (mind as active consciousness).

7. *APo.* I.1.71a8.

8. Recall the analogous senses of potentiality and actuality in perception, using the example from hearing:

Unsounding bell →	Sound from bell (unheard) →	Sound from bell (actively heard)
1st potentiality →	2nd potentiality/ 1st actuality →	2nd actuality
	Transition 1: striking of bell	**Transition 2:** actively hearing ear

9. This claim about memory will be crucial for our interpretation of the closing lines of III.5, where we will discuss the current passage at length.

10. Caston 1999, 210.

11. Ibid.

12. The converse is not necessarily true: just because one cannot find a species that possesses one power but not the other, and consequently both powers always occur together in a being, this does not mean that the powers are indistinguishable. Take the senses for example: though touch can exist apart from the higher senses, one does not have beings with smell but without hearing: yet this does not mean these sensitive powers are indistinguishable. Thus the criterion of separate existence is simply one (particularly good) criterion for distinguishing between powers of the soul among others, for example by the nature of the object of that power.

13. Caston 1999, 209.

14. There are many indications that Aristotle is analyzing human thinking only in III.4. He twice makes clear he is talking about mind as a part of the soul by which one thinks (III.4.429a10; III.4.429a22–23). Rather than employ the verb thinking (νοεῖν) when discussing this part of the soul, he employs γιγνώσκειν and φρονεῖν (III.4.429a10–11) and διανοεῖν and ὑπολαμβάνειν (III.4.429a23), all of which imply a discursive process. He similarly treats Anaxagorean mind by translating the cosmological notion of mind ruling (κρατεῖν) into mind knowing (γνωρίζειν) (III.4.429a19–20).

15. In the discussion of nutrition at II.4.416a32, those who argued against the position that like is fed by like point out that like is unaffected (ἀπαθοῦς) by like, while food is certainly affected in nutrition. They miss how the living organism does remain unaffected (ἀπαθές) in that it transforms its initially foreign object into itself in order to preserve its own determinate nature.

16. This gloss on this Anaxagorean concept of mind ruling shows that Aristotle at this point in the argument is looking at mind in terms of individual human cognition of objects of thought, and not as a principle governing all things. This point is brought out well by Polansky (2000, 67–69), and Kosman, who writes: "More importantly Aristotle makes clear that however correct Anaxagoras was in thinking of mind as a cosmic principle, the present discussion must first come to terms with the nature of mind as determined by the functional psychic definition of Aristotle's treatise . . . Ch. 4 then gives an account of this faculty on the basis of those features that Aristotle agrees with Anaxagoras are important, but restricted to mind as a feature of the human soul" (1992, 352–53).

17. *GC* II.1.329a25 ff. See also *Long. Vit.* III.465b12–13; III.465b30, where he states that all matter immediately has a contrary.

18. Such as those Aristotle mentions in *GC* I.2.316a5–14, when contrasting the natural philosopher and the dialectician, principles which are able to connect and explain a wider range of things.

19. This is perhaps in implicit criticism of Plato's sun and cave allegories, where one returns to the cave blinded by the darkness after having adjusted to the light of higher principles. I am indebted to David Bronstein for this observation. Yet the point of Plato's re-descending blindness seems to be acknowledged by Aristotle's concession that, with a view to action, knowledge seems inferior to experience, at least until the knower is able to connect his theoretical grasp of universals with individuals, since action is concerned with the individual. Compare *Metaph.* I.1.981a12ff.

20. *Eth. Nic.* X.7.1177a23.

21. *Metaph.* XII.9.1074b17–18.

22. The last line, "καὶ αὐτὸς δὴ αὑτὸν τότε δύναται νοεῖν," refers to the mind's knowledge of itself. This is the reading found in the manuscripts and in the Greek commentators. Many modern commentators have followed Bywater's 1885 emendation of "δὴ αὑτόν" to "δι' αὑτοῦ," transforming Aristotle's point to one about the self-initiated character of thinking. Though this is also an important aspect of thinking that distinguishes it from lower activities, it is not sufficient grounds for rejecting the traditional view. For an excellent explanation of the passage interpreted in the traditional way, see Owens (1976).

23. Hence Aristotle's comment in the *Nicomachean Ethics* at X.8.1178b2–5 on how to distinguish the theoretical from the practical life: "But the man who is contemplating the truth needs no such [external things], at least with a view to the exercise of his activity; indeed they are, one may see, even hindrances, at all events to his contemplation." While learning may require certain externals, the one who has learned needs nothing outside of

himself to contemplate. Externality is for the knower seeking to exercise this knowledge mere distraction.

24. Kosman 1992, 348 (italics mine).

25. Ibid., 353; 355n40. Just because there is a distinction throughout *De Anima* between knowledge (ἐπιστήμη) and active contemplation (θεωρεῖν), this does not mean that "contemplative understanding [ἐπιστήμη θεωρητική]" can be viewed interchangeably with active contemplation (θεωρεῖν). The contrast between theoretical and practical ἐπιστήμη is more like the distinction between skill and understanding in *APo.* II.19.100a8–9.

26. Kosman 1996, 352; and above note 6.

27. In thinking, the passive and active moments explained in III.4 and III.5 respectively are easier to isolate than in the explanation of perception, because they can be differentiated into temporally distinct moments. The first actuality of knowing, achieved when the potential knower has learned the nature or essence of some object and thus "become" that object, but is not actively thinking this knowledge, is easily distinguished from the moment of turning one's rational attention to that implicit knowledge and actively thinking it. The receptive and active aspects of mind, though in the fullest actuality occurring together, can be clearly separated through these distinct stages. In contrast, in perception one does not first receive the sensible form of red into one's eye, and subsequently become aware of this affection, but they are two sides of an indivisible activity. In nutrition (in the sense of self-maintaining activity, not digestion, which does admit of these distinctions), one cannot even properly distinguish between potentiality and actuality, let alone first and second actuality. This is why the three-level theory of actuality and potentiality used to explain the lower levels is illustrated through the stages of knowing, which is clearer because more differentiated.

28. To be able to act "itself according to itself [αὐτὸ καθ' αὐτό]" is impossible for sensation, but is ultimately achieved in thought which is active without any relation to an external object. Note how this expression is used by Plato in *Phaedo* 66–67.

29. Cashdollar 1973, 161.

30. Hicks 1907, 487.

31. Aristotle mentions an exception to this distinction between a thing's concrete existence and its intelligible essence: "For some things they [a thing and its essence] are the same" (III.4.429b12). To what does Aristotle refer when he writes that there is not always a distinction between a thing and its essence? He makes it clear later on (III.4.429b18–21) that these are not mathematical truths. As we will learn in III.5, there is a being that alone is that which it is, existing without matter. Is it to this being that Aristotle here refers? I am not sure.

32. In contrast with my reading of this section as a reflection on the three different kinds of sense objects, Hicks sees the examples of quantity (μέγεθος) and water (ὕδωρ) and flesh (σάρκα) as primarily a distinction between objects of mathematics and objects of physics. See Hicks (1907, 486).

33. Hamlyn 1968, 137–38.

34. Bodéüs 1993 calls attention to this passage in the context of the argument in III.4 (1993, 225 fn. 3).

35. *APo.* II.19.100a17. See also *Phys.* I.1.184a21ff., where Aristotle explains how the universal is present in sensation, and that the whole is grasped in a confused manner.

36. This is Aristotle's point at III.4.429b18–21 when he argues that "straight" is like "snub," since straightness is always extended from which its essence is only in mathemat-

ical thinking. The main difference is that the definitions of mathematical objects do not require reference to their matter.

37. *GC* I.7.323b10–15.

38. Ibid., I.7.323b29–324a2.

39. Hamlyn 1968, 138.

40. See Bodéüs 1975, 71.

41. As will become clear when we examine the analogy of active mind with light, the human mind is not itself thinkable except insofar as it has become identical with its objects, so this condition is merely hypothetical and will be denied by Aristotle. Just as light is only visible incidentally (κατὰ συμβεβηκός)—that is, insofar as it is making manifest a colored object which appears through it—the mind is only thought insofar as some object of thought is being made manifest through it. See Wedin (1988, 180n36). How non-epistemic mind (νοῦς) in the case of God is itself thinkable is a separate question.

42. It is an interesting question whether the two analogies Aristotle uses to explain the receptivity of sensation and of thinking—the signet ring's wax and the writing tablet—imply any significant philosophical distinction.

43. Kosman's interpretation of this problem of how to distinguish mind from the merely intelligible and its solution is that it is left unresolved in III.4 and taken up again in III.5 (1992, 344–345). But I do not see how νοῦς ποιητικός (active mind) addresses this "question of the universal presence of νοῦς," nor do I see how it is left at all unresolved by the solution he offers at the end of III.4, through the distinction between the form as its exists as enmattered in its object, and the form as dematerialized in the mind become knowledge (ἐπιστήμη).

44. An image is still required, but as we will explain in a moment, this image is incidental to the already actually understood form (as opposed to the sensible images which underlie the potentially understood intelligible form prior to learning).

45. Recall Aristotle's comparison of sensation to intellect on this score in II.5: "Active sensation is spoken of just like active contemplation [θεωρεῖν]. But it differs in this sense, that what is capable of producing the activity are *external objects*, i.e., the objects of sight and hearing, just like the rest of the sense objects. The reason is that active sensation is of particulars, while knowledge [ἐπιστήμη] is of the universal. And these exist in a sense in the soul. Therefore thinking is up to oneself [ἐπ' αὐτῷ], whenever it wishes, but perceiving is not up to oneself. For it is necessary for the object of perception to be present" (II.5.417b18–26).

46. As Kosman writes, "Given that mind thus knows itself, and therefore does not, as the perceptual faculty does, depend on the existence of an external object, why is it that thinking is not always taking place?" (1992, 354).

47. Polansky 2000, 67–69.

48. "Let me suggest rather than [*sic*] it is this question to which Aristotle turns in the opening lines of ch. 5, and which he elucidates by reference to the analogy of light" (Kosman 1996, 354).

49. See Hamlyn (1968, 138); Hicks (1907, 497); Ross (1961, 295).

50. "Sensation in actuality is spoken of similarly as contemplating [τῷ θεωρεῖν]. But there is this difference, that the producers [τὰ ποιητικά] of the actuality of the sense are external—the object of vision and the object of hearing, and similarly for the rest of the senses" (II.5.417b19–21).

51. See Rist (1966, 519).

52. *Mem.* I.449b19–20.

53. Ibid., I.449b21.

54. Ibid., I.450a13–14.

55. "The image is a πάθος of the common sense. This it is clear that the cognition [γνῶσις] of these belongs to the first sense capacity [τῷ πρώτῳ αἰσθητικῷ]" (Ibid., I.450a10–11).

56. Ibid., I.450a23–26.

57. Caston 1999, 200–202.

58. Kosman 1992, 311. Kosman goes on to note the same strategy is employed at the end of the *Nicomachean Ethics*: Contemplation (θεωρία) is identified as an essential aspect in the happy life, and then by process of elimination this activity is identified with the divine.

59. I agree with Caston (1999) that Ross is too hasty to exclude the possibility that ἐν τῇ ψυχῇ could mean "in the case of soul" rather than "in the soul," meaning within each individual soul. Caston argues that the more general claim is a perfectly plausible reading of the Greek, and that "our only guide, therefore, can be the context itself" (1999, 206). But his argument that "in the case of the soul" is the only possible reading to preserve the parallel structure of the argument between nature and soul seems equally hasty. The parallelism works also if the argument is inferring something about the structure of the soul from nature as a whole because the soul is an instance of natural being.

60. I may be interpreting the force of this inference incorrectly, as the conclusion is surprising to say the least. The soul is the formal principle of natural living beings, but why would the distinction between form and matter exist within the form itself?

61. The matter in each thing is its capacity either to be or not to be all the determinations which it is capable of becoming. See *Metaph.* VII.7.1032a20–22.

62. "For the medical art and the building art are the form of health and of the house; and I call the essence substance without matter" (*Metaph.* VII.7.1032b13–15).

63. "The healthy subject, then, is produced as the result of the following train of thought; since this is health, if the subject is to be healthy this must be first present . . . and the physician goes on thinking thus until he brings the matter to a final step which he himself can take" (ibid., VII.7.1032b5ff.). This knowledge of how to change from the matter without the form to the matter having the form in question is part of the art in question.

64. This is why, as I argued in relation to the hierarchy of senses, we should not think of thinking as being closer to touching just because mind has no medium. Aristotle speaks of mind as touching its object (see *Metaph.* IX.10.1051b17ff.) because in thinking there is no separate medium through which the object appears, but strictly speaking, there *is* a medium in touch; it is simply attached to the organ inside.

65. In Plato's analogy between thinking and seeing, seeing in the light corresponds to thinking intelligible objects, while seeing in the dark corresponds to sensing the merely opinable: "The same is true of the eye by which the soul thinks. When it fixes upon that on which shines truth and being, it thinks and knows and seems to possess mind (νοῦς). But when it is fixed on what is diluted in the darkness, on coming to be and passing away, it opines and is dimmed, changing its opinions back and forth, and then seems not to possess mind (νοῦς)" (*Republic* 508d4ff.). If Aristotle is following and revising the terms of this Platonic analogy, this might explain why he brings up the case of phosphorescent objects, objects which are seen in the dark: "But not everything is visible in the light, but only the proper color of each thing. For some things are not seen in the light, but produce sensation in the dark, such as those things which appear fiery and luminous—these things have no single name—like fungus, the flesh, heads, scales and eyes of fish. But in none of these is the

proper color seen. Why these things are seen is another account, but so much is now clear, that which is seen in light is color" (II.7.419a18). Why bring this up in the treatment of vision without an explanation? Aristotle is arguing that only in light is the proper color seen, just as only in the awareness of mind is the essence or intelligible form thought. But in some cases there are aspects perceived (i.e., thought) in the dark which, although not the proper color (intelligible form), do reveal genuine features of the object. Could Aristotle be making reference here to the fact that one genuinely grasps certain features of objects—though not the intelligible form—in lower modes of cognition than active contemplation (θεωρεῖν)?

66. Michael Frede shows that making colors actual means making them actually seen: "The terms 'colors in act' have a fairly precise significance which can be gleaned from the remarks Aristotle makes in terms of the actuality of sensibles in *De Anima* III.2.425b26ff., especially 426a13–14. The act of the sensible coincides with the act of the sense, and so the act of color is identical with vision, even if there is a formal difference. By producing color in act, then, light produces vision" (1996, 382). On whether Aristotle means the transition from first potentiality to first-actuality colors and seeing or first-actuality to second-actuality colors and seeing when he writes that "light makes potential colors actual colors," see Kosman's discussion (1992, 346–52).

67. Kosman 1975, 518.

68. Ibid., 514.

69. Caston 1999, 202.

70. The distinction here between belonging to the class of "knowers" and those "possessing knowledge" is the distinction between second and first actuality of knowing.

71. 417b29–418a1. In passing, it seems when Aristotle closes II.5 by stating that "there will be a moment later to clarify these things," he is, as has not been recognized, speaking of his analysis of first-potentiality, second-potentiality, and second-actuality knowers in III.4–5.

72. Importantly, since the sentient animal is born with first-actuality perception, both the receptive and the active aspects of sensation occur inseparably—they cannot be separated into distinct minds as in our analysis of thinking. In perception, therefore, awareness as an active cause is not separable (χωριστός) as it is in thinking: it only occurs in the second actuality of perception, which remains dependent upon the external object and its affection of the sense organ. There is no separate transition in perception which *only* involves a change from potentiality to actuality *and no other*. This is why Kosman's (1992) conclusion that knowledge (ἐπιστήμη) is not identical with its object, based upon observing what is true of perception, cannot hold. One cannot measure the higher by the lower automatically in this way.

73. Wedin puts this matter well: "Finally, from the point of view of the person, there is no additional act that effects the transition to active knowing. That is, there are not two acts—the switch at t2 to active knowing and, on the other hand, the active knowing itself that ensues at t2. Rather, the transition occurs simply by virtue of the active exercise of the faculty" (1988, 34).

74. Kosman 1992, 351–52.

75. *Metaph.* XII.6.1071b20.

76. See *Eth. Nic.* X.7.1177a16 and X.7.1177b27–30.

77. *Metaph.* XII.7.1072b21–23.

78. It is disputed whether the two sentences which follow (III.5.430a19–22) should be included in this chapter. Good philological arguments have been made that they should

not, based on the fact that the lines are repeated at the beginning of III.7.431a1–3. I do not know whether or not they were originally included in III.5, but I do think that if one assumes that they were, good sense can be made of them in the developing argument, and in fact this sense does contribute an important point to Aristotle's analysis of the active consciousness in thinking.

79. The claim that understanding is the same as the object (πρᾶγμα) is best understood through a contrast with how sensation works. In sensation, the underlying thing (πρᾶγμα) is not the directly cognized thing, but is rather the sensible quality which belongs to that thing. In thinking, by contrast, the whole object is in the mind as knowledge, and thus the identification of mind and object is far more complete than the partial identification in perception. Kosman explains this beautifully: "In these cases the distinction between immediate and remote object (present in perception) disappears. The πρᾶγμα is nothing but the immediate object of understanding with which the understanding becomes one, and it therefore occupies the place in the economy of importance and value that is occupied in perception by the remote, that is, the ultimate object of perception. This object of understanding is thus without matter—ἄνευ ὕλης. We may if we wish describe such cognition by saying that understanding understands itself, but this should not be interpreted to refer to an act of *reflexive* self-awareness" (2000, 321).

80. It is also plausible to take the claim about the priority in time as follows: though it might *seem* in the development of the human that potential knowing exists before fully active knowing, this fully active knowing, in its eternal and immortal separation from any receptivity, always exists prior to any potential human knower.

81. Caston is absolutely right to argue, against Rist (1966), that the aorist need not indicate past time, forcing us to understand χωρισθείς as referring to a moment in the past when the active intellect becomes separate from the passive part. The aorist is, as Caston argues, "primarily aspectual and need not indicate past time" (1999, 208). Nevertheless, the way I read Aristotle's statement, one need not decide between the past sense or the aspectual sense: both "once it is has been separated" (Rist 1966) and "when it occurs separately" (Caston 1999) work in my interpretation: the active consciousness in our thinking, once we consider it as separate from everything else in us, is the divine activity—which is the subject of this sentence.

82. A startlingly simple interpretation is offered by Caston (1999)—one which seems to me offers a plausible reading of these lines—based on a reinterpretation of the syntax of the sentence. Traditionally, the ὅτι is understood in its causal sense: we do not remember, *because* this mind is unaffected but παθητικὸς νοῦς (mind in its capacity to be affected) is destructible. Caston rightly argues, however, that if one punctuates the sentence differently, removing the comma between δέ and ὅτι, it is perfectly plausible to translate the ὅτι as "that," and the sentence reads "We do not remember that while this cannot be affected, the intellect that can be affected is perishable." Given the extreme similarity of νοῦς ποιητικός (active mind) in human and divine thinking, Aristotle is, in Caston's view, emphasizing the difference between human and divine intellect. The importance of asserting this difference would be even more important in our reading of III.5, where the nature of divine activity is inferred from the fact that νοῦς ποιητικός (active mind) in human thinking is independent of body and the most honorable living activity that exists, meaning that it must also be the way God exists. See Caston (1999, 213–15).

83. Most commentators recognize this clear connection between the passages in III.5 and I.4.

84. Aristotle notes this similarity explicitly: "In those who are strongly moved owing to passion, or time of life, no memory is formed; just as no impression would be formed if the movement of the seal were to impinge on running water; while there are others in whom, owing to the receiving surface being frayed, as happens to old walls, or owing to the hardness of the receiving surface, the requisite impression is not implanted at all. Hence both very young and very old persons are defective in memory; they are in a state of flux, the former because of their growth, the latter, owing to their decay" (*Mem.* I.450b1–8). See *GA* II.5.741b15ff. for the description of life as going around a track where one develops and reaches a certain apex, and then gradually regresses by losing these developments in reverse order.

85. *Eth. Eud.* VII.12.1245b18.

86. *Metaph.* XII.9.1074b35–38.

87. *Eth. Eud.* VII.12.1245a5–9.

88. See Enrico Berti (1996); and Thomas de Koninck (1990). Besides Berti's contribution, there are also two essays on III.6 in *Corps et âme: Sur le De anima d'Aristote*: see the essays by Mario Mignucci (1996) and Michel Fattal (1996) in this book. An excellent and plausible account of the chapter which differs radically from my own is given by Kurt Pritzl (1984). My own treatment has been especially helped by Fattal's admirably clear exposition.

89. As Caston (1996) notes, the question of error is perhaps the main concern in his chapter on imagination.

90. See II.6 and III.3 428b18–30.

91. "In those things in which there are both falsity and truth, there is already some synthesis of thoughts as if they were one" (III.6.430a27–8); "The false is always in a synthesis" (III.6.430b1–2). Harvey (1978) argues persuasively that in both these III.6 passages, only falsity is withheld from indivisible objects, not truth: "Instead of taking Aristotle to be saying that there is composition wherever there is truth and wherever there is falsity, one can take him to be saying that there is composition wherever there is both truth and falsity" (220).

92. "But sometimes by means of the images or νοήμασιν in the soul just as if it were seeing, it reasons and deliberates on things about to be relative to things present" (III.7.431b6–8).

93. "But imagination is different than affirmation and denial. The true and the false are a combination [συμπλοκή] of νοημάτων. But from what will the first thoughts [τὰ πρῶτα νοήματα] differ from the φαντάσματα?" (III.8.432a10–13).

94. See Fattal (1996, 426): "This distinction between καθ' αὑτό and κατὰ συμβεβηκός allows the difference which exists between the ἀδιαίρετα of *DA* III.6.430a26 and the νοήματα of 430a28 to be understood. The indivisibles are objects of thought, νοητά or intelligibles, conceived of in themselves independently of all relation, that is to say without predication. The νοήματα are equally objects of thought, but conceived in their relation to other νοήματα, that is to say in an attributive relation. The former are considered in isolation, the later in 'combination' (σύνθησις)."

95. Aristotle also notes in passing (III.6.430b3–4) that every such synthesis is also a division (διαίρεσις), for judging that Cleon is white collects Cleon into the category of white things and distinguishes him from the category of black things.

96. Note that this noetic judgment that Cleon is white is not to be confused with the incidental perception of the son of Cleon or son of Diares as non-inferentially predicated

of white in Aristotle's exemplary case of that phenomenon. Cashdollar notes that whenever Aristotle discusses noetic examples of predication, he uses proper names (Socrates, Callias, etc.), whereas he refers to objects of perceptual predication using the patronymic (son of Diares or Cleon) or no name at all. Cashdollar speculates, I think rightly, that "its only function would be to indicate the vague and often not substantial form a perceptive predication might have . . . 'son of Cleon' might instead refer to various relational aspects without the implication of τόδε τι" (1973, 168).

97. Most commentators think that when Aristotle claims that the mind is what makes the unity, that this is a general conclusion he draws about thinking. But the very point of the chapter, I argue, is that in the thinking of essence, as well as in definition of an essence or causal explanation (ἀπόδειξις) which uses the essence as its beginning point, it is not the mind that imposes the unity from without, but which apprehends the unity intrinsic to its object.

98. Aristotle takes this ability to distinguish between the true and the false to be the main philosophical achievement of the *Sophist*, since he concedes that Plato solves the problem of making statements (saying of what it is that it is, and what is not that it is not). Yet he also wants to point out the incompleteness of this achievement. He points out that the truth or falsity of something depends upon the relation between two parts of a statement—the combination or separation of a subject and its predicate. It is not in the inherent nature of a thing to be true or false, but it is when a predicate is attached to the subject that a judgment of truth or falsity can be made. Therefore the distinctions only exist *in thought*: "The combination and the separation are in thought and not in the things" (*Metaph.* VII.4.1027b30). In *Metaphysics* VI, limiting the scope of what must be investigated in the study of being as being, Aristotle dismisses the accidental being (the realm of sophistry) and then being in the sense of true and false (Plato's *Sophist*), since they both involve an external reflection upon the inherent essence of things. Aristotle wishes to overcome this externality in the Platonic dialectic, by thinking things together and not apart: "by 'together' and 'apart' I mean thinking them so that there is no succession in the thoughts but they become a unity" (*Metaph.* VII.4.1027b24–25). For Aristotle, Plato cannot define what one thing is in itself; he can only capture the relation of one thing to another, with the connection between the two occurring merely for the subject.

99. *Metaph.* IV.2.1004b29.

100. See also *Metaph.* XII.10.1075a27ff., and for the similar claim in *De Anima*, see I.2.405b23.

101. Of the various attributes and properties of being, Aristotle writes that "those who study these properties err not by leaving the sphere of philosophy, but by forgetting that substance, of which they have no correct idea, is prior to these other things" (*Metaph.* IV.2.1004b8–10).

102. *Metaph.* IV.2.1004b17ff.

103. "We are now examining concerning the soul whether it is directly moved and partakes of motion" (I.3.406a12–13). That the soul is moved insofar as it is in the body and the body is moved—like passengers in a ship—is not problematic for him.

104. "For he clearly intends the soul of the world to be in a way like what is called mind. For it is not like the sense capacity or the desiring capacity, for of these the motion [κίνησις] is not cyclical movement" (I.3.407a3–6).

105. Sensation always involves a moment of receptivity to external sensible form where the organ takes on the quality perceived. This reception of sensible form is like the

transition from ignorance to knowledge in learning, which involves a form of transition (κίνησις) from ignorant to knowing (417a30–417b1). Even this is change (κίνησις) only in a qualified sense, since the very nature of the organ is to receive sensible form—in perceiving red the eye becomes other but does not lose its nature, because it is defined by this very capacity to receive form (see 417b12–16). Thinking, in contrast, in the sense of contemplation of already acquired knowledge, involves only the transition from potency to act with no change in the mind—the mind simply becomes what it already was, only more actively (417b5–7). See also *Physics* VII.3.247b1–248a9.

106. "But these things are the unity of the series, just like number, and not like [the unity of] a spatial magnitude" (I.3.407a8–9).

107. For the translation of ἀπόδειξις as "causal explanation" rather than "proof" or "demonstration," see Kosman (1973, 378). Kosman recalls the root meaning of the word as "showing forth" as revealing or uncovering something for what it is.

108. "If [the line is grasped] as a compound of both, it will be in a time compounded from both" (III.6.430b12–14).

109. While the end of a process (κίνησις) lies outside the process towards it, an *energeia* is in possession of its end during every moment of its activity. And insofar as its activity is complete during every moment it is ongoing, Aristotle argues that its present and perfect tense coincide. An *energeia* is in this way not in time (*Nicomachean Ethics* 1174a14–b14), and so does not admit of quickness or slowness (1177a31–b4). See *Metaphysics* IX.6 1048b18–36.

110. "There is in these things something undivided, but perhaps not separable, which makes the time and the length one. And this is similarly the case in each continuous thing, both in time and in length" (III.6.430b17–19).

111. *Categories* V.3b24.

112. Here is the most explicit indication that the thinking (νόησις) of indivisibles is the thinking (νόησις) of the essence (τὸ τί ἦν εἶναι).

113. The common sensible is perceived incidentally (κατὰ συμβεβηκός) by the proper sense, but intrinsically (καθ' αὑτό) by the sensitive power common to all the senses. See III.1.425a14–23.

114. *Mem.* I.449b13–15.

115. Pritzl 1984, 140.

116. *Metaph.* XII.7.1072b3.

117. *Eth. Nic.* X.7.1177b1.

118. *Metaph.* XII.7.1072b26–31.

119. There is a certain question about exactly how similar the activity of human thinking and divine thinking are. Aristotle argues about the activity of thinking in general: "If God is always in that good state in which we sometimes are, this compels our wonder; and if in a better this compels it yet more. And God *is* in a better state" (*Metaph.* XII.7.1072b24–26). See also *Eth. Eud.* VII.14.1248a27ff. for a similar argument.

120. *Eth. Nic.* X.7.1177b27–1178a1.

121. *Metaph.* XII.10.1075a12–17.

122. *APo.* II.19.99b35.

Chapter 5

1. For the many references to this division in *De Anima*, see my introduction, note 2.

2. See the figure on p. 235 and the discussion which follows it.

3. φαντασία plays an essential role both on the cognitive side and the locomotive side of this division. For this reason Aristotle opens the chapter on imagination with a restatement of this division. See III.3.427a18–20.

4. I am following Moss (2009, 124, fn. 11) in referring to the powers Aristotle groups under τὰ κριτικά as "cognition."

5. When Aristotle turns to the cause of locomotion, this is not his first discussion of κίνησις in *De Anima*. See *De Anima* I.3.406a12 for the enumeration of the primary kinds of motion: change of place, alteration, and growth and diminution. The other two principal kinds of change besides change of place play important roles in *De Anima*. Quantitative change in growth and diminution is caused and controlled by nutritive soul as the λόγος or ratio of the body (see III.9.432b8–11), while qualitative change in sensation is controlled by the sensitive soul as the λόγος or ratio of the sense organ. The correspondence between the hierarchy of emerging causal powers of the soul (nutrition, sensation, movement through space) and the hierarchy of quantitative change, qualitative change, and change of location articulated in *Physics* V.1, VIII.7, and elsewhere suggests a deep systematic connection between the *De Anima* and his general theory of change. But in the discussion of *De Anima* III.9–11, Aristotle is only concerned with self-initiated movement through space. He immediately excludes from view the non-voluntary forms of change – growth and decay, inhalation and exhalation, sleeping and waking, as belonging to another account. See III.9.432b7–13.

6. Aristotle frames this whole investigation in III.9–11 in terms of the question of how the soul moves the body, rather than searching for the causes of practical activity, so that his analysis includes the whole range of desiderative cognitions and behavior these cognitions cause, no matter how primitive. See Labarrière (2004, 175): "When Aristotle turns to the problem of the motive faculty and the search for the desirable, he offers an explanation common to humans and other animals, as is indicated by the assimilation of the desirable to the practical good. It is only on the grounds of this explanation common to local motion strictly defined and to practical activity that that which is proper to the human is drawn out."

7. Moss (2009, 126) uses the term "practical cognition" which she defines as cognition "that plays a crucial role in action . . . cognition of things as good or bad, worthy or unworthy of pursuit." Theoretical cognition by contrast is cognition of the object as it is in itself, irrespective of its relation to the organism cognizing it. I will clarify this distinction through the course of the argument.

8. See especially III.4, where thinking is said to be *either* separate from sensation, or related to it as a bent line is related to itself when it is stretched straight (III.4.429b15–16). This passage can be considered in comparison with Aristotle's image for the relation of sensation and thinking on the practical, desiring side: the convex and concave (*NE* I.13 1102a30–34).

9. As in III.5 where the analysis of the activity of contemplating already acquired knowledge, separate from the body and any externality, moves to a reflection on the pure *energeia* of divine thinking.

10. In this sense I agree with Jennifer Whiting (2002, 176), who writes of "the assumption that the soul is properly divided primarily along the rational/non-rational axis," that "this is precisely the assumption that I take Aristotle to be challenging not simply in this passage but throughout the *De Anima* as a whole." But this is not due, as Whiting (2002, 177) claims, to the methodological concern that "we should not *define* various parts of the

soul in terms of their having or lacking λόγος. We should instead define parts of the soul in terms of their functions and their respective objects." The determinative point is the view Aristotle is developing that the higher power is related to the lower as the actualization of potentiality, or as form to matter (which is also ultimately Whiting's [2002, 199] view).

11. I am arguing that the implicit purpose of *De Anima* III.9–11 on the soul's role in animal movement is the same as the explicit purpose of *De Motu Animalium*, where Aristotle draws attention to the analogy between the way an animal moves itself and the way the unmoved mover moves the eternal moved mover. For an explicit statement of this, see *De Motu* 6.700b30–35. Aristotle also argues at the opening of the treatise (*De Motu* 1.698a12–17) that the first unmoved mover's relation to the self-movement of the eternal circular motion should also be manifested in the parts of the universe, especially in the self-movement of animals. *De Motu* seeks to show how that most universal cause is also present in the inner structure of sensible, particular beings.

12. For example, Ross (1961, 308) notes of Aristotle's promise to investigate this question later: "No passage has been traced in which A. discusses this question." Lawson-Tancred (1986, 249, fn. 125) writes: "It is a question which he neither answers himself nor provides us with the materials for answering." See also Hamlyn (1968, 148): "The promise made in the last sentence is, as far as can be seen, not carried out. It is not altogether clear why the problem arises in the form in which Aristotle expresses it here."

13. The comments on mathematical thinking directly preceding this question (431b12–17) serve to distinguish the separation from sensible bodies in mathematics through abstraction of characteristics not actually separable from the kind of separability of the practical mind he is investigating in what follows. In other words, do the objects of practical mind have a *real* independence from the sensible, not one that would exist only in thought?

14. This can also be expressed as a question about the degree of autonomy of self-movers. As J.-L. Labarrière (2004, 163–64) writes: "If this autonomy approaches zero, then self-moving animals would only be nominally so and everything will happen in them mechanically and automatically without being able to say that they are in some way masters of their own movements, since they will only be set into motion by a mover which remains radically exterior to them, from which it follows that their famous local motions would be nothing but responses to stimuli coming from their environment."

15. The ethical consequences of this problem are clearly brought out in *NE*, where Aristotle dismisses this conclusion by which pleasant objects and not the soul which has become easily caught up by them would be seen as the intiating cause of action. See *NE* III.10 1110b9–15.

16. Another extremely plausible reading of the question which concludes III.7 is the following. After explaining how the mind grasps (1) the essence of sensible objects and (2) mathematical objects, Aristotle goes on to consider how the mind thinks immaterial substance, such as divine self-thinking thought. On this reading Aristotle is wondering how the mind of an embodied being, which needs sensation of its object as a beginning point in the process towards grasping its essence (a process outlined in *Metaphysics* I.1 and *Posterior Analytics* II.19), could think a being that exists in complete independence of the sensible. It seems to me Aristotle never examines this important question anywhere, let alone in what follows in *De Anima*. On my reading, by contrast, whether practical mind can think the separate when it is itself inextricably bound to sensation of extension

becomes the driving question which the whole ensuing argument of *De Anima* III.9–11 seeks to answer.

17. This connects *De Anima* III.9–11 with the discussion in *Physics* VIII, where Aristotle *appears* to be denying that animals are self-movers. There Aristotle entertains the possibility that animals are not self-movers who can set themselves in motion from rest, partly because some part in them is always moving, and partly because the environment and not the animal inititates the movement. Furley (1994) treats the apparent tension in Aristotle's attitude towards whether animals are genuinely self-movers.

18. Aristotle is asking if mind can "think the separate," whereas the emphasis of my interpretation is about whether it can "think separately." But this should not be seen as a confusion. Is the object of practical thinking, my general knowledge that such and such is good for a human being to do, independent of the various desirable objects I perceive through the senses? The questions of the separability of the object cannot be isolated from questions of the separability of the activity which grasps the object, as Aristotle himself states in III.4: "And generally as the objects are separable from matter, in this way also are the things of the mind" (429b21–22).

19. *Metaph.* IX.6.1048b18–26. He follows these examples with two non-theoretical biological activities: living and being happy.

20. *DC* II.6.

21. Ibid., I.4.271a20–22.

22. Ibid., I.9.279b1–3.

23. Ibid., II.6.288a25. *GC* II.10.337a7 (this passage shows how it is not *only* living being that imitates the circular motion of the outermost sphere).

24. *DC* II.4.286b18–23.

25. *GC* 337a32–34.

26. Kosman (1994, 147) writes that circular motion is a "mediating figure that is in one sense clearly motion, but in another virtually a mode of activity that contrasts with motion."

27. Aristotle argues that thinking of the soul's activity in analogy with different kinds of motion through space, even if this motion is circular, still draws the soul into spatial extension.

28. *NE* VI.2.1339b1–5.

29. Jessica Moss (2009) shows how this explains why Aristotle can speak of weakness of will (ἀκρασία) as a kind of perceptual illusion, and that there is ultimately no contradiction in saying that it is both this and a struggle between competing desires.

30. Jennifer Whiting (2002) argues for the same basic point in her article "Locomotive Soul." She argues that there is a single sensitive-locomotive part of the soul, and that the capacities for sensation and movement "constitute a single, functionally integrated part of soul that has two aspects—one an internal, representational aspect and the other an external, behavioral aspect—each aspect being inseparable from the other in so far as an animal's behavior is for the most part an extension of its representational states" (2002, 142). Further: "The locomotive part is simply the same part—considered from a different point of view—as the perceiving part (which Aristotle identifies with the imagining and desiring part): talk of this part as 'locomotive' simply emphasizes the external or behavioral aspects of the internal representational states that are emphasized in talk of it as 'perceptive,' 'imaginative,' and 'desiderative'" (2002, 143, fn. 1). Where I chiefly differ from Whiting is that I think this distinction between the capacity for representational states and the capacity

for behavior and locomotion is more basic for Aristotle than the characteristic division of nutritive/sensitive/intellective. Both the representational and behavioral sides include a sensual power and an intellective power, and nutrition manifests in a primitive but rather precise way the structure of both cognition and behavior production.

31. Whiting (2002, 158) writes that "the perception of something as pleasant or painful simply constitut[es] a form of desire."

32. The passage comes up in the context of showing how just as practical sensations of present objects involve a push or pull on the soul, practical images and thoughts can also exercise a push or pull in the absence of any sensation. The example of the beacon should be understood as an illustration of how a sensation can be practical and cause movement, in contrast to the practically motivating image or thought discussed in what immediately follows the example.

33. This is presumably an instance of incidental perception. One perceives orange, a certain shape and so on, and the remembered image of "fire" is spontaneously associated with the proper sensation. In turn, this kind of fire is associated with the remembered image "beacon," such that a beacon is perceived.

34. Motion is one of the common sensibles.

35. It is because of this implicitly predicative structure that there is the perpetual possibility of practical error—that there is always for practical cognition the possible distance between the apparent good and the real good. As Aristotle states in III.10, νοῦς is always right—here I assume he means theoretical mind's (νοῦς') apprehension of essence, but one could also include the sensation of proper objects. The simple, non-predicative structure of these objects places them beyond falsity—in other words, what *appears* and what *is* for νοῦς in its grasp of intelligible form and the five senses in relation to sensible forms always coincide. The same is not true for our desiderative perceptions: "νοῦς is always right. But desire [ὄρεξις] and imagination [φαντασία] are both right and wrong. Consequently the object of desire always moves, but sometimes this is the good [τὸ ἀγαθὸν] and sometimes the imagined good [τὸ φαινόμενον ἀγαθόν]" (III.10.433a26–29).

36. See also *De Motu* 6.700b17–25.

37. This is, I suggest, the same μεσότης mentioned just a few lines down as the center of all sensitive activities: "the air makes the eye this particular way, and it acts on another, and the same goes for hearing. And the ultimate end is one, and a single mean [τὸ δὲ ἔσχατον ἕν, καὶ μία μεσότης], but its being is many" (III.10.431a17–20). On the search for this principle of awareness in the center of the animal, see *De Motu* 8.702a31–9.703a12.

38. Jennifer Whiting (2002, 163–74) offers a persuasive argument that this is in fact the purpose of the reflection on common sense in the context of a discussion of the relation between the sensitive and desiderative powers of soul.

39. See Whiting 2002, 174–86.

40. See also *De Motu* 6.700b18–21.

41. Contrary to Labarrière 2004, 188ff.

42. This radically undifferentiated unity of cognition and desire will have to be qualified when Aristotle turns to the rationally virtuous human action, in his treatment of the "practical syllogism" which concludes his treatment of desire and locomotion in *De Anima*. There the unmoved cognition is the cognition of an object of rational desire, while the moving desire is the cognition of an object of appetitive desire. See the concluding section below.

43. This unity is conveyed by his definition of choice as desiring mind (ὀρεκτικὸς νοῦς) or thinking desire (ὄρεξις διανοητική) (*NE* 1139b4–5). Yet Aristotle's point in *De Anima*

applies even to animal desires, which could be accurately described as ὀρεκτικὴ αἴσθησις (desiring sensation) or ὄρεξις αἰσθητική (sensual desire) (though Aristotle never describes them as such).

44. "For if there were two movers, mind and desire, they would move according to some common form." III.10.433a22–23. See Whiting (2002, 182) for a similar account.

45. "This moves without itself being moved by being thought or imagined" (433b11).

46. Contrary to Furley (1994, 9): "The unmoved mover is not the soul or any 'part' of the animal but something external to it—the object of ὄρεξις, here identified with the πρακτὸν ἀγαθόν." Although ultimately the practical good does refer to an object outside the soul, for there to be desire there must be the internalized representation of the object, so it is the object as cognized in the soul to which Aristotle here refers. It makes no difference here whether we say this is an "internal image" or "the object itself, perceived in a particular way" (Furley 1994, 13, fn. 14): in either case we are speaking of the soul's cognition. Furley (1994, 12) recognizes this in the article: "But people desire things in the external world, and exert themselves to get them, *under certain descriptions*, and their actions cannot be explained without some notion of what each of their goals means *for them*. The ὀρεκτόν cannot be identified as such independently of the ὀρεκτικόν, and in this sense the ἀρχή of action produced by desire is 'inside' the agent."

47. For the purposes of his argument in *De Anima*, Aristotle does not distinguish between appetite (ἐπιθυμία) and spirit (θυμός). The only mention of spirit (θυμός) in the treatment of desire is in reference to the Platonic tripartition. In contrast, Falcon (2005, 96), Lorenz (2006), and others take Aristotle to be adopting the Platonic tripartition wholesale.

48. Against Labarrière (2004, 194), I would argue that the object of desire must always be interior, even when it is an external sense object grasped by sensation. Sensation is the identity of object and perceiver, and although this inner awareness in sensation is dependent on an external object, the object of desire is just as much inner as outer when it is desired. Although the proper object of desire is external, desiring it requires an interior representation of the object. There can be no desire of an object which is not cognized.

49. The distinction between cognizing a thought as opposed to cognizing an image is made at III.7.431b8, where both are able to consider present ends in the light of future ends, and again at III.10.433b11, where the object of appetite can be one that is thought or imagined.

50. III.7.431b2-5: "So the thinking capacity thinks the forms [τὰ εἴδη] in the images [ἐν τοῖς φαντάσμασι], and just as in those [i.e., the sensing animal] it is defined for it what is to be pursued and fled from, so too outside of sensation [ἐκτὸς τῆς αἰσθήσεως], whenever it is directed towards images, it is moved." See Labarrière (2004, 185–86): "What then to do with the *orekton* in this case? The best course seems to me to be to think that it is, above all else, an object that is *present* and *external* to the animal, the object perceived as desirable . . . That being said, this model seems to me to hold equally when the desirable is apprehended by *phantasia* or by the *nous praktikos*, faculties which have the capacity of (re)presenting the *orekton*, whether it is present or absent."

51. Even the other side of practical thinking—deliberation about means—is essentially just a way of transferring the desirability of the end to the necessary intermediate steps, so that otherwise indifferent ends can exert the pull on us that is necessary for attaining the ultimate end of the reasoning.

52. Moss 2009, 129. She further defines βούλησις or wish as "desire for what one rationally judges good" (2009, 128, fn. 23).

53. Labarrière (2004, 194) seems to conflate these when he writes that "there is a first mover, the desiring faculty, and a second mover, the cognitive faculty, for if this last is indispensable, this is not in order to produce the desire as such, but in order to determine it."

54. Moss brings out the sense of what it means to identify the immediately pleasant with the unqualified pleasant and unqualified good: "This part of the soul simply fails to notice any of the factors that qualify the pleasure and goodness of what it desires" (127).

55. "But for the dianoetic soul the φαντάσματα are just like αἰσθήματα."

56. Cashdollar 1973, 165.

57. The fact that *phantasia* is so hard to place relative to sensation and thinking can be explained through this dual character as perceptual (αἰσθητική) and rational (βουλευτική). See III.9.432a31–432b3.

58. Though it might seem strange to call the image a rational desire (βούλησις), this follows from the view I am trying to articulate about cognition of objects in their practical, interested, desiderative mode. The cognition and the desire are one, and awareness of the object as good *is* the desire.

59. "This is the reason why they [i.e., the other, non-rational animals] seem not to have beliefs, because they do not have [the imagination, i.e., the deliberative or rational imagination] which comes from reasoning, and this imagination does involve belief." The passage is particularly difficult and obscure. For my construal of the text, see below, note 87.

60. The same language is used in chapter I.13 of the *Nicomachean Ethics* devoted to moral psychology. There he notes that one praises the reason (λόγος) or the aspect of the soul which has reason (λόγος) in both continent and incontinent people, blaming their deficiencies on a part of the soul he calls the appetitive capacity (τὸ ἐπιθυμητικόν) or generally, the desiring capacity (ὅλως ὀρεκτικόν). The problem with this way of speaking is that the rational part of the soul seems to be *other* than the desiring part, while the appetitive power of the soul seems to be identified with the desiring power of the soul, as though desire were not a more comprehensive concept than appetite. At the same time, Aristotle speaks of the rational and appetitive parts as a struggle between two impulses (ὁρμαί) (1102b21), and he corrects his original way of speaking at 1103a1: "But if it is necessary to speak of this [appetitive power] as having λόγος, then the part having λόγος will be double, the one side having reason precisely and in itself, the other as able to hear it as from a father."

61. See Whiting 2002, 180, fn. 55: "The idea here seems to be that βούλησις, which is a form of νοῦς, is also a form of ὄρεξις." See also fn. 56. Whiting occasionally speaks as if desire (ὄρεξις) can be contrasted with practical mind (νοῦς)(see for example p. 181), while I prefer to see desire (ὄρεξις) as the genus, with sensual desire (ἐπιθυμία) and noetic desire (βούλησις) as its species.

62. See his definition of choice as ὀρεκτικὸς νοῦς or ὄρεξις διανοητική (*NE* 1139b4–5).

63. See Moss 2009, 129.

64. See Whiting 2002, 180 fn. 56.

65. Whiting (2002, 185) states the matter extremely well: "The answer to the question posed at the start of *De Anima* 3.9 is that what moves the animal is *not* some distinctive part of the soul beyond those mentioned: it is simply τὸ ὀρεκτικόν. But since the desiring part of the soul is one and the same part of the soul as the perceiving part, the imaging part, and the practically thinking part, the identification of the part that moves the animal with

the orectic part demands clarification." All the modes of cognition that have been treated in terms of the theoretical (κριτική) powers exist also in the orectic, locomotive modes.

66. Contrary to Richardson 1992, 178. While nutritive activities are for the sake of something, this end is not present to the organism as something distinct from itself, i.e., it is not *aware* of its end.

67. "ἀλλὰ τῷ γε ἁπλῶς διαφέρει καὶ τινί" (431b12). This distinction between a theoretical and interested cognition is at the heart of Aristotle's example of seeing the beacon discussed above. I see fire – this is an incidental perception which grasps what the object is in itself. I see the fire moving—this is a common sensible, also about what the object is in itself independently of my own good. Seeing a moving fire, I *know* it signifies an enemy—what is known is not what the object is in itself, as "enemy" is essentially related to my own good.

68. On my interpretation of this passage, Aristotle refers to the capacity for deliberating (βουλευτικόν) because deliberation is the original source of any rational desire (βούλησις). On this point, see III.11.434a7–10, and this chapter, n. 86. Although rationally desiring capacity (βουλητικόν) would have more directly supported my reading, my interpretation is also compatible with the text as it stands.

69. Strictly speaking, desire (ὀρέξις) includes both appetitive and rational desire (ἐπιθυμία and βούλησις).

70. This way of dividing up the soul is already present in Aristotle's treatment of the *aporiai* surrounding how to divide the powers of soul at I.5.411a26–b1: ἐπεὶ δὲ τὸ γινώσκειν τῆς ψυχῆς ἐστὶ καὶ τὸ αἰσθάνεσθαί τε καὶ τὸ δοξάζειν, ἔτι δὲ τὸ ἐπιθυμεῖν καὶ βούλεσθαι καὶ ὅλως αἱ ὀρέξεις, γίνεται δὲ καὶ ἡ κατὰ τόπον κίνησις τοῖς ζῴοις ὑπὸ τῆς ψυχῆς, ἔτι δ' αὔξη τε καὶ ἀκμὴ καὶ φθίσις, πότερον ὅλῃ τῇ ψυχῇ τούτων ἕκαστον ὑπάρχει. Notice how knowing (γινώσκειν), sensing (αἰσθάνεσθαί), and opining (δοξάζειν) belongs on one side of the soul's activities, while the orectic powers of appetite (ἐπιθυμεῖν) and rational desire (βούλεσθαι), from which movement through space (ἡ κατὰ τόπον κίνησις) occurs, belong on the other, leaving the nutritive soul's activities (αὔξη τε καὶ ἀκμὴ καὶ φθίσις) as a third distinction prior to the first two.

71. The fundamental unity of the powers of sensation and self-movement might have been confirmed for Aristotle by his observation that when certain insects are divided, both divided parts retain the powers of sensation and movement in space for some time. See I.5.411b19–28. At the very least this shows that the powers of sensation and of locomotion are not distributed to different parts of the body.

72. See II.4.416b3–20.

73. See III.9.432b8–11.

74. *Physics* VIII.5.256b14ff.

75. In fact in plants, the heat does not really belong to the organism, but rather to the environmental heat which transforms the nutriment prior to assimilation—the process in plants is thus more deeply determined from without than for animals, who are in this sense and others far more a center unto themselves.

76. It is important to note how, in moving from nutrition to sensation and desire, one does not move to a distinct body part. Rather, in moving from nutritive heat to the sensitive-desiderative heart, the power of the lower is drawn into the organ responsible for the power of the higher. The heart is as much the center of nutritive heat as the seat of sensible awareness and the origin of the animal's local movement. Aristotle identifies the heart as the center of nutrition, sensation, and locomotion. In contrast with the view

from Plato's *Timaeus* which locates each part of the soul's tripartition in distinct parts of the body, the bodily unity of the soul's various powers is further indication that Aristotle's psychological theory abandons the view of the soul's distinctions as "parts."

77. III.9.432b15–16.

78. See *Parts of Animals* 647a25–b8, as well as Whiting's (2002, 167–68) discussion of this passage.

79. As James Doull (2003, 147) writes, "Each of the principal distinctions is the whole substance, less and more explicit to itself. These distinctions reduce to two, which contain the rest: the soul seeks to know, to find itself in what is presented to itself as other, and to move, to initiate from itself its relations to another."

80. See III.9.432a23ff.

81. *NE* I.13.1102a30–33. He notes at 1102b25 that it makes no difference for his argument how the rational and irrational oppose and resist one another.

82. At III.11 these animals are considered incomplete, while at III.9 the proof that they are *not* incomplete is that they can reproduce, and that they have their own pattern of development and decline.

83. See Yurdin (2009, 72) for a similar view.

84. See on this point Richardson (1992, 385).

85. These are also treated as interchangeable at *NE* 1139a11–14.

86. The deliberative (βουλευτική) image is the object of rational desire (βούλησις), in that this object of practical mind—a general conception of what is good for me—results from deliberation between appetitive desires. It remains unclear to me whether rational desire (βούλησις) in the *De Anima* simply is the rational image, or whether it is a thought which comes from these rational images. If it is the latter, what precisely is the difference between the sensible and rational image? Would the thought need to take the form of an image in order for the good to appear good to the agent?

87. Here I follow Hutchinson's (1990, 8) reading of the notoriously difficult Greek text at 434a10–11: καὶ αἴτιον τοῦτο τοῦ δόξαν μὴ δοκεῖν ἔχειν, ὅτι τὴν ἐκ συλλογισμοῦ οὐκ ἔχει, αὕτη δὲ ἐκείνην·. Hutchinson removes all unnecessary emendations by Ross, and brings out the straightforward sense of the passage: "This is the reason why they [i.e., the other, non-rational animals] seem not to have beliefs, because they do not have [the imagination, i.e., the deliberative or rational imagination] which comes from reasoning, and this imagination does involve belief."

88. Though only weakness of will or incontinence (ἀκρασία) is explicitly mentioned, it seems clear that the first two motions are instances of continence and incontinence.

89. Hutchinson 1990, 9. Hutchinson reports that this reference "has been the subject of controversy for several millennia," divided between camps which have taken Aristotle to mean an analogy with the heavenly spheres, and Simplicius who argues it is one ball striking another. Hutchinson argues that Aristotle means by spheres simply parts of the soul—each part of the soul includes within its sphere a certain kind of object.

90. As Hutchinson (1990, 9) writes: "Simplicius reports that earlier interpreters, probably Alexander of Aphrodisias and before him, Plutarch, had understood the spheres to be Aristotle's heavenly spheres. This was also the view taken by Themistius and Philoponus, and, in modern times, Trendelenburg, Hicks, and the Oxford Aristotle." See Simplicius (1882, 310.34).

91. Falcon 2005, 15.

92. Hutchinson 1990, 17.

93. Ibid., 18.

94. *Metaph.* XII.8.1074a1–2.

95. For a very precise and illuminating explanation of how the counteracting (or "unwinding") spheres work, see Jonathan Beere (2003).

96. Here Aristotle means the moment of knowledge in practical activity, not knowledge (ἐπιστήμη) in its strictest sense which is of objects that cannot be otherwise. This is an example of the "likeness [ὁμοιότης]" to knowledge (ἐπιστήμη) evoked at *NE* 1139b20.

97. This is what Aristotle in the *Ethics* calls φρόνησις, the grasp of practical truth about what is good or bad for oneself and for the human being in general. See *NE* VI.5.1140b5–11.

98. This is an instance of the transformative effect of a higher power on a lower power—ἐπιθυμία is not the same in a non-rational animal as it is in a rational animal. See Whiting's (2002, 187–88) treatment of this feature of Aristotle's psychology: "The idea here is presumably that sight is altered by its association with intellect, so that sight itself—along with its possible objects and the pleasures of its exercise—is rendered more complex . . . Given that Aristotle allows this, it is not surprising that he seems also to allow that the emergence of *practical* intellect alters and informs sight in similar ways, yielding forms of perception complex enough to register what (for example) is noble or what justice requires here and now, forms of perception that go hand in hand with ethical forms of desired and the pleasures associated with their satisfaction."

99. As Moss argues (2009, 137, fn. 37), "The virtuous person has correct non-rational cognition of a kind that all others (except the person with 'natural' virtue—see *EN* VI.13) lack."

100. Of course, even for that virtuous agent, this is only true in a qualified sense. The virtuous agent will encounter things in the environment which are unexpected and unaccountable according to his or her existing practical knowledge.

101. *DC* IV.3.310b14–15.

102. This agrees with Whiting's (2002, 199–200) conclusions.

103. For this reason I think Furley (1994, 14) misses the point of *De Anima* III.9–11 when he writes that Aristotle would have to give up the idea of the soul as an unmoved mover to recognize that there must be some effect of external objects on the soul in self-motion: "The point is that external objects are not in themselves sufficient causes for the voluntary movements of animals. But they do have some effect on the soul, and it would be obstinate of Aristotle to deny that the effect can be called a movement."

104. One might compare this inactive practical knowledge with the example of unexercised productive know-how cited in III.9.433a4–6—besides the universal knowledge, without the sensual awareness of an instance of a certain sickness, there will be no desire to bring the general knowledge into action.

105. See Falcon 2005 and 2009.

106. *DC* II.4.287a23–25.

107. Presumably each of these has an unmoved (cognitive) and moved (desiring) aspect.

108. Labarrière (2004, 184) aptly calls it "une explication commune."

109. Hence I disagree with Labarrière's claim that the idea of "absolute autonomy" is foreign to Aristotle's analysis of self-movers. This complete autonomy and self-sufficiency belongs only to the divine, though human rational self-movement is the closest mortal approximation of this absolute autonomy, while all mortal self-movers fall onto a continuum of degrees of self-initiated movement and autonomy from the external.

110. These two sides of the divine activity are suggestively brought together at *Metaph.* XII.7.1072a27–30. Wondering how something unmoved might move another, Aristotle's answer is twofold, as the object of thought and as the object of desire.

111. *DC* I.9.278b12–14.

112. *DC* I.9 appears to define the divine as these two sides—on the one hand the immaterial beings (the famous reference to the "beings there"—τἀκεῖ) who live "beyond" the outermost sphere in a non-spatial sense, and on the other the circular motion outermost periphery itself which contains all matter and motion within itself: I.9.279a18–b3. See also II.1.284a2–18.

113. *DC* I.2.269a31–33. See also *DC* I.2.269b13–15: "Beyond the bodies here around us there is another which is separate [κεχωρισμένον], having a nature more divine to the same degree that it is more distant from here."

114. *DC* II.1.284a3–6.

115. Kosman 1994, 144.

116. Ibid., 139.

117. Ibid., 150.

118. *DC* II.12.292b1ff.

119. In fact, the correspondence between *De Anima* and the *Nicomachean Ethics* might go even more deeply than the biological grounding of the theoretical/practical distinction in the κριτική / κίνητική distinction. For prior to both cognition and self-movement through space in living beings is the nutritive activity of soul, characterized ultimately by its final goal, which is producing another like itself. Thus its ultimate end (remaining one and the same through its activity) is realized not in itself but in something distinct from itself which it produces. In the *Ethics*, besides the distinction of practical and theoretical reason, Aristotle considers *productive* reason. While practical reason and theoretical reason are activities which contain their ends in themselves, the end of productive reason is a product beyond the activity, and so its activity is subordinate to its product. It is significant that for this reason the life of production is not a candidate in the competition for which human life is the happiest. The life of pleasure, being most intimately connected to contact senses, *is* considered, precisely because the activity of appetitive pleasure does constitute an end in itself.

120. One problem which is not resolved by my interpretation is how, given that the primary division in the soul is that between theoretical and practical cognition, what the unity of these two sides are—what holds together these two sides of the soul? See I.5.411b6–19 for these problems. In terms of the division between nutritive, sensitive, and intellective powers, this is not a question because the higher contains the lower within itself as potentiality to its actuality or matter to form. In terms of the division between κριτική and κινητική cognition, perhaps the question of what draws the two sides together becomes a moot one because sensation, whether theoretical or desiderative, is *sensation*; νοῦς, whether theoretical or practical, remains νοῦς. Aristotle's answer to this problem is not wholly clear to me.

121. *Eth. Eud.* 1244b35ff.

122. The same is true for the productive knowledge of a τέχνη, although with the qualification that activating productive knowledge through desire is under the added constraint of requiring certain external material conditions, in contrast with the possession of purely theoretical knowledge. See *De Anima* III.9.433a4–6: "And generally we see that the one having the art of medicine is not always healing, since there is some other cause respon-

sible for making in accordance with its knowledge, but not the knowledge." For Aristotle, this other cause is the soul's desire.

123. See Davis (2011, 35). Davis draws attention to the tension between the two sides of the "double function of soul," that is, its power of awareness and its power to move: "how can what gives us a motive to act at the same time allow us passively to render what is as it is?"

BIBLIOGRAPHY

Editions of *De Anima*

Bodéüs, Richard. 1993. *De l'âme.* Paris: GF-Flammarion.

Hamlyn, D. W. 1968. *Aristotle's De Anima: Books II and III.* Oxford: Clarendon.

Hett, W. S. 1936. *Aristotle on the Soul.* Trans. London: Heinemann. Loeb Classical Library.

Hicks, R. D. 1907. *Aristotle De Anima.* Cambridge, Eng.: Cambridge University Press.

Lawson-Tancred, Hugh. 1986. *Aristotle De Anima (On the Soul).* New York: Penguin.

Rodier, G. 1900. *Aristote: Traité de l'âme.* 2 vols. Paris: Ernst Leroux.

Ross, W. D. 1956. *De Anima.* Ed. W. D. Ross. Oxford: Clarendon. Oxford Classical Text.

———. 1961. *Aristotle De Anima.* Ed. W. D. Ross. Oxford: Clarendon.

Theiler, W. D. 1959. *Aristoteles über die Seele.* Berlin: Akademie Verlag.

Other Treatises

Barnes, Jonathan, ed. 1984. *The Complete Works of Aristotle.* 2 vols. Princeton University Press.

Hutchinson, D. S., and M. K. Johnson, eds. 2002. *Aristotle: Invitation to Philosophy.* http://www.chass.utoronto.ca/~phl102y/Protrepticus.pdf.

Ancient and Medieval Commentators

Alexander of Aphrodisias. 1887. *De Anima cum Mantissa* and *Aporiai kai Luseis.* Supplementum Aristotelicum, Vol. II, pt. 1. 1st ed. Bruns. Berlin: G. Reimer.

———. 1891. *In Aristotelis Metaphysica.* Ed. M. Mayduck. Commentaria in Aristotelem Graeca 1. Berlin: G. Reimer.

Aquinas, Thomas. 1948. *In Aristotelis librum de Anima commentarium.* Ed. M. Pirotta. Rome: Marietti.

———. 1951. *Aristotle's De Anima in the Version of William of Moerbeke and the Commentary of St. Thomas Aquinas.* Ed. K. Foster and S. Humphries. London: Routledge and Kegan Paul.

———. 1964–1981. *Summa Theologiae: Latin Text and English Translation, Introductions, Notes, Appendices, and Glossaries.* 61 vols. New York: McGraw Hill, Blackfriars.

Averroes. 1999. *L'intelligence et la pensée: Grand commentaire du De anima.* Ed. and trans. Alain de Libera. Paris: Garnier Flammarion.

Philiponus. 1897. *In Aristotelis De Anima libros commentaria.* Ed. M. Hayduck. Commentaria in Aristotelm graeca. Vol. 15. Berlin: G. Reimer.

Simplicius. 1882. *In libros Aristotelis De Anima commentaria.* Ed. M. Hayduck. Commentaria in Aristotelem Graeca. Vol. 11. Berlin: G. Reimer.

Themistius. 1899. *In Aristotelis De Anima.* Commentaria in Aristotelem Graeca, Vol. 5, pt. 3. Ed. R. Heinze. Berlin: G. Reimer.

Secondary Literature

Achard, Martin. 2005. *Épistémologie et pratique de la science chez Aristote: Les Seconds Analytiques et la définition de l'âme dans le De Anima*. Paris: Klincksieck.

Ackrill, J. L. 1972–1973. "Aristotle's Definitions of *Psuche*." In *Proceedings of the Aristotelian Society* 73: 119–33. Reprinted in Barnes, Schofield, Sorabji, *Articles on Aristotle*, 1979, pp. 65–75.

Andersen, Nathan. 2004. "Dynamic Boundaries: Place in Aristotle's Biology." *Graduate Faculty Philosophy Journal* 25, no. 1: 5–29.

Barker, Andrew. 1981. "Aristotle on Perception and Ratios." *Phronesis* 26: 248–66.

Barnes, J., M. Schofield, and R. Sorabji, eds. 1979. *Articles on Aristotle 4: Psychology and Aesthetics*. London: Duckworth.

Beere, Jonathan. 2003. "Counting the Unmoved Movers." *Archiv für Geschichte der Philosophie* 85: 1–20.

Berti, Enrico. 1978. "The Intellection of Indivisibles According to Aristotle: *De Anima* III.6." In Lloyd and Owen, *Aristotle on Mind and the Senses*, 1978, pp. 148–63.

———. 1996. "Reconsidérations sur l'intellection des 'indivisibles' selon Aristote, *De anima* III.6." In *Corps et âme*, ed. Cristina Viano, 391–404. Paris: Vrin.

Besnier, Bernard. 1997. "L'âme végétative selon Aristote." *Kairos* 9: 33–56.

Block, Irving. 1965. "On the Commonness of the Common Sensibles." *Australasian Journal of Philosophy* 43: 189–95.

———. 1988. "Aristotle on the Common Sense: A reply to Kahn and Others." *Ancient Philosophy* 8, no. 2: 235–49.

Blumenthal, H. J. 1976. "Neoplatonic Elements in the *De anima* Commentaries." *Phronesis* 21: 64–87.

———. 1977. "Neoplatonic Interpretations of Aristotle on *Phantasia*." *Review of Metaphysics* 31: 230–41.

———. 1996. *Aristotle and Neoplatonism in Late Antiquity: Interpretations of the De Anima*. Ithaca, N.Y.: Cornell University Press.

Bodéüs, Richard. 1975. "Notes sur quelques aspects de la conscience dans la pensée aristotélicienne." *Phronesis* 20: 63–74.

———. 1990. "L'imagination au pouvoir." *Dialogue* 29: 21–40.

Bolton, R. 1978. "Aristotle's Definitions of the Soul: *De Anima* II 1–3." *Phronesis* 23: 258–78.

Brentano, F. 1867. *Die Psychologie des Aristoteles, insbesondere seine Lehre vom nous poietikos*. Mainz: Franz Kirchheim.

Brogan, Walter. 2005. *Heidegger and Aristotle: The Twofoldness of Being*. New York: SUNY Press.

Brunschwig, Jacques. 1991. "Les multiples chemins aristotéliciens de la sensation commune." *Revue de Métaphysique et de Morale* 96, no. 4: 455–74.

———. 1996. "En quel sens le sens common est-il commun?" In *Corps et âme*, ed. Cristina Viano, 189–218. Paris: Vrin.

Burnyeat, Myles. 1992. "Is an Aristotelian Philosophy of Mind Still Credible? (a Draft)." In *Essays on Aristotle's De Anima*, ed. Martha Nussbaum and Amélie Rorty, 15–26. Oxford: Clarendon.

———. 2001. "Aquinas on 'Spiritual Change' in Perception." In *Ancient and Medieval Theories of Intentionality*, ed. D. Perler, 129–53. Studien und Texte zur Geistesgeschichte des Mittelalters 76. Leiden: Brill.

———. 2002. "*De Anima II* 5." *Phronesis* 47, no. 1: 28–90.

Byl, S. 1991. "Le toucher chez Aristote." *Revue de Philosophie Ancienne* 9, no. 2: 123–32.

Cantin, S. 1946. "Les puissances et les opérations de l'âme végétative dans la psychologie d'Aristote." *Laval Théologique et Philosophique* 2: 23–45.

Cashdollar, S. 1973. "Aristotle's Account of Incidental Perception." *Phronesis* 18: 156–75.

Caston, Victor. 1996. "Why Aristotle Needs Imagination?" *Phronesis* 41, no. 1: 20–55.

———. 1999. "Aristotle's Two Intellects: A Modest Proposal." *Phronesis* 44, no. 3: 199–227.

———. 2005. "The Spirit and the Letter: Aristotle on Perception." In *Metaphysics, Soul, and Ethics in Ancient Thought: Themes from the Work of Richard Sorabji*, ed. Richard Salles, 245–320. Oxford: Clarendon.

Charlton, William. 1980. "Aristotle's Definition of Soul." *Phronesis* 25: 170–86.

Code, Alan, and Moravcsiki, Julius. "Explaining Various Forms of Living." In *Essays on Aristotle's De Anima*, ed. Martha Nussbaum and Amélie Rorty, 129–45. Oxford: Clarendon.

Corcilius, K. 2008. *Streben und Bewegen: Aristoteles' Theorie der animalischen Ortsbewegung*. Berlin: Walter de Gruyter.

Corrigan, Kevin. 1985. "The Irreducible Opposition between the Platonic and Aristotelian Concepts of Soul and Body in Some Ancient and Mediaeval Thinkers." *Laval Théologique et Philosophique* 41, no. 3: 391–401.

Davis, Michael. 2011. *The Soul of the Greeks*. Chicago: University of Chicago Press.

De Corte, M. 1934. *La doctrine de l'intelligence chez Aristote*. Paris.

———. 1939. "La définition aristotélicienne de l'âme." *Revue Thomiste* 45: 460–508.

De Koninck, Thomas. 1990 "La *noesis* et l'indivisible selon Aristote." In *La naissance de la raison en Grèce*, ed. J.-F. Mattéi, 215–28. Paris: Presses Universitaires de France.

Diamond, Eli. 2014. "Aristotle"s Appropriation of Plato's Sun Analogy in *De Anima*." *Apeiron* 47, no. 3: 356–89.

Dörrie, Heinrich. 1961. "Gedanken zur Methodik des Aristoteles in der Schrift *peri psyches*." In *Aristote et les problèmes de méthode*, ed. S. Mansion, 223–44. Louvain: Publications Universitaires.

Doull, James. 2003. "Tragedy, Comedy, and Philosophy in Antiquity." In *Philosophy and Freedom: The Legacy of James Doull*, ed. David G. Peddle and Neil G. Robertson, 21–54. Toronto: University of Toronto Press.

Easterling, H. J. 1966. "A note on *De Anima* 413a8–9." *Phronesis* 11: 159–62.

Everson, S. 1995. "Psychology." In *The Cambridge Companion to Aristotle*, ed. J. Barnes, 168–94. Cambridge, Eng.: Cambridge University Press.

Falcon, Andrea. 2005. *Aristotle & the Science of Nature: Unity without Uniformity*. Cambridge, Eng.: Cambridge University Press.

———. 2009. "The Scope and Unity of Aristotle's Investigation of the Soul." In Van Riel and Destrée, eds., *Ancient Perspectives on Aristotle's De Anima*. Leuven: Leuven University Press.

Fattal, Michel. 1996. "L'intellection des indivisibles dans le *De Anima* III, 6 d'Aristote: Lectures arabes et modernes." In *Corps et âme*, ed. Cristina Viano. Paris: Vrin.

Fraser, Kyle. 2002. "Demonstrative Science and the Science of Being *qua* Being." *Oxford Studies in Ancient Philosophy* 22: 43–82.

———. 2003. "Seriality and Demonstration in Aristotle's Ontology." *Oxford Studies in Ancient Philosophy* 25: 131–58.

Frede, Dorothea. 1992. "The Cognitive Role of *Phantasia* in *De Anima.*" In *Essays on Aristotle's De Anima*, ed. Martha Nussbaum and Amélie Rorty, 279–95. Oxford: Clarendon.

Frede, Michael. 1996. "La théorie aristotélicienne de l'intellect agent." In *Corps et âme*, ed. Cristina Viano, 377–90. Paris: Vrin.

Freeland, Cynthia. 1992. "Aristotle on the Sense of Touch." *Essays on Aristotle's De Anima*, ed. Martha Nussbaum and Amélie Rorty, 227–48. Oxford: Clarendon.

Freudenthal, Gad. 1995. *Aristotle's Theory of Material Substance: Heat and Pneuma, Form and Soul.* Oxford: Clarendon.

Furley, David. 1994. *Self-Movers: Self-Motion from Aristotle to Newton.* Ed. Mary-Louise Gill and James Lennox, 135–53. Princeton, N.J.: Princeton University Press.

Gadamer, Hans-Georg. 1980. *Dialogue and Dialectic: Eight Hermeneutical Studies of Plato.* New Havem, Conn.: Yale University Press.

Gerson, Lloyd. 2004. "The Unity of Intellect in Aristotle's *De Anima.*" *Phronesis* 49, no. 4: 348–73.

Gonzalez, Francisco. 1991. "Aristotle on Pleasure and Perfection." *Phronesis* 36, no. 2: 141–59.

Gregoric, Pavel. 2007. *Aristotle on the Common Sense.* Oxford: Oxford University Press.

Hamlyn, D. W. 1968. "Koine Aisthesis." *The Monist* 52, no. 2: 195–209.

Hankey, W. J. 1987. *God in Himself.* Oxford: Oxford University Press.

Harvey, Peter. 1978. "Aristotle on Truth and Falsity in *De Anima* 3.6." *Journal of the History of Philosophy* 16, no. 2: 219–20.

Heath, Thomas L. 1949. *Mathematics in Aristotle.* Oxford: Oxford University Press.

Hegel, G. W. F. 1971. *Hegel's Philosophy of Mind—Part Three of the Encyclopaedia of the Philosophical Sciences (1830).* Trans. William Wallace and A. V. Millar, foreword by J. N. Findlay. Oxford: Clarendon.

———. 1971. *Philosophy of Nature. Hegel's Philosophy of Nature—Part Two of the Encyclopaedia of the Philosophical Sciences (1830).* Trans. A. V. Millar, foreword by J. N. Findlay. Oxford: Clarendon.

———. 1995. *Lectures on the History of Philosophy.* 3 vols. Trans. E. S. Haldane and Frances H. Simson. Lincoln: University of Nebraska Press.

Heidegger, Martin. 1922. "Phänomenologische Interpretationen zu Aristoteles: Anzeige der hermeneutischen Situation." In *Gesamtausgabe*, vol. 62, *Phänomenologische Interpretationen ausgewählter Abhandlungen des Aristoteles zur Ontologie und Logik*, ed. Gunther Neumann. Frankurt am Main: Vittorio Klostermann.

Hubert, Bernard. 1997. "Le sens commun et l'unité de l'animal chez Aristote." *Revue Thomiste* 94: 694–708.

Hübner, Johannes. 1999. "Die Aristotelische Konzeption der Seele als Aktivität in *de Anima* II 1." *Archiv für Geschichte der Philosophie* 81: 1–32.

Huby, Pamela. 1991. "Stages in the Development of Language about Aristotle's *nous.*" In *Aristotle and the Later Tradition*, ed. H. Blumenthal and H. Robinson, 129–43. Oxford.

Hutchinson, D. S. 1987. "Restoring the Order of Aristotle's *De Anima.*" *Classical Quarterly* 37: 373–81.

———. 1990. "Aristotle and the Spheres of Motivation: *De Anima* III.11." *Dialogue* 29: 7–20.

Hutchinson, D. S., and M. K. Johnson. 2005. "Authenticating Aristotle's *Protrepticus.*" *Oxford Studies in Ancient Philosophy* 29: 193–294.

Johansen, T. K. 1992. "Aristotle on the Sense of Smell." *Phronesis* 41: 1–19.

———. 1998. *Aristotle on the Sense Organs*. Cambridge, Eng.: Cambridge University Press.

Jonas, Hans. 2001. *The Phenomenon of Life: Toward a Philosophical Biology*. Evanston, Ill.: Northwestern University Press.

Kahn, Charles. 1966. "Sensation and Consciousness in Aristotle's Psychology." *Archiv für Geschichte der Philosophie* 48: 43–81.

King, R. A. H. 2001. *Aristotle on Life and Death*. London: Duckworth.

Kosman, Aryeh. 1968. "Predicating the Good." *Phronesis* 13: 171–74.

———. 1969. "Aristotle's Definition of Motion." *Phronesis* 14: 41–62.

———. 1973. "Understanding, Explanation and Insight in Aristotle's *Posterior Analytics*." In *Exegesis and Argument: Studies in Greek Philosophy Presented to Gregory Vlastos*, ed. Lee, Mourelatos and Rorty, 374–392. Assen: Koninklijke Van Gorcum.

———. 1975. "Perceiving That We Perceive: *On the Soul* III, 2." *Philosophical Review* 84: 499–514.

———. 1984. "Substance, Being, and *Energeia*." *Oxford Studies in Ancient Philosophy* 2: 121–49.

———. 1987. "Animals and Other Beings in Aristotle." In *Philosophical Problems in Aristotle's Biology*, ed. J. Lennox and A. Gotthelf, 360–91. Cambridge, Eng.: Cambridge University Press.

———. 1988. "Divine Being and Divine Thinking in *Metaphysics* Lambda." *Proceedings of the Boston Area Colloquium in Ancient Philosophy*. Lanham, Md.: University Press of America.

———. 1992. "What Does the Maker Mind Make?" In *Essays on Aristotle's De Anima*, ed. Martha Nussbaum and Amélie Rorty, 342–58. Oxford: Clarendon.

———. 1994. "Aristotle's Prime Mover." In *Self-Motion from Aristotle to Newton*, ed. Mary-Louise Gill and James Lennox, 135–53. Princeton, N.J.: Princeton University Press.

———. 2000. "*Metaphysics* Λ 9: Divine Thought." In *Aristotle's Metaphysics Lambda, Symposium Aristotelicum*, ed. Michael Frede and David Charles, 307–26. Oxford: Oxford University Press.

———. 2004. "On the Desirability of Friends." *Ancient Philosophy* 24: 135–54.

Labarrière, Jean-Louis. 2004. *Langage, vie politique et mouvement des animaux: Etudes aristotéliciennes*. Paris: Vrin.

Lear, Jonathan. 1988. *Aristotle: The Desire to Understand*. Cambridge, Eng.: Cambridge University Press.

Lloyd, G. E.R., and G. E. L. Owen. 1978. *Aristotle on Mind and the Senses: Proceedings of the Seventh Symposium Aristotelicum*. Cambridge, Eng.: Cambridge University Press.

Lorenz, Hendrik. 2006. *The Brute Within: Appetitive Desire in Plato and Aristotle*. Oxford: Clarendon.

Mansion, S. 1973. "Deux définitions de la vie chez Aristote." *Revue Philosophique de Louvain* 71: 425–50.

Matthews, Gareth B. 1992. "*De Anima* 2.2–4 and the Meaning of Life." In *Essays on Aristotle's De Anima*, ed. Martha Nussbaum and Amélie Rorty, 185–93. Oxford: Clarendon.

Menn, Stephen. 2002. "Aristotle's Definition of Soul in the *De Anima*." *Oxford Studies in Ancient Philosophy* 22: 83–139.

Mignucci, Mario. 1996. "Vérité et pensée dans le *De anima*." In *Corps et âme*, ed. Cristina Viano, 405–22. Paris: Vrin.

Modrak, D. 1981. "*Koine Aisthesis* and the Discrimination of Sensible Differences in *De Anima* III.2." *Canadian Journal of Philosophy* 11, no. 3: 405–23.

———. 1987. *Aristotle: The Power of Perception*. Chicago: University of Chicago Press.

———. 1991. "The *Nous*-Body Problem in Aristotle." *Review of Metaphysics* 44: 755–774.

Moraux, Paul. 1955. "A propos du *nous thurathen* chez Aristote." In *Autour d'Aristote*, ed. Auguste Mansion, 255–95. Louvain: Publications universitaires de Louvain.

———. 1978. "Le *De anima* dans la tradition grecque: Quelques aspects de l'interprétation du traité, de Théophraste à Thémistius." In *Aristotle on Mind and the Senses*. Proceedings of the Seventh Symposium Aristotelicum, ed. G. E. R. Lloyd and G. E. L. Owen, 280–324. Cambridge, Eng.: Cambridge University Press.

Moss, Jessica. 2009. "*Akrasia* and Perceptual Illusion." *Archiv für Geschichte der Philosophie* 91: 119–56.

Murphy, Damian. 2005. "Aristotle on Why Plants Cannot Perceive." *Oxford Studies in Ancient Philosophy* 29: 295–339.

Nussbaum, Martha. 1992. "Introduction A: The Text of Aristotle's *De Anima*." In *Essays on Aristotle's De Anima*, ed. Martha Nussbaum and Amélie Rorty. Oxford: Clarendon.

Nussbaum, Martha, and Amélie Rorty, eds. 1992. *Essays on Aristotle's De Anima*. Oxford: Clarendon.

Nuyens, François. 1948. *L'évolution de la psychologie d'Aristote*. Paris:Vrin.

Owens, Joseph. 1951. *The Doctrine of Being in Aristotle's Metaphysics*. Toronto: Pontifical Institute of Medieval Studies.

———. 1971. "Aristotle's Definition of Soul." In *Philomathes: Studies and Essays in the Humanities in Memory of P. Merlan*, 125–45. The Hague: M. Nijhoff.

———. 1976. "A Note on Aristotle, *De Anima* 3.4, 429b9." *Phoenix* 30, no. 2: 107–18.

Papish, Laura. *Aristotle on Common Perception. Apeiron* 47, no. 3: 342–55.

Peck, A. L. 1943. *Introduction to Generation of Animals*. Trans. A. L. Peck. London: Heinemann, Loeb Classical Library.

Plato. 1997. *Complete Works*. Ed. John. M. Cooper. Indianapolis, Ind.: Hackett.

Polansky, Ronald. 2000. "Analogy and Disanalogy of the Soul's Faculties in Aristotle's *De Anima*." *Proceedings of the Boston Area Colloquium in Ancient Philosophy*. ed. John J. Cleary and Gary M. Gurtler, 57–86. Leiden: Brill Academic.

———. 2007. *Aristotle's De Anima*. Cambridge, Eng.: Cambridge University Press.

Pritzl, Kurt. 1984. "The Cognition of Indivisibles and the Argument of De Anima 3.4–8." *Proceedings of the American Catholic Philosophical Association: Practical Reasoning* 58: 140–50.

Richardson-Lear, Gabriel. 2004. *Happy Lives and the Highest Good: An Essay on Aristotle's Nicomachean Ethics*. Princeton, N.J.: Princeton University Press.

Rist, John. 1966. "Notes on Aristotle, *De Anima* 3.5." *Classical Philology* 61: 8–20.

Rorty, Amélie. 1992. "Introduction B: *De Anima* and Its Agenda." In *Essays on Aristotle's De Anima*, ed. Martha Nussbaum and Amélie Rorty, 7–13. Oxford: Clarendon.

Rosen, S. H. 1961. "Thought and Touch: A Note on Aristotle's *De Anima*." *Phronesis* 6: 127–37.

Russon, John. 1996. "Self-Consciousness and the Tradition in Aristotle's Psychology." *Laval Théologique et Philosophique* 52, no. 3: 777–803.

Schofield, Malcolm. 1979. "Aristotle on the Imagination." In Barnes, Schofield, Sorabji, *Articles on Aristotle*, 1979, 103–32. Reprinted in Nussbaum and Rorty, *Essays on Aristotle's De Anima*, 1992, 249–77.

Shields, Christopher. 1999. *Order in Multiplicity: Homonymy in the Philosophy of Aristotle*. Oxford: Clarendon.

Sorabji, Richard. 1974. "Body and Soul in Aristotle." *Philosophy* 29: 63–89.

Sprague, Rosamond Kent. 1996. "A Missing Middle Term: *De Anima* II.2." *Phronesis* 41, no. 1: 104–8.

Stigen, Anfinn. 1961. "On the Alleged Primacy of Sight." *Symbolae Osloenses* 37: 15–44.

Thomas, Ivo. 1951. Introduction to *Aristotle's De Anima with the Commentary of St. Thomas Aquinas*. London: Routledge and Kegan Paul.

Tracy, Theodore. 1985. "Heart and Soul in Aristotle." In *Essays in Greek Philosophy* II, ed. J. P. Anton and A. Preus, 283–302. Albany: SUNY Press.

Van Riel, Gerd, and Destrée, Pierre, eds. 2009. *Ancient Perspectives on Aristotle's De Anima*. Ancient and Medieval Philosophy, series I 41. Leuven: Leuven University Press.

Viano, Cristina. 1996. "La doxographie du *De anima* (I, 2–5)." In *Corps et âme*, ed. Cristina Viano, 51–79. Paris: Vrin.

———, ed. 1996. *Corps et âme: Sur le De Anima d'Aristote*. Paris, Vrin.

Ward, Julie K. 1996. "Souls and Figures: Defining the Soul in *De Anima* II 3." *Ancient Philosophy* 16: 113–28.

Wedin, Michael. 1988. *Mind and Imagination in Aristotle*. New Haven, Conn.: Yale University Press.

Whiting, Jennifer. 2002. "Locomotive Soul: The Parts of Soul in Aristotle's Scientific Works." *Oxford Studies in Ancient Philosophy* 22: 141–200.

Yurdin, Joel. 2009. "Aristotelian Imagination and the Explanation of Behavior." In Van Riel and Destrée, eds., *Ancient Perspectives on Aristotle's De anima*. Leuven: Leuven University Press.

GENERAL INDEX

In this index *f* refers to a reference on the following page, *ff* to a reference on the following two pages. Principal topics within a chapter are indicated by a reference to the chapter number, e.g., "ch. 1."

INDEX LOCORUM

All works cited are by Aristotle.